FLORIDA
GARDENER'S RESOURCE

ALL YOU NEED TO KNOW TO PLAN, PLANT, & MAINTAIN A FLORIDA GARDEN

Published by Cool Springs Press
P.O. Box 2828
Brentwood, Tennessee 37024

EAN: 978-1-59186-467-7

First Printing 2010
Printed in the United States of America
10 9 8 7 6 5 4 3 2 1

Managing Editor: Paula Biles
Contributing Editors: Robert Bowden and Tom MacCubbin
Art Director: Marc Pewitt
Photography Research Assistant: Matthew Allison
Production: S.E. Anderson

Photography and illustration

Cool Springs Press would like to thank the following contributors to the *Florida Gardener's Resource.*

Thomas Eltzroth: 25b, 26a, 27ab, 28ab, 29ab, 30ab, 31a, 32b, 33ab, 34a, 35ab, 37a, 38ab, 39a, 55b, 56a, 60a, 62ab, 64a, 66b, 67b, 68a, 69b, 86ab, 87b, 88a, 89b, 90b, 143b, 145a, 170b, 171a, 172b, 173a, 174ab, 176a, 178a, 180a, 195b, 199b, 201a, 202ab, 203a, 204ab, 205a, 206a, 207a, 209a, 210b, 211a, 229a, 231ab. 236ab, 237a, 238ab, 240b, 241b, 244a, 260b, 261ab, 262a, 264a, 266b, 267a, 270b, 273a, 274b, 276a, 294b, 296b, 297ab, 301ab, 306a, 307a, 308a, 311b, 321ab, 324ab, 325a, 327b, 330b, 332a

Liz Ball and Rick Ray: 25a, 32a, 36a, 37b, 39b, 56b, 59a, 66a, 96a, 175a, 195a, 198b, 199a, 227b, 228ab, 259b, 264b, 271a, 294a, 332b

Bruce Asakawa: 145b, 235a, 277a, 295b, 331b

Bruce Holst: 179b, 203b, 230b, 269b, 300a

Charles Mann: 177a

Dency Kane: 268b, 330a

David Price: 181b

Georgia B. Tasker: 48, 68b, 230a

iStockphoto and its artists: 84b, 88b, 89a, 91a, 94b, 98a, 99ab, 242b

Jackson & Perkins: 233a, 234b, 235b

Jerry Pavia: 26b, 31b, 36b, 61b, 179a, 206b, 211b, 263b, 270a, 272a, 302a, 307b

Jupiter Images: 18, 59b, 76, 83a, 84a, 85a, 87a, 90a, 92b, 95a, 96b, 97a, 98b, 115b, 116a, 117a, 118ab, 119ab, 121b, 122b, 124a, 125a, 126ab, 136, 162, 188, 196a, 201b, 205b, 220, 252, 286, 314

Kirsten Llamas: 55a, 58a, 63a, 91b, 208a, 237b, 243b, 259a, 265a, 266a, 267b, 268a, 269a, 271b, 273b, 276b, 303a, 327a

Langeveld Bulb Company, courtesy of Armstrong Garden Centers: 57b

Lorenzo Gunn: 92a, 95b, 97b, 171b, 172a, 198a, 234a, 275a, 293a, 306b, 322a, 329a

Michael Dirr: 65b, 262b

Mark Turner ©2002: 58b, 173b

Nan Sterman: 69a, 240a

Paula Biles: 34b, 60b, 169b, 177b, 200ab, 208b, 209b, 210a,

232b, 233b, 239b, 241a, 242a, 260a, 293b, 295a, 296a, 298ab, 299b, 302b, 304b, 305b, 309b, 310ab, 323ab, 326ab, 328ab, 329b

Pam Harper: 176b, 227a, 243a, 263a, 274a, 275b, 311a, 325b, 331a,

Photo courtesy of Proven Winners, www.provenwinners.com: 196b, 197a

Stephen G. Pategas / Hortus Oasis: 169a, 178b, 244b, 272b, 305a

Robert Bowden: 85b, 93ab, 94a, 116b, 117b, 120ab, 121b, 122a, 123a, 124b

Roger Hammer: 175b, 265b

Ralph Snodsmith: 197b

Sacbee: 308b

Tom Koske: 144a

Tom MacCubbin: 143a

W. Atlee Burpee & Co.: 125b

William Adams: 57a, 61a, 63b, 64b, 65a, 67a, 144b, 146ab, 170a, 180b, 181a, 207b, 229b, 232a, 239a, 277b, 299a, 300b, 303b, 304a

FLORIDA
GARDENER'S RESOURCE

ALL YOU NEED TO KNOW TO PLAN, PLANT, & MAINTAIN A FLORIDA GARDEN

TOM MacCUBBIN AND GEORGIA B. TASKER

WITH ROBERT BOWDEN AND JOE LAMP'L

**COOL
SPRINGS
PRESS**

Growing Successful Gardeners™

www.coolspringspress.com

BRENTWOOD, TENNESSEE

CONTENTS

WELCOME TO
GARDENING
in Florida

Whether you are new to the state or just new to gardening, you are about to have lots of fun, enjoy colorful flowers, and reap big harvests from fruit and vegetable plants. Even if you already have some local gardening experience, there is always more to learn and new adventures ahead.

Florida is different from most other states. It's a long state, almost 900 miles from the northernmost point in the Panhandle to the tip of the Keys. There is frost-free growing in the southern part of the state and there are yearly freezes in the north. Before you begin planting, you can learn a little about some other features of our state:

- Most of the soil is sand; gardeners often call it "beach sand."
- May through September are very hot months.
- January and February are the coldest months.
- Summer is the rainy season; the rest of the months are relatively dry.
- Fall and spring are times for warm-season plantings, winter is devoted to cool-season plantings, and summer is the time for plants that don't mind the heat.
- Gardeners on the coast and some isolated inland areas have to deal with salty water.
- Pest problems are similar to those of other climates, but the pests are active year-round.
- By now you have probably gotten the hint that most people can use some help in becoming oriented to Florida growing conditions. Flowers and vegetables are often planted at different times than in other states. You will need to learn about tropical crops and some new varieties of fruits. And we have not even mentioned the incredible variety of plants that are available for a Florida landscape. We live in a gardener's paradise.
- You will be asking lots of questions as you begin gardening in Florida. It's only natural.

FLORIDA'S CLIMATE

Enjoy our Florida climate: the living is easy here. Seldom will you need a heavy winter coat, and you can sell your snow shovel. Most of the state is considered a subtropical climate. In spite of our great growing conditions, gardeners are often concerned about weather.

Luckily, Florida weather tends to be fairly predictable within its three climatic zones. On average, spring and fall are warm and dry, summer hot and humid, and winter cool and dry.

NORTH FLORIDA

- extends northward from State Road 40.
- has about 60 inches of rainfall per year.
- is sure to get frosts and freezing weather in winter.
- has a first frost by late November and last frost during late February.
- has 350 to 650 annual hours below 45 degrees.

- has summers of similar duration to those in temperate areas but are hotter and more humid.

CENTRAL FLORIDA
- lies between State Roads 40 and 70.
- has about 56 inches of rainfall per year.
- has frosts most years and some light freezes in winter.
- has a first frost by mid-December and a last frost during mid-February.
- has 150 to 350 annual hours below 45 degrees.
- has extended summer-like, hot, humid weather in late spring and fall.

SOUTH FLORIDA
- extends below State Road 70 across the state.
- has about 56 inches of rainfall per year.
- has infrequent frosts and no freezes.
- has 50 to 150 annual hours below 45 degrees.
- has extended, summer-like, hot, humid weather into spring and fall.

Our state gets lots of rainfall, but it is not evenly distributed throughout the year. Most arrives during summer.

WINTER HARDINESS

How many USDA plant hardiness zones are in Florida? Most would guess three, but the answer is four, zones 8 through 11. It would be nice to believe that the listed temperatures are accurate for all areas of each zone. But Florida is full of microclimates where temperatures can be much higher or lower than average during cold weather. Nevertheless, hardiness zones are good guides for determining what will grow in your area, as long as you recognize that there may be exceptions.

FLORIDA HEAT

Gardeners often wonder why forsythia and lilacs don't grow well locally and why petunias and snapdragons give out by early summer. Much of the problem is the amount of heat received in a warm climate. It may get too hot for good growth and flowering. If it can be too cold to grow a plant, certainly it can be too hot. Before you make a plant selection, you may want to check to see if a plant can be grown in your region.

SOILS

Understanding soil in Florida is easy: most landscapes are full of sand. The topsoil is usually like the sand used in an hourglass. But don't be too alarmed—you can grow great plants in sands. You just have to supply water and fertilizer. Florida also has some pockets of clays, areas with high organic matter, and rocky soils.

Growing in loose sands has a number of advantages:

- Sands are usually well-drained, except in lower areas where water accumulates.
- Sands offer good aeration for root growth.
- Because sands offer little resistance to root growth, plants become well anchored in the ground.
- Sands make for easy digging when preparing planting sites.
- Sands can be easily amended to improve water-holding and nutrient-supplying ability.

There are some problems you may have when growing in sands:
- Sands hold very few nutrients and the plants need frequent feeding.
- Sands offer little resistance to pests that move through the soil.
- Sands dry quickly and need frequent watering.
- Sands blow about during windy weather and need covering with vegetation or mulch.
- Sands become hot during the summer if they are not mulched or planted.
- Sandy soils are not suitable for all plants.

Wherever possible, amend your soils with organic matter. These additions help the soils hold moisture and supply some nutrients for plant growth. Test the soil pH using a pH kit or have it done at a garden center or Extension Service office.

GENERAL HORTICULTURAL TIPS

A gardener is always adding plants to the landscape. One of the nice things about living in Florida is that plants can be added to the landscape at any time of year.

CONTAINER PLANTINGS

Container-grown plants come from small cell-packs to 30-gallon or larger pots and are easy to transport and plant in a new location. It's a good idea to check the rootballs to make sure they are not potbound at purchase time. If plants have very tightly wrapped root systems, they may not grow out into the surrounding soil and will be short-lived. This is especially true of annuals. Here are a few tips to get container plants quickly established:

- Find a site where the plant will have ample room to grow.
- Dig the hole twice as wide as but no deeper than the rootball.
- Position the plant in the center of the hole and at the same depth it was growing or with the top of the rootball 1 to 2 inches above the ground.
- Adding organic matter to the fill soil is optional.

- Fill in around the rootball with soil, adding water as you plant.
- Create a 4- to 6-inch-high soil berm at the edge of the rootball around the plant to hold water.
- Spread a 3- to 4-inch layer of mulch up to the edge of the rootball of trees and shrubs. Add a light mulch layer over the root system.
- If plants may be affected by winds, add stakes or guy wires.
- Water the planting thoroughly.

WATERING NEW PLANTINGS

Just as important as good planting technique is the care a plant receives once it is in the ground. Remember, Florida can have some dry months, and many landscape plantings are made during the spring and fall season when there is little rain and lots of hot weather.

Most plants need a good watering program until roots are established in the surrounding soil. It takes some time to get trees, shrubs, and other landscape plants established. Their most important need is good watering or rainfalls. Florida's sandy soils dry very rapidly, so daily watering is needed in the beginning. Some gardeners recommend watering trees once a day for six or more months if they are planted in very sandy soils.

For most plants, however, you will do fine if you just water when the surface soil begins to feel dry. Most gardeners water every day for the first few weeks and then back off to an "as needed" schedule, using the surface soil moisture as a guide. (Feel the soil, and if the upper inch is dry, water may be needed.)

Note that it is important to build berms around new plantings. Many plants are grown in highly organic soils and when set in the ground the water tends to run around the rootball. You may think you are doing a good job of watering but sometimes rootballs remain dry. When you fill a berm around the rootball with water, the moisture has to move down and through the rootball before it goes into the surrounding soil. Here are a few more tips for good watering:

- Don't rely on irrigation systems to water new plantings—do it by hand.
- When watering, thoroughly wet the soil.
- Keep a mulch layer in place up to the edge of the rootball and a light layer over the roots.
- Where possible, install drip irrigation systems or use soaker hoses.
- Water during the early-morning hours to conserve water.
- Control weeds.

FERTILIZING

Feeding new plants is also part of the establishment program. You may have noticed that no fertilizer was added to the planting hole. There are products available if you want them, but Florida soils are so heavily watered in the beginning that many added nutrients may be lost during the first few weeks of plant care. It is often best to let the tree, shrub, vine, or ground cover plantings get a start on establishment for four to six weeks, and then make a fertilizer *application*. The type of fertilizer you use is not that important as long as it's meant for landscape plantings. Many garden-ers are using a 16-0-8 or similar product as their main fertilizer.

Slow-release fertilizers are also available—they stretch the time between feedings, and your dollars too. Just follow the label instructions.

Most shrubs, vines, and groundcovers can be fed lightly every 6 to 8 weeks March through October for the first year. After that a regular maintenance program can be followed.

Give trees their first feeding four to six weeks after planting, and then feed in March and June for the first three years. After that, no feedings are normally needed for trees except for fruiting trees.

Annual flowers and perennials require a feeding program that is a little different: they are immediately put on a regular maintenance program. Give annuals a monthly feeding year-round, and give perennials a feeding every six to eight weeks during March through November.

SOIL AMENDMENTS

Florida's sandy soils can grow lots of great plants if you add plenty of water and fertilizer, but you can make gardening even easier by improving sandy sites with organic matter. It's almost impossible to add too much organic matter when preparing flower beds, vegetable gardens, and other planting sites. Some of the organic amendments available for use:

- COMPOST: Make your own at home or pick it up at county landfills. Work 4 to 6 inches into most planting sites including clay soils. Compost produced at landfills is normally alkaline and is not recommended for use with azalea or blueberry plantings.
- PEAT MOSS: Florida has local sources of peat moss that can be purchased through landscape supply companies. Canadian peat moss can also be obtained at garden centers. Work 4 to 6 inches into sandy or clay soils before planting.
- MANURES: Chicken, cow, and horse manure are all readily available.

Use about 25 pounds for each 100 square feet of bed area to be planted, or follow package instructions. Composted manure can be applied to the soil surface. Fresh manure should be tilled into the soil 90 to 120 days before planting.

- POTTING SOILS: A potting soil is a good amendment for small garden spots, but it can be costly to use in large beds.
- TOPSOIL: Florida does not have standards for topsoil. Be careful when ordering to make sure it's not the same sandy soil found in your yard, and that it is free of weeds.

WATERING ESTABLISHED PLANTINGS

Much of Florida's landscape would shrivel and dry without receiving extra water. Many gardeners are practicing "xeriscape planting" techniques to reduce water usage. They use trees, shrubs, and other plantings that need very little watering once established. But even water-wise designs usually include an oasis for plants requiring more moisture.

Let the plants tell you when they need water. Spots in lawns can be used as indicators. Wait until the shrub and perennial foliage shows early signs of wilting. Here are some guidelines for conserving water while maintaining a well-kept landscape:

- Turn irrigation systems on manually and only when plants need water.
- Feel the soil, and if the upper inch is dry, water may be needed.
- Water between 4 and 6 in the morning.
- Apply ½ to ¾ inch of water at each irrigation.
- Water trees and shrubs that use less water separately from lawns and flower beds.
- Use sprinkler heads that keep the water at ground level and off walks and roads.
- Perform monthly tests to make sure the irrigation system is working properly.
- Use microsprinklers and soaker hoses wherever possible.
- Water before freezes are expected.
- Do not water while temperatures are below freezing.

PROPER FERTILIZATION

Plants need nutrients for growth, especially in Florida's sandy soils. Much of the fertilizer supplied is quickly gone in a month or two, used for growth or washed deeper into the ground.

There is much concern about groundwater pollution today, and it's important that only the right amount of fertilizer is applied, and not much more. Many plants actually grow better on a lean fertilizing schedule with fewer insect and disease problems, plus you won't have to mow or prune as much.

Where possible, use slow-releasing fertilizers. These supply the nutrients over a period of weeks or months.

Use your plant as a guide as to when feedings are needed. If it's green

and growing, skip a scheduled feeding. Keep fertilizers off walkways and roads. Keep a fertilizer-free zone at least 20 feet wide around lakes and waterways. Here are some suggested feeding times:

- ANNUALS FLOWERS: Monthly
- PERENNIAL FLOWERS: Every other month, March through November
- CITRUS TREES: March, May, August, and October
- CONTAINER PLANTINGS: Every other week during warmer months
- DECIDUOUS FRUIT TREES: February, June, and August
- GROUNDCOVERS: February, June, and September
- LAWNS: March and September
- ORCHIDS: Every other week, March through November
- ROSES: Monthly
- SHADE TREES: March and June for three years after planting
- SHRUBS: February, June, and September
- TROPICAL FRUITS: March, June, and September
- VEGETABLES AND HERBS: Monthly

WINTER CARE

If your plants are chosen properly they will need very little winter care. Most trees, shrubs, vines, and similar plants go dormant when shorter days signal the season's end.

Much of Florida's real plant damage occurs when warm days are followed by sudden freezes that catch plants in active growth.

Most gardeners do keep some plantings that could be damaged by cold. When cold warnings are sounded, our first urge is to encase plantings with plastic. But plants are not like people: they do not give off heat. Any heat that can warm a plant must be entrapped before the air cools, come from the ground, or be supplied by a heat source. Plants covered with plastic are unprotected. The cold quickly passes through the thin films so plants freeze, and if the wraps are not removed the sun cooks the plant inside the covers.

There are numerous ways to ensure winter survival of cold-sensitive plants:

- Keep the plants in pots that can be moved indoors.
- Dig the plants just before the freeze and put them in pots or burlap to move into warmer locations.
- Mound up soil over the lower stems to protect the buds from freezing. With some plants the tops can be removed a foot or two above ground, then soil mounded over the stems.
- Cover plants with cloth sheets or quilts draped to the ground.
- Surround plants with plastic over stakes held above and away from foliage. Outdoor-approved lights can be added to provide heat.

Perhaps the best advice in planning your landscape is to make most of your plantings cold-hardy ornamentals; for interest, add some of the exotics that might not survive the winter. Remember, not all winters bring freezing weather throughout the state. Many years the plants suffer only minor damage that can be pruned away when spring weather arrives.

HOW TO USE THE FLORIDA GARDENING RESOURCE GUIDE

Each entry in this guide provides you with information about a plant's particular characteristics, habits, and basic requirements for active growth as well as our personal experiences and knowledge of the plant. We have included the information you need to help you realize each plant's potential. Only when a plant performs at its best can one appreciate it fully. You will find such pertinent information as mature height and spread, bloom period and seasonal colors (if any), sun and soil preferences, water requirements, fertilizing needs, pruning and care, and pest information. Each section is clearly marked for easy reference.

SUN PREFERENCES

Symbols represent the range of sunlight suitable for each plant. The icon representing "Full Sun" means the plant needs to be sited in a full sun (8 to 10 hours of sun daily) location. "Part Sun" means the plant likes full sun, but will appreciate a few hours of protection from harsh, late-afternoon sun. "Part Shade" means the plant can be situated where it receives partial sun all day, or morning sun, or dappled shade. "Full Shade" means the plant needs a shady location protected from direct sunlight. Some plants can be grown in more than one range of sun, so you will sometimes see more than one sun symbol.

Full Sun   Part Sun   Part Shade   Shade

ADDITIONAL BENEFITS

Many plants offer benefits that further enhance their appeal. The following symbols indicate some of the more important additional benefits:

 Attracts Butterflies

 Has Fragrance

 Attracts Honeybees

 Attracts Hummingbirds

 Suitable for Cut Flowers or Arrangements

 Provides Food or Shelter for Wildlife

 Provides Edible Fruit

 Long Bloom Period

 Good Fall Color

 Provides Attractive Fruit

 Native Plant

 Drought Resistant

 Good for Containers

 Tropical or Tropical Looking

 Tolerates Seaside Conditions

 Award Winner

USDA COLD HARDINESS ZONE MAP

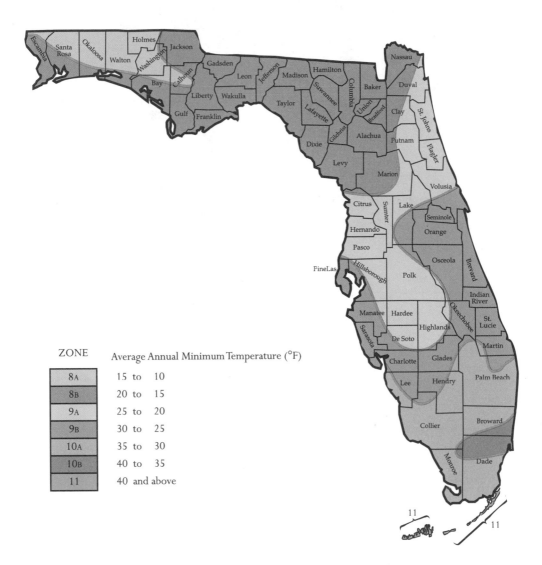

ZONE	Average Annual Minimum Temperature (°F)
8A	15 to 10
8B	20 to 15
9A	25 to 20
9B	30 to 25
10A	35 to 30
10B	40 to 35
11	40 and above

HARDINESS ZONES

Cold-hardiness zone designations were developed by the United States Department of Agriculture (USDA) to indicate the minimum average temperature for an area. A zone assigned to an individual plant indicates the lowest temperature at which the plant can be expected to survive over the winter. Florida has zones ranging from 8A to 11. Though a plant may grow (and grow well) in zones other than its recommended cold-hardiness zone, it is a good indication of which plants to consider for your landscape. Unless otherwise noted, the plants in this book are suitable for Florida.

ANNUALS
for Florida

Florida gardeners have learned that a quick way to add color to the landscape is to use annual flowers. Most can be purchased with blooms at local garden centers to bring home and create an instant garden. And the selection of annuals for the landscape is almost endless. As the name annual implies, the plants last only a season or two, but offer plenty of color for six to eight weeks. A few, including Geraniums, Impatiens, and Coleus, continue growing until seasonal changes in temperature cause decline.

CONSIDERATIONS BEFORE PLANTING

In Florida you have to learn when to plant certain annuals. There are two main types: the warm-season and the cool-season flowers. Warm-season annuals usually grow well between March and November. Then as the days shorten and temperatures dip into the 40s or lower at night, it's time to add the cool-season types. They are usually planted November through February in most areas of Florida.

Most annuals prefer the bright locations with at least six to eight hours of sun. When picking a location for the flower bed, remember the shifting pattern of the sun throughout the year. During the winter, the sun dips down in the horizon to create more shade in many locations.

Because our weather is so mild, it's common in Florida to make three or four annual plantings a year. But be careful which annuals you grow— some prefer the warm months, others the cooler seasons. Be sure to consult the Annuals chart (pages 42 and 43) before planting the garden.

PLANNING FOR ANNUAL FLOWERS

Annual flowers are cheery additions to a home landscape. Some gardeners like to plan large beds and others prefer spots of color.

If you want to plant a large bed of annuals, there is almost no limit to size. It's probably best to start small until you get the knack of caring for the plants, but you will soon find that growing annuals is easy. When you design the bed, keep these things in mind:

- Decide if you want the bed to be viewed from one side or from many sides.
- Design the bed with tall plants in the center or the back, depending on the viewing angles.
- Select low-growing annuals for the border plantings.
- Decide if you want paths through the bed or if you want to plant it solid.
- Plan to plant the bed in one type of annual flower, or plan for clusters of color.
- Select your flowers according to the light they will receive.
- Use a hose or extension cord to form the outline of the bed during the planning stage.
- Draw lines in the ground with a stick or hoe to show where each flower cluster should be planted.

Perhaps you do not have adequate room for a bed of color but still want to enjoy annual flowers. Container gardens could be for you. How about a big pot of color, maybe a planter box or hanging basket? You can also move containers around when company arrives to put the color where needed.

PLANTING

Most annuals grow in Florida's sandy soils. However, it pays to enrich sandy sites with lots of organic matter. First eliminate the weeds by digging them out or by applying a nonselective herbicide that allows planting after the weeds decline. Till the ground to a depth of 6 to 8 inches before planting, working in liberal quantities of compost, peat moss, and composted manure. Also test the soil acidity. All annuals prefer a pH around 6.5. Make adjustments as needed, following test recommendations. (For rocky alkaline soils, build raised beds.) Most gardeners like to scatter a light amount of a general garden fertilizer over the soil surface. When the ground is ready, follow these steps to good planting:

1. Moisten the soil thoroughly a day or two before planting.
2. Loosen the rootballs just a little if any roots are wrapped tightly together.
3. Arrange the plants over the bed at the correct spacing, using labels or charts as a guide.
4. Set the plants in the ground at the same depth they were growing in their containers.

5. Spread a thin layer of mulch over the bed, but keep it away from the base of the plants.

6. Water the entire bed of flowers thoroughly.

Gardeners have the option of sowing annual seeds directly into the ground. Unfortunately, Florida soils dry very rapidly, which makes establishing plantings by seed difficult. You will do much better if you sow the seeds in pots or individual cells of market packs and then add them to the landscape as transplants once they have sprouted.

Planting annuals in containers is easy, but be sure to start with a well-drained potting soil. You can make your own by combining equal parts of peat moss, perlite, and compost. Many gardeners prefer to use a potting soil purchased at a local garden center.

Container gardens can be devoted to one type of annual, or you can create the wildflower look by mixing several together. If you use more than one type, keep the tall flowers to the center or back of the container. You may want to use cascading types around the edges.

IN-GROUND ANNUALS

WATERING

Most annual flowers prefer a moist soil. Water annuals daily for the first week or two until the roots begin to grow out into the surrounding soil. Reduce watering frequency gradually until you are watering only when the surface soil is dry to the touch. Learn which annuals tolerate drought if you want to minimize watering chores.

FERTILIZING

Apply a balanced fertilizer monthly to encourage new growth and flowering. If you would like to take some of the work out of plant care, apply one of the slow-release products that can feed your plants for months. Be sure to follow label instructions.

GROOMING

Many annuals benefit from deadheading (the removal of fading flowers) to encourage additional blooms. If you want to develop fuller plants, nip out the tips of new growth. Lanky annuals can also be cut back to shorten the plant, which sometimes encourages new growth and blooms.

CONTAINER ANNUALS

WATERING

Check containers daily and water when surface soil feels dry to the touch. When plants begin to fill their pots, they may need water once or twice a day.

FERTILIZING

Fertilizer solutions are an easy way to feed annuals growing in containers. Apply a balanced fertilizer every other week. Many gardeners prefer to use a time-release fertilizer that is applied every few months.

GROOMING

Deadhead any faded flowers as needed. Remove declining individual annuals and replant as needed.

PEST CONTROL

Annual flowers have very few pests, but check your plantings frequently to prevent major problems. Holes in leaves, yellow spots, and browning plant parts can all mean pests are active. You may notice some of the following problems:

- Caterpillars can be up to 2 inches long. They chew holes in leaves, stems, and flowers. Many gardeners tolerate caterpillar damage and wait for the pests to be transformed into colorful moths or butterflies. Others handpick the insects from the plants to destroy them, or apply a natural insecticide containing *Bacillus thuringiensis*, or a properly labeled synthetic product.
- Aphids are soft-bodied, pear-shaped insects about ⅛ inch long. Their colors vary depending on the species and the plants they attack. They attack new growth and flower buds. Control with a natural soap spray or a properly labeled synthetic insecticide.
- Leafminers (immature stages of a moth or fly) tunnel inside the leaves of garden flowers.
- Some damage can be tolerated. Control by hanging sticky boards near plantings, or apply a properly labeled synthetic insecticide.
- Mites resemble tiny spiders, about ¹⁄₅₀ inch long, and they turn leaves yellow. Some produce a webbing between the leaves. Control with a soap spray.
- Slugs are slimy pests up to 2 inches long that chew flowers and foliage. They can often be detected by slime trails noticeable during the morning hours. Handpick from the plants or trap in shallow trays of beer or malt beverages, or control with natural slug baits available from garden centers.
- Nematodes are roundworms that live in most Florida soils. They develop large populations that destroy roots among susceptible plants. Use soil solarization to bake out nematodes during the summer. Plant resistant flowers such as marigolds, ageratum, and zinnias in problem sites.
- Root and stem rot problems are caused by several fungal organisms when plants are kept too moist or planted in sites previously infested with these organisms. Water on an "only-as-needed" schedule once plants are established. Replace the soil in heavily infested sites.

- Leaf spots are yellow and brown areas that develop on annual flower foliage because of fungal or bacterial infections. Keep the foliage as dry as possible. Fungicides are also available at garden centers to apply as needed.
- Rabbits can wreak havoc on an annual bed. Exclude with fencing or apply repellents available from garden centers. Plant varieties which are not a favorite food of rabbits.

AGERATUM
Ageratum houstonianum

HARDINESS
A tender warm season annual grown through-out Florida. Any freezing weather can cause major damage.

COLOR(S)
White or blue flowers

PEAK SEASON
Blooms spring to summer

MATURE SIZE
8 inches to over 2 feet tall

WATER NEEDS
Thoroughly moisten soil before and after planting. Water frequently for first few weeks. In sandy soils and containers, water when surface feels dry.

CARE
Space 12 to 18 inches apart to allow for spread.

PROBLEMS
Handpick caterpillars, mites, and garden flea hoppers or treat with recommended pesticide.

USES AND SELECTIONS
Ageratum provides a carpet of blue or pure white blossoms above spreading foliage. It is ideal for compact plantings along walkways or a blanket of border color in front of taller plants. Goes well with backdrops of Bush Daisy, Dusty Miller, Marigolds, Salvia, Snapdragons, and Petunias. Can be planted in beds, container gardens, and hanging baskets.

BABY'S BREATH
Gypsophila paniculata

HARDINESS
Zones 8-10

COLOR(S)
Tiny white flowers

PEAK SEASON
Blooms summer

MATURE SIZE
1½ to 4 feet x 3 to 4 feet

WATER NEEDS
Allow to dry out between waterings.

CARE
Prefers slightly alkaline soil and thrives in lean, well-drained soils. It is also somewhat salt tolerant. Baby's reath is quite easy to grow. It is full and billowing, so allow it sufficient elbowroom. Fertilize monthly for best flower production. Once established, it is an incredibly abundant bloomer, with little button flowers covering the plant. Blooms cut off for flower arrangements will be quickly replaced. Can also be grown as a perennial.

PROBLEMS
If kept too wet may get rot

USES AND SELECTIONS
The little white blooms are often used as accents in bouquets. It can also be used for bedding, borders, containers, and hanging baskets. Improved versions with plusher, double flowers are now common as well as pink or violet-tinged varieties.

CALENDULA
Calendula officinalis

HARDINESS
Cool weather annual used throughout Florida. Declines after day temperatures consistently reach 80° F.

COLOR(S)
Bright yellow, orange

PEAK SEASON
Fall and winter blooms

MATURE SIZE
8 to 24 inches tall, flowers over 2 inches in diameter

WATER NEEDS
Thoroughly moisten soil before and after planting. Water frequently for first few weeks, especially for sandy soil. Check container plantings often; water when surface feels dry.

CARE
Add plenty of organic material to sandy soil. Allow 12 to18 inch spacing. Add light mulch layer. Remove declining blossoms so new ones develop.

PROBLEMS
Planting in well-drained soil prevents most problems. Handpick any caterpillars or treat with pesticide.

USES AND SELECTIONS
Mix with cool season flowers such as Pansies, Snap- dragons, or Petunias. Also looks good with greenery such as Coleus, Dusty Miller, and low-growing shrubs. Good for bright color masses in flower beds, container gardens, and hanging baskets. Suitable for cut flowers.

CELOSIA
Celosia cristata

HARDINESS
A warm season annual used throughout Florida. Protect from frosts and freezes.

COLOR(S)
Yellow, orange, red, pink flowers

PEAK SEASON
Blooms fall to late spring

MATURE SIZE
10 to 18 inches

WATER NEEDS
Thoroughly moisten soil before and after planting. Water frequently for first few weeks, especially for sandy soil. Then water when surface feels dry.

CARE
Plant 10 to 12 inches apart. Remove declining blossoms to keep color coming. Gives about six to eight weeks of good color before needing replacement.

PROBLEMS
Avoid during summer rainy season, when rainy damp weather causes flowers to rot. Handpick any caterpillars or treat with recommended pesticide.

USES AND SELECTIONS
A unique way to add garden color, with brightly colored flowers held high above foliage. There are two flower forms, plume and cockscomb. Plant a bed of mixed colors, combine with other plants, use as backdrop, or plant in containers. Cut flowers good for bouquets or drying.

COLEUS
Coleus x *hybridus*

HARDINESS
In North Florida replant after each winter, unless given extra winter protection. Central and South Florida gardeners may keep plants growing for several years.

COLOR(S)
Various shaped leaves have mixtures of pink, green, yellow, bronze, or red

PEAK SEASON
Year-round foliage

MATURE SIZE
1 to 2 feet tall

WATER NEEDS
Keep new plants moist. Once established, water when soil feels dry. Check container plantings daily.

CARE
Add plenty of organic material to sandy soil. Space 12 to 18 inches apart. Add light mulch layer. With long Florida growing season, Coleus may grow too tall. Cut back to desirable height.

PROBLEMS
May get slugs or caterpillars. Use slug bait, Handpick caterpillars, or treat with pesticide.

USES AND SELECTIONS
Mix many colors together or select flowering plants with blooms to match the Coleus' leaves. Plant with low growing Gingers, Ivy, and Liriope. Use in ground beds and containers. Varieties with greater sun tolerance and ruffled leaves are being introduced.

COSMOS
Cosmos spp.

HARDINESS
Zones 9-10

COLOR(S)
Red, white, pink, purple, yellow flowers

PEAK SEASON
Spring and summer

MATURE SIZE
1 to 7 feet tall

WATER NEEDS
Somewhat drought tolerant once established.

CARE
Easy to grow, thriving even in poor soils, if well-drained. Space 12 to 18 inches apart. Stake taller varieties. Very easy to grow from seeds and to transplant.

PROBLEMS
Virtually pest resistant. If too much fertilizer is applied, they will grow lots of feathery foliage at the expense of flowers.

USES AND SELECTIONS
Cosmos (also called Mexican Aster) is one of the best nectar plants for attracting butterflies. The flowers are also ideal for cut flowers and for pressing. Use taller selections of Cosmos as background or border plants. Use shorter varieties in front of hedges. They are also ideal for wildflower, meadow, and butterfly gardens. There are several species and hybrids available, including the dwarf 'Sonata Series', which is ideal for container plantings.

DIANTHUS

Dianthus x hybrida

HARDINESS
Similar culture throughout Florida. Northern plantings can survive light freeze with little protection. Southern plants are often shorter lived, although some gardeners get plants through summer by using containers moved to cooler locations during hotter months.

COLOR(S)
Pink, white, or red flowers

PEAK SEASON
Blooms fall through spring

MATURE SIZE
8 to 18 inches

WATER NEEDS
After established, water when soil feels dry. Container-grown plants may need more frequent watering.

CARE
Add plenty of organic material to sandy soil. Space 10 to 12 inches apart. Do not plant too deeply. Add light mulch layer. May live for more than one growing season. Deadheading may help keep bed attractive.

PROBLEMS
Handpick any caterpillars or treat with pesticide.

USES AND SELECTIONS
Also called Pinks. Use for large color masses in flower beds or color splashes along walkways or in containers. Good selections are 'Baby Doll', 'Carpet', 'Charms', 'Flash', 'Floral Lace', 'Ideal', 'Magic Charm', and 'Telstar'.

DUSTY MILLER

Senecio cineraria

HARDINESS
In North and Central Florida Dusty Miller often survives to early summer. Southern gardeners may delay planting until late fall's cooler temperatures.

COLOR(S)
Fuzzy gray-green leaves look silvery

PEAK SEASON
Fall through spring

MATURE SIZE
12 to 18 inches tall

WATER NEEDS
After establishing, water when soil feels dry. Container-grown plants may need more frequent watering.

CARE
Add plenty of organic material to sandy soil. Space 10 to 12 inches apart. Do not plant too deeply. Add light mulch layer.

PROBLEMS
Hot, damp weather causes plants to rapidly decline. May have caterpillars as pests. Handpicking is best.

USES AND SELECTIONS
The leaves of Dusty Miller vary from coarsely toothed to lace-like. They add textural interest and are the perfect foil to brightly colored annuals in ground beds and containers. Use plants with contrasting colors, such as red Salvia, purple Petunias, or red Begonias. Good selections are 'Cirrus', 'Silver Dust', and 'Silver Queen'.

GAZANIA
Gazania spp.

HARDINESS
Grows best fall through spring. Tolerates light frosts. Summer rains cause rot problems.

COLOR(S)
Yellow, orange, red flowers; blue-green foliage

PEAK SEASON
Year-round flowering

MATURE SIZE
6 to 12 inches x 12 to 24 inches

WATER NEEDS
Very drought tolerant. Does not tolerate soggy roots.

CARE
Requires well-drained soil. Does best in enriched soil. Thrives in hot, dry areas and needs full sun for blooming. On cloudy days flowers might not open all the way. When used as a ground cover, plant 12 to 18 inches apart. Also grown as a perennial.

PROBLEMS
No pests or diseases are big problems. May get root rot if kept too wet.

USES AND SELECTIONS
The low-growing Gazania provides mounds of blue-green foliage with cheery daisy-like flowers. It is invaluable in sunny, dry areas where other things won't grow. Use as a ground cover, edging, and to control erosion. It is also suitable for xeriscaping, rock gardens, and containers.

GERANIUM
Pelargonium x *hortorum*

HARDINESS
Grow well throughout Florida. Planting can begin in October if winter protection is provided.

COLOR(S)
Foliage can have zonal marking. Blooms are pink, red, and lavender, plus white and blends.

PEAK SEASON
Fall through spring

MATURE SIZE
18 to 24 inches tall

WATER NEEDS
After establishing, water when soil feels dry. Container-grown plants may need more frequent watering.

CARE
Add plenty of organic material to sandy soil. Space 12 to 18 inches apart. Do not plant too deeply. Add light mulch layer. Tolerates some shade, but needs sunny location for best flowering.

PROBLEMS
May have caterpillars as pests. Handpicking is best. Summer rains cause rot and plant decline.

USES AND SELECTIONS
A beloved bedding plant, Geranium produces colorful flower clusters above the foliage. Some genus members are perennials. However, in Florida, Geraniums are treated as cool-season annuals, to be replaced when the summer rainy season starts. Can be planted in ground beds and containers.

GLOBE AMARANTH
Gomphrena globosa

☼ ⚘ ⚘ ⬤ ⚘

HARDINESS
Plant during warmer months. It is damaged by frosts and freezes.

COLOR(S)
Yellow, white, pink, purple flowers

PEAK SEASON
Blooms summer through fall

MATURE SIZE
12 to 24 inches x 6 to 12 inches

WATER NEEDS
Moderately drought tolerant. Water when very dry, but do not overwater.

CARE
This carefree plant tolerates poor soil, heat, and drought. Seeds may be sown directly into the garden or started indoors. To dry these ever-lasting flowers, cut just before they completely open and hang upside down in a warm, dark place. When planted close together they pro-duce longer stems, which are better for drying.

PROBLEMS
Free of most pests and diseases

USES AND SELECTIONS
The showy clover-like flowers of Globe Ama-ranth look good in borders, edging, and mass plantings. They are ideal in containers, along walkways, and in drier areas where color is needed. Many hybrids are available in differ-ent colors and growth habits, including more compact plants.

HOLLYHOCK
Alcea rosea

☼ ⬤

HARDINESS
Plant during fall to experience winter cold.

COLOR(S)
Yellow, white, pink, lavender, maroon, red flowers

PEAK SEASON
Blooms spring and summer

MATURE SIZE
5 to 8 feet x 2 to 3 feet

WATER NEEDS
Somewhat drought tolerant once established. Water during very dry periods. Do not overwater.

CARE
Easy to grow. Shelter tall varieties from wind or stake them. Hollyhocks self-sow, so site them where they can multiply, or deadhead the flowers to prevent volunteers next season.

PROBLEMS
The heat of summer may cause decline. Leaves may develop rust disease and should be removed and destroyed.

USES AND SELECTIONS
Tall, showy Hollyhocks are a cottage garden classic. They are great swaying along a fence or wall. They may also be planted at the back of a perennial bed, in mixed borders, in xeriscape gardens, or near an entryway. Not all varieties are suitable for Florida. Try to find local seed and selections.

IMPATIENS

Impatiens walleriana

HARDINESS

Grow well throughout Florida for most of the year. North and Central Florida gardeners may need to provide winter protection, but cold affected Impatiens may grow back.

COLOR(S)

All color flowers

PEAK SEASON

Blooms year-round

MATURE SIZE

10 to 24 inches tall

WATER NEEDS

Space 12 to 14 inches apart in thoroughly moistened soil. Once established, water when soil feels dry. Container-grown plants may need more frequent watering.

CARE

If Impatiens become tall and lanky, prune back to within 1 foot of the ground.

PROBLEMS

May have caterpillars, slugs, and mites. Hand-pick or use approved pesticide. Nematodes may also be a pest. There is no easy control, so replace soil in infested beds or grow plants in containers.

USES AND SELECTIONS

Impatiens provide color in areas where other plants refuse to bloom. Using Impatiens is an economical way to fill large areas with color. Can be planted in ground beds, containers, and hanging baskets.

JOHNNY-JUMP-UP

Viola tricolor

HARDINESS

Tolerates frosts and freezes. Grows best November through March.

COLOR(S)

Multi-hued flowers of blue, white, lilac, or gold

PEAK SEASON

Blooms late fall through early spring

MATURE SIZE

To 8 inches

WATER NEEDS

Keep moist

CARE

Plant in well-drained, enriched soil. In northern parts of the state may be perennial.

PROBLEMS

These carefree plants don't like Florida's heat and humidity. Most decline in early spring.

USES AND SELECTIONS

The cheery petite faces of Johnny-Jump-Up have long been popular in northern climates. Also called Viola, it is the most frost- and freeze-resistant winter annual in Florida. Plant in hanging baskets, containers, ground covers, or massed in beds. The blossoms are edible cooked or raw; they make great garnishes and cake decorations. Recent All-America Selection winners include 'Skippy XL Red-Gold' and 'Rain Blue and Purple' (colors change as they mature). Florida also has some native blue and white violets.

31

LOBELIA
Lobelia erinus

HARDINESS
Cold tolerant. Survives all but hard freezes.

COLOR(S)
Blue, violet, white, purple flowers

PEAK SEASON
Blooms winter and spring

MATURE SIZE
3 to 12 inches x 12 to 24 inches

WATER NEEDS
Needs plenty of moisture

CARE
Plant these cool-season annuals in rich, fertile, well-drained soil. In warmer parts of Florida, plant in partial shade. When temperatures get too hot, plants decline. Plants are best obtained as transplants during the later fall and winter.

PROBLEMS
If kept too damp, the stem or roots may rot.

USES AND SELECTIONS
Use compact varieties for edgings, borders, or mass plantings. Lobelia with trailing habit can be used in containers, raised beds, or cascading over walls. Many cultivars of this spectacular little plant are available, including 'Cambridge Blue' (compact), 'Crystal Palace' (bronze green leaves), 'Paper Moon' (white flowers), and 'Sapphire' (trailing with purple flowers).

MARIGOLD
Tagetes patula

HARDINESS
North and Central Florida gardeners must wait until cooler weather is over. Frosts and freezes kill Marigolds. In warmer areas they can be grown year-round.

COLOR(S)
Yellow, orange, red, maroon, white flowers

PEAK SEASON
Blooms spring through fall

MATURE SIZE
8 to 12 or more inches

WATER NEEDS
Space 10 to 18 inches apart in thoroughly moistened soil. Once they're established, water when soil feels dry. Container-grown plants may need more frequent watering.

CARE
Be prepared to protect Marigold plantings from frosts.

PROBLEMS
May have caterpillars, garden flea hoppers, mites, and leaf miners. Handpick or use approved pesticide.

USES AND SELECTIONS
Use African and American (*Tagetes erecta*), and French Marigolds in combination with warm-season annuals and perennials. Their color and compact size go well with Ageratum, Salvia, Torenia, Zinnias, herbs, and vegetables. Marigolds can be planted in ground beds and containers. Suitable for flower beds or along walkways.

MELAMPODIUM

Melampodium divaricatum
(synonym *M. paludosum*)

HARDINESS
Grows best during warmer months. Damaged by freezes.

COLOR(S)
Yellow flowers

PEAK SEASON
Blooms summer through fall

MATURE SIZE
10 to 36 inches x 15 to 48 inches

WATER NEEDS
Drought tolerant once established

CARE
Plant in well-drained soil. This carefree plant loves heat and blooms prolifically. The bushy mounds are filled with self-cleaning flowers so deadheading isn't required; is self-branching, so trimming isn't needed either. Fertilize every two weeks for maximum blooms. It readily self-seeds, providing lots of new seedlings.

PROBLEMS
Pest and disease free

USES AND SELECTIONS
Plant Melampodium in beds, borders, in mass plantings, and as edging. Create a bold look by planting with dark leafed Coleus, Ornamental Pepper, or 'Blackie' Ornamental Sweet Potato. Make interesting color combinations when mixed with red Zinnias or Salvia. Use shorter, compact selections as ground covers and in containers. Cultivars only 10 inches tall are 'Compact Million Gold', 'Lemon Delight', and Derby'.

MEXICAN SUNFLOWER

Tithonia rotundiflora

HARDINESS
Plant during warmer months. Damaged by frosts and freezes.

COLOR(S)
Brilliant red-orange flowers

PEAK SEASON
Blooms spring through fall

MATURE SIZE
5 to 6 feet x 3 to 4 feet

WATER NEEDS
Drought tolerant. Water when dry.

CARE
Plant in well-drained soil. Does best in full sun. The stems and leaves are covered with soft fuzz. Heat tolerant and grows quickly. In a single season it can self-seed for a second generation. Allow plenty of room.

PROBLEMS
Tithonia diversifolia (also called Mexican Sunflower or Giant Mexican Sunflower) is invading into native Florida areas and should not be planted.

USES AND SELECTIONS
An excellent butterfly plant. Use in border and beds. Popular cultivars 'Torch' and 'Fiesta del Sol' (dwarf) were All-America Selections. Another dwarf variety, 'Goldfinger', is also ideal for smaller gardens, growing to 3 feet tall. When cutting flowers for arrangements, carefully cut them with a sharp knife to prevent damaging the delicate stem.

NICOTIANA
Nicotiana alata

HARDINESS
In North and Central Florida limit plantings to spring. In South plant both spring and early fall. Nicotiana does not grow well in hot summer or cooler winter months.

COLOR(S)
Red, pink, white flowers

PEAK SEASON
Blooms spring and fall

MATURE SIZE
18 to 24 inches

WATER NEEDS
Space 12 to 18 inches apart in thoroughly moistened soil. Once established, water when soil feels dry. Container-grown plants may need more frequent watering.

CARE
Extend flowering by keeping plant from going to seed. As soon as flowering stalks finish blooming, cut them back.

PROBLEMS
Hot, rainy weather destroys flowers. Handpick any caterpillars, apply *Bacillus thuringiensis*, or use other approved pesticide.

USES AND SELECTIONS
Plant in ground beds and containers. Suitable as bedding plant alone or as backdrop for other plants. Striking as accent in center of container with other plants down the sides. Mix with warm season flowers including Celosia, Marigolds, Salvia, Torenia, and Zinnias.

ORNAMENTAL PEPPER
Capsicum annuum

HARDINESS
Plant during warmer months. Damaged by frosts and freezes.

COLOR(S)
White, yellow, orange, red, purple fruit

PEAK SEASON
Fruiting from late spring to frost

MATURE SIZE
12 to 20 inches x 12 to 18 inches

WATER NEEDS
Water regularly

CARE
Plant in well-drained, enriched soil. Grow in full sun or partial shade. Fruit can be round, short and stubby, or long and narrow.

PROBLEMS
Generally pest free. Although edible, peppers are far too hot for most to tolerate, so tell children not to eat them.

USES AND SELECTIONS
With peppers always on the plant in varying stages of ripeness, Ornamental Pepper is often a riot of color. (They remain for a long time.) Use in containers, mass plantings, borders, and mixed with flowers in beds. Many cultivars are developed for fruit size, shape, and color. Several have been All-America Selections, including 'Black Pearl' (dark fruit with black-purple leaves), 'Holiday Time', 'Chilly Chili', and 'Candlelight'.

PANSY
Viola x *wittrockiana*

HARDINESS
Hardy throughout Florida. After Florida's coldest weather, pansies may be the only flowers blooming. Needs really cool weather and grows best when night temperatures are in the 50s. Wait until there is a consistent chill in the air before planting.

COLOR(S)
All color flowers

PEAK SEASON
Blooms fall and winter

MATURE SIZE
10 to 12 inches tall

WATER NEEDS
Space 6 to 8 inches apart in thoroughly moistened soil. Pansies fill in slowly.

CARE
Remove old blossoms to keep new flowers forming.

PROBLEMS
May have aphids and slugs as pests. Handpick or use approved pesticide. Decline when hot spring weather arrives.

USES AND SELECTIONS
Can be planted in ground beds, containers, and hanging baskets. As cut flowers, they are perfect for bouquets. Edge borders or fill entire gardens with mix of Pansy colors. Or use just a single selection to contrast with other cool-season annuals like Dianthus, Dusty Miller, Petunia, and Snapdragons.

PETUNIA
Petunia x *hybrida*

HARDINESS
Plant when weather cools. North Florida plantings have longer season (into early summer), but need protection from occasional severe freezes.

COLOR(S)
Flowers all colors and blends

PEAK SEASON
Fall through spring blooms

MATURE SIZE
12 to 18 inches tall

WATER NEEDS
Space 10 to 12 inches apart in thoroughly moistened soil.

CARE
Often grow lanky and full of old blossoms and seedpods. Periodically prune to remove old portions and encourage new growth.

PROBLEMS
May have caterpillars and aphids as pests. Handpick or use approved pesticide.

USES AND SELECTIONS
Plant in ground beds, containers, and hanging baskets. Varieties range from just over 1-inch flowers to over 4 inches across. They take light frosts and provide spring color when gardens need it most. Mix with greenery, other cool season plants, shrubs, or bulb plantings. Good companions include Calendula, Dianthus, Nicotiana, Salvias, and Snapdragons. 'Wave' hybrids can last into warmer months.

PORTULACA
Portulaca grandiflora

HARDINESS
Provides color in sun-drenched areas when Florida's summer sun withers other plants. Cool weather causes decline, so South Florida plantings start earlier and end later each season.

COLOR(S)
Brilliant reds, pinks, oranges, yellows, creams, white flowers

PEAK SEASON
Blooms spring through summer

MATURE SIZE
3 to 6 inches tall

WATER NEEDS
Space 8 to 10 inches apart in thoroughly moistened soil.

CARE
Don't worry if you skip a watering or two for this warm-season flower; Portulaca is quite drought tolerant. Portulacas will flower (in sunny locations) for six to eight weeks before gradually declining.

PROBLEMS
May have mites. Apply a soap spray or use approved pesticide. Excessive moisture causes rot.

USES AND SELECTIONS
Also called Mexican Rose and Moss Rose. Plant in ground beds, containers, and hanging baskets. Portulaca is best used as a border, to highlight beds of greenery, or in hanging baskets with taller plants. Also suitable for rock gardens or desert-look plantings.

SALVIA
Salvia splendens

HARDINESS
Provides almost year-round color throughout Florida. In Southern regions Salvia can be grown as a perennial. In Central Florida cover during cold weather, and in Northern areas it is likely to be damaged by frosts and freezes.

COLOR(S)
Bright red, salmon, pink, purple, and white flowers

PEAK SEASON
Blooms year-round

MATURE SIZE
8 to 18 inches tall

WATER NEEDS
Space 10 to 16 inches apart in thoroughly moistened soil. Once established, wait until soil surface feels dry, then soak.

CARE
When buying Salvias, avoid potbound plants. Keep plants attractive and encourage new shoots by periodically removing old flower heads and extra-long stems. May reseed.

PROBLEMS
May have caterpillars, mites, and slugs. Hand-picking is best.

USES AND SELECTIONS
Also called Scarlet Sage, it can be planted in ground beds and containers. A bed of different Salvia types and colors displays well, as do clusters planted with Dusty Miller, Marigold, Petunia, Snapdragon, and Wax Begonia.

ON

light freezes. In North
…ovide protection for
…uth Florida, wait for
…nt.

…thoroughly
…d, wait until

…flower spikes.
…ds encour-
…apid decline

…es or garden
…dpicking

…s and containers,
…e. A good planting
…Hollyhocks with
…ias. New Snap-
…mpact, only 8 to
…arieties (like 'Rocket'
…buquets.

Handwritten note: AMANDA PIKE — Transferrins

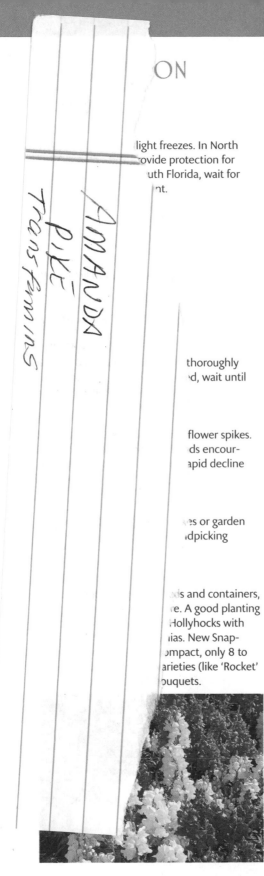

SUNFLOWER
Helianthus annuus

HARDINESS
Plant during warmer months in North Florida, year-round in Central and South Florida.

COLOR(S)
Yellow, orange, red flowers

PEAK SEASON
Blooms best spring through fall

MATURE SIZE
2 to 15 feet

WATER NEEDS
Drought tolerant

CARE
Plant in organically enriched soil. Fertilize every 3 or 4 weeks, with adequate potassium for strong stems. To harvest seeds, cut flower after it dries. Hang upside down in well-ventilated place. When completely dry remove seeds for eating by you or local wildlife.

PROBLEMS
Bugs may damage foliage and flowers. Hand-pick to control.

USES AND SELECTIONS
Sunflowers are a native American crop of global importance, grown for oil, snack seed, birdseed, garden flowers, and cut flowers. Plant for borders, screening, and along fences. They are also good in wildlife and children's gardens. Some new cultivars have shorter heights and different colors. All American Selection winners include 'Soraya' and 'Ring of Fire' (bi-colored petals). Florida has several native *Helianthus*.

TORENIA
Torenia fournieri

HARDINESS
Also called Summer Pansy and Wishbone Flower, start planting Torenia as soon as cold weather is over. It needs similar care throughout the state, with Northern gardeners delaying until consistently warm weather arrives.

COLOR(S)
Lavender, white, blue, and pink combinations

PEAK SEASON
Blooms spring through fall

MATURE SIZE
Sprawling plants 6 to 12 inches tall

WATER NEEDS
Space 8 to 12 inches apart in thoroughly moistened soil. When established, wait until soil surface feels dry, then soak.

CARE
A vigorous grower that tolerates heat, rain, and light shade. Torenia produces one flush of blooms after another for the entire warm season.

PROBLEMS
May have caterpillars and slugs. Handpicking is best. Use *Bacillus thuringiensis*, slug bait, or other recommended control.

USES AND SELECTIONS
Can be planted in ground beds, containers, and hanging baskets. Torenia can be used as a groundcover or as edging with Celosia, Marigolds, Nicotiana, and Vinca in the middle.

VERBENA
Verbena x hybrida

HARDINESS
Cold sensitive and may be damaged by frosts and freezes in North and Central Florida. Grows best in spring and fall.

COLOR(S)
Deep green leaves with blue, purple, red, white, and cream flowers

PEAK SEASON
Spring through early winter blooms

MATURE SIZE
Wide-spreading plants 10 to 12 inches tall

WATER NEEDS
Space 10 to 14 inches apart in thoroughly moistened soil. When established, wait until soil surface feels dry, then soak.

CARE
Most selections give six to eight weeks of good flowering before needing to be replaced.

PROBLEMS
May have caterpillars, mites, and garden flea hoppers. Handpick or use recommended pest controls. Blooms may be damaged by summer heat and rains.

USES AND SELECTIONS
Use in ground beds, containers, and hanging baskets. Ideal as colorful groundcover or in containers. Verbena also makes attractive edging for borders or to spill over sides of hanging baskets. Plant with Begonias, Celosia, Dusty Miller, Geraniums, Marigolds, and Snapdragons.

WAX BEGONIA
Begonia x *semperflorens-cultorum*

☼ ☼ ☼ ☼ 🌿 🌿

HARDINESS
In South Florida plant year-round. In North and Central areas, plant March through May so they can establish before days become consistently hot.

COLOR(S)
Foliage is green, variegated, or bronze. Single or double flowers are all shades of pinks and reds, plus pure whites.

PEAK SEASON
Blooms year-round

MATURE SIZE
12 to 18 inches tall

WATER NEEDS
Space 10 to 12 inches apart in thoroughly moistened soil. Once established, wait until soil surface feels dry, then soak.

CARE
Begonia is a dependable, minimal-care plant that thrives in many conditions. May grow for several seasons before declining. If plants become lanky, prune to renew compact shape.

PROBLEMS
May have caterpillars and slugs. Use BT, soap spray, slug bait, or other recommended pest controls. May be damaged by excessive moisture.

USES AND SELECTIONS
Can be planted in ground beds or containers. Create a Begonia bed or combine with Ageratum, Dianthus, Dusty Miller, Torenia, Verbena, and Zinnias.

ZINNIA
Zinnia elegans

☼ 🦋 🐝 🏺 🌿 💧

HARDINESS
Plant before weather gets too hot and humid. The North Florida season is longer. Early plantings in Central and South Florida give six to eight weeks of flowering.

COLOR(S)
Pink, red, orange, plum, white flowers

PEAK SEASON
Blooms spring

MATURE SIZE
8 to 36 inches tall

WATER NEEDS
Space 10 to 20 inches apart in thoroughly moistened soil. Once established, wait until soil surface feels dry, then soak.

CARE
A carefree plant with big, long-lasting blossoms. Extend flowering period by removing declining blossoms.

PROBLEMS
Plant in spring to avoid diseases. May have caterpillars, leaf spot, and powdery mildew. Handpick caterpillars or treat with Bt. Apply copper fungicide or other approved fungicide.

USES AND SELECTIONS
Use both tall and short varieties in ground beds or containers. Plant smaller selections as edging and taller types as focal points. Newer varieties tolerate summer heat and rains. Attractive when mixed with Marigolds, Salvia, and Verbena. Excellent as cut flowers.

ANNUALS

Variety	Flower Color	Height (Inches)	Spacing (Inches)	Cold Hardiness	Light Level
Ageratum	White, blue, pink	6 – 18	10 – 12	Tender	Sun to light shade
Alyssum	White, pink, purple	6 – 12	10 – 12	Tender	Sun to light shade
Amaranthus	Red	36 – 48	12 – 18	Tender	Sun
Aster	White, pink, blue	18 – 24	12 – 18	Tender	Sun to light shade
Baby's Breath	White, pink	18 – 36	18 – 24	Hardy	Sun
Balsam	White, red, purple	18 – 24	12 – 18	Tender	Sun to light shade
Browallia	White, purple	12 – 18	10 – 12	Tender	Sun to light shade
Calendula	Orange, yellow	12 – 18	10 – 12	Hardy	Sun
California Poppy	Yellow, orange	18 – 24	12 – 18	Hardy	Sun
Celosia	Orange, red, yellow	8 – 24	10 – 12	Tender	Sun
Cleome	White, pink	36 – 48	18 – 24	Hardy	Sun
Coleus	Insignificant	12 – 30	12 – 18	Tender	Sun to light shade
Cosmos	White, pink, yellow	18 – 36	12 – 18	Tender	Sun
Dahlberg Daisy	Yellow	6 – 8	8 – 12	Tender	Sun
Delphinium	White, pink, purple	24 – 36	12 – 18	Hardy	Sun
Dianthus	White, pink, red	12 – 18	8 – 12	Hardy	Sun to light shade
Dusty Miller	Yellow	12 – 24	10 – 12	Hardy	Sun to light shade
Foxglove	White, pink, purple	24 – 36	12 – 18	Hardy	Sun to light shade
Gazania	Orange, red, yellow	12 – 18	8 – 12	Tender	Sun
Geranium	White, red, lavender	18 – 24	12 – 24	Tender	Sun
Globe Amaranth	Pink, purple	12 – 24	12 – 18	Tender	Sun
Hollyhock	White, pink, purple	48 – 60	18 – 24	Hardy	Sun
Impatiens	White, pink, purple	12 – 24	12 – 18	Tender	Shade
Johnny-Jump-Up	Yellow, pink, blue, purple	8 – 12	6 – 10	Hardy	Sun
Lobelia	White, blue, purple	8 – 12	8 – 12	Tender	Sun to light shade
Marigold	Yellow, orange	10 – 36	12 – 18	Tender	Sun

ANNUALS

Variety	Flower Color	Height (Inches)	Spacing (Inches)	Cold Hardiness	Light Level
Melampodium	Yellow	18 – 24	12 – 18	Tender	Sun
Mexican Sunflower	Orange	36 – 48	18 – 24	Tender	Sun
Nasturtium	White, yellow, orange	12 – 24	12 – 18	Tender	Sun
Nicotiana	White, pink, red	12 – 24	12 – 18	Tender	Sun
Nierembergia	White, purple	8 – 12	10 – 12	Tender	Sun to light shade
Ornamental Kale or Cabbage	Yellow	10 – 12	12 – 18	Hardy	Sun
Ornamental Pepper	Cream	12 – 18	10 – 12	Tender	Sun
Pansy	Yellow, orange, purple	6 – 8	8 – 10	Hardy	Sun
Periwinkle	White, pink, purple	12 – 18	12 – 24	Tender	Sun
Petunia	White, pink, red, purple	8 – 16	12 – 18	Hardy	Sun to light shade
Phlox (Annual)	White, pink, purple	12 – 18	8 – 12	Hardy	Sun
Purslane	White, yellow, pink	8 – 12	12 – 18	Tender	Sun
Rose Moss	White, yellow, pink, orange	6 – 10	8 – 12	Tender	Sun
Scarlet Sage	White, red, pink, purple	12 – 24	12 – 18	Tender	Sun to light shade
Silk Flower	Pink, red	18 – 24	12 – 18	Tender	Sun
Snapdragon	White, pink, yellow, red	10 – 36	10 – 12	Hardy	Sun to light shade
Stock	White, pink, purple	12 – 24	10 – 12	Hardy	Sun
Strawflower	Red, yellow, orange	18 – 24	10 – 12	Tender	Sun
Sunflower	Yellow, orange	12 – 124	12 – 24	Tender	Sun
Sweet Pea	White, pink, red, purple	18 – 72	8 – 12	Hardy	Sun
Torenia	White, pink, blue, purple	10 – 18	12 – 18	Tender	Sun to light shade
Verbena	White, red, purple	8 – 12	12 – 18	Tender	Sun
Wax Begonia	White, pink, red	12 – 18	8 – 12	Tender	Sun to shade
Zinnia	White, yellow, orange, red	12 – 36	12 – 24	Tender	Sun

ANNUAL PLANTING TIMES BY REGION

Variety	North	Central	South
Ageratum	March – May September – November	February – May	November – March
Alyssum	February – March September – November	February – April	October – March
Amaranthus	March – May	March – May	October – March
Asters	March – April	February – April	October – March
Baby's Breath	February – March October – December	February – March	August – December
Balsam	March – June	February – June	February – May
Browallia	March – May	March – April	February – March
Calendula	February – April	November – March	November – March
California Poppy	November – January	November – February	November – February
Celosia	March – May September – November	March – May September – November	March – May
Cleome	March – June September – November	March – May	February – May
Coleus	April – September	March – September	March – October
Cosmos	April – May	March – April	November – March
Dahlberg Daisy	April – June	March – June	March – June
Delphinium	February – March	November – January	November – February
Dianthus	November – March	November – March	November – February
Dusty Miller	February – May	November – May	November – April
Foxglove	February – March	December – March	December – February
Gazania	March – May September – November	March – May	November – May
Geranium	March – May	November – April	November – March
Globe Amaranth	March – September September – October	March – May September – November	March – May
Hollyhock	March – April	November – December	Not recommended
Impatiens	March – September	March – November	March – November
Johnny-Jump-Up	November – February	November – February	November – January
Lobelia	March – April	November – March	November – February

ANNUAL PLANTING TIMES BY REGION

Variety	North	Central	South
Marigold	April – June September – October	March – June	October – March
Melampodium	March – July	March – July	February – August
Mexican Sunflower	April – July	March – June	February – June
Nasturtium	March – April	November – March	November – March
Nicotiana	March – May September – October	March – April September – October	February – April
Nierembergia	April – July	March – July	March – July
Ornamental Kale or Cabbage	November – February	November – March	November – February
Ornamental Pepper	March – June September – October	March – May	September – April
Pansy	November – February	November – February	November – January
Periwinkle	March – June	March – October	March – October
Petunia	November – March	November – April	November – March
Phlox (Annual)	October – November	October – December	October – December
Purslane	April – July	April – June	April – June
Rose Moss	April – July	March – May	March – May
Scarlet Sage	March – June September – November	March – May September – November	February – May
Silk Flower	April – July	April – July	March – July
Snapdragon	October – March	November – March	November – March
Stock	March – April	November – March	November – March
Strawflower	March – May	March – April	November – March
Sunflower	February – May September – October	February – May	November – April
Sweet Pea	October – February	November – February	November – February
Torenia	March – June September – October	March – June September – October	February – May
Verbena	March – May October – November	March – April October – November	February – March
Wax Begonia	March – June September – November	March – May	October – April
Zinnia	March – May September – October	March – April September – October	February – March

JANUARY

• It's great planting weather. Check garden areas that need replanting and add your favorites. It will soon be too late for some cool-season annuals. Pansies and Violas must be planted now since they need cooler temperatures to survive.

• When warm-season annuals start to fade, add cool-season color. If frosts and freezing weather have damaged some plants, make replacements.

• Annuals grow a little more slowly during cooler months, but check at least once a week for pests and water needs. Cold weather could appear at any time, so be prepared to protect plants that need it.

• Plants that have been growing for a few months may be getting lanky or forming seedheads. Stretch their life by pruning faded flowers, cutting spindly stems, and applying monthly fertilizer.

• January is one of the driest months, so provide extra waterings, but only if necessary.

• Pests may still be affected by caterpillars. Handpick or use *Bacillus thuringiensis* insecticide.

FEBRUARY

• This is rejuvenation month for most annual flower beds. As you remove old plants, try to determine if they had any problems, such as weeds, nematodes, or insects. Careful preparation of new beds can help prevent some problems.

• This is the last time to plant some of the flowers that need cool weather.

• With longer and warmer days, annual flowers should start making more active growth. Good care is needed now to help old beds keep blooming and new beds to fill in quickly.

• This is still the cool-but-dry season. Plants use moisture slowly, but will need some extra water when surface begins to dry.

• If you are using a general or liquid fertilizer, it's time for the monthly application for plants that are in bloom. There is no need to fertilize beds you are about to remove.

• Check for pests weekly, especially caterpillars and mites. Look for cutworms when preparing new beds.

MARCH

• Planting annuals from pots is simple. If they are potbound, fluff apart the roots without tearing large root sections. Try not to use the same plants in the same spot year after year, which builds up pests specific to one plant.

• Water new plantings daily for a week or two. Don't count on an irrigation system. Reduce watering to an as-needed schedule when plants grow into surrounding soil. Overwatering causes root and stem rots.

• If you are using slow-release fertilizer check the label for application rate and schedule to be reapplied. Note the date on your calendar but check the plants' condition for any additional feedings. If using regular fertilizer, follow a monthly program.

• As weather becomes warmer, pest problems will become more intense. Watch for mites, aphids, leafminers, caterpillars, slugs, and snails.

APRIL

• Now is a good time to start Sunflower seeds. They are favorites of many, especially kids. Use normal planting techniques for other flower beds and container gardens.

• Check for any plants that need staking. Renew mulch that is too thin and keep it a few inches from the base of annuals.

• If the rain doesn't last enough to soak into the soil, look for signs of wilting and water if the surface inch is dry.

• Continue with monthly feeding program (unless using slow-release fertilizer), even though many annuals are reaching full size and creating colorful displays. Apply with liquid fertilizer, scatter dry fertilizer over dry foliage and water immediately, or reach among leaves to place handfuls of fertilizer at ground level.

• Keep an eye out for aphids, garden flea hoppers, mites, whiteflies, slugs, and snails.

MAY

• Most annuals last only a few months, set seed, and then decline. When cool-season annuals stop flowering, remove the top and underside growths. Prepare soil by working in organic matter and a light feeding of general fertilizer. Set new plants at the proper spacing, then water.

• To sow from seed, press big seeds into pots or cell-packs of germination mix and sprinkle small seeds on surface. Keep moist, in bright light. Fertilize weekly with half-strength solution. Transplant when seedlings are 4 to 6 inches tall, about four to six weeks.

• Stake tall plants. Replace severely damaged plants.

• Water if rain isn't sufficient. Don't overwater, which might cause flower damage and stem and root rots. If in doubt, keep plants a little dry.

• Apply fertilizer regularly.

• This month could start the rainy season and reduce the mite problem. Aphids, garden flea hoppers, grasshoppers, whiteflies, slugs, and snails like hotter weather.

JUNE

• Record annuals' performance and your preferences as a guide for choosing plants next year.

• Replant during summer months to correct problems and replace dying flowers. When filling in bare spots, remove declining plant stems, leaves, and roots.

• Weed after watering. Hand pulling is a good, quick method. Spot-kill with herbicide that permits use around growing plants. Other control methods are mulch, landscape fabric, newspaper, and preemergence herbicide.

• Use adequate fertilizer during summer to compensate for increased growth and rains washing away nutrients. See if plants' growth slows or foliage yellows. They may need extra feeding.

• Leaf spots increase with the rains. Especially susceptible are Impatiens and Salvias. Reduce watering to an as-needed schedule, and keep foliage as dry as possible.

JULY

• In this rainy season some annuals, like Petunia and Celosia, fade. More rain-tolerant hot-weather annuals include: Coleus, Globe Amaranth, Impatiens, and Melampodium.

• Summer can be difficult to establish a new flower bed, since hot days quickly dry out plants. Keep new plantings moist.

• Summer annuals are often kept too wet or too dry. Watch for their moisture needs and for any damage that requires pruning or replanting.

• Growing plants need a constant nutrient source. Follow your regular feeding schedule, but watch for nutritional deficiencies, like yellow foliage, which require additional fertilizer.

• Rot problems are big summer concerns. Few annuals can stand wet feet. Note problem areas so future plantings can be modified. Look for flea hoppers, grasshoppers, nematodes, whiteflies, slugs, and snails.

AUGUST

• Many gardeners take a break this hot time of year and allow annuals to gradually decline. Others continue with full replacement. After mid-August is a good time to start the first fall warm-season flowers, like Marigolds, Salvia, Nicotiana, Verbena, and Sunflowers.

• Some long-lived annuals, including Wax Begonias, Impatiens, and Coleus, may become lanky and overgrown. Trim back a foot or more to let new shoots sprout from base.

• August can be the wettest month. Turn off irrigation systems and let nature do the watering. Closely watch moisture levels of hanging baskets and containers.

• Continue the scheduled monthly feedings. Newly planted annuals or those in containers may need special feedings.

• Leaf spots and stem disease continue to be a problem. Consider changing to other selections in problem areas or use soaker hoses for watering (they are less likely to wet the foliage).

• Watch for garden flea hoppers, grasshoppers, nematodes, whiteflies, slugs, and snails.

SEPTEMBER

• Many flowers can be added to the early-fall annual gardens.

• Container gardens may begin to decline after long summer growing season. Many have run out of room and set seed. Replant as soon as they begin to decline.

• Now is the time for major bed renovation. The beginning of the month is also a good time to start seeds of quick-growing warm-season annuals.

• Keep existing plants growing until new beds can be planted. Weeding, staking, pruning, and feeding can keep the plants attractive for longer.

• Early September is usually damp but by month's end rains can quickly taper off. Water when the surface inch begins to dry. Make sure your irrigation system will be ready when needed.

• Expect leaf spot and stem disease to continue until rains subside. Watch for garden flea hoppers, grasshoppers, nematodes, slugs, snails, and whiteflies.

OCTOBER

• Cooler weather starts arriving, marking the in-between time of warm- and cool-season flowers. The transition can be handled four ways: 1) Continue planting warm-season annuals during early October, then gradually work in cool-season plants. 2) After warm-season flowers finish, let beds lie fallow until after mid-October, when you can plant cool-season plants. 3) Take a chance on the month being cool and jump directly into planting cool-season annuals. 4) Continue planting warm-season annuals and wait until November or December to change.

• This is an easy month to care for new plantings. Keep weeds out and check for moisture levels and pests.

• The dry season is here, so watch moisture levels.

• As weather turns cool, plants will not use as much fertilizer. Feed less frequently.

• Mites are back with the drier weather. However, root rot and leaf spot should decrease, and nematodes are less active. Watch for garden flea hoppers, grasshoppers, whiteflies, slugs, and snails.

NOVEMBER

• Pansy may be the most eagerly awaited annual in Florida. November is the earliest you can count on them to beat the heat and survive until early spring.

• Most cool-season annuals are frost-resistant unless making lots of tender new growth. These plants need coolness to flower, but not freezing weather. If in doubt, provide frost protection, such as a temporary blanket or hay covering. Don't use plastic.

• Cooler temperatures mean annuals will not use as much water. However during this drier season, check all flower beds and container gardens for moisture levels.

• The plantings will slow their growth during cooler weather, so the intervals between fertilizer applications can be lengthened. If the weather is warmer than expected, an extra feeding might be required.

• Insect populations grow less during cooler months. Keep up frequent garden visits to check for pests and other problems. Check for root rots, garden flea hoppers, grasshoppers, nematodes, slugs, snails, and whiteflies.

DECEMBER

• Create some festive holiday season plantings. Red and white combinations work well, including petunias and dianthus. Also combine silvery Dusty Miller with red flowered annuals or Poinsettias.

• Start early to fill empty flower spots. Garden centers concentrate on holiday plants and forget about annual flowers. Annuals may be purchased even though they aren't needed right away. Keep them healthy by placing in appropriate light level, feeding weekly with balanced fertilizer, keeping no more than a month before planting, and checking water needs daily.

• Be on guard for cold weather. Few freezes arrive at this time, but frosts are common. Control winter weeds and stake taller-growing plants if needed.

• Fertilize according to schedule. Most feeding schedules can be lengthened by a week or more during cooler weather.

BULBS, CORMS, RHIZOMES, & TUBERS
for Florida

Close your eyes, and think of some plants that grow from bulbs. What immediately comes to mind? Admit it: you see tulips, daffodils, crocus, and hyacinths.

Now erase that image, because most Northern bulbs don't grow well in Florida. You can force a few, but forcing is a chore. You are about to discover a wide selection of bulbs that you can grow easily right in your own landscape.

We use a broad definition of bulb in this chapter. A true bulb resembles an onion, has some residual roots, a small stem portion, and lots of leaves packed closely together. (Some true Florida bulbs are Amaryllis, Crinum, and Rain Lilies.) Many other plants that we call bulbs are technically classified as stems and include corms, tubers, tuberous roots, and rhizomes.

CORMS: These are tightly compressed, often flattened, stems. If you look closely, you will see the plant portion has a central bud, and there are many smaller buds around the stem portion. The Gladiolus is a corm.

TUBERS: Look for the buds of this stem on the surface. There is a central bud and many smaller buds. The skin of the tuber is leather-like. The Caladium is a tuber.

TUBEROUS ROOTS: These are swollen, fleshy, usually underground roots, such as the sweet potato. The buds that develop into new plants from most tuberous roots are present only at the stem end. An example of a flowering plant we grow from a tuberous root is the Dahlia.

RHIZOMES: Plants that grow from rhizomes come from thickened horizontal stems. Some grow just at the surface of the soil, while others form slightly underground. The roots grow from the bottom of the rhizomes. Plants that grow from rhizomes include Canna, Calla Lily, and Daylily.

Now that you have become acquainted with the different kinds of plants in this group, let's settle on just one term: bulb. All these plants grow in a similar manner, forming a clump or cluster from which arise attractive foliage and, often, colorful flowers. Happily, you will find that some of our Florida favorites rival their Northern relatives. Some can be in bloom at just about any time of year. Many have extended flowering seasons in our state, so you might see them in bloom several times a year.

You can plant entire beds of bulbs, or use them for small spots of color. A few kinds grow very well in containers and can be moved into the home or to patios, porches, or balconies when in bloom. Only a few lend themselves to naturalization. If you want them to naturalize, do not mow the areas until flowering and foliage growth is over.

PLANTING

Most Florida bulbs can stay in the ground for several years before being replanted. While some grow well in sandy soils, all seem to prefer an improved planting site. A few like damp, poorly drained soil, but most do not like to have their roots in water.

Check to make sure the bulbs you plan to add will receive appropriate light. Some, like Caladiums, grow in either sun or shade, but Amazon and

Blood Lilies prefer some shade. You might change your bulb or the planting site just to ensure a good display.

You should also select a planting site that is free of noxious weeds. It is very difficult to pull weeds out of the planting site year after year. One of the best ways to start any new bed is by controlling perennial weeds. They can be hand dug, but you will never really get many of the underground shoots this way. The best way is with a nonselective herbicide that allows replanting after the weeds decline.

Once the weeds are under control, you are ready to prepare the bed for your next bulb planting. Follow these few steps to getting the soil ready:

1. Remove all weeds and associated debris.
2. Till the soil deeply. If you have a power tiller available, use it to turn the soil 6 to 8 inches deep.
3. Check the soil acidity and adjust if needed. Most bulbs grow well at the 5.5 to 7.5 pH range. If a soil test indicates that pH correction is needed, dolomitic lime or soil sulfur can be used to make the correction.
4. Enrich sandy and clay soils with liberal quantities of organic matter. Some good sources are compost, peat moss, and manures. Fresh manure should be tilled into soil 90 to 120 days before planting.
5. Apply up to 2 pounds of 6-6-6 or similar fertilizer to 100 square feet of the soil surface, and work it into the ground lightly. Some gardeners prefer to add bonemeal, a traditional product for bulb plantings. It contains some quickly available nitrogen and lots of slowly available phosphorus.

You are now ready to plant. Florida bulbs come in different forms. Bulbs may come in a mesh or plastic bag. Some local bulbs can be purchased in pots; many have flowers already or buds ready to open. Some are dug up in clumps or separated into individual plants and shared between friends. It really does not matter how you obtain your bulbs. But if you obtain growing plants, be sure to give them water and the proper light level until the ground is ready for planting.

The best planting recommendation are to read and follow the label that comes with the bulbs—or consult our planting chart on pages is 70 and 71. Proper spacing and planting depth is important. Some bulbs do not flower or multiply well if planted too deep. Many like to grow close to the soil line. Keeping the proper planting depth in mind, follow these final planting suggestions:

1. Dig a hole or trench to receive the bulbs.
2. Fill in around the bulbs with soil and water. If the soil is extra dry, make a muddy paste out of the fill soil.
3. Finish filling in around the bulbs.
4. Add a thin mulch layer over the planting site or around bulbs that might be added in containers.
5. Water well.
6. Mark and label the site so you will know where the bulbs are growing before they begin to sprout. Include the variety and the planting date on the label.

CARE

It's easy to care for the bulbs you can easily see. They will need watering to prevent leaf loss during drought, feeding to encourage growth, pest control, and some grooming as leaves yellow and fruiting structures begin to mature. But some bulbs won't really be noticed until they begin to grow and flower; this doesn't mean they should be forgotten. They are living plants that need some care, including water, weed control, pest prevention, and sometimes cold protection.

WATERING

Most bulbs prefer uniformly moist soil, and this means you must water during drier months of the year. Mulch helps stretch the time between waterings. Use hay, coarse compost, bark, pine straw, or similar mulch to help hold in moisture and reduce weeds. You can also cover the soil with landscape fabric, but leave room for the bulbs to grow up within the covering. You can make an "X" or cut out a circle for the bulbs to grow through the fabric. Louisiana iris, native iris, and some cannas like a damp-to-wet soil. These plants grow best in bog conditions, which may have to be created in Florida's sandy soils.

FERTILIZING

Most bulbs are not heavy feeders. Two or three applications per year of a complete fertilizer is normally adequate. Perhaps the real secret of Florida bulb care is to feed when the bulbs are making active growth and can use the nutrients.

Any general garden fertilizer can be used. Many gardeners use a balanced fertilizer at the annual flower or perennial rate. Some bulb products are also available—these usually contain a little less nitrogen in the analysis and more phosphorus and potassium. Here are a few tips for fertilizing different types of bulbs:

- SPRING-FLOWERING BULBS AND THOSE THAT LOSE THEIR FOLIAGE AFTER FLOWERING: Feed once in March and once in June.
- TROPICAL BULBS THAT GROW SPRING THROUGH FALL: Feed lightly every six to eight weeks. Gardeners can also apply a slow-release fertilizer at the perennial plant rate and repeat as recommended on the label.
- CONTAINER PLANTINGS DURING PERIODS OF ACTIVE GROWTH: Feed every other week with a 20-20-20 or similar fertilizer solution. Some gardeners prefer natural fertilizers. Organic products including composted manure tea, composts, and composted manures can be substituted for synthetic fertilizer products. Some may have to be applied more frequently to properly feed bulb plantings.

PEST CONTROL

Bulbs have only a few pests. Luckily, most seem to be resistant to nematodes—but it is still a good idea to plant in soils as free as possible of these roundworms. The best advice is to control other pests as noted. Just check the foliage and flowers during garden walks and handpick pests from the plants (you may first apply a natural control if you like). If needed, synthetic pesticides are available for insect and disease control.

AFRICAN IRIS
Dietes spp.

HARDINESS
8B–10. Hardier than other tropical bulbs, can be grown in pots to overwinter inside in North Florida.

COLOR(S)
White, cream, yellow flowers

PEAK SEASON
Blooms spring and summer; foliage evergreen

MATURE SIZE
2 to 4 feet tall, 1 to 3 feet spread

WATER NEEDS
Although African Iris will grow in sandy soils without much water, they flower best in rich, moist soil.

CARE
Can be planted any time during the year, spaced 18 to 24 inches apart. Need soil with good drainage. Very carefree and only requires a light fertilization once or twice a year.

PROBLEMS
Grasshopper and snails may occasionally be a problem. Handpick or use recommended pest control.

USES AND SELECTIONS
Use this versatile perennial as an edging or border plant, in mass plantings, or in containers. The stiff leaves radiate in a dense fan pattern and make the plant attractive as an accent or groundcover.

AFRICAN LILY
Agapanthus africanus

HARDINESS
Zones 8–10. Grows best in North and Central Florida. Protect from severe freezes. Plantings in South Florida are usually short-lived.

COLOR(S)
Blue, white flowers

PEAK SEASON
Blooms spring and summer; strap-like leaves evergreen

MATURE SIZE
3 feet tall; 1 to 2 feet spread

WATER NEEDS
Will grow in sandy soils but needs plenty of water and nutrients. Enrich and mulch soil to maintain moisture and make more drought-tolerant plantings.

CARE
Rhizomes best planted from October through March, spaced 12 inches apart. Does best in areas with morning sun and afternoon shade. Needs well-drained soil. Fertilize in March, May, and September. After flowering, cut old stalks near ground.

PROBLEMS
Caterpillars and grasshoppers may be a problem. Handpick or use recommended pest control.

USES AND SELECTIONS
Also called Lily-of-the-Nile. Excellent as an accent plant, in perennial beds, for spot color throughout landscape, or in containers. Makes nice backdrop for annuals, tropicals, and other bulbs.

ALSTROEMERIA
Alstroemeria spp.

HARDINESS
Zones 8 -10. Check with local sources to get hardiest types for South Florida.

COLOR(S)
Green/red, pink, yellow, white, lavender flowers

PEAK SEASON
Blooms spring and early summer

MATURE SIZE
18 to 24 inches tall

WATER NEEDS
Will grow well in sandy soil with plenty of water and nutrients. Enrich soil and use mulch to retain moisture. Less water is needed during winter months.

CARE
Best planted from later winter through spring, 6 to 9 inches deep and 1 foot apart. Need light feeding in March and May. Cut old stalks back to ground after flowering or allow seeds to develop.

PROBLEMS
May be affected by slugs and cutworms. Handpick or use recommended pest control.

USES AND SELECTIONS
Also called Peruvian Lily. Use Alstroemeria in areas with filtered light, in mixed beds or by themselves. It also does well in containers. When used as a cut flower, it has a long vase life.

AMARYLLIS
Hippeastrum hybrids

HARDINESS
Zones 8–10. Protect from freezing.

COLOR(S)
Red, pink, orange, salmon, white flowers

PEAK SEASON
Blooms winter and spring

MATURE SIZE
2 feet tall

WATER NEEDS
Use enriched soil and mulch to maintain moisture. Withhold water during resting stage.

CARE
Plant in fall to early spring, spaced 12 inches or more apart. Fertilize at least three times a year. After flowering, cut old stalks near ground before seeds form. Keep watering until leaves turn yellow. If plants die back to a resting stage, withhold water for a while or dig and refresh planting bed.

PROBLEMS
Grasshoppers and snails may damage leaves. Handpick or use recommended pest control.

USES AND SELECTIONS
A favorite Christmas present for Florida gardeners, Amaryllis can be planted as border plants, in a bed of their own, or in containers. They are useful at the feet of leggy shrubs.

AMAZON LILY
Eucharis grandiflora

HARDINESS
Zones 9–11. Restrict plantings in colder Florida gardens to containers.

COLOR(S)
White flowers

PEAK SEASON
Sporadic winter and early spring blooms; large green leaves evergreen

MATURE SIZE
1 foot tall

WATER NEEDS
Use enriched soil and mulch to maintain moisture

CARE
Plant bulbs any time of year, spaced 3 to 4 inches apart. In an 8-inch pot, add 3 to 4 bulbs. Fertilize in March, May, and September. Encourage flowering by alternating moist and dry periods for about a month, followed by a feeding to start growth and flowers. After flowering, cut old stalks near ground.

PROBLEMS
Caterpillars and slugs may be pests. Handpick or use recommended pest control.

USES AND SELECTIONS
Amazon Lily (also called Eucharis Lily) can be used in beds or pots. Plant with Caladiums, Gingers, Impatiens, and Begonias or use it as a ground cover in front of other greenery. Can be used as a substitute for Hostas.

AZTEC LILY
Sprekelia formosissima

HARDINESS
Zones 8–11. In areas with frost, protect Aztec Lily bulbs with heavy mulch.

COLOR(S)
Scarlet red flowers; green leaves

PEAK SEASON
Spring and summer blooms

MATURE SIZE
Flower about 5 inches across on 15-inch stalk. Strap-like leaves grow to 20 inches.

WATER NEEDS
Provide lots of water when growing new leaves and blooming. Keep dry when dormant.

CARE
Plant container-grown plants any time. Divide and plant bulbs in fall, with top of bulb just above ground level. Fertilize in March, May, and September. When crowded and allowed to occasionally dry out, it may bloom several times during summer.

PROBLEMS
None

USES AND SELECTIONS
Aztec Lily blooms look like a cross between an Amaryllis and an Orchid. It has several common names: Jacobean Lily, St. James Lily, and Orchid Lily. This is the only species in the genus, with several cultivars. It can also grow in containers.

BLOOD LILY
Scadoxus multiflorus

HARDINESS
Zones 8–11. Use extra mulch in northern regions for cold protection.

COLOR(S)
Red flowers

PEAK SEASON
Spring and early summer blooms; leaves dormant in winter

MATURE SIZE
18 to 24 inches tall; flower ball 6 inches or larger

WATER NEEDS
Will tolerate sandy soils but mulched and amended soils retain moisture better.

CARE
Plant from January through March, spaced 6 to 8 inches apart. Fertilize lightly in March, May, and August. After flowering, cut old stalks near ground.

PROBLEMS
Caterpillars and slugs may be pests. Handpick or use recommended pest control.

USES AND SELECTIONS
Blood Lily can be used in beds or pots. Plant with other bulbs and perennials, in front of shrubs, or as a specimen where it can be viewed up close. Combine with Amaryllis, Crinum, Impatiens, Gingers, and African Iris. Grows best with filtered sun but can also grow in more intense shade under trees.

BLUE FLAG IRIS
Iris virginica

HARDINESS
Zones 8–10

COLOR(S)
Lavender to purple flowers

PEAK SEASON
Blooms briefly in spring; sword-like leaves evergreen

MATURE SIZE
3 feet tall

WATER NEEDS
Requires very moist or wet conditions

CARE
Plant in late summer or fall, spacing rhizomes 8 inches apart. Keep them within 2 inches of the surface, using regular potting soil with fertilizer added. Cover with rocks to keep the fish out and the soil in. Fertilize later in the season with tablets. Divide rhizomes in fall or early winter.

PROBLEMS
This Florida native has few problems.

USES AND SELECTIONS
Blue Flag Iris (Southern Blue Flag) should be planted in low-lying swales, pots submerged in ponds, or bog conditions. The upright Iris looks elegant when seen against the flat, round leaves of water lilies and other horizontal foliage. For best viewing, keep it visually removed from other upright plants. Louisiana Iris, another warm-growing iris, comes in a wide range of colors.

CALADIUM

Caladium x hortulanum

☼ ☼ ☼ ☼ 🌱 💧 🌴

HARDINESS
Zones 9-11

COLOR(S)
Red, rose, pink, white, silver, bronze, green leaves

PEAK SEASON
Summer foliage

MATURE SIZE
18 to 24 inches

WATER NEEDS
Plant 1 to 2 inches deep in late winter or spring using enriched soil. Water sparingly until leaves emerge, then keep it moist.

CARE
Caladiums are far more durable than they look, tolerating Florida's summer heat and humidity. They look best with some shade from midday heat, waterings two or three times a week, and monthly fertilizing. After the leaves die back each fall, reduce watering. Keep bulbs in the ground or dig up and dry them for replanting in April. Under poor growing conditions, may need replacing after about three years.

PROBLEMS
None

USES AND SELECTIONS
Caladiums' complex color forms look best in masses. They can be used in ground beds, around the base of trees, or in containers. The long lasting leaves are good for flower arranging.

CALLA

Zantedeschia spp.

☼ ☼ ☼ 🦋 🌱 🌿

HARDINESS
Zones 8–10. Container culture best for South Florida.

COLOR(S)
White, pink, yellow, cream, lavender, purple, and almost black flowers; green and variegated leaves

PEAK SEASON
Blooms in spring; foliage dormant fall and winter

MATURE SIZE
6 to 36 inches

WATER NEEDS
Will grow in sandy soils with plenty of water and nutrients. Enhance the soil and use mulch to retain moisture. In containers use loose potting mix. In ponds, keep at surface level.

CARE
Plant from September through January in enriched soil, 1 to 2 inches deep. Fertilize lightly in March, May, and August. After flowering, cut old stalks near ground.

PROBLEMS
Spider mites and thrips may be pests. Use recommended pest control.

USES AND SELECTIONS
Create a tropical look with cluster of Calla Lilies among warm climate plants, such as Philodendrons, Caladiums, Anthuriums, Gingers, Canna, and Bananas. Use cut flowers and leaves for bouquets.

CANNA
Canna hybrids

HARDINESS
Zones 9–11. *C. flaccida* to Zone 8.

COLOR(S)
Green, bronze, and striped leaves; red, orange, yellow, pink, cream, white, and bicolored flowers

PEAK SEASON
Blooms spring and summer

MATURE SIZE
2 to 4 feet

WATER NEEDS
Cannas love rich, moist soil. The native *C. flaccida* is an aquatic. Many hybrids can be acclimatized to grow in ponds.

CARE
To be vigorous they require frequent fertilizing.

PROBLEMS
Leaf rollers, moth larva, spider mites, and rust may be problems, especially in South Florida. Inspect regularly and use recommended pest controls.

USES AND SELECTIONS
The tropical leaves and bright flowers of Canna are often used as a focal point in ground beds and containers. They are also used in combination with other broad-leafed tropicals like Bananas or Gingers. In water gardens they are used as tall background plantings.

COSTUS
Costus spp.

HARDINESS
Zones 9b–11

COLOR(S)
Yellow, orange, white flowers

PEAK SEASON
Blooms summer

MATURE SIZE
4 to 8 feet x 4 to 5 feet

WATER NEEDS
Keep moist, with less water in winter

CARE
Locate in high, light shade where shallow-rooted Costus can clump and spread. Mulch and use acid-forming fertilizer. Once stems have flowered and bracts faded, cut out parent stem. Every few years Costus benefits from digging and refreshing the beds with organic material. Grow in protected areas or containers in cold-sensitive areas.

PROBLEMS
Costus tends to look haggard in winter .

USES AND SELECTIONS
Use Costus as an accent, in containers, or as mass plantings. Also called Spiral Ginger, try Costus beneath Oaks with stands of red and pink Gingers. *Costus speciosus* is 8 or 9 feet tall with white flowers from red bracts. Use as a screen. There is a Costus with variegated leaves.

CRINUM LILY
Crinum spp.

HARDINESS
Zones 8–11. Recover quickly from killing frosts in northern regions.

COLOR(S)
White, pink, rose, or striped flowers; green or burgundy foliage

PEAK SEASON
Blooms spring; leaves evergreen

MATURE SIZE
To 5 feet tall x to 5 feet wide

WATER NEEDS
Tolerant of most conditions, from wetland to dry areas. Somewhat drought tolerant.

CARE
Leave plenty of space between the large bulbs. Plant any time, but winter is best. Those in high shade look nicer. Fertilize in spring, summer, and fall. Moderately salt tolerant.

PROBLEMS
Fungus and lubber grasshoppers occasionally a problem.

USES AND SELECTIONS
Plant Crinum Lilies throughout the landscape, from water garden accents to mass plantings in dry areas. Use in groupings to accent their large fragrant flowers. There are several species and popular selections with rose and striped flowers, plus the white Florida native (*C. americanum*). They look good with Ferns or as large specimen plants. Also use as a cut flower.

DAHLIA
Dahlia spp.

HARDINESS
Zones 8–10

COLOR(S)
All flower colors from white to almost black

PEAK SEASON
Blooms spring through early summer

MATURE SIZE
1 to 6 feet x 1 to 2 feet

WATER NEEDS
Needs constant moisture

CARE
Plant tubers and growing plants in enriched, well-drained soil with heavy mulch. Dahlias require lots of maintenance. Provide high-nitrogen fertilizer in spring and high potassium fertilizer in summer. For large, numerous flowers remove spent blossoms and clip out the side buds. Stake tall varieties.

PROBLEMS
Susceptible to many diseases and pests, requiring regular treatments. Blooms often damaged by summer heat and rains.

USES AND SELECTIONS
Dahlias can be planted throughout the garden. The showy flowers provide beautiful color at different times of year, depending upon your Florida location. Use in mass plantings, in mixed beds, as borders, and for cut flowers. Plant dwarf varieties in containers. Over 20,000 cultivars exist, with new hybrids constantly available.

DAYLILY
Hemerocallis hybrids

HARDINESS
Zones 8–10. In South Florida, check local garden centers for best selections.

COLOR(S)
Flowers in yellow, orange, pink, red, lavender, and blends

PEAK SEASON
Blooms spring and summer

MATURE SIZE
To 2 feet

WATER NEEDS
Grows in sandy soils with enough water and nutrients. Does better with enriched soil and mulch to conserve moisture.

CARE
Add at any time of year. Set with base of foliage at or above soil level. Feed lightly in March, May, and September.

PROBLEMS
Handpick any caterpillars, aphids, thrips, and grasshoppers or treat with recommended pest control.

USES AND SELECTIONS
Although blossoms last one day, numerous buds result in continual blossoms throughout the season. Use in beds, rock gardens, perennial borders, and containers. Fill entire beds with Daylilies or mix with annuals, perennials, and shrubs. The best Daylilies for Florida are evergreen and semievergreen types. Florida has some of the nation's most popular breeders and growers.

ELEPHANT EAR
Alocasia spp.

HARDINESS
Zones 9–11

COLOR(S)
Green and dark green, often with colored veins

PEAK SEASON
Evergreen foliage

MATURE SIZE
2 to 12 feet tall x 8 feet wide

WATER NEEDS
Provide plenty of water in spring. Water twice weekly if it doesn't rain.

CARE
Use slow-release fertilizer two or three times a year, once in spring if in pots. Supplement with foliar spray to bolster nutrients. If leaves yellow, use micronutrient spray or fish emulsion. Damaged by cold in northern regions, and during prolonged cold in South Florida. Prune away damaged leaves in early spring.

PROBLEMS
May bleach out when in sun all day

USES AND SELECTIONS
The enormous Elephant Ear leaves proclaim tropical in a garden. Use in the center, a corner, or toward the back for dramatic effects. Also attractive in pots and ponds. Varieties come in all sizes and veination patterns. Some take more sun than others. Often confused with Taro, also called Elephant Ear.

GINGER
Alipinia spp.

HARDINESS
Zones 9–11

COLOR(S)
Red, pink, purple, white flowers

PEAK SEASON
Blooms summer; foliage evergreen

MATURE SIZE
3 to 15 feet x various

WATER NEEDS
Requires good soil moisture

CARE
Locate in high shade, allowing room to grow. Gingers are fast growers and prefer to be well fertilized. They will spread and form big clumps. Maintain by cleaning out old, brown stems. In Central and North Florida, use in containers, protected from chilling winds.

PROBLEMS
Too much light causes yellowing.

USES AND SELECTIONS
This useful plant says welcome to the tropics. There are about 1,000 species, with new ones being discovered all the time. The flowers are lovely amid the broad tropical foliage. A popular Pink Ginger contrast nicely with the Red. Use mass plantings of dwarf and variegated forms in understory beds and as ground covers. The true Ginger, *Zingiber officinale*, can be grown in partial sun and is fragrant.

GINGER LILY
Hedychium coronarium

HARDINESS
Zones 8–11

COLOR(S)
White flowers

PEAK SEASON
Summer blooms

MATURE SIZE
2 to 4 feet x various

WATER NEEDS
Loves moist soil. Mulch is essential.

CARE
Allow enough space, especially in shaded locations, for this assertive grower. Like other Gingers, its rhizome grows fairly close to the surface. Slow-release fertilizer is practical for nutrients throughout growing season. Fewer flowers are produced in deep shade.

PROBLEMS
Freezing weather kills them back, but they may resprout from rhizomes.

USES AND SELECTIONS
Plant a group of Ginger Lilies (Butterfly Gingers) near entryways and patios to enjoy their lovely aroma. Grow in containers on patios and around pools. Also use as fillers around waterfalls and ponds. They are tall enough to be visible over Lilies, Coleus, Begonias, and other low-lying shrubs. Group with other water-thirsty plants to avoid over-watering the entire landscape. There are about fifty species, including white *H. coronarium*, which flowers for up to six weeks.

GLADIOLUS
Gladiolus hybrids

HARDINESS
Zones 8–11. Plant any time in South Florida, in North and Central Florida plant spring and summer.

COLOR(S)
Flowers in all colors and blends

PEAK SEASON
Blooms spring and summer

MATURE SIZE
To 2 feet

WATER NEEDS
Enriched soil with good drainage. Will grow in sandy soils with plenty of water and nutrients. Add mulch to conserve moisture.

CARE
Plant corms 2 to 3 inches deep and 4 to 6 inches apart. Fertilize lightly each month while growing. After stalks develop, stake to prevent wind damage. Plants gradually decline for rest period after a few months of flowering, before starting new growth.

PROBLEMS
Handpick any caterpillars, grasshoppers, and thrips or treat with recommended pest control.

USES AND SELECTIONS
Often planted in rows. Also attractive with other bulbs, perennials, and shrubs. Mix with Canna, Crinum, Society Garlic, and Zephyrlilies. Excellent as cut flowers, lasting up to a week. Both tall and short forms are available.

GLORIOSA LILY
Gloriosa spp.

HARDINESS
Zones 8–11. Goes dormant in cooler regions when affected by cold.

COLOR(S)
Flowers are crimson-banded and yellow.

PEAK SEASON
Blooms spring through summer

MATURE SIZE
To 6 feet

WATER NEEDS
Likes enriched, well-drained soil. Grow in sandy soils with plenty of water and nutrients. Mulch to conserve moisture. Withstands drought but dies back, resuming growth with damper weather.

CARE
Plant V-shaped tubers 2 to 4 inches deep and 12 to 18 inches apart. Trim vines to keep in bounds. After flowering, cold, or drought the plants die back. Trim dead vines and wait for new growth.

PROBLEMS
It's poisonous if ingested. Handpick any caterpillars or treat with recommended pest control.

USES AND SELECTIONS
Also called Climbing Lily. Best trained to a trellis. Plant as accent near patio or home entrance. Use as backdrop, along fence or wall, or among perennials that decline during winter. Plant with shorter growing African Iris, Crinum, and Gingers.

HELICONIA

Heliconia spp.

☀ ☀ ☀ 🌱 🌿 🪴 🌴

HARDINESS
Zones 9 (if protected) –11

COLOR(S)
Yellow, orange, scarlet flowers

PEAK SEASON
Blooms spring and summer

MATURE SIZE
2 to 15 feet x various

WATER NEEDS
Once established, water twice weekly if it doesn't rain. In sunny or windy conditions water more often.

CARE
Requires good drainage and some protection from cold and wind. Leaves get yellow on hungry plants. To feed their big appetites use slow-release fertilizer combined with periodic micronutrient sprays and compost. In clumps the outer stems may lean. Stake from within so flowers can show.

PROBLEMS
Handpick snails. Use fungicide to control root and stem rot.

USES AND SELECTIONS
These fascinating plants, also called Lobster Claw, have become important tropical plants in Florida. Use at garden's edges, as specimen plants, along walls, and behind Shrimp Plants. Plant for accents or in mass plantings. Use dwarf varieties in containers, especially in colder areas. The cultivars and color forms number in the hundreds.

HURRICANE LILY

Lycoris spp.

☀ ☀ 🍃 💧

HARDINESS
Zones 8–10

COLOR(S)
Red flowers; blue-green foliage

PEAK SEASON
Blooms August and September; foliage fall and winter

MATURE SIZE
Blooming stalk to 24 inches; flower cluster to 8 inches across

WATER NEEDS
Prefers moist soil but doesn't need regular watering

CARE
Plant dormant bulbs in late summer and autumn. Growing Lilies can be planted any time. Not picky about soil, but prefer enriched soil. Let leaves die completely in spring, do not cut off. Divide every few summers to maintain best flowering.

PROBLEMS
Delicate flowers last longer if protected from wind and sun. The bulbs may be slightly toxic.

USES AND SELECTIONS
Flowers appear suddenly (before foliage) after heavy rains. Plant under trees, in mixed borders, or in front of shrubs. Use in clusters for fall color. There are numerous *Lycoris* species and hybrids. The most common for Florida is *L. radiata* var. *radiata*, with red-orange flowers. It blooms better and produces more bulbs.

KAFFIR LILY
Clivia miniata

HARDINESS
Zones 9–11. Grow in containers in North and colder areas of Central Florida. Protect all plantings from freezing.

COLOR(S)
Bright orange, yellow flowers

PEAK SEASON
Blooms spring; deep green foliage evergreen

MATURE SIZE
18 to 24 inches

WATER NEEDS
Likes enriched coarse soil with excellent drainage. Does not like to be soggy. Keep plants drier during winter months.

CARE
Plant bulbs just below soil surface, 18 to 24 inches apart. Fertilize lightly in March, May, and September. After flowering, cut old stalk near ground. New plants multiply rapidly, but take three years to flower.

PROBLEMS
May be affected by caterpillars and grasshoppers. Handpick or treat with recommended pest control.

USES AND SELECTIONS
Kaffir Lily (Clivia) does well in lower light where flowering plant sections are limited. Best in clusters for perennial beds, among shrubs, in containers for showy displays, or indoors. Combine with Alstroemeria, Begonias, Caladium, Eucharis Lily, and Impatiens.

LOUISIANA IRIS
Iris hybrids

HARDINESS
Zones 8-9

COLOR(S)
Yellow, blue, red, reddish/brown, white, and purple flowers

PEAK SEASON
Spring blooms; strap-like leaves evergreen

MATURE SIZE
To 3 feet tall

WATER NEEDS
Best planted in or near standing water. Will also grow in drier conditions if kept moist, using enriched soil and mulch.

CARE
Plant spring through summer in soil, with rhizomes above the water surface. Space 8 to 12 inches apart with roots in the ground. Feed in March, May, and September. Cut old stalks back to ground after flowering.

PROBLEMS
Rhizomes in ponds should be kept slightly above the water surface. May be affected by caterpillars and grasshoppers. Handpick or use recommended pest control.

USES AND SELECTIONS
Thrives in wetland conditions but also does well in terrestrial plantings if kept moist. Use along pond edges or plant in containers. Mass plantings make dramatic statements. Both flowers and leaves are often used in flower arrangements.

PRIDE OF BURMA
Curcuma roscoeana

HARDINESS
Zones 9–11. Grow in containers where freezing occurs. Some hybrids do well in cooler climates.

COLOR(S)
Pink, lavender, yellow, orange, white flowers

PEAK SEASON
Blooms spring

MATURE SIZE
To 3 feet

WATER NEEDS
Like enriched soil with good drainage. Keep soil evenly moist. Use loose, leafy mulch to retain moisture.

CARE
Plant rhizomes in late winter to early spring, within 2 or 3 inches of the soil surface. Plant in partially shady location; morning sun is ideal. Fertilize with slow-release fertilizer. Dig and separate rhizomes in fall as plant begins to go dormant. In winter some *Curcuma* go dormant.

PROBLEMS
None

USES AND SELECTIONS
Also called Curcuma Ginger, Hidden Ginger makes good understory planting for a palm, or as a soft foil for shade-loving Bromeliads. The broad tropical foliage is nice enough to use seasonally when blooms are finished.

RAIN LILY
Zephyranthes spp.

HARDINESS
Zones 8 -11

COLOR(S)
White, yellow, pink flowers

PEAK SEASON
Blooms spring to early fall; thin leaves usually evergreen

MATURE SIZE
To 12 inches tall

WATER NEEDS
Very drought tolerant, although foliage may die back without adequate water. Grow best in moist soil. Less water is needed during winter than during hotter, drier months.

CARE
Flowering for Rain Lily (also called Zephyr Lily) begins with the rainy season. Plant 1 to 2 inches deep, spaced 3 to 4 inches apart. Need light feeding in March, May, and September. Cut old stalks back to ground after flowering or allow seeds to develop. Seeds germinate quickly when sown in loose potting mix.

PROBLEMS
May be affected by caterpillars and grasshoppers. Handpick or use recommended pest control.

USES AND SELECTIONS
Best planted in clusters as if naturalized in flower and perennial beds. Also use along walkways, as groundcover, in containers, and in water gardens.

SNOWFLAKE

Leucojum spp.

☼ ☀ 🛢 💧

HARDINESS
Zones 8–9

COLOR(S)
Flower white with colored tips

PEAK SEASON
February to March blooms; dormant in summer

MATURE SIZE
1 to 2 feet high

WATER NEEDS
Water during spring growth and flowering. Tolerates drought during summer dormancy. Also tolerates soggy soils.

CARE
Plant these carefree bulbs in organic enriched, well-drained soil, from September through November. Leave in the ground for about 10 years before digging and dividing.

PROBLEMS
None

USES AND SELECTIONS
Snowflake is easy to grow and multiples freely. They are ideal for naturalizing. The arching thin leaves and delicate nodding flowers look best in large clumps. Although sometimes called Summer Snowflake, the blooms usually appear in late winter or early spring. (In Zone 9, it may bloom in fall and winter.) Plant in meadows, under shrubs or trees, or in other places that would benefit from their springtime flush of blooms. The flowers have a faint fragrance. There are about ten species.

VOODOO LILY

Amorphophallus spp.

☼ ☀ 🛢 💧

HARDINESS
Zones 8–11, with winter mulch as cold protection for less hardy varieties

COLOR(S)
Reddish-brown flowers

PEAK SEASON
Blooms spring; leaves dormant in winter

MATURE SIZE
Leaves to 6 feet tall; some flowers to 8 feet or more

WATER NEEDS
Grows in sandy soils with plenty of water and nutrients. Use enriched soil and mulch to retain moisture. Avoid planting in areas that flood.

CARE
Plant 3 to 4 inches deep, 1 foot or more apart. Use enriched well-drained soil. Feed lightly in March, May, and August. After flowering, remove shriveled blossom.

PROBLEMS
Handpick any caterpillars and grasshoppers or use recommended pest control.

USES AND SELECTIONS
This unusual plant grows quickly in spring, is among the world's largest flowers, and emits a foul odor. It's best featured with perennials and shrubs for summer interest or as an accent in containers. Surround with African Iris, Bird-of-Paradise, Crinums, Heliconias, and Philodendrons.

WALKING IRIS

Neomarica spp.

HARDINESS
Zones 10b-11. Grow in pots in North Florida. In Central Florida will die back if damaged by freezes, but regrow in spring.

COLOR(S)
White, yellow, blue, brown blossoms

PEAK SEASON
Year-round blooms

MATURE SIZE
To 3 feet tall

WATER NEEDS
Walking Iris has a low tolerance for drought conditions, so use enriched soil, water regularly, and apply mulch.

CARE
Plant any time of year in partial shade. Fertilize in spring, summer, and fall. To hasten the rooting of small plantlets, bend over flower stalks and anchor them in place. Occasionally clean out old stolons and leaves from beds to allow new plantlets to root.

PROBLEMS
None

USES AND SELECTIONS
Use this as a tallish ground cover around trees or palms, or in a Japanese garden where the fan shape of the flat leaves can be highlighted. It also does well in foundation planters or a shrub bed where a vertical element is desired.

WATSONIA

Watsonia spp.

HARDINESS
Zones 9–10

COLOR(S)
Intense pink, mauve, red, orange, white flowers

PEAK SEASON
Blooms late spring and summer; evergreen foliage in some species

MATURE SIZE
3 to 5 feet x 2 to 3 feet

WATER NEEDS
Drought tolerant once established

CARE
Plant corms September through May in well-drained soil. These tough plants do not need much care. Feed with slow-release fertilizer. Do not divide until they become crowded.

PROBLEMS
No serious pests or diseases

USES AND SELECTIONS
This tall clump-forming plant has thin upright foliage with long flower spikes to 5 feet, each with up to forty tubular blooms. Like its cousin Gladiolus, Watsonia is ideal for cut flowers. The blooms are fragrant. Use these showy plants as specimens, as borders, at the back of perennial beds, or in xeriscape plantings. There are many species and cultivars. Common names are Bugle Lily and Cape Bugle Lily.

BULBS, CORMS, RHIZOMES, & TUBERS

Variety	Area of Florida	When to Plant	Depth (Inches)	Spacing (Inches)	Light Needs	Blooms
Achimenes	NC	Feb.–April	1	2–3	Light shade	June–Sept.
African Lily	NCS	Year-round	Tip at soil	12–14	Sun to light shade	May–July
Alstroemeria	NCS	Jan.–Mar.	4–6	10–12	Sun to light shade	June–July
Amaryllis	NCS	Year-round	Tip at soil	12–14	Sun to light shade	Mar.–June
Amazon Lily	CS	Feb.–June	Tip at soil	10–12	Light shade	Dec.–Mar.
Anemone	NC	Oct.–Dec.	1	6–8	Sun to light shade	Mar.–April
Aztec Lily	NCS	Year-round	3–4	8–10	Sun	April–Aug.
Blackberry Lily	NCS	Feb.–Oct.	1	6–8	Sun	May–July
Blood Lily	NCS	Mar.– May	Tip at soil	8–10	Light shade	June–July
Blue Flag Iris	NCS	Sep.–Nov.	1–2	8–10	Sun to light shade	Mar.–May
Caladium	NCS	Feb.–May	2–3	12–14	Sun to light shade	Insignificant
Calla Lily	NC	Sept.–Mar.	3–4	12–24	Sun to light shade	Mar.–May
Canna	NCS	Feb.–Aug.	1–2	12–18	Sun to light shade	April–Nov.
Costus	S	Feb.–April	2–4	12–24	Light shade	June–Sep.
Crinum	NCS	Year-round	Neck at soil	18–24	Sun to light shade	Mar.–Nov.
Crocosmia	NCS	Feb.–Oct.	1–2	3–4	Sun	May–Sept.
Dahlia	NC	Feb.–May	4–6	12–24	Sun	May–Aug.
Daylily	NCS	Year-round	Stem at soil	12–24	Sun to light shade	April–June
Elephant Ear	NCS	Mar.–Nov.	3–4	24–48	Sun to light shade	Insignificant
Ginger	CS	May–Aug.	2–4	12–24	Light shade	May–Oct.
Ginger Lily	CS	Feb.–April	1–3	12–24	Sun to shade	May–Oct.
Gladiolus	NCS	Year-round	2–3	4–6	Sun	In 3 months
Gloriosa Lily	NCS	Feb.–April	2–4	12–18	Sun to light shade	April–Sept.
Heliconia	S	May–Oct.	Stem at soil	12–18	Sun to light shade	April–Oct.

BULBS, CORMS, RHIZOMES, & TUBERS

Variety	Area of Florida	When to Plant	Depth (Inches)	Spacing (Inches)	Light Needs	Blooms
Hurricane Lily	NC	Dec.–Feb.	3–4	8–10	Sun to light shade	Sept.–Oct.
Kaffir Lily	NCS	Year-round	Tip at soil	12–18	Light shade	Mar.–May
Lapeirousia	NCS	Oct.–Dec.	1	3–4	Sun to light shade	Feb.–Mar.
Lily	NC	Feb.–April	4–6	10–12	Sun to light shade	April–July
Louisiana Iris	NC	Year-round	1–2	10–12	Sun to light shade	April–June
Moraea	NCS	Year-round	1–2	6–8	Sun	April – Aug.
Narcissus	NC	Sept.–Dec.	2–4	6–8	Sun to light shade	Mar. – April
Pineapple Lily	NCS	Oct.–Nov.	5–6	10–12	Sun	June–July
Pride of Burma	CS	Feb.–April	2–3	8–12	Light shade	April–June
Rain Lily	NCS	Feb.–Sept.	1–2	4–6	Sun to light shade	May–Sept.
Shell Ginger	CS	Year-round	1	12–24	Sun to light shade	April–Oct.
Snowflake	NC	Sept.–Nov.	3–4	4–6	Sun to light shade	Feb.–Mar.
Society Garlic	CS	Year-round	1–2	6–8	Sun	Mar.–Nov.
Spider Lily	NCS	Year-round	3–5	12–18	Sun	April–Aug.
Tiger Flower	NC	Feb.–Mar.	3–4	4–8	Sun to light shade	June–Aug.
Tritonia	NCS	Jan.–Mar.	2–3	2–3	Sun	April–Aug.
Tuberose	NC	Jan.–Mar.	1–2	10–12	Sun	April–Aug.
Tuberous Begonia	NC	Jan.–Mar.	1–2	10–12	Light shade	May–July
Voodoo Lily	NCS	Jan.–Mar.	4–6	12–24	Sun to light shade	May–June
Walking Iris	NCS	Year-round	Stem at soil	12–14	Light shade	April–Oct.
Watsonia	NCS	Oct.–May	3–4	6–8	Sun to light shade	In 3 months

N = North Florida   C = Central Florida   S = South Florida

JANUARY

• Prepare bulb beds. Dig out or spot-kill all perennial weeds. Till deeply, adding organic matter to sandy and clay soils. Also add light fertilizer or bonemeal.

• Be ready to move container-grown and less-hardy bulbs inside. Most others may have their foliage damaged by severe cold, but can be left in the ground and expected to survive in most parts of the state.

• Freeze damage to in-ground plantings may be prevented by covering the plants with blankets.

• Moisten soil when it feels dry. Renew mulch to a 2- to 3-inch layer.

• During warm winters, check for insects. Use a soap spray to control aphids attacking new growth and handpick any caterpillars.

• To get a jump start on the growing season, start some bulbs in pots, such as Canna, Caladiums, or Blood Lily. Keep them moist and warm. Fertilize every other week after growth begins with liquid fertilizer. Move into garden when weather is suitable.

FEBRUARY

• Plant new bulbs and those from friends or relocated from the landscape. If growing plants are added, cut back lanky foliage or provide staking.

• Prune out declining and winter-damaged foliage.

• As the weather warms, water moisture needs increase. Water when the surface inch of soil feels dry. Apply ½ to ¾ inch of water for each irrigation. Maintain 2 to 3 inches of mulch. Check the irrigation systems and install a microsprinkler or soaker hoses.

• When growth begins, start spring feeding. Use granular fertilizers, liquids, or composted manures at the labeled rates. Fertilizer can be applied on top of mulch. Water after feedings.

• Pests may start to appear. Aphids can be controlled with a soap or synthetic spray. Use the soap spray to also control mites. Apply a synthetic insecticide to combat thrips.

MARCH

• This is bulb planting season. Early this month is the best time to transplant Canna, Caladiums, and Blood Lilies so they will be ready to bloom on time.

• Bulbs that are now blooming (including Amaryllis and Swamp Lily) will go to seed after flower. Unless you want to collect a few seeds, cut off seedpods to keep from wasting energy that could be going into the bulbs.

• Keep the soil moist now to ensure good blooms.

• Provide major feeding for bulbs that were not fed earlier. Use special bulb product, general garden or slow-release fertilizer, or composted manures. Scatter over the soil surface. Keep granules away from foliage. Water immediately after feedings.

• Some pests are hatching, like lubber grasshoppers. After hatching they are black with yellow and red lines. They are also very hungry and possible to control, unlike fully grown adults. Handpick or apply synthetic grasshopper insecticide. Other pests are aphids, mites, and thrips.

APRIL

• Container-grown bulbs give a quicker start than bulbs in the dormant stage. Plant the same as normal bulb planting, although increased distance between plants may be possible. Keep soil moist until roots grow out. Remove any faded flowers or damaged foliage. Stake if needed. Apply first feeding a week or two after planting.

• Remove flower stalks after blossom fade. When foliage fades, cut old leaves (which may encourage pests) to main stem or ground.

• Although bulbs are somewhat drought resistant, it is best not to let them reach the wilt stage. Container plantings will need more frequent waterings.

• Keep warm-season bulbs fertilized. Feed with slow-release fertilizer or every six to eight weeks with general garden or bulb fertilizer.

• Slugs and snails can be a major problem, as evidence by early-morning slime trails. Handpick, use shallow trays of beer, or apply slug and snail baits. Also watch for aphids, grasshoppers, and mites.

MAY

• Begin transplanting. Divide and replant Daylilies, Gladiolus, Louisiana Iris, Kaffir Lilies, Shell Ginger, Society Garlic, Watsonia, and Walking Iris. Keep growing bulbs moist. Apply first feeding in two to three weeks.

• If weather turns windy, tall flowering stalks may blow over after a storm. Keep stakes and tape handy for their support. When stems are severely damaged, use them as lovely cut flowers.

• Keep your eye on Louisiana Iris, Caladiums, and some Canna selections. Keep them moist for good flowering. Pay special attention to bulbs in pots or planters; they can become dry in a day, especially if root bound.

• Stay on fertilizing schedule. If weather is exceptionally dry, you might delay feeding until rains return. Dormant bulbs can be delayed until growth begins.

• Red blotch disease may appear on amaryllis and crinums. Infected foliage should be pruned. Watch for aphids, grasshoppers, mites, and thrips.

JUNE

• Add Daylilies to the landscape, either individual plants or clumps. Plant in sunny area, although some can tolerate light shade. Tops can be cut back to within 6 or 8 inches of the base. Keep moist for best growth and flowering, even though they tolerate drought.

• As other flowering bulbs die back, divide and replant Gladiolus and Watsonia.

• Cut bouquets to display in the home. It's a good way to enjoy the blooms without having to remove the spent flowers later on.

• You won't have to water as often with the frequent summer rains. Most bulbs don't mind extra water but a few, such as Tuberous Begonias, can drown without well-drained soil.

• Watch for grasshoppers, mites, thrips, slugs, and snails. Aphids are a special problem for Daylilies. Red blotch disease may occur on Amaryllis, Swamp Lily, and other bulbs.

JULY

• Don't be afraid to move bulbs that are in full growth or flowering. You will not severely damage the plants, although you could affect flowering. If bulbs are in the way or need to be divided, summer is a good time. Most make rapid growth afterwards.

• Help your Gloriosa Lily climb, but keep it off nearby shrubs and trees since it can get out of control. Gingers grow very rapidly and may encroach on other plantings. Prune out new shoots, or dig some to share.

• Summer rains should do most of the watering, but there may be dry times. Keep mulched and check soil frequently for dry spots.

• Check your calendars to maintain scheduled feedings, especially during this time of maximum growth. Consider using slow-release fertilizers.

• During summer rains, some bulbs may need to be moved or they will rot from excess moisture.

• Watch for red blotch, aphids, grasshoppers, mites, thrips, and slugs and snails.

AUGUST

• Container bulbs may need transplanting, especially if root bound. Do not transplant bulbs that may be going dormant. Allow Calla Lilies to go dormant by withholding water and fertilizer. Keep potted Calla Lilies on the dry side during dormancy, until growth resumes.

• Remove older yellowing leaves to make plant more attractive and keep down diseases. Remove faded flowers and old stalks. If you are not going to grow from seed, remove old seedpods.

• If rains are less frequent, check plantings for moisture. It only takes a few days without water during hotter months for wilting to begin.

• Keep feedings on schedule, making sure to water immediately after fertilizing.

• A few bulbs, like Canna, suffer from rust. Light infestations can be tolerated, but heavy fungal damage requires a fungicide. Watch for red blotch, aphids, grasshoppers, mites, thrips, and slugs and snails. The leaf roller caterpillar can damage Canna leaves. Handpick to control.

SEPTEMBER

• It may be best to stick with good Florida bulbs for the most part. Fall normally starts with Amaryllis and Zephyr Lily for early plantings. Continue your transplanting as needed. If bulbs are wounded during digging, allow the spots to dry before replanting.

• If bulb plantings are overgrown, don't be afraid to do some rejuvenation pruning.

• Early September normally has plenty of rainfall for bulbs. Then suddenly the rains stop and you have to use the irrigation system. Use early September to make sure it is working properly.

• Reduce the feedings to an only-as-needed basis to keep the foliage green and flowers coming. Make the final slow-release feeding of the year.

• Stay alert and keep checking for damage on foliage and flowers. With drier weather ahead, expect mites to become more active. The most prevalent pests are red blotch, aphids, caterpillars, grasshoppers, thrips, and slugs and snails.

OCTOBER

• A few true daffodils grow and flower in Central and North Florida. Add them (and others that need just a short period of cold) during fall months, starting in October.

• Check other bulb plantings. Many may have filled beds and can be divided or transplanted. Outdoor temperatures are much more comfortable at this time of year.

• As many bulbs decline, remove old stems. Mark the bed areas so you will not disturb them. These areas can be planted with annual flowers for temporary color.

• It's the dry time of year, but fortunately temperatures are cooler so bulbs need minimal waterings. Check the soil every 3 or 4 days.

• If you have not provided a fall feeding, now is the time.

• Some pests know it's fall and start to decline. Continue to keep an eye out for reduced numbers of grasshoppers, slugs, and snails. Also watch for the persistent aphids, caterpillars, mites, and thrips.

NOVEMBER

• Some bulbs that can be planted at this time of year are Swamp Lily, Daylily, Kaffir Lily, and Louisiana Iris. Almost any bulb growing a clump of foliage can be divided and moved.

• If Amaryllis does not flower well in spring, it may be due to continuous growth of bulbs. Withholding water during fall is one technique to encourage late-winter flowering.

• Cleaning up declining bulb portions may be the biggest chore at this time of year. Bring container plantings of Caladiums and similar bulbs inside to a shady, well-ventilated spot.

• It's a dry, but cool, time of year. Usually seasonal rains provide adequate moisture. Check any bulbs with green foliage. Give soaking if dry.

• Feedings are just about over for all except the active tropical bulbs. If growth becomes yellow, give a light feeding.

• Handpick any of the few insects that may still be active.

DECEMBER

• Happy holidays! It's a great time to share your love of bulbs. Give a bulb-planting kit, complete with container, soil, fertilizer, and bulbs or starter plants.

• Begin new beds while the weather is cool. Till the soil, adjust the acidity, add organic matter, and let rest until planting.

• Check the bulb beds for declining plant portions and pests. Check bulbs in storage. Keep Caladiums at about 70 degrees F. Other bulbs can be stored in the 40- to 60- degree range.

• It's still the drier time of year and fairly cool in all areas of the state. Most plantings can go for a week or more without waterings. However check soil for moisture levels.

• Skip feedings of all but actively growing and tropical bulbs in southern part of state. These only require light fertilizing.

• Inspect for pests every week or two. Aphids, mites, and thrips may still be active.

CITRUS, NUTS, & OTHER FRUITS
for Florida

by Robert Bowden & Tom MacCubbin

You can really make your Florida landscape pay by adding fruiting trees and shrubs that provide food. It's easy to replace some or all of the ornamental plants in any design. Just look for fruiting plants with similar growth habits. Many would recommend that if you plant only one fruit tree, make it a citrus. These reliable trees require little care from you. Here are some ways you can use fruiting trees and shrubs:

- Create shade, screen a view, block winds, and still bear a good crop.
- Create accents with fruiting plants so you can enjoy the flowers and colorful fruits.
- Plant fruits to attract wildlife.
- Create natural hedges and other space dividers with shrubs and small trees.
- Add citrus near the patio to cast shade and to hang orchids from.
- Plant small citrus in a container for patio shade or at an entrance.
- Plant a grove with selections to fruit throughout most of the year.

PLANNING

Consider how much room the plantings need to be productive. Some, like avocados, grapefruits, and oranges, can grow quite large. Unless plants have other features that make them good landscape additions, plan to plant only what your family can use as food. You may select a fruiting tree or shrub just because it's a favorite even if it doesn't give very high yields. But to really make the additions worth the effort, most of the plantings should produce a bumper crop each year.

Consider the hardiness and heat tolerance of the plants. Plants that grow only in the northern or central regions of the state probably cannot stand intense heat or extended warm weather. Many must have some cold. Others, limited to central and southern zones, are usually damaged by winter cold. These freeze-sensitive plants can be protected from cold or sometimes grown in containers and moved to a warm location.

- Look at pest problems associated with the crop, including any special pests.
- Make sure you have the needed room. Don't cram the plants close together just because you want the fruits.
- Realize there may be pruning, thinning, and other chores required. If your time is limited, pick the plants that need the least amount of extra care.

You may be better off selecting only one or two favorites and getting good production. Look at our fruiting plant list (pages 100 to 103). Note the harvest times and plan for year-round fruit harvests. You don't want too much in production at one time of the year. Most fruits have numerous varieties that can be planted to get production over the entire harvest time. Often you have a lot more to pick from than what is in our charts. Check these out at your local garden centers or fruiting tree nurseries.

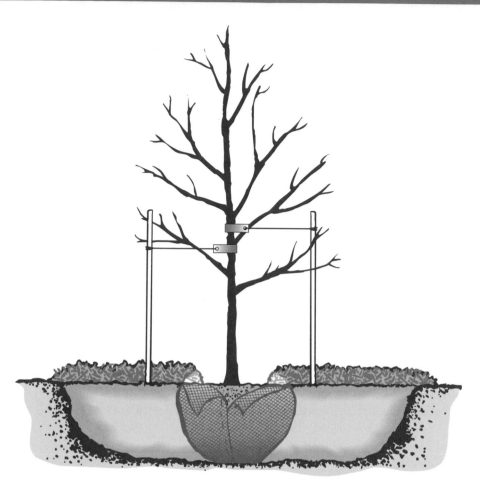

PLANTING

Normal planting procedures are used. Actually, the work is probably a bit less than for some ornamentals. Only a few have special soil needs. Most fruiting plants, especially citrus, grow fine in any well-drained Florida soil.

If the site is not immediately ready for your new plant, it can be grown for a short while in the nursery container. It is best if the wait is not too long.

- Find a spot with the proper light level. Citrus trees need sunny locations.
- Check to make sure there is plenty of growing room and no overhead wires in the case of large trees.
- Dig a hole that is one to two times wider but no deeper than the rootball. For citrus, the hole should be a little wider than the rootball.
- Set the plant in the ground with the top of the rootball at or slightly above the ground line.
- Fill in around the rootball with water and soil from the hole. There is no need to work organic matter in the soil except for figs.

- Build a berm of soil 4 to 6 inches high around the edge of the root-ball to hold water.
- Water the planting and add a mulch layer to the soil surface around the edge of the rootball, except for citrus.

Some fruiting plants are received bare root. These should be timed to arrive during the winter months so they can become established before hot spring weather. Planting is similar to that of container plants, except the roots are spread out over a mound of soil as the plant is positioned so it sets at the same level it grew in the nursery.

CARE

Citrus needs very little pruning to maintain their natural rounded shape, with lower limbs growing to the ground. Dead limbs or sprouts growing from below the grafted area should be removed. Some other fruiting plants have very specific pruning needs. The yearly "as needed" trimming is usually performed to improve fruit production and keep the crop within reach. Get familiar with each crop to know the care needed to provide the best yields.

It's suggested that some form of weed control be practiced. With trees, it may be keeping the weeds and grass away from the base by a foot or two. Shrubs and perennials may be clean-cultivated. You can add a landscape fabric. Except for citrus trees, all can be mulched.

WATERING

Young plantings need a good start, and this includes plenty of water. For the first few weeks, water daily. Then gradually taper off the waterings, but keep the soil moist until the plantings are well established.

Most fruiting plants are very drought tolerant. However, care is needed for younger plantings during drier times. Deep-rooted types can go weeks without rain or irrigation. When water is lacking, however, the plantings may start to drop their fruits. It's best to provide water to all established fruits when the surface inch of soil begins to feel dry. Some, like figs, need a constantly moist soil.

- When watering, apply ½ to ¾ inch of water.
- Use soaker hoses or microsprinklers when possible under the spread of the plants.
- Water during the early-morning hours.
- Keep plantings (except citrus) mulched to conserve moisture.

Making sure citrus trees have an even moisture supply ensures good growth and prevents some physiological problems. A problem known as fruit splitting is often increased by intermittent periods of moisture.

FERTILIZING

Fruiting plants vary as to fertilizer needs. You can develop special schedules or stick to a general feeding program. All appear to grow best when fed more than once a year. If the plants are growing among turf, flowers, or shrubs, they may receive an adequate nutrient supply with the feedings given these plants. In general, gardeners like to give the fruiting plants special feedings. Unless you work out a special schedule for your plantings, an application two or three times a year is fine, except for citrus.

- Apply a 6-6-6, 8-8-8, or similar fertilizer that also contains minor nutrients. If desired, citrus fertilizers may be used for citrus trees, Mangos, and Avocados.
- Feed new fruit tree plantings lightly every six to eight weeks from March through September. Use ¼ pound of fertilizer per plant, scattered under the spread of the branches.
- This may be gradually increased to ½ pound as the plants begin to grow. Citrus tree feedings should be increased to provide 1½ pounds at the end of the first year, 2½ pounds at the end of year two, and 4 pounds at the end of year three.
- Feed established citrus trees four times a year—in March, May, August, and early October. Use ¼ pound of a citrus fertilizer for each inch of trunk circumference, measured 6 inches above the ground.
- Feed established other fruit trees in March, June, and September at the rate of 1 pound for each 100 square feet of area.
- Scatter fertilizer under the spread of the tree and out past the drip line.
- Apply the fertilizer over mulches.

APPLE

WHEN TO PLANT
Apple trees are grown in 3- to 5- gallon containers and can be planted any time of year.

WHERE TO PLANT
Plant in full sun with well-prepared, well-drained soil.

HOW TO PLANT
Place the rootball 1 inch higher than the soil level to compensate for settling. Create a saucer with remaining soil and water every other day for four to five weeks or until well-rooted.

WATER NEEDS
Apple tree prefers moist, well-drained soil. Drought can cause leaf drop and premature fruit drop.

CARE
Apples are traditionally grown in cooler climates so growing apples in Florida is not an easy task. Keep well watered and fertilize with a general 6-6-6-2 (NPKMg) fertilizer four times a year.

PROBLEMS
Watch for apple scab (looks like blotches on fruit with leaves that are gnarled and twisted) and fireblight (a serious disease that can be spread from tree to tree).

HARVEST
Apples can be harvested when they separate from the tree when gently pulled.

SELECTIONS
For Florida gardens try 'Anna', 'Dorsett Golden', and tropic 'Sweet'.

AVOCADO

WHEN TO PLANT
Plant at any time.

WHERE TO PLANT
Needs well-drained soil in full sun. Position 15 to 20 feet from buildings, sidewalks, and streets. Also used as landscape tree.

HOW TO PLANT
Place 1 inch above the soil line. In areas prone to flooding, plant on mounds.

WATER NEEDS
Established trees require watering only during severe drought—but for best production, water weekly.

CARE
Feed new trees every other month. Fertilize established trees in February, April, June, and September with Avocado-type fertilizer.

PROBLEMS
Diseases and pests don't usually affect the number of fruit produced. Pick fruit before squirrels get them.

HARVEST
Avocados do not ripen on the tree. They are picked at maximum size, ripening about a week later. They don't have to be picked at the same time. Harvest seasons range from May to March, depending on variety.

SELECTIONS
There are numerous varieties developed for Florida, some with moderate cold hardiness. They have different ripening seasons and sizes. Check with local gardeners or your Extension Service to find out which work best in your area.

BANANA

WHEN TO PLANT

In South and Central Florida plant March through May. Where heavy freezes occur, plant small varieties in pots that can be brought indoors for cold protection.

WHERE TO PLANT

Plant in full sun (best for fruit production) to part shade in well-drained, compost-enriched soils. Protect from strong winds. Also plant for tropical foliage.

HOW TO PLANT

Place rootball 1 inch above soil line to compensate for settling. Mulch to maintain moisture.

WATER NEEDS

Bananas like plenty of water but not standing water.

CARE

Fertilize lightly every two months, increasing amount as plant grows. Annual micronutrient spray is helpful.

PROBLEMS

Without enough fertilizer the fruit weight may cause stalk to buckle. For best fruiting, thin the stand to 1 foot between trunks.

HARVEST

Blooms after 10 to 18 months. Fruit ripens about 5 months later. After bananas form and the first hand that formed begins to turn yellow, cut entire bunch and ripen off the main stalk.

SELECTIONS

'Goldfinger', 'Lady Finger', 'Manzano', 'Mysore', 'Rajapuri'. Dwarf: 'Dwarf Cavendish', 'Dwarf Orinoco', 'Dwarf Red'.

BLACKBERRY

WHEN TO PLANT

Plant bare root in December to February, immediately after purchased. Plant container-ized any time.

WHERE TO PLANT

Prefer mildly acidic, well-drained soil

HOW TO PLANT

Clip roots of bare-root plants to about 6 inches and plant with crown just above soil level. Containerized plants should also be set slightly above soil level. Provide ample growing room.

WATER NEEDS

Always mulch to retain moisture and prevent weeds.

CARE

After the first year, prune main canes down to 36 inches, to initiate new canes. Fruit is produced on old canes—more pruning results in more berries. Don't prune more than 1/3 of the canes down to the ground each season. Erect-type Blackberries are easier to grow than trailing, which need support. Apply light fertil-izer (with micronutrients) in spring or summer, 18 inches away from plant centers to protect shallow roots.

PROBLEMS

Plants withstand very cold temperatures but flowers are very susceptible to cold.

HARVEST

Blackberries fruit in summer. Trailing types ripen earlier, with smaller berries.

SELECTIONS

'Brazos' is most popular selection. Thornless varieties: 'Apache', 'Choctaw', and 'Ouachita'.

BLUEBERRY

WHEN TO PLANT
During winter

WHERE TO PLANT
In highly acidic (pH 4.5 to 5.2), well-drained soil high in organic matter. Need full sun, with plenty of room.

HOW TO PLANT
Add lots of sphagnum peat moss. Plant a few inches above soil level. To improve soil condition and acidity, place bands of pine bark (2 feet wide) around every plant and renew regularly.

WATER NEEDS
Needs 45 inches of rain each year but dies if roots flood or stand in water.

CARE
Once established, provide a little fertilizer often. Four times annually apply 2 ounces per plant of azalea-camellia fertilizer, in 2 foot circle. Gradually increase dose to 4 ounces per year and spreading circle to 4 feet .

PROBLEMS
Improper pH leads to plant decline. If planted near hardwood trees or within 20 feet of structures, will produce less fruit.

HARVEST
Late spring and early summer

SELECTIONS
Only use varieties specifically for Florida: southern highbush (good for Central and South Florida) and rabbiteye. Southern highbush: 'Emerald', 'Gulf Coast', and 'Sharpblue'. Rabbiteye: 'Beckyblue', 'Bonita', and 'Woodruff'.

CARAMBOLA
(STAR FRUIT)

WHEN TO PLANT
Plant at any time

WHERE TO PLANT
In full sun with well-drained soil. Although the small tree withstands some cool weather it prefers hot and humid Central and South Florida.

HOW TO PLANT
Plant rootball with top slightly above soil level. Water well and add mulch. If you live where flooding occurs, plant in a mound.

WATER NEEDS
While too much water hinders fruit production, Carambola is not tolerant of drought. Provide at least one inch of water per week. If leaves begin to wilt, it's not getting enough water.

CARE
Fertilize young trees with ½ pound of complete 10-10-10-2 (NPKMg) fertilizer six times per year. Spray trees in alkaline soils with micronutrient spray containing manganese and zinc.

PROBLEMS
Virtually trouble free. Use stream of water to wash off occasional aphids. Keep fruit picked to avoid fruit flies. Star fruits are high in oxalic acid, so by-pass them if you have kidney disease.

HARVEST
Depending on variety, may produce several crops per year

SELECTIONS
'Arkin', 'Fuang Tung', 'Kari', 'Sri Kembangan', 'Thai Knight'

COCONUT PALM
Cocos nucifera

WHEN TO PLANT
Plant from sprouted nuts in early summer. Plant container-grown trees any time.

WHERE TO PLANT
In full sun, zones 10 and 11. Plant in good drainage,where large crown won't be crowded.

HOW TO PLANT
Bury the sprouted nut about halfway, placed sideways in thick, damp layer of mulch.

WATER NEEDS
Keep new tree moist. Tolerates drought once established.

CARE
Water in about 3 pounds of fertilizer every four months for the first year. After that, feed two or three times annually.

PROBLEMS
Very sensitive to cold weather. New varieties are resistant to lethal yellowing disease.

HARVEST
Once old enough to fruit (5 to 10 years), coconuts are produced throughout the year. Fruits take approximately one year to develop. Production is 50 to 200 coconuts per year, depending upon cultivar and climate.

SELECTIONS
The Coconut Palm is one of the world's most useful trees. It is also used to provide a tropical look to landscapes. Young trees can be planted in large containers. 'Dwarf Green', 'Golden Malayan', 'Maypan', 'Red Spicata'.

FIG

WHEN TO PLANT
Plant bare-root figs in fall, containerized figs any time

WHERE TO PLANT
In full to part sun, with plenty of room to grow. Need well-drained soil. Keep away from standing water or soggy soils.

HOW TO PLANT
Dig a hole twice as wide and deep as the root mass. Place a few inches above the soil line. Water thoroughly and add good mulch layer.

WATER NEEDS
Water daily for first two weeks. Gradually reduce frequency to once or twice weekly during hot weather.

CARE
Figs have a healthy fibrous root system so deep cultivation is not recommended. Maintain mulch layer. Fertilize monthly during growing season. Pruning is generally not required. Figs enjoy an annual dose of calcium once established. Apply one cup of calcium nitrate under the canopy, increasing the amount as the plant gets larger.

PROBLEMS
Plant in nematode-free soil. There are no insect pests to speak of but figs are highly prized by birds.

HARVEST
July and August ('Celeste') or July through fall ('Brown Turkey')

SELECTIONS
'Celeste' is best; 'Brown Turkey' also popular

GRAPE

WHEN TO PLANT
Any time of year

WHERE TO PLANT
In full sun in well-drained soil with a clay base

HOW TO PLANT
Place individual plants 8 feet apart in rows at least 6 feet apart. Plant a few inches above the soil line. Rows on a north-south axis maximize sunlight.

WATER NEEDS
Water every few days after planting. Gradually reduce frequency. Then provide plenty of water before harvest.

CARE
Grapes produce fruit on new wood. However, too much new wood and grapes will be small in size and quantity. Special trellises and year-round pruning ensure good fruit production and easy harvesting. In the first year apply ¼ pound of 8-8-8 fertilizer per plant. Increase amount annually to 4 pounds.

PROBLEMS
Bunch grapes may need fungicide spray program for anthracnose.

HARVEST
June through September, depending on variety

SELECTIONS
Scuppernong, muscadine, and bunch grapes are all Florida grapes. They can be eaten fresh or used for wine. Purple: 'Conquistador', 'Blue Lake', 'Black Spanish'. Green: 'Stover', 'Blanc Du Bois', 'Suwannee'. Red: 'Daytona'.

GRAPEFRUIT

WHEN TO PLANT
The best times to plant Grapefruit trees are from the end of winter until midsummer.

WHERE TO PLANT
Plant in full sun, in zones 9 – 11. Select a location with excellent drainage and easy access to all sides for harvesting.

HOW TO PLANT
Situate tree in planting hole even with soil surface

WATER NEEDS
Water weekly during droughts

CARE
Keep grass and weeds from growing under tree. Feed bearing trees four times a year (March, May, August, and early October) using citrus fertilizer with extra magnesium. Prune deadwood from crowns as needed.

PROBLEMS
Not all varieties come true from seed. Use insecticidal soap against sucking insects (such as aphids, mealybugs, and whiteflies) that may be attracted to new leaves. They excrete sticky honeydew that grows sooty mold.

HARVEST
When grown from seed, may take six to ten or more years to fruit. Ripens November through winter, depending upon variety. Fruit can remain on the tree for long periods.

SELECTIONS
'Duncan', 'Flame', 'Marsh', 'Redblush' (new name for 'Ruby'), 'Thompson'

GUAVA

WHEN TO PLANT
Plant at any time

WHERE TO PLANT
In full sun. Must have well-drained soil; intolerant of wet feet even for a short time.

HOW TO PLANT
In sandy soils plant a few inches above soil level. In mucky soils plant on mound.

WATER NEEDS
Water new plant daily for two weeks then gradually taper off. Water 1 to 1½ inches weekly.

CARE
Fertilize with one pound 8-8-8-2 (NPKMg) every two months. Increase to five pounds, four times per year after year five. Once established, apply foliar nutritional spray containing boron, manganese, zinc, and copper four times per year. If soil is alkaline apply chelated iron annually.

PROBLEMS
Intolerant of cold; growth and fruit production stop when temperatures reach 60°F.

HARVEST
Pick pink or red guava when peel begins turning light green or yellow. Pick white varieties when light green, before a fully ripe yellow. Allow fruits to ripen without refrigeration until ready to eat.

SELECTIONS
Often grown as a landscape specimen. Pink: Homestead, Hong Kong Pink, Barbi Pink, Patillo. Green: Webber, Crystal, Lotus, Supreme.

JABOTICABA

WHEN TO PLANT
Can be planted any time. Freeze tolerance is variable, so don't grow where freezing temperatures are common.

WHERE TO PLANT
Plant in full to part sun (part sun reduces number of fruit) in well-drained, deep, sandy soil. May also be planted as a specimen tree.

HOW TO PLANT
Place 1 inch above the soil line (to compensate for settling). Plant in mounds if holes are difficult to dig.

WATER NEEDS
Roots are quite shallow so supplement rainfall and use mulch.

CARE
Apply general 8-8-8-2 (NPKMg) fertilizer four times annually. Pruning is rarely needed but they can be trimmed into a hedge without significant fruit reduction. In alkaline soils add mulch and semi-annual chelated iron drench.

PROBLEMS
Deer may eat new foliage. Squirrels and raccoons enjoy the fruit.

HARVEST
Harvest when dark purple or black, and soft.

SELECTIONS
Jaboticaba produces fruit the size of large grapes that erupt from the main trunk, which has unique flaking bark. 'Paulista' has large, sweet fruit, 'Rajada' has green skin, and 'Sabra' produces up to four crops in South Florida.

JACKFRUIT

WHEN TO PLANT
Any time of year

WHERE TO PLANT
Plant in full sun where flooding is not a problem and frosts rarely occur. Plant at least 30 feet from houses and trees.

HOW TO PLANT
Place 1 inch higher than the soil level.

WATER NEEDS
Does not like soggy soil

CARE
Trees can reach 40 feet tall but can be pruned to 10 or 15 feet without significant fruit reduction. During first year apply one pound of fertilizer (8-8-8 with micronutrients) five times. Afterwards apply 5 pounds annually 5 times. Apply micronutrient spray four times annually. In alkaline soils apply chelated iron once per year.

PROBLEMS
Virtually pest free although scale can affect leaves and stems. The latex-like sap can stain clothes and may cause skin irritation in some people.

HARVEST
Jackfruits are very large (to 60 pounds) with two parts, one of which is inedible. Harvest when fruit develops a pungent odor. It will ripen in four to seven days.

SELECTIONS
Varieties good for Florida gardens include 'Black Gold', 'Cheena', 'Chompa Gob', 'Honey Gold', and 'Lemon Gold'.

KUMQUAT

WHEN TO PLANT
Plant container-grown trees at any time

WHERE TO PLANT
As the most cold-tolerant citrus, the small Kumquat tree can be grown in areas that freeze. Plant in full sun. It is compact and ornamental enough to be planted in containers.

HOW TO PLANT
If well-drained soil isn't available, plant on mounds. Water daily for two weeks then taper off.

WATER NEEDS
Water established trees once or twice a week during dry times.

CARE
For young trees apply half to full pound citrus fertilizer, 4 or 5 times per year. Feed established trees once in March, May, August, and early October with ¼ pound per inch of trunk circumference. Scatter fertilizer under branches and out past drip line. Also apply citrus nutritional spray.

PROBLEMS
Remove weeds beneath entire tree canopy where possible. Can often be grown without pesticides, since many pests affect appearance only, not quality.

HARVEST
Usually October through February, depending upon hybrid. Some are sweet when ripe, others are tart.

SELECTIONS
Several species and hybrids are available, including limequats and orangequats.

LEMON

WHEN TO PLANT
Plant container-grown citrus at any time.

WHERE TO PLANT
Lemons are one of the most cold-sensitive citrus. Grow below a line from Daytona Beach to Crystal River. Plant in full sun. Can also be grown in containers.

HOW TO PLANT
If well-drained soil isn't available, plant on mounds. Water daily for two weeks then taper off.

WATER NEEDS
Water established in-ground trees once or twice a week during dry times.

CARE
For young trees apply half to full pound citrus fertilizer, four or five times per year. Feed established trees once in March, May, August, and early October with ¼ pound per inch of trunk circumference. Scatter fertilizer under branches and out past drip line. Also apply citrus nutritional spray.

PROBLEMS
Remove weeds beneath entire tree canopy where possible. Can often be grown without pesticides, since many pests affect appearance only, not quality.

HARVEST
Varies by selection. If picked before maturity, can be stored for long periods.

SELECTIONS
'Avon', 'Bearss', 'Eureka'. 'Ponderosa' is large and grown for show.

LIME

WHEN TO PLANT
Plant container-grown Lime trees any time

WHERE TO PLANT
The most cold-sensitive Citrus. Grow below a line from Daytona Beach to Crystal River. Plant in full sun. Don't plant close to house or septic fields. May be grown in containers.

HOW TO PLANT
If well-drained soil isn't available, plant on mounds. Water daily for two weeks then taper off.

WATER NEEDS
Water established trees once or twice a week during dry times.

CARE
For young trees apply half to full pound citrus fertilizer, 4 or 5 times per year. Feed established trees once in March, May, August, and early October with ¼ pound per inch of trunk circumference. Scatter fertilizer under branches and past drip line. Also apply citrus nutritional spray.

PROBLEMS
Remove weeds beneath tree canopy where possible. Can often be grown without pesticides, since many pests affect appearance only, not quality.

HARVEST
Pick Limes when starting to change color. Tahitian Limes mature from June to September, Key Limes almost year-round.

SELECTIONS
Tahitian (Persian) Limes tolerate more cold than Key (Mexican) Limes

LOQUAT

WHEN TO PLANT
At any time

WHERE TO PLANT
Produce most fruit in full sun. Not finicky as to soil type and are even somewhat salt tolerant. However, they do not like wet or water-logged soils.

HOW TO PLANT
Place rootball a few inches above the soil (to compensate for settling).

WATER NEEDS
Water young trees frequently, then gradually reduce waterings.

CARE
Loquat trees do not require pruning. Feed one-year-old plants one pound general fertilizer 8-8-8-2 (NPKMg) four times annually. Increase to 5 pounds, four times per year, as tree gets bigger. Apply micronutrient foliar spray four times annually. If grown in alkaline soil apply chelated iron soil drench twice per year.

PROBLEMS
Fire blight may be a problem. Cut out damaged portions and spray with fungicide.

HARVEST
Generally produce fruit in spring; in warmer areas may have two or three crops. Fruit ripens in approximately 120 days. Let ripen on tree.

SELECTIONS
Also popular as a small shade tree. 'Advance', 'Champagne', 'Emanuel', 'Golitch', 'Juda', 'Judith', 'Oliver', 'Thales', 'Thursby', 'Wolfe'

LYCHEE

WHEN TO PLANT
Plant any time of year. More mature trees better withstand freezes.

WHERE TO PLANT
Grow best in full sun, with well-drained, well-composted soil and plenty of room. Also planted as landscape tree.

HOW TO PLANT
Place top of rootball 1 inch above soil line. More Lychees have been killed by planting too deep than for any other reasons.

WATER NEEDS
Water daily for first three weeks. Established trees are somewhat drought tolerant, but for best fruit production, water weekly. Cannot tolerate any standing water.

CARE
Feed four to six weeks after planting and continue alternate months for first year. Then fertilize in March, May, and early October. In limestone soils, add minor nutrient foliar spray two or three times annually.

PROBLEMS
If scale becomes a problem, apply a recommended fruit tree spray. Lychees are not strong enough for ladder picking (like citrus). Use long poles with sharp clippers.

HARVEST
The entire cluster of Lychees is harvested when bright red in late spring through summer. Individual fruits are clipped from the cluster.

SELECTIONS
'Mauritius', 'Brewster'

MACADAMIA

WHEN TO PLANT
Macadamia trees are grown in 3- to 5-gallon containers and can be planted at any time of the year.

WHERE TO PLANT
Plant in full sun with well-prepared, well-drained soil in areas of Florida where hard freezes are not reoccurring.

HOW TO PLANT
Place the rootball 1 inch higher than the native soil level to compensate for settling.
Create a saucer with remaining soil and water every other day for four to five weeks or until well rooted.

WATER NEEDS
Prefers moist soil. Although drought tolerant, extended periods of drought will cause premature nut drop.

CARE
Macadamia trees are long-lived rainforest trees from Australia and require high humidity and high temperatures. Young trees may be killed during cold periods but adult trees may withstand temperatures to 28°F without damage. Requires no special care.

PROBLEMS
Occasional scale insects are not serious.

HARVEST
Fruits mature in fall. The nuts are protected by a thick sheath that falls off when mature, exposing a very hard, brown shell.

SELECTIONS
None specific for Florida

MANGO

WHEN TO PLANT
Plant at beginning of rainy season, in frost-free zones.

WHERE TO PLANT
Plant in full sun with well-drained soil, at least 30 feet from buildings. Allow plenty of room for the tree's height (30 to 50 feet) as well as for its extensive root system. Often planted as beautiful evergreen shade trees, with new leaves showing a red flush.

HOW TO PLANT
Place with top of rootball 1 inch above the soil line. Keep mulched.

WATER NEEDS
Water daily for two weeks and taper off as plant becomes established. Established trees can withstand drought. However, for best fruit production water periodically during its development.

CARE
Avoid planting expensive or rare plants beneath it because of fruit and leaf drop. Use fertilizer with extra magnesium three times a year during growing season and an iron drench once annually.

PROBLEMS
Although anthracnose may be a problem, no harm is usually done to the fruit.

HARVEST
Fruits (hanging on long stalks) mature May to September, depending upon type.

SELECTIONS
'Carrie', 'Carrie Atkins', 'Dunkin', 'Edward', 'Florigon', 'Keitt', 'Parvin'

NECTARINE

WHEN TO PLANT
Plant any time

WHERE TO PLANT
In full sun and well-drained soil. Allow plenty of room for growth.

HOW TO PLANT
Plant a few inches above soil level.

WATER NEEDS
Water daily for three weeks then gradually taper off

CARE
The tree must be open in the middle with upward growth. It takes discipline, but for good nectarine quality and quantity some initial hard pruning is essential. Cut the primary single upright leader about 36 inches above the ground to encourage side branching. As tree matures, remove sprouts and branches in the center. New fruit grows on one-year-old wood, so annual pruning is necessary.

PROBLEMS
Alkaline or marl soils can cause poor overall growth, leaf drop, and insect infestations. Use elevated beds of good soil and liberal sprinkling of granulated sulfur each spring.

HARVEST
Ripens early to mid-May

SELECTIONS
Growing nectarines in Florida was formerly possible only in northern areas. However, a new variety is good for fruit and ornamental characteristics. 'Sunhome' can be grown everywhere in the state and has purple new growth.

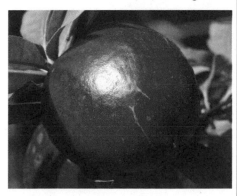

ORANGE

WHEN TO PLANT
Plant container trees any time. Best planted from May to August.

WHERE TO PLANT
In full sun, zones 9 to 11. In northern range, plant in southern location to protect from cold winds.

HOW TO PLANT
Situate tree in planting hole so it sits even with the soil

WATER NEEDS
Requires good drainage; cannot endure wet feet. Water once or twice a week during dry times.

CARE
Fertilize new trees frequently (four or five times from March to October) starting with ½ pound and ending with 1½ pounds. Trees three years and older should be fed once in March, May, August, and early October with one quarter pound of citrus fertilizer per inch of trunk circumference. Prune back cold damage in spring. Otherwise, little pruning is needed.

PROBLEMS
Use insecticidal soap or horticultural oil sprays if leaves turn black from whitefly secretion.

HARVEST
Fruit ripens from October to March, depending upon variety.

SELECTIONS
All varieties bloom in the spring. Small Orange trees are suitable for townhouses or apartment patios, and can be grown in large containers.

PAPAYA

WHEN TO PLANT
Start seeds in fall. Plant containerized papayas or transplants in spring.

WHERE TO PLANT
In full sun with average soil where no danger of frost. Can also grow in large containers.

HOW TO PLANT
Plant containerized papayas in average soil. Purchase plants 2 to 3 feet tall. Larger plants are frequently root bound. They quickly grow to 8 feet and produce in about ten months.

WATER NEEDS
Need plenty of water

CARE
Plants can be male, female, or bisexual. Females produce the best fruit, bisexuals' fruits are smaller, and male plants are good for cross pollination. Apply ¼ pound of general fertilizer while young. Increase to 1 to 2 pounds every two months during warmer time of year as plants get larger. Feed a foliar or ground micronutrient application at least twice annually.

PROBLEMS
Susceptible to nematodes and several other pests, including papaya fruit fly, papaya webworms, spider mites, papaya whitefly, two-spotted mite, papaya ring spot, and powdery mildew.

HARVEST
Produced throughout the year

SELECTIONS
'Sunrise Solo', 'Red Lady', 'Maradol'

PASSION FRUIT

WHEN TO PLANT
Any time of year. In northern areas, plant in containers and provide winter protection.

WHERE TO PLANT
In full sun with fast-draining enriched soils for best fruit production. May also be planted as ornamental vines or in butterfly gardens.

HOW TO PLANT
Place top of rootball about 1 inch higher than the soil line

WATERING
Keep roots well irrigated until vine is growing vigorously

CARE
Passion Vines are quick growers, requiring an arbor. Feed with a balanced slow-release, or Palm fertilizer. Too much nitrogen may result in foliage only. In very alkaline soils may become chlorotic, needing an iron drench or micronutrient foliar spray.

PROBLEMS
They are not woody but will run away if you don't control them. Passion fruits are relatively pest free.

HARVEST
Both the purple and yellow fruits change color rapidly as they ripen. For the best taste, leave on the vine until they drop. Pick up often so they don't attract animals.

SELECTIONS
Edible species are *Passiflora edulis* and *P. edulis flavicarpa*. There are a few Florida native species.

PEACH

WHEN TO PLANT
Plant any time

WHERE TO PLANT
In full sun and well-drained soil. Allow plenty of room.

HOW TO PLANT
Set rootball a few inches above soil level

WATER NEEDS
Water daily for three weeks then gradually taper off

CARE
The tree must be open in the middle with upward growth. It takes discipline, but for good peach quality and quantity some initial hard pruning is essential. Cut the primary single upright leader about 36 inches above the ground to encourage side branching. As tree matures, remove sprouts and branches in the center. New fruit grows on one-year-old wood so annual pruning is necessary.

PROBLEMS
Alkaline or marl soils can cause poor overall growth, leaf drop, and insect infestations. Use elevated beds of good soil and liberal sprinkling of granulated sulfur each spring.

HARVEST
Ripen early to mid-May

SELECTIONS
Growing peaches in Florida had been possible only for northern areas. New varieties enable gardeners everywhere in the state to grow peaches with only 150 hours of cold chill. Low chill: 'FloridaGlo', 'FloridaPrince', 'UF Beauty'

PECAN

WHEN TO PLANT
Plant in fall

WHERE TO PLANT
Pecans, which can grow to 70 feet, need plenty of room, well-drained soil, and full sun. Plant at least thirty feet away from structures.

HOW TO PLANT
Plant either bare-root or containerized plants. Apply a single application of diluted white latex paint to the trunk 4 feet high to reduce bark sunscald.

WATER NEEDS
Water at least three times weekly for two months. Reduce waterings until warm weather returns.

CARE
Apply 1 pound fertilizer (10-10-10-3 NPKMg) after planting. Apply 1 pound fertilizer per 1 inch of trunk diameter in early March and June. Once nut production begins apply 2 to 4 pounds in February and June. If planted as a single leader, reduce by $2/3$ and train to have symmetrical branches. Containerized and mature trees are seldom pruned.

PROBLEMS
Spraying may be necessary for caterpillars and other pests. Barriers on the trunk may deter squirrels.

HARVEST
Takes four to twelve years for nuts, depending on variety. Best Pecans are grown in North Florida.

SELECTIONS
'Cape Fear', 'Elliott', 'Moreland'

95

PERSIMMON

WHEN TO PLANT
Plant at any time.

WHERE TO PLANT
Need well-drained soil. Plant in full sun or slightly dappled shade. Native persimmons grow to 30 feet tall, Asian to 8 feet.

HOW TO PLANT
Plant in a hole twice as wide and deep as the containerized rootball

WATER NEEDS
Water three times a week for first month. Reduce the amount as tree becomes established.

CARE
Keep weeds and turf at least three feet away. Do not fertilize during first year. Apply 10 pounds of 10-10-10-3 (NPKMg) fertilizer to mature trees four times per year.

PROBLEMS
Blemishes on foliage and fruit don't usually affect fruit quality and can be ignored.

HARVEST
There are astringent and non-astringent varieties. In Florida astringent varieties are picked, peeled, skewered, and dried. The dried fruit is sweet and delicious. Non-astringent account for most Florida trees. Pick in fall when hard or soft and eat fresh.

SELECTIONS
Persimmons make nice landscape plants. American native persimmons aren't as tasty as Asian selections, listed here. Astringent: 'Ormond', 'Saijo', 'Sheng', 'Tenenashi'. Non-astringent: 'Fuyu', 'Hana Fuyu', 'Izu', 'Suruga'.

PINEAPPLE

WHEN TO PLANT
Plant at any time.

WHERE TO PLANT
Plant in any soil in full sun. Pineapples make great container plants.

HOW TO PLANT
Cut pineapple 1 inch below the very top and let air dry for a few days. Many plant directly into the garden but it's recommended to plant into a container first. Plant in good potting soil so only the spiky top is sticking out. After 45 to 60 days plant into the garden. In frost-prone areas bring the container indoors when nighttime temperatures reach 55°F.

WATER NEEDS
Water daily for first month or two

CARE
Fertilize with 1 to 2 ounces of 6-6-6-4 (NPKMg) every 8 weeks. Gradually increase to 6 ounces as the plant grows. Stake the fruit stalk if necessary.

PROBLEMS
Root rot can be deterred by not overwatering and planting in well-drained sandy soil. Combat mealy bugs by applying 1 teaspoon Ivory soap per quart of water to the soil, not in the spike.

HARVEST
Harvest when bottom starts to change from green to yellow, before critters get to it.

PLUM

WHEN TO PLANT
Plant at any time.

WHERE TO PLANT
In full sun and well-drained soil. Trees can reach 10 to 12 feet tall and 12 feet wide so give them plenty of room.

HOW TO PLANT
Plant a few inches above soil level to allow for settling. In areas where pH is high, plant in elevated beds made of good garden soil. A liberal sprinkling of granulated sulfur once each spring will help lower the pH as well.

WATER NEEDS
Water daily for three weeks then gradually taper off

CARE
Prune to grow from a central leader

PROBLEMS
Alkaline or marl soils can cause poor overall growth, leaf drop, and insect infestations. Use raised beds. Make sure insecticides are labeled for use on fruit trees.

HARVEST
Ripens early to mid-May

SELECTIONS
Growing plums in Florida once was only possible in northern areas. However, new varieties are now available that can be grown throughout the state. They only need 150 hours of cold chill with temperatures below 50°F. 'Gulfbeauty', 'Gulfblaze', 'Gulfrose', 'Gulfgold', 'Gulfruby'

POMEGRANATE

WHEN TO PLANT
Plant at any time.

WHERE TO PLANT
In full sun in most deep, well-drained soils. Grown as shrubs or trees.

HOW TO PLANT
Place rootball slightly higher than soil line

WATER NEEDS
Tolerant of minor, short-term flooding

CARE
Very easy to grow. Fruits are borne on new growth so lightly trim branch ends before July 1 to create buds for next year. Four times a year, apply one cup of fertilizer. Use 8-8-8-4 (NPKMg) with micronutrients. After the plant is two years old fertilize use 2 cups once in fall and in spring. Use 3 cups in year three and 4 in year four. However, too much food can cause fruit drop so be careful with the "groceries."

PROBLEMS
Pomegranates are virtually pest free. Scale and mealy bugs may occur.

HARVEST
Fruits range from 2 to 5 inches in diameter and in North and Central Florida mature from July to November. In South Florida they may produce year-round.

SELECTIONS
The shrub makes a welcome addition to any landscape. 'Purple Seed', 'Spanish Ruby', 'Wonderful'

SEA GRAPE

WHEN TO PLANT
At any time in South and coastal Central Florida

WHERE TO PLANT
In full sun with well-drained soil. Very salt tolerant. Sea Grape is more often grown in the landscape as a large shrub or small tree. It is used as a hedge, for soil stabilization, in native gardens, and for its exotic look.

HOW TO PLANT
Plant at the same depth as in container and add 2- to 3-inch mulch layer.

WATER NEEDS
Water every day for first few weeks, then gradually taper off to watering as needed. Sea Grape is drought tolerant once established and only needs watering during severe drought.

CARE
Feed after four to six weeks. Continue applying fertilizer in March and June for next three years.

PROBLEMS
Virtually pest-free

HARVEST
Long fruit clusters are generally produced from summer through fall. Fruits ripen only a few at a time and turn purple. They are tastier to wildlife than to people, who occasionally use them for preserves and for wine.

SELECTIONS
Only the native species is available in Florida.

STRAWBERRY

WHEN TO PLANT
Plant bare-root plants in fall for up to three production cycles

WHERE TO PLANT
In full sun in rich, very well-composted, well-drained soil

HOW TO PLANT
Grow in raised linear beds about 8 inches high with irrigation just below the surface, and covered with opaque plastic. Insert plants through slits in the plastic, which is necessary to prevent weeds during entire season. The only alternative are mounds covered with newspaper and hay, with or without soaker hoses.

WATER NEEDS
Keep soil moist.

CARE
Incorporate fertilizer with ½ slow-release nitrogen and micronutrients into the bed before planting. Protect fruit and flowers from freezing.

PROBLEMS
Try growing strawberries. However, buying them may be easier and cheaper. Use fine mesh netting to keep out birds and animals. Use beer traps for the common slugs. For spider mites and insects apply Neem oil.

HARVEST
Pick frequently, especially during spring, to defeat insects and birds. A plant can produce 1 to 2 pints per season.

SELECTIONS
'Camarosa' (best for North Florida), 'Festival', 'Sweet Charlie' (best for Central Florida)

TAMARIND

WHEN TO PLANT
Tamarind trees are grown in 3- to 5-gallon containers and can be planted any time of year.

WHERE TO PLANT
Plant in full sun with well-prepared, well-drained soil. Tamarind trees are tropical and should only be planted where freezes do not occur.

HOW TO PLANT
Place the top of the rootball 1 inch higher than the soil level to compensate for settling.

WATER NEEDS
Water every other day for four to five weeks, or until well-rooted. Tamarind trees prefer moist, well-drained soil.

CARE
These slow-growing, long-lived tropical trees require high humidity and high temperatures. Young trees may be killed during cold periods but adult trees may withstand temperatures to 28°F without damage.

PROBLEMS
Generally free of pests and diseases

HARVEST
Fruits mature in late spring to early summer. Ripe fruit is sometimes attacked by beetles and fungi, so harvest mature fruit and store under refrigeration. Tamarinds may be eaten fresh, but they are most commonly used to make a cooling drink or to flavor preserves and chutney.

SELECTIONS
'Manilla Sweet', 'Markham Waan'

TANGERINE

WHEN TO PLANT
Add container-grown plants any time, although cooler times are best ·

WHERE TO PLANT
In full sun, Zones 9 – 11. In northern range, plant in southern location to protect from cold winds.

HOW TO PLANT
Plant in hole about two times wider than rootball (but no deeper), at same depth as in container.

WATER NEEDS
Requires good drainage; grows well in Florida sandy soils. New trees need frequent watering.

CARE
Fertilize new trees frequently (four or five times March to October) for first two or three years. Beginning in fourth year, feed with citrus fertilizer in March, May, August, and early October with ¼ pound per inch of trunk circumference. Prune lower limbs to make maintenance and harvesting easier. Citrus sometimes suffers cold damage in Central Florida. Mound soil around trunk to protect grafted portions from freezing.

PROBLEMS
Control caterpillars by hand picking or applying *Bacillus thuringiensis* (Bt) spray. Spray aphids and whiteflies with oil spray or other recommended controls.

HARVEST
Ripens fall to spring, depending upon variety

SELECTIONS
Often called Mandarin. 'Sunburst', 'Dancy'

SELECTED CITRUS PLANTINGS

Name	Area of Florida	Ready to Eat	Seeds per Fruit	Fruit Size (Inches)	Remarks
ORANGES					
Ambersweet	CS	Oct. – Dec.	0 – 15	3 – 3½	Easy to peel, good juice quality
Cara Cara	CS	Oct. – Jan.	0 – 6	3 – 3½	A red-fleshed navel selection
Gardner	CS	Jan. – Mar.	6 – 24	2½ – 3	Good juice quality
Hamlin	CS	Oct. – Jan.	0 – 6	2¾ – 3	Early juice orange
Midsweet	CS	Jan. – Mar.	6 – 24	2½ – 3	Good juice quality
Navel	CS	Oct. – Jan.	0 – 6	3 – 3½	Very popular, eat fresh or juice
Parson Brown	CS	Oct. – Jan.	10 – 20	2½ – 2¾	Low fruit yields but early
Pineapple	CS	Dec. – Feb.	15 – 25	2¾ – 3	Excellent juice but seedy
Rhode Red	CS	Mar. – June	0 – 6	2¾ – 3	A red-fleshed Valencia selection
Sunstar	CS	Jan. – Mar.	6 – 20	2½ – 3	Good juice quality
Valencia	CS	Mar. – June	0 – 6	2¾ – 3	Excellent juice quality
GRAPEFRUIT AND RELATED FRUITS					
Duncun	CS	Nov. – May	30 – 70	3½ – 5	An old variety, white flesh
Flame	CS	Nov. – May	0 – 6	3¾ – 4½	Most popular, dark red flesh
Foster	CS	Nov. – May	30 – 50	3½ – 5	Good older variety, pink flesh
Marsh	CS	Nov. – May	0 – 6	3½ – 4½	Very popular, white flesh
Pink Marsh	CS	Dec. – May	0 – 6	3¾ – 4½	Also called Thompson, pink flesh
Pummelo	CS	Nov. – Feb.	50	5 – 7	May be a parent of the grapefruit
Ray Ruby	CS	Nov. – May	0 – 6	3½ – 4	Dark red flesh
Redblush	CS	Nov. – May	0 – 6	3½ – 4½	Also called Ruby Red, red flesh
Star Ruby	CS	Dec. – May	0 – 6	3½ – 4	Dark red flesh
MANDARINS AND HYBRIDS					
Dancy	CS	Dec. – Jan.	6 – 20	2¼ – 2½	Easy-to-peel-and-section tangerine
Fallglo	CS	Oct. – Nov.	30 – 40	3 – 3½	Easy-peeling Temple hybrid

SELECTED CITRUS PLANTINGS

Name	Area of Florida	Ready to Eat	Seeds per Fruit	Fruit Size (Inches)	Remarks
MANDARINS AND HYBRIDS					
Minneola	CS	Dec. – Jan.	7 – 12	3 – 3½	A tangelo, often called Honeybell
Murcott	CS	Jan. – Mar.	10 – 20	2½ – 2¾	A hybrid with a unique flavor
Nova	CS	Nov. – Dec.	1 – 30	2¾ – 3	A hybrid with good flavor
Lee	CS	Nov. – Dec.	10 – 25	2¾ – 3	A hybrid with good flavor
Orlando	CS	Nov. – Jan.	0 – 35	2¾ – 3	A heavy producing tangelo
Osceola	CS	Oct. – Nov.	15 – 25	2¼ – 2¾	A hybrid with good flavor
Ponkan	CS	Dec. – Jan.	3 – 7	2¾ – 3½	Good flavor, easy-to-peel tangerine
Robinson	CS	Oct. – Dec.	1 – 20	2½ – 2¾	Good flavor, tangerine
Satsuma	NCS	Sept. – Nov.	0 – 6	2¼ – 2½	A hybrid with sweet taste
Sunburst	CS	Nov. – Dec.	1 – 20	2½ – 3	A tangerine with sweet taste
Temple	CS	Jan. – Mar.	15 – 20	2¼ – 3	Sweet, easy to peel
ACID CITRUS					
Calamondin	CS	Year-round	6 – 10	1 – 1½	A heavy producing small tree
Key Lime	CS	Year-round	12 – 20	1 – 1½	A small tree with good production
Kumquat	NCS	Year-round	6 – 10	¾ – 1	A small tree, several varieties
Lemon	S	July – Dec.	1 – 6	2 – 2½	Numerous varieties
Limequat	CS	Year-round	0 – 16	1 – 1½	Hybrid of key lime and kumquat
Meyer Lemon	CS	Nov. – Mar.	10	2½ – 3	Grows as a bush
Ponderosa Lemon	S	Year-round	20 – 30	4 – 5	A hybrid to grow as a small tree
Tahiti Lime	S	June – Sept.	0	1¾ – 2½	A hybrid also called Persian lime

N = North Florida   C = Central Florida   S = South Florida

SELECTED FRUIT CROP PLANTINGS

Name	Growth Habit	Height (Feet)	Area	Harvest Time	Best Use of Fruits
Apple	Small tree	20 – 25	NC	May – June	Fresh, juice, baking
Atemoya	Small tree	15 – 20	S	Aug. – Oct. Nov. – Jan.	Fresh, drinks, ice cream
Avocado	Large tree	40 – 50	CS	May – Mar.	Fresh, salads, sauces
Banana	Large perennial	12 – 15	CS	Year-round	Fresh, baking, ice cream
Barbados Cherry	Shrub	15 – 20	S	April – Oct.	Fresh, juice, jelly
Blackberry	Perennial	4 – 6	NCS	April – May	Fresh, jelly, baking
Black Sapote	Large tree	40 – 50	S	Dec. – Mar.	Fresh, desserts
Blueberry	Large shrub	5 – 15	NC	May – June	Fresh, salads, baking
Canistel	Small tree	15 – 25	S	Year-round	Fresh, baking
Carambola	Medium tree	25 – 35	CS	June – Oct. Nov. – Feb.	Fresh, salads, juice
Carissa	Shrub	8 – 10	CS	Year-round	Jelly, juice
Cattley Guava	Large shrub	15 – 20	CS	July – Aug.	Fresh, juice, jelly
Coconut	Palm	50 – 60	S	Year-round	Fresh, baking
Feijoa	Large shrub	12 – 15	NCS	July – Aug.	Fresh, preserves
Fig	Small tree	10 – 15	NCS	June – Aug.	Fresh, salads, baking
Grapes	Vines	15 – 20	NCS	June – Aug.	Fresh, juice, jelly, wine
Guava	Medium tree	20 – 30	CS	Aug. – Oct. Nov. – Feb.	Fresh, salads, jam
Jaboticaba	Medium tree	20 – 30	CS	Year-round	Fresh, jelly, wine
Jackfruit	Large tree	40 – 50	S	Year-round	Fresh
Longan	Large tree	40 – 50	S	July – Aug.	Fresh, dried
Lychee	Large tree	35 – 45	S	June – July	Fresh, salads
Macadamia	Large tree	40 – 50	CS	Aug. – Oct.	As nuts, baking
Mamey Sapote	Large tree	40 – 50	S	May – July	Fresh, jelly, ice cream
Mango	Large tree	40 – 50	S	May – Oct.	Fresh, salads
Miracle Fruit	Shrub	4 – 6	S	Year-round	Fresh
Monstera	Vine	15 – 20	CS	Aug. – Oct.	Fresh, salads
Nectarine	Small tree	15 – 20	NC	May – June	Fresh, salads
Papaya	Tree-like	15 – 20	CS	Year-round	Fresh, salads, juice

SELECTED FRUIT CROP PLANTINGS

Name	Growth Habit	Height (Feet)	Area	Harvest Time	Best Use of Fruits
Passion Fruit	Vine	15 – 20	CS	June – Dec.	Fresh, juice
Peach	Small tree	15 – 20	NCS	May – June	Fresh, salads, baking
Pear	Medium tree	20 – 30	NC	July – Aug.	Fresh, canned, cooked
Pecan	Large tree	50 – 60	NC	Oct. – Nov.	As nuts, baking
Persimmon	Small tree	15 – 20	NC	Sept. – Oct.	Fresh, baking
Pineapple	Perennial	2 – 3	CS	Year-round	Fresh, salads, baking
Plum	Small tree	15 – 20	NC	May – June	Fresh, baking
Pomegranate	Large shrub	10 – 15	NCS	Year-round	Fresh, juice, jelly
Prickly Pear	Cactus	4 – 6	NCS	Aug. – Sept.	Fresh
Sapodilla	Large tree	40 – 50	S	Feb. – June	Fresh, juice, jelly
Sea Grape	Large shrub	15 – 20	CS	July – Aug.	Fresh, jelly
Star Apple	Large tree	40 – 50	S	Feb. – May	Fresh
Sugar Apple	Small tree	15 – 20	S	July – Sept. Nov. – Jan.	Fresh, ice cream
Surinam Cherry	Large shrub	10 – 15	CS	May – Aug.	Fresh, salads, jelly
Tamarind	Large tree	40 – 50	S	April – June	Drinks, sauce, chutney
Wampee	Small tree	15 – 20	S	June – Aug.	Fresh, pie
White Sapote	Medium tree	25 – 30	S	May – Aug.	Fresh

N = North Florida   C = Central Florida   S = South Florida

JANUARY

• This is the height of the citrus harvest season.

• January and February are the coldest months of the year. Be prepared to protect cold-sensitive fruit plants. Lemons and limes are the most vulnerable citrus. Mound a foot of soil around the base to protect the tree, but not the upper portions, which will later regrow.

• Bare-root trees can be planted. Planting container-grown fruits is best delayed until later, unless in warmer regions.

• Prune deciduous plants during dormancy. In warmer parts of the state, Peaches and Nectarines are beginning to bud and need pruning. Delay trimming Citrus for another month.

• Keep young trees moist after planting. Water daily for first few weeks. Then gradually decrease watering to keep the soil moist. Mature trees need limited watering.

• Check for scale insects and sooty mold. If needed, apply an oil spray. Follow all instructions.

FEBRUARY

• Citrus trees are very cold sensitive and need protection this month. Many Citrus are ready to harvest although they can be stored on the tree for extended periods.

• Some fruit trees need cold weather to produce fruit. When selecting trees, make sure the varieties will fruit in your area. Other fruits need special pollinators.

• When purchasing container-grown plants, select ones where the ball is starting to develop a web of roots around the soil. Citrus can be planted once temperatures reach the 70s. Protect from freezing when necessary.

• Prune grapes before the vines sprout new buds. Prune citrus before spring growth begins.

• Begin fertilizing in late February or March. Use a special fertilizer for your fruit instead of general garden product.

MARCH

• Harvest grapefruit now, when they get sweet.

• This is a good time to plant Citrus. Unlike other fruiting trees, Citrus do not need amended soil or mulch. When planting other fruits, add organic material. Some crops have special needs. For example, Blueberries require very acidic soil.

• Trim figs if needed. Most gardeners grow them as multitrunk trees. To produce large Peaches and Nectarines, thin fruit when the size of a quarter.

• March is dry and watering is important to mature the crops. Keep the soil moist for new plantings until roots grow into the surrounding soil. For established plantings, water when the surface inch feels dry to the touch. Bananas and Figs need extra moisture.

• Feed new plantings lightly every six to eight weeks March through September. Feed established plantings in March, June, and September. Fertilize Citrus this month.

• Begin insect and disease spray programs using products specifically for home fruit trees.

APRIL

• Continue planting container-grown stock. Discontinue bare-root plantings until winter. In northern areas, plant Citrus in moveable containers for winter protection.

• It's a dry month and water is important now. Make sure the irrigation system is working. Use soaker hoses and microsprinklers where possible. Water only during early morning hours.

• If you missed the spring feeding, fertilize in April. Citrus should have been fertilized in March.

• Some evergreen trees drop much of their foliage in spring, but new leaves quickly follow. Some of the leaves may have spots or pests, but no control is needed.

• Bunch grapes may need a spray program. Pests like aphids and caterpillars may start to appear on other fruits. Control only as needed. Keep up any spray programs that have been started for Apple, Peach, and Nectarine plantings. Most Citrus problems do not significantly affect fruit production.

MAY

• Continue planting trees, shrubs, and Citrus from containers. Hurry for a good selection.

• Some plants send up suckers that should be removed. Check your Citrus, Lychee, Mangoes, and similar plants for shoots from beneath the graft union. These can usually be rubbed off or trimmed back flush with the trunk.

• May can be very dry, with hot days. Pay special attention to water needs of all plantings, especially new ones.

• Except for Citrus, wait one more month for a major fertilizing. New plantings should continue an every-other-month schedule. All fruits growing in containers need every-other-week to monthly feedings, unless using a slow-release fertilizer.

• Lace bugs may appear on Avocado foliage, with yellow spots then leaves that turn brown. Some damage may be ignored. When needed, oil spray will provide control. Caterpillars may be chewing holes in leaves of many plantings. Damage is unsightly but often minimal. If needed, use a natural spray containing *Bacillus thuringiensis*.

JUNE

• All containerized fruiting plants may be planted now.

• Citrus fruits may drop. It's a normal process to thin fruit and will reoccur in June and September.

• Many plantings have finished fruiting and have produced new growth. Prune as needed.

• Apply fertilizer. Use a balanced fertilizer with minor nutrients or a special product for your fruit. Feed new plantings lightly every six to eight weeks scattered under the branches. Feed established plants under and out past the branches. Apply fertilizer over mulch. If the May Citrus feeding was missed, apply it now.

• When Peach, Nectarine, and Plum crops are harvested and general spraying stops, stay alert for borers. Many other fruiting plants may be infested with caterpillars. Most gardeners ignore them since treatment in large trees is difficult. If treatment is done for Citrus problems, be sure to use sprays labeled for use with Citrus.

JULY

• All container-grown fruiting plants can be planted in summer, although fruits may be lost or damaged because of transplant shock.

• Finish pruning this month so stems can mature during remainder of season. Harvest fruit as they ripen and remove those on the ground.

• Get props ready for heavy-bearing Citrus trees when unable to pick extra fruits to lighten the load on limbs.

• If you missed the June feeding, apply fertilizer this month. Use a fertilizer made for your crop or a general garden product with minor nutrients. Feed container plants monthly using liquid fertilizer. Only container-grown Citrus need feeding this month.

• Ripening Nectarines, Peaches, and Guavas attract Caribbean fruit fly, as well as the papaya fruit fly. Watch for leaf spots, aphids, scales, lace bugs, caterpillars, and trunk borers. Control only as needed to prevent major plant decline. Rounded brown spots in Citrus fruit may be caused by pecking birds. The fruits usually ripen normally.

AUGUST

• Plant Citrus and vining fruits this month. Choose vining plants that are not heavily entwined, or prune them back and wait for new shoots to develop.

• Immediately after fruiting, Blackberries and Blueberries need pruning. All pruning should be finished early this month. Other plantings may need pruning too. Remove Citrus limbs that might interfere with maintenance or foot traffic. Support young Citrus limbs that are loaded with fruit to prevent breaking.

• Only container and new plantings receive feeding now, except for Citrus. This is a regular month to fertilize Citrus.

• Caterpillars may be noticeable in the taller trees, although it's almost impossible to reach the tops with sprays. Check for grasshoppers, katydids, lace bugs, scales, and trunk borers. On Citrus most damage can be ignored unless the tree is small or unhealthy.

SEPTEMBER

• New fruit trees can still be planted. Avoid trees susceptible to cold damage, but hardy plants can become well established. Plant Papaya seeds now for next year. Sow two or more per container and when they germinate, thin to one.

• If desired, prune back large trees immediately after fruiting. Either top and trim the sides, or selectively remove limbs. Expect a lower yield next season, but easier to harvest fruits. Prop up Citrus limbs overladen with fruits. If needed, remove some of the fruits.

• Rains may diminish, with more waterings required.

• Now is the time to apply last fertilizing of the year, so new growth can mature before cooler winter weather.

• Watch for papaya fruit fly. Many fruits are making the final growth of the year. Look for caterpillars, grasshoppers, scale, and mites. Apply pesticides only as needed. Blemishes on Citrus usually affect appearance, not flavor. It's too late to apply a chemical control.

OCTOBER

• Most fruiting plants can still be added. But if they are cold sensitive, now is not the right time. Container-grown Citrus can be planted then protected during cold or kept in the container until late winter.

• Check for cool-season weeds.

• This is the dry season. Luckily temperatures are a little lower and days are shorter, reducing moisture needs. Check plantings every few days to see when watering is required. Container-grown fruits still need daily waterings.

• Fertilizing is over for most fruits unless you forgot the fall feeding, which should be applied early in the month. Also feed Citrus early in the month. Continue to feed all plants in containers.

• Twigs on the ground may be caused by the twig girdler. Damage is minimal. However, destroy the twigs. Many deciduous trees will have leaves with spots. This is normal. Citrus pests should be tolerated, since it's best not to spray while you are consuming the fruit.

NOVEMBER

• Continue planting the cold tolerant fruits in central and northern portions of the state. Add cold sensitive plants only in southern locations. Bare-root Citrus can be planted.

• Besides harvesting fruits still ripening, especially Citrus, limited work is required as plants head into dormant season. You should still take weekly walks among plants to determine any needs. Remove damaged limbs. To discourage pests, remove any fruits on the ground. Control weeds and renew mulches.

• As plants become dormant they need less water. Still, if soil becomes dry in upper inch, apply water. Watering of container plants will also become less frequent.

• Feeding time is over for all but the container plantings. And if these are dormant or making little growth, fertilizing is over for them too.

• Pests are less active in the cooler portions of the state, but you might find aphids, lace bugs, and similar pests feeding where temperatures are warm.

DECEMBER

• Except for Citrus and a few fruits ripening in cooler locations, fruiting is over. Plan to protect cold-sensitive trees. Move container plants when cold warnings are sounded. Mound up soil around tree trunk bases to protect graft unions from freezing. Add cold tolerant plants.

• Remove broken limbs. Some deciduous fruit trees, may start to bloom. Delay their pruning until January.

• It's dry, but luckily it's cool. Check by touch to see if plants need watering. Do not water during freeze conditions. Make sure the soil is moist before freezing weather. Also water as plants recover from freezes.

• Feeding is over for the year. Even container plants are dormant. Some growth may continue in the southernmost portions of the state, and plants will benefit from light feedings.

• A few insects still found in the warmer areas are aphids, lace bugs, and scales. Where needed apply pesticide. Most spraying can be discontinued until spring.

HERBS &
VEGETABLES
for Florida

by Robert Bowden

Most gardeners will say there is no better tomato than the one you produce at home. And that is true of just about all vegetables. Corn is never sweeter than when it is picked from the stalk and dunked immediately in boiling water. The same is true of herbs. Stems, with their spicy flavors, are best when gathered right from your own patch.

Most plantings need a sunny location. The general rule: If the plant produces a fruit, pod, or similar edible portion, it needs six to eight hours of sun a day. Herbs and vegetables with roots can often get by with four to six hours of sun, or a day of lightly filtered sun.

PLANTING

Florida has a year-round season, but you have to select the proper times to plant various crops. If you plant at the wrong time, you could face failure. Look at our planting chart on pages 128 to 129, then decide what to plant.

It's a good idea to sketch the planting plan on paper. Decide what you are going to plant, when, and where in the garden site, using traditional in-ground or raised-bed plantings.

1. Make beds 6 inches above the ground or higher with lumber, plastic beams, concrete blocks, or similar materials. In Florida, use materials that are resistant to rot and termites. A convenient size is four feet wide and as long as you like.
2. Fill the beds with soil. You can use existing landscape soil or mix organic matter, including compost, peat, and composted manure with sand and clay soils. Many gardeners also like to fill small beds with potting soils that are pest-free.
3. To avoid compaction and the introduction of pests, avoid walking on the soils.

For in-ground plantings:

1. Select a predominantly sunny site. Check for possible shade at different times of the year. In Florida, the sun dips way to the south by midwinter.
2. Till the soil deeply and work in liberal quantities of organic matter with sand and clay soils.
3. Scatter a light application of garden fertilizer over the site and till into the ground.
4. Test the soil acidity and adjust the pH with lime or soil sulfur if needed.

If you are using containers, make a list of what you want to grow and when. Then follow these steps:

1. Select a container big enough to accommodate the root system of the plants. Small herbs can grow in 4- to 5-inch pots, but most vegetables need gallon containers. The containers can be fairly shallow, as most roots only grow 6 to 8 inches deep.

2. Fill the containers with a pest-free potting soil. Don't risk bringing in soilborne organisms with these small gardens. After preparing your beds or containers, you will be ready to plant the vegetables and herbs. Use our table as a guide for spacing and planting techniques. If you are cramped for space, use the closer spacings.

HERBS IN A POT

Don't let the rainy weather spoil your herb plantings. Keeping your plants in a well-drained potting mix in a container is a good way to avoid the problem. Growing herbs in containers is also a good way to make use of available patio, balcony, and porch space. The plants can be used as foliage plants to move about as needed. Keeping Mint plants in containers is a good way of maintaining control. Here are some tips:

- Use a container big enough to hold the plant and allow for some growth.
- Consider planting several different herbs in the same container.
- Use a good potting mix, available from your garden center.
- Set the plants in the soil at the same depth they were growing in their pots.
- Keep the planting container in the proper light for growth.
- Feed every other week with a liquid fertilizer solution.
  Here are some quick ways to preserve a portion of the herb crop:
- Gather small bundles of herbs and hang them upside-down in a paper bag. The bag will keep the herbs dust-free.
- Strip leaves from the stem and dry them on a flat screen in a well-ventilated shady spot. Space leaves so they do not touch. Store in a bottle or plastic bag when dry.
- Microwave between two sheets of paper towel. Dry only four or five sprigs at a time, for two or three minutes. They will become brittle and flaky.
- Gather herbs to freeze. Wash and pat dry, and store in a plastic bag in the freezer.

CARE FOR YOUR GARDENS

If you set out on a five-minute walk in the garden, you will often end up actually spending thirty minutes to an hour. It's just fun to watch the plants grow. Here are some things to think about during your strolls:

- Use the walks to decide what to plant next.
- Check to see when to harvest the plantings.
- Do minor staking and training along the way.
- Decide when to water and feed.
- Spot pests and beneficial insects. Decide if a control is needed.

WATERING

Good gardens need plenty of water, but that doesn't mean you should not conserve. Just by enriching sandy soil with organic matter prior to planting, you reduce the need for moisture. Keeping a good mulch over the soil also helps. Here are some tips to stretch the time between waterings:

- Water deeply at each irrigation. Feel the soil.
- When the surface inch begins to dry, it's time to water.
- Apply ½ to ¾ inch of water at each irrigation.
- Use microsprinklers and soaker hoses where possible.
- Control weeds, which use water and compete with the crops.
- Adjust your watering schedule to the time of the year.

Hot, dry spring and fall months use more water than the cooler winter and rainy summer months.

Water during the early-morning hours to prevent loss due to evaporation and winds.

FERTILIZING

Productive gardens need regular feedings to produce lots of foliage, fruits, and root crops. Most plantings tell you when they have run out of nutrients with yellowing leaves and little growth. Often by the time you notice the deficiency symptoms, it's too late to help this season's crop. It's usually best to get on a regular feeding program with most crops.

Liquid fertilizers provide instant food for the plantings. Most need to be reapplied every two to three weeks.

Granular feedings can offer both quick- and slow-release nutrients. Most general garden fertilizers are applied every three to four weeks. Slow-release products may last for months.

Manures have both slow- and quick-release qualities. They are of a low analysis and must be applied frequently in large quantities to be effective. Composted manures can be applied to the surface or made into a tea for drenching around plants. Fresh manure should be tilled into the soil 90 to 120 days before planting.

PESTS

Florida vegetable and herb plantings have the same types of pests found in most other areas of the world. Here they remain active for longer periods and the numbers can be greater than those found in a cooler climate. They tend to be most active during warmer times of the year.

One pest that is new to many gardeners is the root knot nematode. All nematodes that affect gardens are microscopic roundworms that live in the soil. The root knot nematode causes roots to swell and become ineffective at absorbing water and nutrients. Some controls include planting resistant varieties, using pest-free soils, planting nematode-retarding cover crops, and practicing soil solarization during the summer.

BASIL

WHEN TO PLANT
Basil cannot tolerate cold weather. Planted in successive plantings, two to three weeks apart, spring through fall.

WHERE TO PLANT
Plant basil in full sun, in well-prepared, well-drained soil.

HOW TO PLANT
Basil seeds can be direct sown in garden rows and thinned to 12 to 14 inches apart or as transplants with the same spacing.

WATER NEEDS
Basil prefers moist but not wet soil. Although it is drought tolerant, leaf edges may turn brown after wilting. It's still good enough for cooking—it just doesn't look as nice.

CARE
Basil is a very easy herb to grow. Give it plenty of water and a dash of 20-20-20 water-soluble fertilizer every two to three weeks and basil will grow very well. Remove flower buds as they appear to encourage branching.

PROBLEMS
Other than an occasional leaf-chewing insect (which can be removed as they appear), basil is trouble free.

HARVEST
Basil leaves can be harvested at any time.

SELECTIONS
Good varieties for Florida include 'Dark Opal', 'Genovese', 'Lettuce Leaf', 'Siam Queen', 'Spicy Globe', and 'Sweet'.

BEANS

WHEN TO PLANT
In North Florida grow March through November. In Central and South Florida grow February through May and August through October.

WHERE TO PLANT
Need at least eight hours of full sun. Beans grow in about any soil. However, good, rich compost provides bountiful results.

HOW TO PLANT
Direct sow in garden. Provide pole beans with support.

WATER NEEDS
Need lots of water

CARE
Fertilize monthly, but go easy—too much produces more leaves and fewer beans.

PROBLEMS
With good soil and ample water, beans can be pest free. They may get rust and birds may eat the seedlings.

HARVEST
Harvest Bush, Green, and Wax beans while pods are still tender. Pole beans produce multiple crops, provided you pick every pod.

SELECTIONS
Beans are a great way to introduce children to gardening. With adequate light and ample water, beans can grow in containers. Some of many good varieties for Florida are 'Contender', 'Greencrop', and 'Tendergreen Improved' (Bush); 'Cherokee Wax' and 'Improved Golden Wax' (Wax); and 'Blue Lake', 'Kentucky Wonder', and 'White Half Runner' (Pole).

BROCCOLI

WHEN TO PLANT

Plant at the onset of cooler weather. A second planting can grow until warm weather returns. Brocolli bolts with too much heat.

WHERE TO PLANT

In full sun, with well-drained, moist soil with added organic matter

HOW TO PLANT

Place one or two seeds per pot containing ¼ inch soil. Cover with fine soil. Place container in shallow water until soil becomes saturated. Thin to one seedling per container. Keep moist in full sun. Plant into garden after three mature leaves develop. Allow plenty of room with plants 24 inches apart, in rows 24 inches apart.

WATER NEEDS

Give plenty of water

CARE

Feed every two to three weeks with general-purpose fertilizer

PROBLEMS

Keep army worms from young transplants with a 3-inch heavy paper collar pushed partially into the ground.

HARVEST

After head matures, but before individual flowers expand, cut the center head about 6 inches below the flower head. Continue to feed and water so small flower florets will sprout for additional smaller broccoli.

SELECTIONS

'Green Comet', 'High Dividend', 'Packman' (early season)

CABBAGE

WHEN TO PLANT

This cool-season crop hates warm weather. Plant one crop in late fall and another 30 to 45 days later to stagger availability. Stop planting in March.

WHERE TO PLANT

In full sun, in average, well-drained soil

HOW TO PLANT

If sown directly into the ground, thin to proper spacing for good growth—too close will yield small, weak plants.

WATER NEEDS

Lots of water

CARE

Provide high-nitrogen fertilizer application every three weeks

PROBLEMS

Remove weeds. Occasionally army worms cut tender stems of new sprouts or transplants at night. Make barriers of heavy paper and push them half way into the ground. Once seedlings get a little older (and tougher) remove the collars.

HARVEST

Harvest at any stage

SELECTIONS

Easy-to-grow Cabbage is great for beginners, but there numerous unique varieties for advanced gardeners. Check with neighborhood gardeners for their best selections. Try 'Bonnie's Hybrid', 'Copenhagen Market', 'Mammoth Red Rock' (red cabbage), 'New Jersey Wakefield', or 'Savoy Chieftain' (densely curled). Chinese cabbages may even be used in ornamental plantings.

CANTALOUPE

WHEN TO PLANT
Plant after frost danger has passed, the earlier the better. Start seeds indoors two weeks before planting.

WHERE TO PLANT
In full sun in well-drained, organically enriched soil. Good air circulation is necessary to discourage diseases.

HOW TO PLANT
Plant seeds or seedlings either in rows 48 inches apart with individual plants 24 inches apart, or in hills 48 to 60 inches apart with four to five seeds per hill.

WATER NEEDS
Provide ample water until fruit begins to ripen. Then hold off a little for better-tasting melons.

CARE
Use plastic or fabric weed barrier over entire vine area.

PROBLEMS
Place half-grown fruit on boards or cans to reduce slug or insect damage. Or grow on vertical supports with fruits held by panty hose to prevent slugs and keep fruit easy to monitor.

HARVEST
Pick immediately when ripe, when fruit is fragrant and melons release from vine.

SELECTIONS
Cantaloupes are worth the effort and real estate. 'Ambrosia' is still the best hybrid, with intense flavor and disease-resistant vines. 'Minnesota Midget' has three-foot-long vines.

CARROT

WHEN TO PLANT
Multiple sowings any time between September and mid-March

WHERE TO PLANT
Plant in well-drained, enriched soil, with all rocks and roots removed. Need at least eight hours of full sun.

HOW TO PLANT
Fluff soil at least a foot deep. Sow very small amount of seed in ¼-inch furrow. DO NOT COVER and gently water with a watering can. Even if careful, you probably sowed too many seeds. Seedlings MUST be thinned to one plant every three inches. Gently pull seedlings sideways or cut at ground level to minimize damage to remaining seedlings.

WATER NEEDS
Keep moist

CARE
Carrots past their prime are woody and inedible, so plant crops four weeks apart.

PROBLEMS
Rotate crop locations annually. Too long in one spot encourages wire worm infestations. To be safe, when preparing soil, sprinkle in wood ashes, which repel root worms.

HARVEST
Anytime after reaching 3 inches long

SELECTIONS
Tasting their garden carrots gets children interested in eating veggies and in gardening. 'Chantenay Royal', 'Imperator 58', 'Nantes Half Long', 'Tendersweet' ; unusual varieties: 'Cosmic Purple', 'Snow White'

CHIVES

WHEN TO PLANT
Chives can tolerate low temperatures to the mid 20s. Plant at any time of the year.

WHERE TO PLANT
Plant chives in full sun, in well-prepared, well-drained soil. With their lovely light lavender flowers, chives can be planted as a border plant in flower gardens.

HOW TO PLANT
Given their reluctance to grow quickly, it's recommended that many chive seeds be planted in small containers with good potting soil then later planted into the garden after they have reached sufficient size.

WATER NEEDS
Chives prefer moist soil but can also survive drought conditions and be revived with regular applications of water.

CARE
Chives are very easy to grow. Provide plenty of water and a dash of 20-20-20 water-soluble fertilizer every two to three weeks and chives will grow very well.

PROBLEMS
None

HARVEST
Chives can be harvested by pulling individual stems or by cutting what's needed with scissors or clippers.

SELECTIONS
There are no known specific varieties of regular chives. However, garlic chives (a separate species all together) perform well in Florida too.

CORN

WHEN TO PLANT
In North Florida plant February through April. In Central Florida plant January through April. In South Florida plant October through March.

WHERE TO PLANT
Full sun, in well-drained soil

HOW TO PLANT
Start with fresh seed. Plant in blocks, not long rows, to increase pollination.

WATER NEEDS
Requires large quantities of water

CARE
Fertilize regularly throughout entire growing season. To increase chances pollen will reach the ear, shake entire plant several times a day when pollen first appears.

PROBLEMS
Given the number and kinds of bugs that attack corn, after one season most gardeners decide it's easier to buy a few ears. Bottom line—growing corn is not easy in most areas of Florida. Weeds compete for water and nutrients. Some important corn pests are birds eating seedlings, Fall Army worms, and corn earworm.

HARVEST
Check for ripeness when silks turn brown all the way to the husk or if top kernels squirt "milk" when pushed with a thumbnail.

SELECTIONS
'Early Sunglow' and 'Golden Cross Bantam' (yellow); 'Silver Queen' and 'Sweet Ice' (white)

CUCUMBER

WHEN TO PLANT
In North Florida plant seeds August through September and February through April. In Central Florida plant seeds September and January through March. In South Florida plant seeds September through October, November through December, and January.

WHERE TO PLANT
Full sun in well-drained, enriched soil

HOW TO PLANT
Sow seeds ½ inch deep in rows or grow on strings like pole beans. The upright method keeps fruits cleaner and more visible for harvesting at the proper time. Upright plants also require less space, have better air circulation, and are easier to fertilize.

WATER NEEDS
Maintain a regular watering regimen to prevent misshapen fruit

CARE
Keep a detailed garden journal to review the next time around

PROBLEMS
The worst problem is powdery mildew. Lessen it by increasing air circulation, reducing overhead watering, and watering in early morning. Walking amongst wet plants transfers the disease. Oils can protect and eradicate powdery mildew but cannot be used when temperatures reach 90°F.

HARVEST
Varies

SELECTIONS
For pickling: 'Cherokee', 'Dasher II', 'Ohio MR 17', 'Pixie', 'Straight Eight'; or 'Burpee's Bushmaster' (smaller)

DILL

WHEN TO PLANT
Dill can be planted for fall or spring gardens and tolerates both extreme heat and freezing temperatures.

WHERE TO PLANT
Plant dill in full sun, in well-prepared, well-drained soil. It can also be planted in butterfly gardens as a caterpillar host plant.

HOW TO PLANT
Dill seed can be direct sown into the garden at 9-inch intervals in rows that are 14 to 16 inches apart. Seedlings produce very fine foliage so care must be taken when weeding for the first four to five weeks.

WATER NEEDS
Dill prefers moist soil but can also survive drought conditions and be revived with regular applications of water.

CARE
Dill is a very easy herb to grow. Provide plenty of water and a dash of 20-20-20 water-soluble fertilizer every two to three weeks and dill will grow very well. Once flowers begin to bloom, foliage production stops.

PROBLEMS
None

HARVEST
Dill foliage can be harvested by cutting individual lacy leaves or collecting the seeds for use in recipes.

SELECTIONS
For Florida gardens try 'Fernleaf', 'Hercules', and 'Super Dukat'.

EGGPLANT

WHEN TO PLANT
Plant seeds of this warm-season vegetable six weeks before outdoor planting date. Eggplants love heat.

WHERE TO PLANT
Full sun in average, well-drained soil

HOW TO PLANT
Uncommon varieties are usually only available from seed. Sow seeds ¼ inch deep and provide bottom heat when possible. Plant individual plants 30 inches apart, in 30- to 36-inch-wide rows. Space smaller types closer.

WATER NEEDS
Although eggplants can withstand drought, production is severely curtailed when plants go dry. Keep soil moist. Add mulch to conserve moisture.

CARE
Apply 12-0-12 fertilizer when planting, again halfway through the season, and immediately after the first fruit is picked.

PROBLEMS
Eggplants are virtually pest free. Occasional aphids, scale, flea beetles, or spider mites occur, but only if plants are stressed. Keep heavy fruits off the ground by gently tying individual branches to a pole.

HARVEST
Harvest while still glossy. Leave the calyx (the green star at the top) on fruit to prolong shelf life.

SELECTIONS
'Black Beauty', 'Calliope', 'Casper', 'Cloud Nine','Florida High Bush', 'Green Goddess'

LETTUCE

WHEN TO PLANT
Plant seeds indoors four to five weeks before planting outdoors. Plant every two weeks for season-long supply. In North Florida plant September through October and February through March. In Central Florida plant September through March. In South Florida plant September through January.

WHERE TO PLANT
Needs at least eight hours of full sun, in enriched, deeply-tilled, and well-drained soil.

HOW TO PLANT
Sow seeds directly or plant by transplants. Sprinkle a seed every two to three inches apart into a ¼-inch furrow and barely cover with fine soil. *Gently* water with a watering can. Carefully thin seedlings to distance specified on packet.

WATER NEEDS
Keep moist but not wet. Mulch retains moisture and keeps leaves cleaner.

CARE
Use fresh seed and refrigerate opened seed packets for later sowings. Water with a little fertilizer when transplanting, then feed every two weeks during growing season.

PROBLEMS
Cover if cold weather threatens. If plants are kept too wet, slugs can occur.

HARVEST
Pick outer leaves or entire head

SELECTIONS
'Black-Seeded Simpson', 'Buttercrunch', 'Oak Leaf', 'White Boston'

MINT

WHEN TO PLANT
Able to withstand extremes in temperatures and can be planted at any time of the year.

WHERE TO PLANT
Mint is a very vigorous grower and it's recommended that it only be planted in containers where it can be controlled. Plant mint in full sun to part shade, in well-prepared, well-drained soil.

HOW TO PLANT
Mint can be direct sown into containers with a good-quality, well-drained potting soil. Mint can also be planted with annuals and perennials for an attractive mixed ornamental planter.

WATER NEEDS
Mint prefers moist soil but can also survive drought conditions and be revived later with regular applications of water.

CARE
Mint is a very easy herb to grow. Give it plenty of water and a dash of 20-20-20 water-soluble fertilizer every two to three weeks and mint will grow very well.

PROBLEMS
Mint is very aggressive and invasive. Plant in containers only.

HARVEST
Mint foliage can be harvested by cutting individual leaves at any time.

SELECTIONS
For Florida gardens try peppermint, spearmint, apple mint, pineapple mint, and chocolate mint.

OKRA

WHEN TO PLANT
Will grow in Florida's summer heat and humidity. In North and Central Florida plant seed March through August. In South Florida plant in August and September.

WHERE TO PLANT
Plant in full, hot, blazing sun in deeply-tilled, well-drained soil.

HOW TO PLANT
Direct sow seed one inch deep after frost danger has passed and soil has warmed. Or start early by sowing seeds in peat cups indoors. Give okra plenty of room—plant seed 24 inches apart, in rows 36 inches apart.

WATER NEEDS
In well-drained soil you can't water okra too much.

CARE
Unpicked pods remaining on the plant cause it to stop making new pods.

PROBLEMS
Harvest pods with clippers. Don't twist them off or leave unpicked.

HARVEST
Pods longer than three inches are virtually inedible so pick okra every day or two.

SELECTIONS
Varieties include 'Alabama Red', 'Baby Bubba' (for small gardens and containers), 'Clemson Spineless', 'Cow Horn', 'Evertender', 'Little Lucy' (burgundy dwarf), 'Red Burgundy', and 'White Velvet'. Okra is pretty enough to grow as an ornamental.

121

ONION

WHEN TO PLANT
Onions prefer cool weather. Plant September through March throughout Florida.

WHERE TO PLANT
Onions enjoy full sun in a well prepared, deeply tilled, sandy loam or muck soil. Any amount of organic matter will enrich the flavor and increase the size.

HOW TO PLANT
Onions can be planted three ways. Place individual bulb onions (sets) half way into prepared soil, 4 inches apart. Grow onions from seed then transplant into the garden. (Buy "short day" seeds, not "long day" varieties grown in northern states.) Direct sow seeds into prepared beds, usually reserved for bunching onions (scallions). Plant ½ inch deep and thin when they get about 4 inches tall.

WATER NEEDS
Average water needs

CARE
Onions are heavy nitrogen feeders. Add 12-0-12 fertilizer about every three weeks or water-soluble 20-0-20 weekly.

PROBLEMS
Weeds are the biggest problem. Cultivating is difficult around the thin plants so extreme care is needed.

HARVEST
Onions can be harvested and eaten any time in their development.

SELECTIONS
'Crimson Forest Bunching', 'Crystal Wax Bermuda', 'Excel', 'Granex', 'Red Creole', 'White Lisbon Bunching'

OREGANO

WHEN TO PLANT
Oregano cannot withstand freezing temperatures and must be planted spring through fall.

WHERE TO PLANT
Oregano is a low-growing herb with ¼-inch-long leaves. Plant oregano in full sun to part shade, in well-prepared, well-drained soil.

HOW TO PLANT
Oregano seeds can be direct sown into containers with a good quality, well-drained potting soil. It can be grown from transplants or seeds. Oregano can also be planted with annuals and perennials for an attractive mixed ornamental planter.

WATER NEEDS
Oregano prefers moist soil. If permitted to completely dry out it might not survive.

CARE
Oregano is a very easy herb to grow. Give it plenty of water and a dash of 20-20-20 water-soluble fertilizer every two to three weeks and oregano will grow very well.

PROBLEMS
Oregano is quite well behaved with no known problems.

HARVEST
Oregano foliage can be harvested by cutting individual leaves at any time.

SELECTIONS
For Florida gardens try 'Greek' oregano, 'Hot and Spicy' oregano, 'Harrenhausen', and 'Kent Beauty'.

PEPPER

WHEN TO PLANT
Peppers enjoy warm temperatures. In North and Central Florida plant February through March and again July through September. In South Florida, plant August through September.

WHERE TO PLANT
Needs at least eight hours of full sun. Not particular about soils, but perform best in compost amended, well-drained soil.

HOW TO PLANT
Growing from seed is easier indoors than out-doors. Follow spacing specified on packet.

WATER NEEDS
Peppers like moist but not wet soil. Mulch helps moderate soil temperatures and retains moisture.

CARE
Peppers are major feeders, preferring little bits of fertilizer often. An 8-0-8 fertilizer applied every three weeks is ideal. As they begin to set fruit, reduce nitrogen fertilizer and increase potassium level.

PROBLEMS
Prevent brittle stems with fruit from breaking by staking plants. Occasionally aphids appear on emerging growth.

HARVEST
Can be picked before mature color develops

SELECTIONS
Sweet: 'Big Bertha', 'Gypsy', 'Pimento', 'Purple Beauty', 'Sweet Banana', 'Yolo Wonder'; hot: 'Caribbean Red', 'Habañero', 'Scotch Bonnet', 'Super Chili'. Peppers can also grow in containers.

POTATO, SWEET

WHEN TO PLANT
Plant March through June

WHERE TO PLANT
Plant in full sun, in compost-enriched soil. Avoid areas that have been fallow or where sweet potatoes have grown in the last three years.

HOW TO PLANT
Prepare soil properly before planting. Create 10-inch tall, 12-inch wide linear mounds. Sprinkle 2 to 3 pounds fertilizer (10-10-10) on soil to make the mounds, which should last for the entire season. Place rooted slips into the top of mounds 12 to14 inches apart, in rows 48 to 60 inches apart.

WATER NEEDS
Provide adequate water. In final two weeks reduce irrigation amount.

CARE
Require very little care

PROBLEMS
Sweet potatoes perform best where soil was turned over two or three months before planting to reduce nematodes. Deer may occasionally eat leaves, which won't have an adverse affect on tubers' size or quality.

HARVEST
Tubers can be harvested at any time. Cut vines away, gently remove soil, and cure in sun for two or three days. They will continue growing as long as tops are green.

SELECTIONS
'Beauregard', 'Hernandez', 'Picodito' (boniato)

ROSEMARY

WHEN TO PLANT
Rosemary can withstand the extremes in Florida temperatures and can be planted into the garden at any time.

WHERE TO PLANT
Depending on the selection, Rosemary can grow either as a groundcover or as low-growing shrub to 48 inches tall. Plant rosemary in full sun to part shade, in well-prepared, well-drained soil.

HOW TO PLANT
Rosemary should be planted into the garden as a labeled transplant.

WATER NEEDS
Rosemary prefers soil that is watered well and allowed to dry out between waterings.

CARE
Rosemary is a very easy herb to grow. More rosemary plants are killed from too much water than anything else. Just pretend it doesn't exist and it will perform well in the garden. Give it a dash of 20-20-20 water-soluble fertilizer once a month and rosemary will grow very well.

PROBLEMS
Do not overwater!

HARVEST
Rosemary can be harvested by removing individual leaves and stems at any time.

SELECTIONS
For Florida gardens try upright rosemary, creeping rosemary, white rosemary, 'Blueboy', 'Dancing Waters', and 'Spice Island'.

SPINACH

WHEN TO PLANT
This cool-weather vegetable "bolts" in heat. In North and Central Florida plant in October and November. In South Florida plant October through January. Plant successive crops every three weeks for continuous yield.

WHERE TO PLANT
Needs enriched, well-drained, deep loamy soil. Requires full sun and good air circulation. If necessary, plant in aboveground containers or raised beds.

HOW TO PLANT
Start seeds indoors or direct sow into the garden

WATER NEEDS
Keep moist but not wet

CARE
Feed lightly with 12-0-12 fertilizer every two to three weeks. Provide occasional 20-20-20 liquid feeding.

PROBLEMS
Weed often. Apply hay to reduce weeds, conserve water, and keep leaves cleaner.

HARVEST
Harvest single outside leaves or entire plant. Watch for flower stalks, then harvest immediately before it becomes bitter.

SELECTIONS
Good plain-leaf Spinach varieties for Florida include 'Giant Nobel', 'Olympia', and 'Space'. Of the crinkled (savoyed) leaf varieties, 'Bloomsdale Longstanding' performs well. Other savoyed varieties include 'Melody', 'Tyee', and 'Vienna'. Spinach also works well as a border plant or filler in a container of bedding plants and perennials.

SQUASH

WHEN TO PLANT

For summer squash, in North Florida plant March through April and August through September; in Central Florida plant February through March and August through September; in South Florida plant January through March and September through October. For winter squash (usually vining types), in North Florida plant March and August; in Central Florida plant February and March; in South Florida plant January through February and September.

WHERE TO PLANT

In full sun with compost enriched and deeply tilled well-drained soil

HOW TO PLANT

Plant in rows, two or three seeds 24 inches apart, in rows 36 to 48 inches apart.

WATER NEEDS

Water in the morning and provide good circulation to prevent powdery mildew.

CARE

Very easy to grow

PROBLEMS

For stem borers apply light rotenone dusting every two weeks to deter them. Another serious problem is powdery mildew. Correct usage of oils, sulfur, and fungicides can be effective when applied under specific circumstances.

HARVEST

About 45 days from seed

SELECTIONS

'Caserta', 'Cocozelle', 'Eightball', 'Early Butternut', 'Peter Pan', 'Prolific Straightneck', 'Summer Crookneck', 'Spaghetti', 'Table King'

THYME

WHEN TO PLANT

Thyme cannot withstand the heat of Central and South Florida during the summer. In those locations plant thyme fall through spring. In north Florida plant thyme any time.

WHERE TO PLANT

Plant thyme in full sun to part shade, in well-prepared, well-drained soil.

HOW TO PLANT

Thyme should be planted into the garden as a labeled transplant. The seeds are so tiny they have to be sown indoors to start.

WATER NEEDS

Thyme prefers moist, well-drained soil.

CARE

Thyme is a very easy herb to grow. More thyme plants are killed from too much water than anything else. Just pretend it doesn't exist and it will perform well in the garden. Give it a dash of 20-20-20 water-soluble fertilizer once a month and thyme will grow very well.

PROBLEMS

No known problems

HARVEST

Thyme can be harvested by removing individual leaves and stems at any time.

SELECTIONS

There are over one hundred varieties of thyme, with the most common being Garden Thyme and Lemon Thyme.

TOMATO

WHEN TO PLANT
North Florida: after last frost through March and again in August. Central Florida: January through March and September. South Florida: August through March.

WHERE TO PLANT
Plant in the ground or large containers, in eight or more hours of full sun. Use enriched, well-drained soil.

HOW TO PLANT
Sow seeds indoors 6 to 8 weeks before last frost. Plant transplants (taller ones are better) with only top 4 inches above soil.

WATER NEEDS
Prefers constantly moist soil. Cannot tolerate soggy roots.

CARE
Tomatoes are commonly staked, grown in cages, or supported like pole beans.

PROBLEMS
Tomatoes are highly susceptible to several diseases. Do not pick fruit or groom plants when leaves are wet. In names, the letters "VFN" indicate built-in resistance: "V" for Verticillium wilt, "F" for fusarium wilt, and "N" for nematodes.

HARVEST
60 to 90 days, depending on variety

SELECTIONS
The two groups are indeterminate (grow to indeterminate height) and determinate (grow to predetermined height). 'Better Boy' (VFN), 'Sun Coast' (VF), 'Walter' (F), 'Floramerica' (F), 'Red Cherry', 'Sweet 100', 'Floragold', 'Florida Petite'

WATERMELON

WHEN TO PLANT
North Florida: plant seeds March through April and July through August. Central Florida: plant seeds January through March and August. South Florida: January through March and August through September.

WHERE TO PLANT
Most soils except muck, in full sun.

HOW TO PLANT
Plant seeds 1½ inch deep, 36 inches apart, in rows 7 to 8 feet apart.

WATER NEEDS
Needs lots of water

CARE
To retain moisture, keep out competing weeds, and keep fruit clean, plant seeds through black plastic. A tillable newspaper/hay layer also works.

PROBLEMS
Aphids and cucumber beetles carry diseases and should be controlled. Apply rotenone dust in late afternoon or dusk. Worms can be controlled with Dipel (*Bacillus thuringiensis*).

HARVEST
Matures in 80 to 100 days from seed, depending on variety. Although difficult to determine ripeness, check when the melon bottom turns bright golden yellow or the closest tendril turns from green to brown.

SELECTIONS
Florida is the nation's leading watermelon producer. Large watermelons: 'Charleston Grey 133', 'Crimson Sweet', 'Jubilee' (Florida Giant). Smaller melons: 'Mickeylee', 'Sugar Baby'.

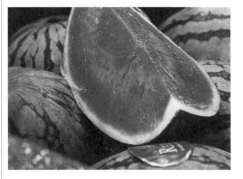

HERBS

Name	Time to Plant	Height (Inches)	Growth Habit	Spacing (Inches)	How to Start	Part Used
Anise	Oct. – May	18 – 24	Spreading	18	Seed	Seeds when ripe
Basil	Oct. – May	18 – 24	Rounded	12	Seed	Leaves any stage
Bay Laurel	Year-round	60 – 72+	Upright	48	Cuttings	Leaves any stage
Borage	Oct. – May	18 – 24	Sprawling	24	Seed	Leaves and flowers
Caraway	Oct. – May	18 – 24	Upright	12	Seed	Seeds
Cardamom	Oct. – May	36 – 48	Clumping	24	Divisions	Seeds
Chervil	Oct. – May	18 – 24	Spreading	12	Seed	Leaves any stage
Chives	Oct. – May	12 – 18	Clumping	10	Seed, division	Leaves any stage
Coriander	Oct. – May	12 – 36	Spreading	12	Seed	Leaves and seed
Cumin	Mar. – April	8 – 12	Spreading	4	Seed	Seeds
Dill	Oct. – May	48 – 60	Upright	12	Seed	Leaves and seed
Fennel	Oct. – Mar.	24 – 36	Upright	12	Seed	Leaves and seed
Garlic	Oct. – Dec.	24 – 30	Upright	6	Cloves	Bulbs and leaves
Ginger	Year-round	24 – 36	Clumping	12	Rhizomes	Rhizomes
Horehound	Year-round	12 – 24	Spreading	12	Seed, cuttings	Leaves before flowers
Lemon Balm	Oct. – May	18 – 24	Clumping	12	Seed, cuttings	Leaves any stage
Lovage	Oct. – Mar.	24 – 36	Upright	12	Seed	Leaves any stage
Marjoram	Oct. – May	6 – 8	Spreading	12	Seed	Leaves any stage
Mint	Year-round	12 – 24	Spreading	18	Seed, cuttings	Leaves any stage
Nasturtium	Nov. – Feb.	12 – 18	Spreading	6	Seed	Leaves and flowers
Oregano	Year-round	6 – 8	Spreading	12	Seed, cuttings	Leaves any stage
Rosemary	Year-round	24 – 36	Upright	24	Seed, cuttings	Leaves any stage
Sage	Oct. – April	18 – 24	Spreading	18	Seed, cuttings	Leaves any stage
Savory	Oct. – Mar.	10 – 12	Upright	12	Seed	Leaves any stage
Tarragon	Year-round	24 – 36	Upright	18	Seed, cuttings	Leaves young
Thyme	Year-round	4 – 12	Spreading	12	Seed, cuttings	Leaves any stage
Watercress	Oct. – Mar.	6 – 8	Spreading	6	Seed, cuttings	Leaves young

COOL-SEASON VEGETABLES

Name	Time to Plant North	Time to Plant Central	South	Planting Method	Spacing (Inches)	Days to Harvest
Asparagus	Year-round*	Year-round		Crowns	12 – 18	2 years
Beets	Sept. – Mar.	Oct. – Mar.	Oct. – Feb.	Seed	3 – 5	50 – 65
Broccoli	Aug. – Feb.	Aug. – Jan.	Sept. – Jan.	Seed, plants	12 – 18	55 – 90
Brussels Sprouts	Sept. – Dec.	Oct. – Dec.	Nov. – Dec.	Seed, plants	18 – 24	75 – 90
Cabbage	Sept. – Feb.	Sept. – Jan.	Sept. – Jan.	Seed, plants	12 – 24	70 – 100
Carrot	Sept. – Mar.	Oct. – Mar.	Oct. – Feb.	Seed	1 – 3	65 – 80
Cauliflower	Jan. – Feb. Aug. – Oct.	Oct. – Jan.	Oct. – Jan.	Seed, plants	18 – 24	55 – 90
Celery	Jan. – Mar.	Sept. – Feb.	Oct. – Jan.	Seed, plants	6 – 10	80 – 125
Chinese Cabbage	Oct. – Jan.	Oct. – Jan.	Nov. – Jan.	Seed, plants	8 – 12	60 – 90
Collards	Feb. – Mar. Aug. – Dec.	Sept. – April	Sept. – Feb.	Seed, plants	10 – 18	40 – 80
Endive/ Escarole	Feb. – Mar. Sept.	Jan. – Feb. Sept.	Sept. – Jan.	Seed	8 – 12	80 – 95
Kale	Oct. – Feb.	Oct. – Feb.	Nov. – Jan.	Seed	8 – 16	50 – 60
Kohlrabi	Mar. – April Oct. – Nov.	Feb. – Mar. Oct. – Nov.	Nov. – Feb.	Seed	3 – 5	70 – 80
Lettuce	Feb. – Mar. Sept.	Sept. – Mar.	Sept. – Jan.	Seed, plants	8 – 12	40 – 90
Mustard Greens	Sept. – Mar.	Sept. – Mar.	Sept. – Mar.	Seed	1 – 6	40 – 60
Onion	Sept. – Dec.	Sept. – Dec.	Sept. – Nov.	Seed, plants	4 – 6	110 – 160
Parsley	Feb. – Mar.	Oct. – Jan.	Sept. – Jan.	Seed	8 – 12	70 – 90
Peas, English	Jan. – Mar.	Oct. – Feb.	Oct. – Feb.	Seed	2 – 3	50 – 70
Potato	Jan. – Mar.	Feb. Sept. – Oct.	Sept. – Jan.	Seed pieces	8 – 12	85 – 110
Radishes	Sept. – Mar.	Oct. – Mar.	Nov. – Mar.	Seed	1 – 2	25 – 30
Radishes, Winter	Sept. – Oct.	Sept. – Nov.	Sept. – Dec.	Seed	4 – 6	60 – 70
Rhubarb	Year-round	Aug. – Oct.	Aug. – Oct.	Seed, divisions	24 – 30	100 – 150
Spinach	Oct. – Nov.	Oct. – Dec.	Oct. – Jan.	Seed	3 – 5	45 – 60
Strawberry	Sept. – Oct.	Sept. – Oct.	Oct. – Nov.	Plants	10 – 14	90 – 110
Swiss Chard	Sept. – Mar.	Sept. – Mar.	Sept. – Mar.	Seed, plants	8 – 10	40 – 60
Turnip	Jan. – April Aug. – Oct.	Jan. – Mar. Sept. – Nov.	Oct. – Feb.	Seed	4 – 6	40 – 60

*not recommended for South Florida

WARM-SEASON VEGETABLES

Name	North	Time to Plant Central	South	Planting Method	Spacing (Inches)	Days to Harvest
Bean, Lima	Mar. – Aug.	Mar. – June Sept.	Aug. – April	Seed	3 – 4	65 – 75
Bean, Snap	Mar. – April Aug. – Sept.	Mar. – May Sept. – Oct.	Sept. – April	Seed	3 – 4	55 – 70
Cantaloupe	Mar. – April	Mar – April	Feb. – Mar. Aug. – Sept.	Seed, plants	24 – 36	65 – 90
Corn, Sweet	Mar. – April Aug.	Feb. – Mar. Aug. – Sept.	Aug. – Mar.	Seed	12 – 18	60 – 95
Cucumber	Feb. – April Aug. – Sept.	Feb. – Mar. Aug.–Sept.	Sept. – Mar.	Seed, plants	12 – 24	40 – 70
Eggplant	Feb. – July Aug. – Sept.	Feb. – Mar. Aug. – Oct.	Dec. – Feb.	Seed, plants	24 – 36	75 – 100
Okra	Mar. – July	Mar. – Aug. Aug. – Sept.	Feb. – Mar.	Seed	6 – 12	50 – 75
Peanut	Mar. – May	Mar. – April	Feb. – Mar.	Seed	24 – 48	75 – 150
Peas, Southern	Mar. – Aug.	Mar. – Sept.	Aug. – April	Seed	2 – 3	60 – 90
Pepper	Mar. – April July – Aug.	Mar. – April Aug. – Sept.	Aug. – April	Seed, plants	12 – 24	60 – 100
Potato, Sweet	Mar. – June	Mar. – July	Feb. – July	Plants	12 – 14	120 – 140
Pumpkin	Mar. – April July – Aug.	Mar. – April July – Aug.	Jan. – Feb. July – Sept.	Seed, plants	36 – 60	80 – 120
Squash, Summer	Mar. – April Aug. – Sept.	Mar. – April Aug. – Sept.	Jan. – Mar. Sept. – Oct.	Seed, plants	24 – 36	35 – 55
Squash, Winter	Mar.	Mar. Aug.	Jan. – Feb.	Seed, plants	36 – 48	70 – 110
Tomato	Mar. – April Aug.	Mar. Aug. – Sept.	Aug. – Mar.	Seed, plants	18 – 24	75 – 110
Watermelon	Mar. – April July – Aug.	Feb. – Mar. Aug.	Jan. – Mar. Aug. – Sept.	Seed, plants	15 – 60	75 – 95

MAKING VEGETABLES FUN

Planting vegetables can also be fun. Here are some different ways to grow them. Use these methods as an excellent way to introduce children to gardening. They also can stimulate a child's interest in eating the results of their efforts, which just so happens to be good for them.

PLANTING IN A SACK

This is a fun project for kids young and old that starts with a stop at the garden center. Pick up a large bag of good potting soil and some seeds or transplants. Place the sack of soil in a sunny location, following these steps:

- Lay the sack flat on the ground.
- Make two 1- and 2-inch horizontal cuts in the sack near the ground line on each side for drainage.
- Decide where you want to plant the herbs or vegetables in the top of the bag.
- Make an X-shaped slit in the bag, 4 to 6 inches long, at each planting site.
- Plant the seeds or transplant through the slit, and water.
- Keep the soil moist and feed weekly with a fertilizer solution through the openings.

Your sack garden will grow just as well as the crops planted in the ground. When the harvest is over, add the soil to your in-ground gardens and start over with another sackful.

TRELLISING CROPS

Crops like Tomatoes, Cucumbers, and Pole Beans grow better and resist disease if they are kept off the ground. Check seed packets to make sure you have a climbing variety.

Tomato fruits that rest on the ground almost always rot. Trellising makes picking easy, saves space, and allows easier spraying when necessary. It also keeps fruit cleaner and makes it easier to see when it's getting ripe. Here are some ways to get your plants up off the ground:

- Set up chicken wire between posts. Space the posts 6 to 8 feet apart and use a 4- to 5-foot-high wire netting.
- Make rings of concrete wire up to 2 feet in diameter, and set the plants inside to climb. This is best used with tomatoes.
- Buy ready-to-use wire rings around plants that need the support.
- Make a teepee of bamboo stakes or wood to support the crop.
- Plant the crops near a chain-link fence or wooden picket fence.
- Cantaloupe can also be grown on vertical supports with fruits held by panty hose.

THE THREE SISTERS

Here is a fun planting technique that can save space and produce vegetables at the same time. It's a great project for kids, teaching them how the American Indians planted Corn, climbing Beans, and bush Squash. All you need is a sunny garden spot and seeds of each crop. Prepare the soil for planting, with plenty of organic matter and composted manure, then follow these steps:

- Form a rounded planting site about a foot or more in diameter. Create as many of the rounded sites as you want, 4 feet apart.
- Plant seeds of the three crops, spacing them 2 inches apart in the rounded sites. Sow three or four seeds of each.
- Water the soil and apply a thin layer of mulch. Water again whenever the soil begins to dry.
- While the seedlings are still small, remove all but one or two of each crop.
- Train the Beans to climb on the Corn stalks, and the Squash to grow under the Corn and Beans.
- Feed the plantings monthly to help produce crops.

The plants should produce Corn, Beans, and Squash at about the same time to complete this enjoyable gardening project.

JANUARY

• This is the middle of Florida's cool-season gardening. South Florida gardeners can plant mixes of cool- or warm-season crops.

• Almost-daily harvesting will be your major chore. If you don't know when to pick a crop, check the grocery store displays for an example.

• During this cool but drier time, crops will use less water. Keep up your regular checks for moisture needs. Do not overwater or root rot may result.

• All edible crop plants need regular feedings. Mark the calendar and apply fertilizer on a regular schedule. Or use your judgment to see if a plant is not growing vigorously or with a good green color. Use liquid fertilizer once or twice a month, scatter granular fertilizer every 3 or 4 weeks, or apply composted manure as a sidedressing.

• Insects and diseases are not a major winter problem. However caterpillars stays active. Handpick or apply natural control. Aphids, nematodes, or whiteflies may also appear.

FEBRUARY

• Prepare weed-free soil for warm-season crops. Dig out deep-rooted perennial weeds, apply herbicides that permits replanting of vegetables after use, use landscape fabric, apply mulch, and remove weeds from rest of garden.

• Start seeds. Mist to keep them moist. Begin weekly feeding of half-strength liquid fertilizer when seedlings sprout. Provide plenty of air movement. Increase fertilizer to full strength when seedlings reach garden size with 4 to 6 true leaves. Transplant to garden when weather warms.

• Since it is still cool, plants don't require as much moisture. However, regularly check the garden to see if surface soil is dry.

• Keep fertilizing even if crop is producing. Many plants continue to grow and give good yields. Stop feeding only when production is almost over.

• Whiteflies are a major problem during winter. Control with soap spray, especially on undersides of leaves, when first noted. You may also see aphids, caterpillars, mites, and root knot nematodes.

MARCH

• Although it's time for warm-season crops, central and northern growers can plant cool-season plants. Most seedlings should be ready to transplant. If you have not yet sown seeds of peppers, tomatoes, or eggplant, make it a first-of-the-month priority.

• Follow instructions on seed packets for most plants.

• Keep up harvests and remove plants when production drops.

• Make sure soaker hoses and microsprinklers are working. These are the two best systems to use in the garden. They conserve water and put it only where needed.

• Corn and Beans are plants that might need special fertilizer attention. Corn may need extra feedings. However, beans may need fewer to keep from producing lots of foliage but not as many flowers or fruit.

• Pests become more active this month. The leafminer finds Tomatoes, Basil, Melons, Beans, and Cucumbers attractive. Severe tunneling can be treated with insecticides. You may also notice aphids, caterpillars, mites, root knot nematodes, slugs, and snails.

APRIL

• Plant the last Corn, Melons, and other spring crops that need only around 50 days. Reliable hot-weather herbs include Basil, Dill, Oregano, Chives, and Thyme.

• As cool-season crops finish up, add new plantings. You can start Sweet Potatoes at home from sprouting potatoes.

• When adding herbs, plant some in containers. Some that have trouble surviving the hot rainy season survive in pots that can be moved. Control spreading herbs by harvesting, sharing with friends, or feeding the compost pile.

• It's hot and dry. Make sure plants get moisture needed for production.

• Maintain feeding schedule.

• Tomatoes are most affected by insects and diseases. The worst are wilts and leaf spots (blight). The only controls for wilts are replanting with resistant varieties, planting in another area, or growing the next crop in containers. Control leaf spots with a fungicide. You may also see aphids, caterpillars, mites, slugs, snails, root knot nematodes, and whiteflies.

MAY

• Crops that take heat are Cherry Tomatoes, Hot Peppers, Okra, and Sweet Potatoes. Many herbs are in full growth, but as hot rainy weather arrives, they often decline. Gather and preserve them now.

• Stop warm-season plantings. Rains foster too many diseases and insects run rampant. Continue with hot-season crops. When crops finish, many gardeners give up for the summer. If you do, don't allow weeds to take over. Plant a cover crop of French Marigolds or legumes to reduce nematodes and diminish weeds.

• Harvest crops as needed. Crops left in the garden attract critters.

• Keep watering as needed.

• Don't stop fertilizing until the crop plant is obviously declining. After Corn and Melons form, no more fertilizer is needed. Most remaining warm-season crops should be fed regularly.

• Stay alert to numerous pests and control as needed. Look for aphids, caterpillars, leaf spots, mites, root knot nematodes, slugs, snails, and whiteflies until crop production is finished.

JUNE

• Keep warm-season crops growing as long as you reap a harvest. Continue to plant summer crops. Try some real tropical crops like Boniato, Calabaza, Chayote, Dasheen, Jerusalem Artichoke, or Malanga. Start them from produce found at your local food store. They are quite ornamental and can be grown in vegetable gardens or added to flower beds.

• Keep up harvests of warm-season crops. Preserve or share excess with friends. Do not allow them to decline in the garden.

• Less watering will be required during the rainy season. Check garden whenever a day or two passes between rains.

• Feed crops that are still actively growing with granular or liquid fertilizer, or a sidedressing of composted manure. Do not feed crops that are about finished with production.

• A few of the more common pests at this time of year are caterpillars, garden flea hoppers, leaf spots, root knot nematodes, slugs, snails, and whiteflies.

JULY

• Prepare beds for new plantings. Remove unproductive herbs or vegetable plants, enrich the soil with organic matter, use weed prevention measures, and solarize soil against nematodes.

• In mid-month, start seeds of Tomatoes, Eggplants, and Peppers for an August planting. Feed seedlings weekly with half-strength balanced fertilizer.

• Don't let summer crops get out of control. Prune to keep in-bounds and they will still produce a good crop.

• Summer rains may provide necessary watering, but also areas that are too wet. Consider raised beds for the next crop.

• Keep up monthly fertilizing schedule. Container plantings may need additional feedings if growth slows or foliage yellows.

• Pests are still active, but summer crops are durable. They won't mind a few chewed leaves or some missing sap. If necessary, control grasshoppers with handpicking or insecticide formulated for use on vegetables. Look for caterpillars, garden flea hoppers, leaf spots, root knot nematodes, slugs, snails, and whiteflies.

AUGUST

• Get ready for nine months of great gardening. The first crops are warm-season types, followed by cool-season crops (planted in fall), then another round of warm-season crops (planted when spring arrives). This is very different for gardeners used to planting first crops in early spring.

• Start easy-to-grow crops from seeds. Add a little fertilizer to water used to start new seeds. Apply first feedings two to three weeks after planting. Keep granular fertilizer or composted manure away from stems.

• If growing transplants, look for varieties with strong stems and bright-green leaves. Avoid spindly or damaged plants.

• Explore the garden daily for water needs and potential pest problems.

• Do not allow newly seeded areas or transplants to get dry. Water when surface inch feels dry, and mulch.

• Beware of cutworms. Place paper collar around the base of transplants to protect them. Other pests to watch for are aphids, caterpillars, mites, slugs, snails, and whiteflies.

SEPTEMBER

• Warm-season gardens begun last month in Central and North Florida should be completed as soon as possible. These regions will soon become too chilly for good production.

• Although it is traditional to plant in rows, it's not necessary. Some prefer using small paths between the crops.

• Check for and remove weeds. Be careful not to remove sprouting seedlings.

• The rainy season may end shortly. Make sure irrigation system and sprinklers are working. Consider using soaker hoses and microirrigation. Apply irrigation during early morning hours to conserve water.

• Feeding schedules are important now. Mark your calendar with next scheduled feeding. You can always skip a feeding if plants are growing adequately. Overfeeding can reduce production in fruiting crops.

• Caterpillars may be your major pest this time of year. Handpick or control with natural or synthetic insecticide. More pests found in the fall warm-season garden are aphids, grasshoppers, mites, slugs, snails, and whiteflies.

OCTOBER

• The chill in the air signals the end of warm-season and beginning of cool-season crops everywhere but South Florida. Fall also means herb-growing season.

• Lots of cool-season crops can be planted from seeds. It takes about 4 to 8 weeks for transplant size. Cover the seeds to keep them moist and speed germination. When first sprouts are noticed remove covering and check for pests. Transplants are easier and quicker than seeds.

• Thick mulch reduces the need for cultivation, keeps out weeds, and retains moisture.

• Growth during cooler weather is slower, so less water is needed. Allowing several days between waterings helps plants develop deeper pest-resistant root systems. Check to see if plants need moisture, especially container plantings.

• As long as the weather remains warm, maintain regular feedings.

• Stay alert to mite problems. Control with soap spray or miticide for vegetable use. Other pests to watch for are aphids, caterpillars, grasshoppers, slugs, snails, and whiteflies.

NOVEMBER

• Don't let one garden area sit without a growing crop. If you want to take a break, consider sowing a cover crop of Rye Grass. Scatter seed over any tilled soil and water it in. It can be mowed down and tilled in at planting time.

• As one warm-season crop finishes, have seeds or transplants of the next vegetable ready. Continue planting herbs in the garden and containers. This is the time of most rapid growth. Don't forget, any area that has even a small open spot is a good place for herbs.

• November can produce bountiful harvests. Most warm- and cool-season crops are starting to mature. Keep crops picked to encourage new production.

• Check plants and containers frequently during this cool but dry time of year.

• Keep to your regular feeding program.

• Insects are less active during cooler days. A few to still watch for are aphids, caterpillars, slugs, snails, and whiteflies.

DECEMBER

• Happy holidays! Your harvest can add to the big family feast.

• Use seeds and transplants in small pots or cell-packs to keep the garden growing when a spot becomes available. Start cool-season vegetables, which take three or more months to produce a crop.

• Keep protective covers handy, as many North and Central Florida areas may get a frost or freeze this month. A blanket or some hay may be enough to hold in some heat. Young plants can be protected with an overturned pot, box, or garbage can.

• Continue checking for water needs of the plants. Both in-ground and container plants can go a bit longer between waterings.

• The plants are still active. Maintain feeding schedules with minor variations. Increase the time between feedings.

• Most pests don't like the really cold weather. Most active will be caterpillars in big-leafed crops. Control by handpicking or using insecticide with *Bacillus thuringiensis*. Synthetic sprays are available.

LAWNS
for Florida

Most homeowners take pride in growing a healthy green lawn. While they may complain about mowing the grass, they are usually happy to tell others what they do to fight off bugs and keep the turf thick. A lawn is an all-American bragging topic for most weekend gardeners.

The home turf is also a playground, supporting family football games, inviting croquet, or simply being the spot to tumble with a family pet. Many gardeners simply appreciate the open space created by turf.

A number of homeowners may not realize it, but their lawns are also producing oxygen, holding the soil in place, and helping moisture percolate down through the ground to replenish the freshwater supply.

Not everyone wants a large lawn. The latest trend is to grow only the grass one really needs and intends to care for. After all, there is work involved!

PLANNING THE LAWN

The best lawns grow in full-sun locations. Some Florida turf varieties, mainly some of the St. Augustines, tolerate light shade. But in general, the less shade the better. Many cultural problems can be eliminated by planting grass only where it gets a full day of sunshine.

It's also best to keep lawns away from trees that cast heavy shade. Not only are light levels too low under most of the canopy, the turf also has to compete with tree roots. It is better to leave these areas for more shade-tolerant and vigorous groundcovers.

SOIL CONSIDERATIONS

Most Florida soils are suitable for growing turf. Soils rich in organic matter or clay hold more moisture than sandy soils, but both are capable of growing a great lawn. Avoid low areas that may accumulate water and hold it for more than a few hours. Such wet locations encourage shallow root systems and disease problems.

All turf sites should have the proper soil pH. Most grasses like a slightly acidic to nearly neutral soil.

A soil in the 5.5 to 7.5 pH range is generally ideal. Only Bahia turf benefits from soil in the acid range of pH 5.5 to 6.5. In this acidic soil, extra iron is available for growing turf—Bahia seems to need this iron more than other grasses. Soil acidity can be adjusted by following soil test recommendations. In Florida, dolomitic lime is usually used to raise the soil pH, soil sulfur to lower it. Follow information from the test recommendations to properly change the acidity.

It may be impossible to make a permanent change in acidity in the very alkaline soils of South Florida, and in pockets of organic soils throughout the state. If the soil pH cannot be changed, gardeners should grow the turf type best suited to the area. And be prepared to periodically add minor nutrients that might be depleted by the extremes in acidity levels.

THE FIRST STEP

Starting a new lawn is similar to filling bare spots in older turf. First, remove debris and weedy growths. Unwanted vegetation can be dug out or killed with a non-selective herbicide. Choose a product that permits planting the turf immediately after the weeds decline. Once weeds are removed, the soil is tilled. This is the time to incorporate lime or sulfur if needed. Some gardeners also like to incorporate organic matter, including aged manure, into sandy soils.

Adding organic matter is beneficial, but usually only practical when dealing with small sites. While the matter is present, it does help hold moisture and provide some nutrients for beginning turf growth, but it quickly breaks down and leaves mainly the original sandy soil. After tilling, smooth out the ground to establish a uniform planting surface as final preparation for planting. This can be performed with a rake or a drag.

STARTING FROM SEED

Seed a lawn during March through September, when the grass makes quick growth. In Florida, Bahia is usually the only grass that is seeded to start the home lawn. It gives the best germination with minimal care. Some Bermuda, Centipede, and Zoysia varieties can also be seeded. For each area of the lawn, divide the amount of seed needed in half. Move back and forth across the lawn, spreading the first portion. Then move across the lawn in a perpendicular direction and spread the remaining seed. Rake the lawn to cover the seed. Bahia seed germinates best if covered with soil ¼ to ½ inch deep. Seeded lawns need frequent watering. Water daily to keep the surface of the soil wet until the grass begins to sprout. As the roots spread out into the surrounding soil, watering can be reduced to "as needed."

STARTING FROM PLUGS

Plugs of grass—well-established sections of grass 2 to 4 inches square—can be used for all but Bahia turf. Some gardeners simply kill out the existing weeds and old grass, then insert the plugs. Good lawns can be established this way, but they appear to fill in more slowly than when the ground is cleared before planting. Add the plugs to moist soil. Most are spaced 6 to 12 inches apart. The closer the spacing, the quicker the grass fills in to establish the lawn.

Some people like to add a slow-release fertilizer to the planting hole. It may be beneficial, but it is also time-consuming. A good feeding shortly after plugging seems to give a similar response.

Keep the planted area moist and the plugs will begin to grow rapidly. After two to three weeks of growth, gardeners may apply a fertilizer to encourage the grass to form the lawn.

STARTING FROM SOD

All turf types can be established by sod, which gives an instant lawn and helps shut out weeds that may grow among seeded and plugged turf.

Most sod is sold in rectangular portions. It can be purchased by the piece or on a pallet. A pallet of sod may contain 400 to 500 square feet, so ask about the quantity before you buy.

Have the soil prepared and damp when the sod arrives. If for some reason the sod cannot be immediately installed, keep it in a shady location. Sod that sits on the pallet for longer than forty-eight hours quickly declines. Install the sod by laying pieces next to each other, abutting the edges. Cut sections to fill in any small spaces. After the sod is laid, water the turf thoroughly. A good rule to keep the sod moist is to water every day for the first week. The second week, water every other day, and the third week every third day. After three weeks, water only as needed to keep the turf from wilting.

Gardeners should note that sod laid in the shade needs less water than sunny locations. Too much water, especially during hot and humid weather, can cause the turf to rot and the sod will be lost. After the sod has been growing for three to four weeks, the first application of a lawn fertilizer can be administered. After this initial feeding, assume a normal care program.

THE ONE DEMAND OF LAWNS

Home lawns do demand one thing: frequent mowing during the warmer months. From March through October, most lawns need cutting at least once a week. During the cooler months, cutting may not be necessary at all in North Florida, and just every other week or so in Central and South Florida. The general rule is to remove no more than one-third of the grass blade at any one time. This keeps the grass from being burned after too close a mowing. Another good mowing tip is to keep a sharp blade and mow in different directions across the lawn at each cutting.

BAHIA GRASS
Paspalum notatum

☼ 🦋 💧

HARDINESS
Throughout Florida

MOWING HEIGHT
3 to 4 inches

WATER NEEDS
Drought tolerant once established. With drought will turn brown but revives once seasonal rains return.

CARE
Provide first feeding in three to four months. Apply 16-0-8 fertilizer around March and September, with iron feeding in early spring. Prefers acidic soil with pH between 5.5 and 6.5. If pH above 7, add extra iron and micro-nutrients. Tolerates filtered open shade.

PROBLEMS
Mole crickets have to be controlled. Apply baits in summer. To deter weeds use cultural controls to encourage dense growth, or apply herbicide.

USES AND SELECTIONS
Bahia Grass is a good-looking lawn requiring minimal care. It's one of Florida's most drought tolerant turf types, tough enough for backyard football games. Bahia is a multi-purpose turf, growing well from seed and establishing easily from sod. Plant Bahia Grass in sunny spots, surrounded with trees, shrubs, and Palms. Different varieties are available.

BERMUDAGRASS
Cynodon spp.

☼ 🦋 💧 🌊

HARDINESS
Throughout Florida. Turns brown with frost but recovers with warm weather.

MOWING HEIGHT
To 2 inches

WATER NEEDS
Drought tolerant once established

CARE
Provide first feeding in three to four months. Apply 16-0-8 fertilizer around March, May, and September to this high maintenance lawn. Supply nitrogen feedings every other month during summer and fall. Tolerates pH extremes if supplied with trace elements. Remove thatch layer.

PROBLEMS
Test soil for nematodes and avoid planting in infested areas. Pests include sod webworms and mole crickets. Diseases include dollar spot, brown patch, and leaf spots. An established Bermuda lawn is weed resistant.

USES AND SELECTIONS
This finely textured turf is popular on golf courses and athletic fields. It is also drought and salt tolerant. It establishes an impressive look when surrounded with flower beds, Palms, and tropical plants. 'FloraTeX' needs fewer feedings, has some nematode tolerance, and has good potential as a carefree home lawn.

CARPETGRASS

Axonopus affinis

☀ ☀ 🦋

HARDINESS
Throughout Florida. Tolerates heat but turns brown with frost and slowly re-greens in warmer weather.

MOWING HEIGHT
2 to 3 inches

WATER NEEDS
Poor drought tolerance. Needs abundant water. Tolerates wet soil.

CARE
This wide bladed turf grows in acidic soil (pH 5.0 to 5.5). It is low-maintenance but with a little care produces good green color and dense growth. Needs less fertilizer than other lawn turf.

PROBLEMS
Produces numerous seedheads, which must be mowed often in summer. Has poor nematode and cold resistance. Also susceptible to armyworm, cutworm, grubs, mole crickets, brown spot, and dollar spot.

USES AND SELECTIONS
Carpetgrass is also called Flatgrass and Louisianagrass. This is the grass for wet, poorly drained soil. It has a shallow root system, so it needs abundant water. It does have some shade tolerance but is not as good as St. Augustinegrass in lower light locations. Grows from sprigs, seeds, and sod.

CENTIPEDE GRASS

Eremochloa ophiuroides

☀ ☀ 🦋 💧

HARDINESS
Throughout Florida

MOWING HEIGHT
2 to 3 inches

WATER NEEDS
Keep new plantings moist to encourage growth. Some drought tolerance once established, for deep-rooted lawns. Shallow-rooted lawns may need frequent waterings.

CARE
Feed at half recommended rate four to six months after new growth begins. Fertilizer in March, and fall if desired. Prefers slightly acidic soil (pH of 6.0). If pH cannot be altered, add minor nutrients. Tolerates light shade.

PROBLEMS
Gardeners in North Florida grow best-looking Centipede Grass, with fewest pests. In sandy, warm soils nematodes are problems and high pH requires periodic iron applications.

USES AND SELECTIONS
Centipede Grass is sometimes called Poor Man's Turf due to its ability to grow in infertile soils with minimal feedings. It has good green color, grows in light shade, and can tolerate drought. It can be quite vigorous with the right care and can grow from seed, plugs, or sod. Different varieties are available.

RYEGRASS
Lolium spp.

☼ ☀

HARDINESS
Throughout Florida

MOWING HEIGHT
2 to 3 inches

WATER NEEDS
Keep moist during growing season, fall through early spring.

CARE
Sow seed soon after cooler weather arrives for best growth and longest time to enjoy the bright green lawn. Use about eight to ten pounds for every 1,000 square feet. Germinates in ten to fourteen days. It is best sown on prepared planting soil. Till the soil, rake it smooth, and then scatter the seeds. After sowing, rake the seeds into soil lightly and then moisten. Fertilize during growing season.

PROBLEMS
Ryegrass is a cool-season grass and cannot take heat. No matter which species you choose, it will decline during spring as the weather warms.

USES AND SELECTIONS
Both the annual (*L. multiflorum*) and perennial (*L. perenne*) species are fast-growing lawns that survive during winter months. Ryegrass is ideal for overseeding and establishing a temporary lawn, and can be used to quickly fill bare spots.

SEASHORE PASPALUM
Paspalum vaginatum

☼ 💧 🌊

HARDINESS
Throughout Florida

MOWING HEIGHT
2 to 2½ inches

WATER NEEDS
Drought tolerant. Can be irrigated with lower-quality recycled water or salty water found in many coastal wells. Periodically flush with less saline water—such as from rainfall—to prevent salt toxicity.

CARE
This turf has a fine leaf blade and is dark green. It is tolerant of wear, cold, heat, varying soil acidity, and high salt levels. Seashore Paspalum spreads rapidly. It prefers frequent and light feedings. The turf also benefits from extra potassium.

PROBLEMS
Needs frequent mowing. Susceptible to army worm, billbug, cutworm, mole crickets, sod webworm, spittlebug, and white grubs. Nematodes may also be a problem.

USES AND SELECTIONS
Ideal for use in seaside plantings or other areas where water may be salty. It can be mowed close to give a well-manicured turf look. Several new varieties were released in the 1990s. Grows from sprigs and sod.

ST. AUGUSTINE GRASS

Stenotaphrum secundatum

☀ ☀ 🦋

HARDINESS
Throughout Florida

MOWING HEIGHT
To 4 inches

WATER NEEDS
Keep new plantings moist to encourage growth. Requires irrigation during drier weather.

CARE
Provide first feeding in three to four weeks. Apply complete fertilizer once in spring and fall. In southern areas, an extra feeding or two may be desired. If turf become slightly yellow in summer, apply iron.

PROBLEMS
Check for chinch bugs, caterpillars, and brown patch during warmer months.

USES AND SELECTIONS
This is probably the best all-around Florida turf. Although coarser bladed than northern turfs, it has good shade tolerance (up to 25 percent filtered sun) and pest resistance. Gardeners like the blue-green color and vigor. Grow with mixture of shade-and-full-sun-loving plants. St. Augustine Grass has several selections suited to differing conditions, including shade, pest, and cold tolerance, as well as color and mowing height. May be grown from plugs or sod.

ZOYSIA GRASS

Zoysia spp.

☀ ☀ 💧 🌀 🌊

HARDINESS
Throughout Florida. In northern sections of Florida will turn brown with cold.

MOWING HEIGHT
1 to 2 inches

WATER NEEDS
Very drought tolerant but during dry weather will turn brown without adequate water

CARE
Sunny sites are best, but can tolerate light shade. It grows in all soil types and tolerates alkaline soils. Apply 16-0-8 once during spring and once during fall. Add nitrogen applications in April, June, August, and November. Mechanically remove thatch as needed from this slower growing turf.

PROBLEMS
Billbugs can cause decline in patches. Use a chemical control.

USES AND SELECTIONS
This is a fine-bladed grass for a well maintained look. Once established, it can beat out weeds and withstand wear. It's also drought tolerant, cold hardy, and resistant to salt levels. Many varieties are available as plugs or sod and one type as seed. The selection 'Empire' has a wider blade and more compact growth habit.

TURFGRASS COMPARISONS

CONSIDERATIONS

Florida is a long state, almost 900 miles from the tip of the panhandle to the last island of the Keys, and as you would expect there are climatic differences. Select a turfgrass that will give the look you want, keeping in mind how it will perform during winter in your zone, and how much water and work will be needed to maintain it.

Coastal gardeners must deal with saltwater sprays and underground intrusion into their irrigation wells. Some inland residents also deal with pockets of salty water that affect irrigation water during drier months. In these areas it's important to select a turf type that tolerates higher salt levels.

Home lawn size has been about 5,000 square feet, but concerns for water shortages in recent years may affect future plantings. People are being encouraged to plant only what lawn they need for family activities and devote the rest of the landscape to drought-tolerant ornamentals.

IT'S TIME TO WATER

Everyone is concerned about conserving water. Wouldn't it be nice to have an easy way to tell exactly when it is time to water? You do, and it's the turf itself.

Home lawns start to wilt when they begin to dry past the point that the roots can supply water. At first you might notice the lawn turning a gray-green. Then, if you look closely, you will see that the grass blades are folded. You might say the grass is wilting. If you walk on the lawn, the tracks are clearly visible and the blades stay flattened.

You will probably also notice that the whole lawn does not become dry at the same time. Does it hurt a lawn to wilt just a little? Usually not. In fact, University of Florida studies show that a lawn that is wilting just a little grows a little longer root system. This means the roots can grow a bit further into the soil and possibly absorb additional moisture. But you cannot let the turf wilt too much or for too long without some damage.

The best time to water is when you notice some spots showing signs of wilting. Then water the entire lawn.

HOW MUCH TO WATER

Determining how much to water is one of the more difficult parts of lawn care. Gardeners often ask, "Do I water for a half hour, or how about an hour or two?" There is no way to just tell you how long to water.

Normally the recommendation is to apply half to three-fourths of an inch of water at each watering. This should do a good job of wetting the upper foot of soil, which can hold about an inch of water. This good soaking should be all that is needed, without wasting water.

To find out when you have applied this amount, place shallow straight-sided containers throughout the lawn to catch water while irrigating. Measure the amount collected in fifteen minutes and use that to determine how long you must water.

WHEN TO WATER

In recent years Florida has had to deal with a lack of water. Water management districts and local communities have helped conserve water with regulations that restrict watering to certain times and days. They are related to the amount of available water and season of the year. Check with your water management district or local Extension Service for rules in your area.

In most areas, watering is not permitted between 10 a.m. and 4 p.m. Actually this is best because water can be lost to evaporation during the hotter portions of the day, before it can infiltrate into the ground. The best time to water is usually between 2 a.m. and 8 a.m., when there is little evaporation and air movement.

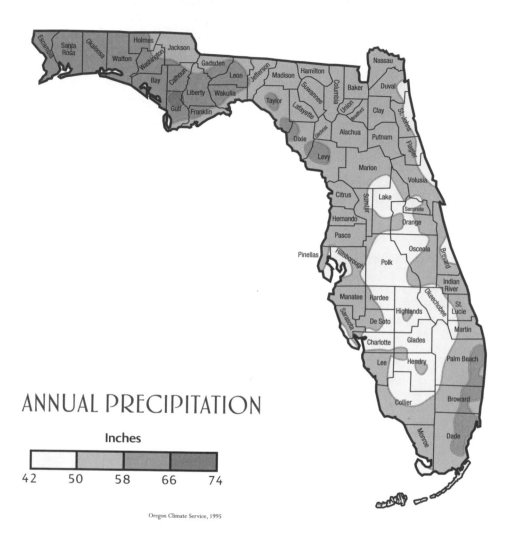

ANNUAL PRECIPITATION

Inches

42   50   58   66   74

Oregon Climate Service, 1995

HOW MUCH DROUGHT CAN A LAWN TAKE?

Perhaps another way to state this question is, "How much brown can you tolerate?" Most lawns are fairly drought tolerant, but if Florida residents are going to endure dry times, they may have to tolerate a less-than-perfect lawn. Keeping a lawn green and lush requires one to two inches of water per week, especially during hot dry weather.

With severe watering restrictions in effect in some locations, gardeners want the toughest turf for their lawn. They are also considering using grass only where it's needed for family activities.

Florida's most drought-tolerant turfgrasses are Bahiagrass, Bermudagrass, Seashore Paspalum, and Zoysiagrass. All can turn brown and survive months of drought, then regrow when rains return or irrigation water is provided. Carpetgrass, Centipedegrass, and St. Augustinegrass are susceptible to drought, with extended drought causing decline and death.

FLORIDA TURF MAINTENANCE AT A GLANCE

LAWN FERTILIZER 101

Fertilizer recommendations have changed rapidly in Florida. Excess phosphorus, along with other nutrients, have been running off lawns into our rivers, bays, and aquifers. They pollute the waterways, affecting water quality. Algal blooms and fish kills are just two of the many consequences. To help stem this nutrient overload, there is a new fertilizer label rule and many counties have added restrictions or recommendations as to when you can feed the lawn and what can be used. Check with your local University of Florida Extension Office for current local recommendations.

In general, the amount of nitrogen and phosphorus that can be applied to the lawn by home-owners and maintenance companies are affected. You will notice some new fertilizer formulas like 16-0-8, 15-0-15, and 32-0-10 on lawn products. Most lawns do not need an application of the nutrient phosphorus (the middle number) so it is not included in many products. When included, the amount of phosphorus that can be applied is also limited by the new fertilizer label rule.

With some products the rate of application may be lower and adjustments have been made in the instructions. So follow the spreader setting suggested on the fertilizer bag. There will also be recommended times of application on the bag that you should follow when deciding when to feed your lawn with the product purchased. Some counties have added what are called "black out" periods or times when you cannot feed lawns. This is normally during the summer months when rains might wash nutrients into the aquifer if not properly applied. Most products also contain slow-release features that release the nutrients over a longer period, which results in better fertilizer use and less pollution.

HOW MUCH FERTILIZER IS ENOUGH?

Fertilizer can turn grass green. Fertilizer can also promote excessive growth that leads to lots of mowing, aboveground runner growth, spongy lawns, and disease and insect problems.

Fertilizers are also being singled out as one of our major causes for water pollution in the state. Most Florida soils are very porous so nutrients can be washed through to the drinking water supply. They can be washed down streets into retention ponds, lakes, and waterways.

So do you really need to fertilize a lawn? The answer is usually yes, but maybe not as frequently as you might think. Most lawns do quite well on a lean diet of no more than two or three feedings a year. Will you have a really green lawn with lots of growth? Probably not. But you will have a tough lawn—one that is more resistant to chinch bugs, diseases, and nematodes.

New guidelines establish various degrees of feeding based on nitrogen fertilizer applications—gardeners can pick from low, medium, and high maintenance levels. You decide what you want. Low to medium feedings are probably best for most home lawns. They require less work and may promote fewer pests. Most gardeners don't need extra work and Florida definitely does not need fertilizers entering our water resources.

MOWING

Mowing is not a chore that everyone loves. But gardeners do seem to take a lot of pride in a manicured lawn. We must not truly mind mowing or we wouldn't have as much lawn!

How often you mow is up to you. Most gardeners find once a week adequate. During the rainy season the grass may grow faster and need more frequent mowing. In general, if the turf produces new growth equal to one-third the desired height, it's time to mow. Removing more than one-third of the leaf blade can stress turfgrass, make lots of clippings, and result in yellowing of the grass.

Forget bagging your grass unless you have a very good reason. Leaving the clippings on the lawn avoids adding it to the landfill plus clippings contain nutrients the turf can use. So don't allow this free lawn food to be hauled away to the dump.

WEEDS

Creating a thick and vigorously growing turf can help keep unwanted vegetation out of the grass—but not always. You don't have to do anything wrong to get weedy plants growing in your lawn. Quick action on your part can keep out weeds. Getting an early start on weed control can prevent an infestation and the need to use chemical controls.

It's not necessary to know each weed by name. By knowing the general type of weeds you are dealing with, a control can usually be determined.

Broadleaf weeds are usually the easiest to spot and control. They have large, oblong to round leaves. They can be annuals or perennials and grow year-round. Some common broadleaf weeds include Brazil pusley, dollarweed, and oxalis.

Grassy weeds may look somewhat like your turf. They normally have long, narrow to wide leaf blades. Grassy weeds can be annuals or perennials and grow year-round. Some grassy turf invaders include crabgrass, goosegrass, and Alexandergrass.

Sedges may be the most shiny, bright green, and upright-growing weeds in your lawn. They look like grass but have triangular stems. They can be annuals or perennials. Some Florida sedges include nutsedges, globe sedge, and green kyllinga.

Gardeners need a strategy when controlling weeds. The first part of the plan is to establish a vigorous, durable turf. The next part is to remove weeds when they first occur by digging or pulling them out. Once established, some are difficult to control. At that point the plan calls for chemical products.

One type of weed control product, selective herbicide, removes the weeds without major damage to the turf. Another type is nonselective herbicide. These show no respect for your turf and kill both weeds and grass. They are most commonly used when renovating lawns or controlling spot infestations.

Read the labels to know which weeds are controlled. All herbicides must be applied according to the instructions, including following the precautions. Remember that herbicides are meant to kill plants and could affect trees, flowers, and other plants growing near your turf.

INSECTS

Nowadays most gardeners would like to avoid applying pesticides, especially insecticides. The trend is to manage insect populations at levels that are least damaging to plant materials, including the turf. It involves knowing your plants and the pests that could cause damage. It also includes monitoring the plants for these pests, and for beneficial insects and other natural controls. Pesticides may be used when a pest reaches a predetermined threshold and other options have been exhausted.

When you spot a pest, determine if control is needed. A few insects may be normal. If a pesticide is needed, select the least toxic product first. Various natural pest control products can be used to help with lawn pests. As always, follow the label instructions.

Controlling turf pests does not necessarily mean spraying the entire lawn. Consider treating only the affected area plus a five-foot section surrounding it. That way you are just treating the infestation and leaving the rest of the lawn free of pesticide, and protecting beneficial insects.

TURFGRASS DISEASES

Plant diseases are a mystery to most homeowners. They seem to show up overnight and are not like insects or weeds that you can see. But diseases are real and destructive, often quickly causing yellowing and decline of the turf.

Plant diseases can be caused by a fungus, bacteria, virus, or mycoplasma, but with turf all you normally have to consider are fungal problems. The pathogens that cause disease are everywhere—in soil, on your shoes, and in the air.

For the disease to occur, several factors must be present: the pathogen, a susceptible turf type, and the right environmental conditions. Most often your best control is altering the environment. Simple changes such as reduced watering, avoiding excessive feedings, and providing more sunlight can stop a disease. At other times you may have to use a fungicide to help make conditions unfavorable for the disease.

Just as you must stay alert to weed and insect problems, you must look for the start of disease symptoms. If you need help with identification, check with a local garden center or Extension Service.

If corrections of the environmental conditions do not solve the problem, fungicides may help prevent and sometimes cure a disease. However, they are short lived since the pathogens are usually always present. Use the fungicide specific to your problem and follow label instructions.

Some alternative remedies and naturally derived products are also becoming available as older fungicides are removed from the market. Check with the Extension Service for recommendations. As always, read the labels and follow all instructions.

Fertilizer Maintenance Program—Central Florida*

Turfgrass	Maintenance Level**	Total lbs. of actual nitrogen per 1000 sq. ft. per year	Feb.	Mar.	Apr.	May	Jun.	Jul.	Aug.	Sep.	Oct.	Nov.	Dec.
Bahiagrass	Low	2.5		1LF	0.5WS					1LF			
	Medium	3.0		1LF	0.5WS	0.5WS				1LF			
	High	3.5	1LF		0.5WS		0.5WS		0.5WS		1LF		
Bermudagrass	Low	2.5		1LF		0.5WS				1LF			
	Medium	3.5	1LF		0.5WS		1SR			1LF			
	High	5.5	1LF	0.5WS		1LF	1SR			1SR		1LF	
Carpetgrass	Low	1.0		1LF									
	Medium	1.5		1LF			0.5SR						
	High	2.0		1LF						1LF			
Centipedegrass	Low	2.0		1LF						1LF			
	Medium	2.5		1LF		0.5WS				1LF			
	High	3.5		1LF	0.5WS		1SR			1LF			
Seashore Paspalum	Low	3.0		1LF			1SR			1LF			
	Medium	3.5		1LF		0.5WS	1SR			1LF			
	High	4.0	1LF				1SR		1SR		1LF		
St. Augustinegrass	Low	2.5		1LF		0.5WS				1LF			
	Medium	4.0		1LF		1SR			1SR		1LF		
	High	4.5	1LF		0.5WS	1SR			1SR			1LF	
Zoysiagrass	Low	3.0		1LF		1SR				1LF			
	Medium	4.0		1LF		1SR			1SR		1LF		
	High	5.0	1LF		0.5WS	1SR			1SR	0.5WS		1LF	

*The boundary between North and Central Florida follows state road 40 and the boundary between Central and South Florida state road 70 from coast to coast.
**A maintenance program should incorporate recommendations from soil test results.
***See the Recommended Fertilizer Amounts table to determine the quantity of formulated fertilizer needed.
LF = Lawn fertilizer with 50% of the nitrogen in a slow-release form; **WS** = Water soluble nitrogen only fertilizer; **SR** = Slow-release nitrogen only fertilizer
Note: Iron only applications may be applied as needed to renew green color without encouraging growth.

Adaped from University of Florida IFAS Extension turfgrass recommendations.

Fertilizer Maintenance Program–North Florida*

Turfgrass	Maintenance Level**	Total lbs. of actual nitrogen per 1000 sq. ft. per year	Months to apply actual nitrogen and amounts needed per 1000 sq. ft.***										
			Feb.	Mar.	Apr.	May	Jun.	Jul.	Aug.	Sep.	Oct.	Nov.	Dec.
Bahiagrass	Low	2.0		1LF						1LF			
	Medium	2.5		1LF		0.5WS				1LF			
	High	3.5	1LF		0.5WS		1SR			1LF			
Bermudagrass	Low	2.5		1LF		0.5WS				1LF			
	Medium	4.0		1LF		1SR			1SR		1LF		
	High	5.5	1LF	0.5WS	1SR	1LF			1SR		1LF		
Carpetgrass	Low	1.0		1LF									
	Medium	1.5		1LF			0.5SR						
	High	2.0		1LF					1LF				
Centipedegrass	Low	2.0		1LF						1LF			
	Medium	2.0		1LF						1LF			
	High	3.0		1LF		1SR				1LF			
Seashore Paspalum	Low	2.0			0.5LF		0.5WS		0.5WS	0.5LF			
	Medium	2.5		1LF			0.5WS		0.5WS	0.5LF			
	High	3.0			1LF	0.5WS		0.5WS		1LF			
St. Augustinegrass	Low	2.0		1LF						1LF			
	Medium	3.0		1LF		1SR				1LF			
	High	4.5	1LF		0.5WS	1SR		1SR			1LF		
Zoysiagrass	Low	2.0		1LF						1LF			
	Medium	4.0		1LF		1SR			1SR		1LF		
	High	4.5	1LF		0.5WS	1SR			1SR		1LF		

*The boundary between North and Central Florida follows state road 40 and the boundary between Central and South Florida state road 70 from coast to coast.

**A maintenance program should incorporate recommendations from soil test results.

***See the Recommended Fertilizer Amounts table to determine the quantity of formulated fertilizer needed.

LF = Lawn fertilizer with 50% of the nitrogen in a slow-release form; **WS** = Water soluble nitrogen only fertilizer; **SR** = Slow-release nitrogen only fertilizer

Note: Iron only applications may be applied as needed to renew green color without encouraging growth.

Adapted from University of Florida IFAS Extension turfgrass recommendations.

Fertilizer Maintenance Program–South Florida*

Turfgrass	Maintenance Level**	Total lbs. of actual nitrogen per 1000 sq. ft. per year	Months to apply actual nitrogen and amounts needed per 1000 sq. ft.***										
			Feb.	Mar.	Apr.	May	Jun.	Jul.	Aug.	Sep.	Oct.	Nov.	Dec.
Bahiagrass	Low	2.0	1LF								1LF		
	Medium	2.5	1LF		0.5WS							1LF	
	High	4.0	1LF		0.5WS	1SR				0.5WS		1LF	
Bermudagrass	Low	3.5	1LF		0.5WS		1SR				1LF		
	Medium	3.5	1LF		0.5WS		1LF				1LF		
	High	5.5	1LF		0.5WS	1SR	1LF			1SR		1LF	
Carpetgrass	Low	2.0	1LF						1LF				
	Medium	2.5	1LF				0.5SR		1LF				
	High	3.0	1LF				1SR		1LF				
Centipedegrass	Low	2.0		1LF							1LF		
	Medium	2.5	1LF		0.5WS						1LF		
	High	3.5	1LF		0.5WS		1SR					1LF	
Seashore Paspalum	Low	3.5		1LF		1SR			0.5WS		1LF		
	Medium	4.0	1LF		0.5WS		1SR		0.5WS		1LF		
	High	4.5	1LF		0.5WS		1SR		1SR		1LF		
St. Augustinegrass	Low	2.5		1LF		0.5WS				1SR		1LF	
	Medium	4.0	1LF		1SR				1SR			1LF	
	High	4.5	1LF		0.5WS		1SR		1SR		1LF		
Zoysiagrass	Low	3.0		1LF		1SR				1LF			
	Medium	4.0	1LF		1SR		1SR		1SR		1SR		1LF
	High	4.0	1LF		0.5WS	1SR				0.5WS			1LF

*The boundary between North and Central Florida follows state road 40 and the boundary between Central and South Florida state road 70 from coast to coast.

**A maintenance program should incorporate recommendations from soil test results.

****See the Recommended Fertilizer Amounts table to determine the quantity of formulated fertilizer needed.

LF = Lawn fertilizer with 50% of the nitrogen in a slow-release form; **WS** = Water soluble nitrogen only fertilizer; **SR** = Slow-release nitrogen only fertilizer

Note: Iron only applications may be applied as needed to renew green color without encouraging growth.

Adapted from University of Florida IFAS Extension turfgrass recommendations.

JANUARY

• Gardeners usually delay adding new turf until it's a little warmer, when seeds germinate and freezes aren't a problem for young grass. But working outdoors now is comfortable, so get areas ready. Remove all weeds, till, rake, and adjust acidity if necessary.

• In warmer areas of the state, begin sodding and plugging.

• Mowing every few weeks keeps unwanted greenery under control and the mower in good shape.

• If grass is brown or not making much growth, little water is needed. Turn off automatic system and check soil to determine water needs.

• January is usually a fertilizer-free month for permanent grasses. If weather is mild and grass begins to grow, some yellowing may indicate a need for half the regular fertilizer feeding.

• Don't expect many pest problems during winter. If weather is warm, areas affected by brown spot disease can be controlled with fungicide. Control cool-weather weeds manually, or with herbicide that permits replanting.

FEBRUARY

• Now is the time to establish new lawns. Prepare the site for planting. If using sod, order it to arrive the day it's needed so it isn't left on pallets. If picking it up, find out when new shipments arrive so you can get fresh sod. Soak the prepared soil before planting. Fit the pieces closely together. Water it as it is laid out so it never dries out. Start a watering program.

• Mow all lawns as needed.

• Established turf won't need a lot of water at this time of year. Help extend the time between waterings by mowing at the highest recommended height.

• First-of-the-year feedings start in South Florida and work their way northward this month. Apply fertilizer when the blades are dry, then water.

• Crabgrass is a problem this month. The trick to eliminate it is to prevent seed germination. Watch for brown spot in lawns and chinch bugs in St. Augustinegrass lawns.

MARCH

• Plugs make starting a new lawn convenient. Have the planting site weed-free and prepared for planting. (Less favorable is to plant through old turf.) Purchase the plugs you can plant in a day or two. Water plugged areas after installing a tray or two. Mow as needed and give first feeding in three to four weeks.

• Lawns grow rapidly this month. Begin mowing at desired height.

• Now that weather is warmer, check irrigation system to make sure it hits all areas of the lawn. Adjust and replace heads, as needed.

• Complete all spring feedings. This is one of two times all lawn types should get a complete fertilizer with all three major nutrients. It is best to select a fertilizer with the minor nutrients also, including iron and magnesium. If lawn turns yellow immediately after feeding, it could have iron deficiency.

• Chinch bugs are becoming very active in St. Augustinegrass lawns.

APRIL

• When seeding, start with a well-prepared planting site, then scatter half the seeds in one direction and the remainder in a perpendicular direction. Rake in lightly. Many gardeners like to add a thin layer of weed-free hay or straw. Keep the seeded area moist. Light watering may be needed two or three times a day. After germination, water less frequently but longer to encourage deep roots.

• Watering requirements vary for different lawn types. Some can survive on only rain, but don't look lush. Stretch time between waterings by waiting until spots turn gray-green and leaves curl. Give a thorough soaking. Stop feedings during very dry times. Keep mower at highest setting. Do not apply weedkillers to drought-stressed lawns.

• Complete spring feedings by early in the month.

• This is last chance to do selective weed control without affecting your turf. Lawn caterpillars may be starting to appear. The most common are sod webworm, army worm, and grass looper.

MAY

• All grass types can now be added. Whether you choose seed, sod, or plugs, prepare the soil properly. Shortcuts like laying sod over dead grass or weeds may not work.

• Mowing is now your major chore. Keep the lawn mower blade sharp and mow when the lawn is dry to prevent slipping and clogging. Cut at the same recommended height year-round. Mow in different directions each time to prevent ruts. Leave clippings on the lawn.

• The rainy season may return this month. Until it does, water as usual. Recheck your irrigation system and loom for dry spots.

• Some vigorous and shallow-rooted grasses are ready for another feeding. Give Bermudagrass another complete fertilizer application and Zoysiagrass a nitrogen-only feeding.

• It's the beginning of the mole cricket season for Bermuda, Bahia, and Zoysia lawns. Other pests may be very active too. Check for chinch bugs, dollar spot, lawn caterpillars, mushrooms, and slime mold.

JUNE

• During heavy rains, suppliers may not harvest sod, so you may have to wait. Be selective and make sure you get high-quality sod. Reject any yellow sod. Don't let it sit for over twenty-four hours on a pallet.

• Summer is a great time to fill in with plugs and seed because Mother Nature often does the watering.

• Keep the mower blades sharp, especially for Bahia lawns.

• Check any brown spots that may indicate inadequate water. Make sprinkler adjustments or hand water.

• If you missed spring feeding, you can catch up with a light application during June. Some yellowing and lighter-green-colored turf can be expected. A quick remedy can be an iron-only application, or a product with iron as a major ingredient.

• Mole crickets are becoming more obvious. Check to see if chinch bugs or lawn caterpillars are present. Using weedkillers during hot weather can damage turf. Dig out, mow, or spot-kill weeds with herbicides.

JULY

• When adding new turf, prepare the soil. Eliminate weeds, till, then check acidity and adjust if necessary. Keep all new turf and seeded areas moist. Check for pests that may hitchhike on new turf.

• Give your lawn mower a midsummer checkup.

• Has your lawn turned yellow or lighter green? This is normal in July. Some gardeners don't mind and it may be more pest-resistant turf. Most gardeners prefer bright- to dark-green lawns and use an iron-only application. Two evenly spaced applications are recommended.

• Both Zoysia and Bermuda lawns are scheduled for a nitrogen-only feeding at this time.

• One disease that runs rampant during summer is "Take-All Root Rot." It affects lawns that receive too much water, are competing with other plants, have nematodes, and are under general stress. Many other problems may affect summer lawns. Check for chinch bugs, lawn caterpillars, and mole crickets. Mow, dig out, or spot-kill weeds.

AUGUST

• All lawn grasses can be established during summer by seeding, plugging, or sodding. Grasses commonly grown from seed include Bermudagrass, Carpetgrass, Bahiagrass, and Centipedegrass.

• Water newly seeded lawns whenever the surface feels dry. Gradually reduce watering to an as-needed basis after six to eight weeks. Mow as needed.

• Summer rains can be counted on for most of the water. Turn the sprinkler on periodically to make sure it is operating properly.

• Most lawn grasses will not receive a major feeding at this time, unless you forgot an earlier application.

• A healthy lawn is more resistant to pest problems, but somehow sod webworms, root rots, and others still cause some damage. Check the lawn weekly for signs of decline. Look for chinch bugs, lawn caterpillars, mole crickets, and the fungus called "Take-All Root Rot." When early damage is noted take the appropriate control. Delay use of selective weed-control products another month or two.

SEPTEMBER

• By the end of October, Bahia stops producing new shoots, but most grasses grow very well during fall. To fill bare spots, try adding plugs or sections of sod.

• Don't let up on your mowing. If you go on vacation, have someone do the job. Cutting it when overgrown is a real shock to the grass. Leave clippings on the lawn, unless they form piles due to infrequent mowing.

• September is a damp month, at least for the first few weeks. When drier weather starts you may have to do the watering.

• Most lawns are ready for the fall feeding of a complete fertilizer with nitrogen, phosphorous, and potassium.

• Summer pests will affect your lawn for at least another month. Look for declining turf weekly. Take steps to control chinch bugs, lawn caterpillars, mole crickets, and "Take-All Root Rot." Wait until the later part of the month to begin selective weed control.

OCTOBER

• It's too late to start a new permanent lawn from seed, but you can continue with sodding and plugging.

• Keep up the mowing. The grass will not stop producing new growth until the weather really gets cool. Check your lawnmower. The blade should be sharpened monthly.

• It is getting drier. However, downpours or storms may dump many inches of water, which may cause some root damage. Water as needed, letting the lawn tell you when it is dry.

• If you forgot the September feeding or have been waiting to apply a weed-and-feed product, now is the time. Bermudagrass lawns are ready for nitrogen-only feeding.

• Some pests may be slowing down. There are still a few pests that linger on: chinch bugs, lawn caterpillars, and mole crickets.

• Mowing, digging out, or spot-killing weeds with nonselective herbicides can continue. You can also apply some of the selective weed-control products. Follow label directions carefully.

NOVEMBER

• Gardeners often want to improve sandy soils for turf by adding organic matter, such as compost or peat moss. However, this can be costly and of short-lived benefit. Another way to increase water-holding ability is by adding colloidal phosphate at the rate of 1 to 2 cubic yards for 1,000 square feet lawn surface.

• Except for the northern part of the state, mowing continues as usual.

• Suddenly it's the dry time, with only a few rainy days each month. Grass grows slower during cooler, shorter days. Water when the lawn tells you it is dry with folded blades and gray-green color.

• Zoysia lawns might get an extra nitrogen feeding, but the other grasses should be fine unless you missed a feeding. Many gardeners like to increase winter hardiness of Bahia and St. Augustine lawns. Apply a potassium-only fertilizer about thirty days before the first frost.

• Looks for grubs, chinch bugs, lawn caterpillars, and mole crickets.

DECEMBER

• Most temporary winter lawns in Central and North Florida are planted with Ryegrass, but other grasses can be utilized. They are normally not planted until cool weather is here.

• Mowing is continued as needed to maintain the normal height year-round.

• It's a dry but cool time. Most lawns only need one or two waterings a week. If cold weather is expected, it's best to water the lawn to prevent drying from associated winds. Only Bermudagrass normally needs feeding at this time of year. Use a nitrogen-only fertilizer.

• Only brown patch is active now. Gardeners are more likely to experience frost or freeze damage in cooler areas of the state. After the grass is damaged, maintain a moist but not abnormally wet soil. Do not apply special feeding to encourage growth. Mow as needed at normal height. Refrain from making pesticide applications. Do not panic, most will recover with warm weather. Some gardeners overseed with Ryegrass.

ORNAMENTAL GRASSES & GROUND COVERS

for Florida

An area may be too small for trees or too narrow for shrubs, or you may want some plants to spread out rather than grow upright. You may want something green and durable in an area, but it may be too shady for turfgrass. These are all spots for a groundcover or ornamental grass.

You are probably familiar with groundcovers, which can hide bare spots, fill in for turf, and make easy maintenance out of the more-difficult-to-care-for landscape areas. They can be colorful and at times eye-catching accents.

But what about ornamental grasses? They have been around for a long time, but many gardeners just don't know what to do with them. In fact, you can use them like shrubs or groundcovers, they add a natural look to the landscape, and many are quite colorful. Most are also low maintenance, which makes them of real value in modern landscaping.

PLANNING

GROUNDCOVERS: Some grow very upright and others spread out across the soil surface. Groundcovers provide extra greenery in the landscape, often becoming transition plantings. They form a bridge between the trees, shrubs, and lawn areas.

- Many grow in shady spots where grass, shrubs, and flowers can't survive.
- Use them under trees to compete with the roots.
- Fill in the hard-to-mow spots or areas where it is difficult to maintain plantings.
- Use groundcovers in dry spots, areas of poor soil, and on banks.
- Some make excellent seaside plantings in areas where salt levels prevent other plants.
- Add them to containers for spots of greenery or combined with flowers.
- Use groundcovers to fill in large open areas where a low-maintenance planting is needed.

ORNAMENTAL GRASSES: You are familiar with turfgrasses—now meet their relatives. These are grasses with a clumping growth habit that grow tall and often have attractive inflorescence. They add a prairie and meadow look to the landscape, and are often used in naturalist settings. Ornamental grasses are usually low maintenance and provide wildlife food and homes.

- Create a view barrier or hedge from the taller-growing grasses.
- Use as an edging, or plant in a mass as a groundcover.
- Create accent features that sport showy inflorescence or colorful foliage.
- Mix together wildflowers and grasses.

PLANTING

Groundcovers and ornamental grasses aren't very particular about planting sites. Most do like a well-drained soil, but it can be sandy, clay, or peaty. Care is made a lot easier if the soil is enriched with organic matter, but in fact you can pop these plants in the ground just about anywhere. When their root systems become established, most are very drought tolerant. Here are a few tips for the best preparation:

- Spot-kill weeds with a non-selective herbicide that permits replanting.
- Till compost, peat moss, and composted manure into sandy or clay sites.
- Check the soil acidity and adjust to a slightly acid pH.
- Level the planting site . . . and you are ready to plant.

It is important to learn a little about the plant to be added to the landscape. If you are going to use more than groundcover and ornamental grass, give them adequate room to grow. Make sure you learn which is going to spread out and will need more room. Most of this information is found on plant labels or can be obtained from garden center employees. Now you can put the plants in the ground:

- Open a hole big enough to hold the root system plus some growing room.
- Position the plant so the rootball is even with the surface of the soil.
- Fill in around the rootball with water and soil.
- Add a 2- to 3-inch layer of mulch to conserve water and prevent weeds.
- Keep the planting site moist with frequent waterings.

CARE

Primary care involves guiding the growth of the new plants and keeping older plants in-bounds.

Groundcovers may need their runners directed across the soil. If needed, creeping groundcovers can have their ends pinched back to cause branching and new growth. They may also need periodic trimming to stay in-bounds. Some seem to want to invade other plants, cross walkways, or climb trees. You may need to check these plantings monthly for errant growth during warm weather.

Grasses usually get a major trimming during the winter months, after the stems have turned brown and flowering is over. Most can be cut back to near the ground to await spring growth.

WATERING

Groundcovers and ornamental grasses are a hardy bunch. Once established, most can exist with seasonal rains. After planting, however, you should give each enough water to establish a root system and begin growth out into the surrounding soils.

Hand water individual plants to maintain a moist rootball and surrounding soil. In water-resistant soil, it may be necessary to build small berms around the plants to catch and hold water.

- Apply ½ to ¾ inch water at each irrigation.
- Water daily for the first few weeks. Then reduce the waterings to every other day for a few more weeks.
- Gradually reduce the waterings to an as-needed schedule.
- Maintain a 2- to 3-inch mulch layer over the root system.
- Water during the early-morning hours.

When the plants begin growth and roots can be found in the surrounding soil, watering can be reduced to an as-needed schedule. Too much water can cause many groundcovers and grasses to develop root rot problems. Feel the soil, and if it's dry in the upper inch, it may need watering. Reapply the ½ to ¾ inch of water.

FERTILIZING

Feeding is needed only to encourage growth, usually during the establishment period. After groundcovers grow together and grasses produce spring growth, little fertilizer is needed. All can be fed lightly about three times a year to help the plantings produce new shoots, leaves, and flowers.

- Apply a 6-6-6, 10-10-10, or 16-4-8 fertilizer at the general rate for garden use once in March, July, and September if needed to encourage growth. Low or no phosphorus fertilizers are also becoming available for soils that have an adequate supply of this nutrient.
- Scatter the fertilizer over the surface of the soil or mulch in the planted area.
- Do not place the fertilizer near the stems.
- Water after feeding to move the nutrients into the soil.
- Feedings can be continued on a yearly schedule as needed to maintain growth. If the plantings are making adequate growth, feedings can be skipped. Many groundcover and ornamental grass plantings are never fertilized. They obtain nutrients from decomposing mulches and fertilizer applied to nearby plantings.

PEST CONTROL

Many groundcovers and ornamental grasses grow pest free. Seldom do you have to spray, as they can tolerate the few leaf spots and holes made by pests. Sometimes a few get out of control, and these hot spots can be spotted during walks in the landscape. Handpick from the plants or treat with natural sprays.

APHIDS: Small pear-shaped insects of numerous colors usually feeding in new growths and flower buds. They may be associated with ants that feed on their excreta. Small populations can be tolerated and may be controlled by beneficial insects. Where needed, control with a soap spray following the label instructions.

CATERPILLARS: The immature stage of moths and butterflies, of many different colors and sizes. May be found feeding on foliage and stems. Best handpicked or controlled with a natural *Bacillus thuringiensis* spray available at garden centers.

GRASSHOPPERS: Large brown to green insects with big legs that hop or fly between plants. They chew large holes in leaves or entire plant portions. Best controlled by handpicking or use of synthetic insecticides.

LEAF SPOTS: Yellow to brown spots forming on plant foliage, usually caused by a fungus. Often prevalent on weakened plants and at leaf drop time. Can usually be ignored. If needed, control with a natural copper-containing fungicide or a synthetic fungicide following label instructions.

MEALYBUGS: White to gray scale-related insects to ⅛ inch long. Often associated with sooty mold. The insects reduce plant vigor and cause decline. Control with a soap or oil spray as needed, following label instructions.

MITES: Small pinpoint-size arachnids that suck juices from foliage. May be clear or tan to reddish color. They cause leaves to yellow and drop. Control with a soap or oil spray as needed.

POWDERY MILDEW: A white fungal growth on the surface of plant foliage. Most prevalent during the spring season. Can cause yellowing and leaf drop. Usually ignored unless excessive and plant damage is noted. If needed, control with a natural copper-containing fungicide or a synthetic fungicide, following the label instructions.

SCALE INSECTS: Brown to white specks to dime size bumps on leaf surfaces and stems. Many are associated with the dark sooty mold fungus living on excreta from the insects. If minor they can be removed by hand, but most need an oil or synthetic insecticidal treatment to obtain control.

ARTILLERY PLANT
Pilea microphylla

☼ ☀ 💧

HARDINESS
Zones 10–11, with winter protection in colder areas

COLOR(S)
Finely textured foliage is lime green. Flowers are inconspicuous.

PEAK SEASON
Evergreen

MATURE SIZE
6 to 10 inches x 18 inches

WATER NEEDS
Requires well-drained soil. Water well for first few weeks if it doesn't rain. Established plants will tolerate some drought.

CARE
For groundcovers space about 18 inches apart. Fertilize lightly. Periodically remove older woody stems or renew plantings. Easily propagates from cuttings.

PROBLEMS
This durable plant holds up well in heat or cold, as well as dry and wet weather. Snails may appear but are not usually a problem. Can become weedy since seeds are easily spread. Do not mix with other groundcover plantings.

USES AND SELECTIONS
Artillery Plant fills in quickly and can be planted in ground beds or containers. Use under Palms or other trees, or near fall flowering herbaceous perennials such as Bananas.

BAMBOO
Clump-forming genera and species

☼ ☀ ☀ 🪴 💐

HARDINESS
Zones 8–11

COLOR(S)
Brown, green, yellow, black, variegated canes

PEAK SEASON
Evergreen foliage

MATURE SIZE
6 to 50 feet high

WATER NEEDS
Water new plantings regularly for first few seasons. Once established may be slightly drought tolerant. Does best if watered during drier times. Bamboo in containers, especially if rootbound, needs deep and frequent watering.

CARE
Actually a grass, Bamboo requires well-drained soil and does not tolerate soggy soil. The first year after planting it sleeps; the second year it creeps; the third year it leaps.

PROBLEMS
To avoid invasive Bamboo, plant only clump varieties, not running types. Under dry conditions canes may get scale and foliage get mites.

USES AND SELECTIONS
Most clump-forming Bamboos are tropical or subtropical, unlike the running, grove-forming ones. They come in all heights and foliage density. They can be used as accents, background plantings, hedges and screens, or to lend an Oriental flavor to a garden.

BLUE DAZE
Evolvulus glomeratus

HARDINESS
Zones 9b–11, may not survive hard freeze

COLOR(S)
Abundant flowers are blue, foliage is silvery blue-green

PEAK SEASON
Flowering and foliage year-round

MATURE SIZE
12 inches x 24 inches

WATER NEEDS
Once established, it is moderately drought resistant.

CARE
Space about 12 to 18 inches apart. Fairly fast growing in almost any soil, requiring almost no maintenance. Fertilize lightly. In partial shade it flowers a little less.

PROBLEMS
Requires good drainage. If kept too wet, fungus may set in.

USES AND SELECTIONS
This multipurpose plant blooms in the morning. It can be used in containers (draping over the sides), hanging baskets, or in the ground. It looks good cascading down a wall, in mass plantings, in borders, and as a groundcover. Since it is salt tolerant, it also serves well in seaside gardens or oceanfront balconies.

BROAD SWORD FERN
Nephrolepis biserrata

HARDINESS
Zones 9–11

COLOR(S)
Green leaves

PEAK SEASON
Year-round foliage

MATURE SIZE
To 6 feet x 4 feet

WATER NEEDS
Will take some drying but looks better when kept moist. In winter, water weekly.

CARE
Plant near soil surface. Mulch heavily. Space large ferns about 24 to 36 inches apart, smaller ferns on 12-inch centers. Apply foliar spray three or four times per year for maximum green.

PROBLEMS
Large clumps are not suitable for small yards. Two non-natives (both have little tubers) are invasive and overtaking the native *N. biserrata* (Giant Sword Fern) and *N. exaltata* (Sword or Boston Fern). Pull out the invasives whenever possible.

USES AND SELECTIONS
Plant beneath tree canopies and Palms, since they prefer some shade. The Giant grows much larger but is only hardy in South Florida. It is best suited for a spacious naturalistic garden. Numerous other species and cultivars are grown indoors and out.

BUGLE WEED
Ajuga reptans

☀ ☀ ☀ ☀ 🌾 💧

HARDINESS
Zones 8–10; Southern plantings prefer more shade.

COLOR(S)
White, pink, purple flowers; dark-green, bronze, or purple foliage

PEAK SEASON
Spring through summer

MATURE SIZE
10 inches x spreading runners

WATER NEEDS
Drought tolerant but makes best growth in enriched moist soil. Water during severe droughts. Does not tolerate soggy soil.

CARE
Plant in well-drained soil, spaced 10 to 12 inches apart. Mulch to retain moisture and control weeds. Feed in spring, summer, and early fall.

PROBLEMS
This slow grower needs good drainage and air movement to prevent root rot, especially in summer. Handpick any caterpillars and slugs or use recommended pest control. May slowly invade nearby plantings.

USES AND SELECTIONS
Useful for edging, groundcovers, and mass plantings. Best suited for smaller spaces or gardens where the dense, tight foliage covers the ground in front of or around shrubs. Use around patio stones or plant in containers.

CAST IRON PLANT
Aspidistra elatior

☀ ☀ 🌱 🪺 💧

HARDINESS
Zones 8–11; leaves are cold sensitive. Prune off any freeze-damaged leaves before spring growth begins.

COLOR(S)
Large dark-green leaves

PEAK SEASON
Foliage year-round

MATURE SIZE
2 to 3 feet x 2 feet

WATER NEEDS
Drought tolerant but makes best growth in moist soils. During severe drought, water weekly.

CARE
Space about 12 to 18 inches apart. Provide the first feeding four to six weeks after planting. Thereafter, fertilize in spring, summer, and early fall. Cast Iron Plant is slow growing, requiring almost no maintenance.

PROBLEMS
Prefers well-drained soil. Resistant to most pests. Protect from cold winter winds.

USES AND SELECTIONS
It is very durable, takes most soil conditions, and even tolerates deep shade. Dense tropical leaves make good backdrop for smaller plants or as a groundcover. Use near patios, along walkways, in containers, or wherever greenery is desired. There are varieties with variegated, striped, and spotted leaves.

CREEPING FIG
Ficus pumila
☼ ☼ ☼ ☼ 🌿 💧

HARDINESS
Zones 8–11

COLOR(S)
Bright green leaves; inconspicuous flower

PEAK SEASON
Year-round foliage

MATURE SIZE
6 to 8 inches x 3 feet or more

WATER NEEDS
Drought tolerant but makes best growth in moist soils. During severe drought, water weekly.

CARE
Space about 12 to 18 inches apart. Fertilize in spring, summer, and early fall. Juvenile plants have small oval leaves, 1 inch long. On older plants the leaves are oblong, 2 to 4 inches long.

PROBLEMS
Prefers well-drained soil. Is an aggressive plant that can climb trees, shrubs, and nearby buildings. Periodic trimming is needed to keep plantings in-bound. Pests are usually few.

USES AND SELECTIONS
Use as a groundcover leading up to turf and walkways, as a wall covering, in hanging baskets, to cover water garden rocks, or to cover topiaries. It forms an excellent backdrop for sunny annuals or shade-loving perennials. Some varieties have variegated or lobed leaves.

DWARF CARISSA
Carissa macrocarpa
☼ ☼ ☼ 🍐 🌿 🫙 💧 🌀

HARDINESS
Zones 9b–11

COLOR(S)
Dark green leaves; fragrant white flower; red fruit

PEAK SEASON
Spring and summer blooms; evergreen foliage

MATURE SIZE
1 to 2 feet x 2 to 4 feet

WATER NEEDS
Drought tolerant. During severe drought or windy conditions, water more often.

CARE
For groundcover, space about 2 feet apart in any kind of well-drained soil. Fertilize three times per year.

PROBLEMS
Most varieties of Dwarf Carissa have thorns. Use soapy water or other recommended pest control for any scale outbreaks.

USES AND SELECTIONS
This salt-tolerant plant thrives in sandy alkaline soils and is ideal for seaside plantings, with thick, waxy leaves that aren't damaged by wind. Also good for small areas around a patio or pool, in containers, or as a groundcover. The fruits are attractive to wildlife. There is also a full-sized Carissa.

ENGLISH IVY
Hedera helix

☼ ☀ ☼ ☀ 🌱 💧

HARDINESS
Zones 8–9; does not grow well in South Florida.

COLOR(S)
Green leaves

PEAK SEASON
Evergreen foliage

MATURE SIZE
10 to 12 inches x trailing

WATER NEEDS
When established is drought tolerant, although grows best in moist soil. During severe drought water weekly.

CARE
For groundcover, space about 18 to 24 inches apart in well-drained soil. Fertilize three times per year.

PROBLEMS
Prune periodically to keep in-bounds and off trees or buildings. Treat scale or mites with recommended pest control. Use landscape selections to avoid summer rot problems.

USES AND SELECTIONS
Use where quick-growing greenery is needed, even in problem areas with low-light, dry spots, or poor soil. Good on banks and areas along walkways too small for turf. Plant in shady spots as a lawn substitute or in beds. Combine with a backdrop of shade loving perennials, like Cast Iron Plant, Begonias, Bromeliads, and Ferns. It can also be trained to walls and fences, and used in hanging baskets.

FLORIDA GAMMA GRASS
Tripsacum floridana

☼ ☀ 🦋 🌱 🌿 Ⓝ 🍃 💧

HARDINESS
Zones 8–11; in colder areas turns brown in winter.

COLOR(S)
Golden-brown flowering stems; foliage green

PEAK SEASON
Summer and fall flowering; year-round foliage in most of Florida

MATURE SIZE
1 to 2 feet x 2 feet

WATER NEEDS
Once established is drought tolerant. Does best if watered during drier times. Tolerant of a wide range of conditions, from dry to wet.

CARE
Plant in enriched soil 24 to 36 inches apart. Fertilize in February, June, and September. Cut back in late winter to within 6 inches of the ground. After pruning apply winter feeding.

PROBLEMS
Pests are seldom a problem.

USES AND SELECTIONS
This Florida native is also called Dwarf Faka-hatchee Grass. Use as groundcover for native plant settings with Asters, Gaillardia, Coreopsis, Iris, and other grasses. It also grows in wetland conditions. The full-size native Fakahatchee Grass grows to 4 feet and has wider leaves.

FOUNTAIN GRASS
Pennisetum setaceum

HARDINESS
Zones 8–11; in North and Central Florida, turns brown with first frosts and freezes. Prune in late winter for rejuvenation.

COLOR(S)
Pink to purple flowering stems; foliage green

PEAK SEASON
Fall flowering; year-round foliage in warmer parts of Florida

MATURE SIZE
3 feet x 3 feet

WATER NEEDS
Once established is drought tolerant. Add mulch to retain moisture. Does best if watered during drier times.

CARE
Plant in enriched soil 24 to 30 inches apart. Fertilize in February, June, and September.

PROBLEMS
Caterpillars may appear but are seldom a serious problem.

USES AND SELECTIONS
Plant as a groundcover, a colorful landscape accent, or backdrop for annual and perennial flowers or shrubs. Can also be used for a natural Florida-style planting or as barrier planting to block unwanted views. Dwarf forms do well in containers. Other varieties include a popular purple form, which grows to 5 feet tall, plus reddish and copper-leaved forms.

KALANCHOE
Kalanchoe blossfeldiana

HARDINESS
Zones 10–11; protect from freezing

COLOR(S)
Red, yellow, orange, white, salmon blooms; dark-green scallop-edged leaves

PEAK SEASON
Winter and spring blooms; evergreen foliage

MATURE SIZE
1 foot x 1 foot

WATER NEEDS
These succulents are drought tolerant when established. Regular watering in spring and droughts makes them more robust.

CARE
Space 6 to 10 inches apart in well-drained, sandy soil. Fertilize in spring and fall. Cut back flower heads after bloom period. Start from cuttings or new plantlets that grow on leaves.

PROBLEMS
Protect from summer's intense midday sun

USES AND SELECTIONS
Kalanchoes are good for winter color in areas that are hard to water. Use as edging when highlighted against gravel, mulch, or greenery. An excellent groundcover for use around Palms, with Dusty Miller for contrast, and with taller plants such as Agave, Bromeliads, and Cycads. Use in succulent or rock gardens with Aloes, Agave, and Portulaca. There are many cultivars available.

LIRIOPE
Liriope muscari

☼ ☼ ☼ ◊

HARDINESS
Zones 8–10

COLOR(S)
Lavender, white, pink, blue flowers;
green leaves

PEAK SEASON
Summer blooms; evergreen foliage

MATURE SIZE
1 foot x 1 foot

WATER NEEDS
Drought tolerant when established. Water in
extremely dry weather.

CARE
Space 8 to 10 inches apart in well-drained
soil. Plant dwarf types closer. Some shade
is preferred for most varieties. Fertilize in
spring. Divide full container-bought plants
before planting.

PROBLEMS
May get lubber grasshoppers in early spring.
Step on them when young or use recommended pest control. Use insecticidal soaps or
horticultural oil to combat scale.

USES AND SELECTIONS
Also called Lilyturf, this slow-growing plant is
one of the best all-purpose groundcovers. It is
also useful as a border plant and when planted
with shrubs such as Crotons, Brugmansia, or
even planted with non-living garden elements
such as decks, steps, or boulders. Several cultivars are sold, varying in size, leaf coloration,
and sun tolerance.

LOPSIDED INDIAN GRASS
Sorghastrum secundum

☼ ☼ 🦋 🌱 🌿 Ⓝ 🌰 🍃 ◊

HARDINESS
Zones 8–11; throughout the state, this native
Florida grass turns golden brown in the fall and
declines after flowering.

COLOR(S)
Golden brown flowering stems; green foliage

PEAK SEASON
Fall flowering

MATURE SIZE
2 feet (foliage) 6 feet (flowers) x 2 feet

WATER NEEDS
Once established is drought tolerant. Add
mulch to retain moisture. Does best if watered
during drier times. Is tolerant of a range of conditions, including damp soils and light shade.

CARE
Plant in enriched soil 18 to 24 inches apart.
Fertilize in February, June, and September.
Give a rejuvenation pruning by late winter.

PROBLEMS
Caterpillars may appear but are seldom a serious problem.

USES AND SELECTIONS
Plant clusters to create a groundcover for
a golden fall accent or mix with perennials
including Gaillardia, Black-Eyed Susans, showy
Primrose, Goldenrod, and Asters for a native
Florida look. The large seed stalks of this native
may be used in flower arrangements.

MEXICAN HEATHER

Cuphea hyssopifolia

☀ ☀ ☀ 🌿 💧

HARDINESS
Zones 8b–11; in spring cut back freeze-damaged branchlets and they will resprout.

COLOR(S)
Purple, pink, white flowers; small green leaves

PEAK SEASON
Spring and summer blooms; evergreen foliage

MATURE SIZE
12 inches x 30 inches

WATER NEEDS
Somewhat drought tolerant when established. However, it does best in enriched, well-irrigated soil. Apply mulch and do not allow to dry out completely.

CARE
Space about 18 inches apart in well-drained soil. Fertilize three times per year.

PROBLEMS
May get nematodes. Vigorously growing plants are less susceptible. Blue metallic beetles feed on foliage and may need control.

USES AND SELECTIONS
Also called False Heather, use this dwarf shrub massed as a groundcover, as edging, or toward the front of a planting bed, where readily visible. Also looks good in a container when used alone or as edging for a larger plant. Several cultivars are available.

MONDO GRASS

Ophiopogon japonicus

☀ ☀ ☀ 💧

HARDINESS
Zones 8–10

COLOR(S)
Dark-green leaves

PEAK SEASON
Year-round foliage

MATURE SIZE
3 to 4 inches

WATER NEEDS
Drought tolerant when established. Grows in any well-drained soil. However, it does best when it is enriched. Apply mulch to retain moisture and keep down weeds. Water during severe drought.

CARE
Space about 8 to 10 inches apart. Fertilize in spring, summer, and early fall. Although slow growing, may invade nearby areas.

PROBLEMS
Does not take foot traffic. May be infected by scale. Apply recommended pesticide.

USES AND SELECTIONS
Mondo Grass can substitute for grass among steppingstones, in shady areas under trees, or on hard-to-mow slopes. The ¼-inch-wide leaves have a turflike look. Plant as filler along walkways, in large beds, or in Oriental gardens. It is an excellent groundcover for shady areas where other plants cannot take the drier or shadier conditions. Several selections are available, including a dwarf form.

MUHLY GRASS
Muhlenbergia capillaris

HARDINESS
Zones 8–11; throughout the state, this native begins to decline in the fall and turn brown after flowering.

COLOR(S)
Pink to purple flowering stems; green foliage

PEAK SEASON
Fall flowering

MATURE SIZE
3 feet x 3 feet

WATER NEEDS
Once established is drought tolerant. Add mulch to retain moisture. Does best if watered during drier times of the year.

CARE
Plant in enriched soil 12 to 18 inches apart. Fertilize in February, June, and September. Give a rejuvenation pruning by late winter to produce attractive spring growth.

PROBLEMS
Caterpillars may appear but are seldom a serious problem.

USES AND SELECTIONS
Also called Pink Muhly, it provides mounds of fine, delicate foliage with flowering stalks high above them. Good as an accent, as a border planting, in perennial gardens and natural settings, or as groundcover, even in dry areas. Enjoy the fall color when mixed with other grasses, Asters, Goldenrod, and Daisies.

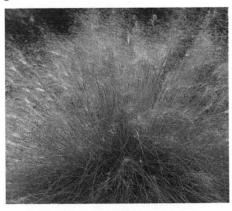

ORNAMENTAL SWEET POTATO
Ipomoea batatas

HARDINESS
Zones 9–11; often declines in winter and tends to die back in colder areas of North and Central Florida.

COLOR(S)
Foliage chartreuse, dark purple, multi-hued

PEAK SEASON
Warm-season foliage; summer blossoms

MATURE SIZE
1 to 2 feet x trailing

WATER NEEDS
Once established, underground tubers retain some moisture.

CARE
Plant in well-drained soil. Keep pruned to control the vigorous vines and to encourage branching. Grows well in full sun, but does better with some shade.

PROBLEMS
Holes caused by beetles may be ignored in this fast-growing plant. Control with insecticide. Keep the plant within bounds.

USES AND SELECTIONS
Varieties come in several colors and are often planting together for maximum visual impact. It makes a colorful groundcover in both sun and partial shade. It also does well around the rocks and sides of water gardens. Use it to make a bold statement in container plantings, especially when cascading over the edges.

PAMPAS GRASS
Cortaderia selloana

HARDINESS
Zones 8–11; in warmer areas may remain evergreen. In cooler regions turns brown after first cold.

COLOR(S)
White to pink flowering stems; green foliage

PEAK SEASON
Blooms late summer and fall

MATURE SIZE
8 feet x 8 feet

WATER NEEDS
Drought tolerant once established. Add mulch to retain moisture. Does best if watered during drier times.

CARE
Plant in enriched soil 36 to 48 inches apart. Fertilize in February, June, and September. Prune before spring growth begins.

PROBLEMS
Keep sharp foliage away from pedestrian traffic. Caterpillars may appear but are seldom a serious problem.

USES AND SELECTIONS
Form an eye-catching accent, view barrier, or garden backdrop. Add other grasses or contrasting native shrubs, perennials, and annual flowers for accents. Good to grow in coastal areas and for dried flower arrangements. Several varieties are available, including dwarf and variegated forms as well as pink foliage. The dwarf may be used in containers and perennial beds.

PURPLE LOVEGRASS
Eragrostis spectabilis

HARDINESS
Zones 8–10; foliage turns reddish in fall and declines after flowering, later in South Florida than North and Central areas.

COLOR(S)
Reddish-purple flowering stems; green foliage

PEAK SEASON
Flowers in fall

MATURE SIZE
2 feet x 2 feet

WATER NEEDS
Drought tolerant once established. Add mulch to retain moisture. Does best if watered during drier times.

CARE
Plant in enriched soil 12 to 18 inches apart. Fertilize in February, June, and September. Prune by late winter to renew spring growth.

PROBLEMS
Caterpillars may appear but are seldom a serious problem.

USES AND SELECTIONS
May be Florida's most attractive grass, forming compact mounds with flowers a foot above foliage which turns reddish each fall. Use in clusters as a groundcover, add it to natural landscape areas for a Florida look, or plant for a late summer accent of color. Mix with native shrubs or wildflowers of Gaillardia, Asters, Daisies, Goldenrod, and Black-Eyed Susans.

PURPLE QUEEN

Tradescantia pallida

☀ ☀ ☀ 🌱 💧

HARDINESS
Zones 8–11; prune out freeze damage in spring.

COLOR(S)
Pink flowers; purple foliage

PEAK SEASON
Year-round blooms and foliage

MATURE SIZE
1 foot x 1 to 2 feet

WATER NEEDS
Drought tolerant but makes best growth in enriched soil with regular watering

CARE
Plant in well-drained soil, spaced about 6 inches apart to keep out weeds. Mulch to retain moisture and control weeds. Tolerant of wide range of soils and conditions. Fertilize in spring and fall. Propagates easily from cuttings.

PROBLEMS
May take a few years to cover, so keep well mulched. Like other groundcovers, Purple Queen does not tolerate foot traffic. Snails may be a problem. Handpick or use recommended pest control.

USES AND SELECTIONS
Useful for edging, groundcovers, and mass plantings. Can be used to contrast with flowers and other foliage (like Begonias) or complement green plantings. Also called Purple Heart, it does well in containers and hanging baskets.

SAND CORDGRASS

Spartina bakeri

☀ 🌷 🌱 Ⓝ 💧 🌊

HARDINESS
Zones 8–11; foliage turns brownish and declines in fall.

COLOR(S)
Brown flowering stems; green foliage

PEAK SEASON
Flowers in May through June

MATURE SIZE
4 feet x 5 feet

WATER NEEDS
Tolerates both wetland conditions and, once established, drought.

CARE
Plant in enriched soil 48 to 60 inches apart. Fertilize in February, June, and September. Prune by late winter to renew spring growth.

PROBLEMS
Once established, this thin-leafed grass forms bunches. It needs room to spread and may not be suitable for small gardens.

USES AND SELECTIONS
Ideal for wetlands, marshlands, lakes, detention ponds, and canal-side plantings. It even tolerates brackish water. This very tolerant plant can be used to create a view barrier, accent planting, space divider, or backdrop with seasonal flowers as accents. Also use as a groundcover grouped with Dwarf Yaupon Holly, Indian Hawthorn, and Junipers. This Florida Native is also called Switchgrass and Marsh Grass.

SHORE JUNIPER
Juniperus conferta

☀ 🪹 💧 🌀

HARDINESS
Zones 8–10A

COLOR(S)
Finely textured blue-green leaves

PEAK SEASON
Year-round foliage

MATURE SIZE
2 feet x 6 to 8 feet

WATER NEEDS
Drought tolerant when established. Grows in sandy or well-drained soil.

CARE
Space about 18 inches apart. Carefree and tolerant of infertile soils. Can also be trained as a bonsai.

PROBLEMS
Do not overwater or prune. Mites occur in dry weather and may be a problem in southern areas. To combat them, use hard spray of water before trying a miticide.

USES AND SELECTIONS
Plant to cascade over sides of low containers, drape over edges of terraces, as a low-lying groundcover, or in rock gardens. The fresh Juniper smell, plus its wind, salt, and drought tolerance make this an excellent seaside planting. Mix with other salt-tolerant plants, such as Agave, Necklace Pod, and shore natives. Several cultivars are available, including trailing and compact forms.

SMALL-LEAF CONFEDERATE JASMINE
Trachelospermum asiaticum

☀ ☀ ☀ ☀ 💧

HARDINESS
Zones 8–10

COLOR(S)
Flowers inconspicuous; glossy dark-green leaves

PEAK SEASON
Year-round foliage

MATURE SIZE
1 foot x trailing

WATER NEEDS
Drought tolerant but makes best growth in moist soil. Add enrichment and mulch to retain moisture. Water where extra growth is needed and during severe drought.

CARE
Space about 24 inches apart in well-drained soil. Feed in spring, summer, and early fall.

PROBLEMS
Easy to grow but vines need periodic trimming to keep in-bounds. No serious pests.

USES AND SELECTIONS
Ideal for difficult conditions and areas, such as a lawn substitute, wall covering, ground-cover under trees, or on slopes. Only a few of this versatile plant are needed to densely fill large areas. Can be used to hang over walls or cascade from planters. It grows low and is not as rampant as common Confederate Jasmine. Varieties are available with dwarf, variegated, and reddish foliage.

WEDELIA
Wedelia trilobata

☀ ☀ ☀ ☀ 🦋 🌱 💧 🌊

HARDINESS
Zones 9–11; mow or shear freeze-damaged plants in spring.

COLOR(S)
Yellow flowers; bright green leaves

PEAK SEASON
Year-round

MATURE SIZE
12 inches x 18 inches

WATER NEEDS
Drought tolerant but makes best growth in moist soil. Water during severe droughts.

CARE
Plant in well-drained soil, spaced 10 to 12 inches apart. Mulch to retain moisture and control weeds. Feed in spring, summer, and early fall.

PROBLEMS
Plantings in deep shade do not flower as well. Wedelia grows quickly and may need periodic trimming to control. May be affected by caterpillars, grasshoppers, and mites. Handpick or used recommended pesticide. May potentially be invasive in your area.

USES AND SELECTIONS
Plant for its durable greenery and pretty flowers or use in difficult situations as turf substitute. Plant under trees, on slopes, in hard-to-mow areas, containers, or hanging baskets. Is salt tolerant and can be used in seaside plantings. Combine with Blue Salvias or Pentas.

WIREGRASS
Aristida beyrichiana

☀ 🌿 🌱 Ⓝ 🌰 🍃 💧

HARDINESS
Zones 8–11; during fall, native Wiregrass declines after producing flowers and seedheads.

COLOR(S)
Yellow flowering stems; green foliage

PEAK SEASON
Flowers in summer

MATURE SIZE
30 inches x 30 inches

WATER NEEDS
Although drought tolerant, prefers water during droughts

CARE
Plant in sandy soil 12 to 18 inches apart. Does best with minimal maintenance, which prevents weeds. Fertilizer is not needed, but a light feeding in February, June, and September can speed growth. Give a rejuvenation pruning annually.

PROBLEMS
Caterpillars may appear but are seldom a problem.

USES AND SELECTIONS
This bunch-type grass is best for coverage of wide-open spaces with wildflowers or used alone as groundcover. Since it grows in poorer soils, it's ideal for site restoration. Create a Florida look with clusters of Wiregrass beds among other native plantings of Wax Myrtle, Hollies, Asters, Goldenrod, Pines, and Palmettos. Leaves are thin and wiry, with plants eventually growing to a mounded shape.

GROUNDCOVERS

Name	Area of Florida	Height (Inches)	Light Needed	Flowers Color/Season	Best Uses
Asiatic Jasmine	NCS	08–12	Sun, shade	Seldom flowers	Under trees, open areas
Beach Morning Glory	CS	4–60	Sun	Purple/ Summer-fall	Banks, seashores
Beach Sunflower	NCS	12–24	Sun	Yellow/ Year-round	Open areas, seashores
Bromeliads	CS	6–36	Light shade	Variable/ Year-round	Under trees
Bugleweed	NC	06–10	Sun, light shade	Purple/ Summer	Under trees, edging
Cast-iron Plant	CS	18–30	Shade	Purple/Spring	Under trees
Confederate Jasmine	NCS	10–18	Sun, shade	White/Spring	Under trees, open areas
Coontie	NCS	12–24	Sun, light shade	Inconspicuous	Under trees, open areas
Creeping Fig	NCS	8–12	Sun, light shade	Inconspicuous	Banks, open areas
Daylily	NCS	12–24	Sun, light shade Spring-summer	Numerous/	Open areas
Dichondra	NCS	1–20	Sun, light shade	Inconspicuous	Under trees, open areas
Dwarf Gardenia	CS	6–12	Sun, light shade	White/Spring	Under trees, open areas
Holly Fern	CS	12–18	Shade	None	Under trees
Ivy, Algerian	NCS	6–10	Light shade, shade	Inconspicuous	Under trees, banks
Ivy, English	NC	6–10	Light shade, shade	Inconspicuous	Under trees, banks
Juniper, Chinese	NC	12–24	Sun	Inconspicuous	Banks, open areas
Juniper, Shore	NCS	12–24	Sun	Inconspicuous	Banks, open areas
Lantana, Trailing	CS	18–24	Sun	Lavender	Banks, open areas
Leatherleaf Fern	CS	18–24	Light shade, shade	None	Under trees
Lilyturf	NCS	12–24	Sun, light shade	Purple-white/ Summer	Under trees, edging
Lilyturf, Creeping	NCS	6–18	Sun, light shade	Purple-white/ Summer	Under trees, edging

ORNAMENTAL GRASSES

Name	Growth Habit	Height (Inches)	Inflorescence Color/Months	Best Use
Chalky Bluestem	Upright	12–18	White/Sept.–Oct.	Groundcover
Elliott Lovegrass	Mounded	12–24	Silver/Aug.–Sept.	Groundcover
Fakahatchee Grass	Arching	24–36	Gold/June–Sept.	Groundcover
Florida Gammagrass	Arching	12–24	Gold/Sept.–Oct.	Groundcover, accent
Fountain Grass	Arching	36–48	Purple/Aug.–Oct.	Groundcover, view barrier
Giant Plumegrass	Upright	24–30	Pink, purple/ Sept.–Oct.	Groundcover, accent
Great Dame	Upright/ creeping	6–12	Green/Year-round	Groundcover
Lopsided Indiangrass	Upright	12–24	Gold/Sept.–Oct.	Groundcover
Muhly Grass	Mounded	24–30	Pink/Sept.–Oct.	Groundcover, accent
Pampas Grass	Upright	72–96	White, pink/ Aug.–Oct.	Accent, view barrier
Pineland Dropseed	Mounded	18–24	Maroon/June–July	Groundcover
Purple Lovegrass	Mounded	12–24	Pink/Aug.–Sept.	Groundcover, accent
Sand Cordgrass	Upright	48–60	Brownish/May–June	Groundcover, view barrier
Short-spike Bluestem	Arching	12–24	Golden/Sept.–Oct.	Groundcover
Wiregrass	Upright	12–18	Bronze/June–Oct.	Groundcover

N = North Florida   C = Central Florida   S = South Florida

JANUARY

• Groundcovers and ornamental grasses may need some grooming. Trim off dead and declining portions. Trim top of brown grasses to the basal clumps, within 6 to 12 inches of the ground. Edge groundcovers creeping over walkways.

• Water new plantings daily for first few weeks. Groundcovers and ornamental grasses usually become established very quickly. Established plants only need to be watered during drought.

• In South Florida, many plants may begin growth and spring feedings can begin. Feed only if you want to encourage growth. Use a general garden fertilizer scattered across the soil surface, then water. In Central and North Florida wait until February or March.

• Most insects do not become active until growth begins. However, scale can appear at any time. Winter is a good time to control with oil spray, if applied when temperatures are above 40 degrees. Insects and sooty mold slowly flake off after a month or more.

FEBRUARY

• Most groundcovers and ornamental grasses are tough, needing little site preparation.

• Prune ornamental grasses just before their spring growth. You don't have to prune every year, but if there is a lot of brown among plants, do a major pruning job. Be sure to cover your arms and legs since grass blades are often sharp. Fertilize and mulch after pruning.

• Water new plantings every day for the first week or two. For the next few weeks, water every day or two. Hand water to make sure moisture runs through the root system. Use soaker hoses or microsprinklers where possible. Established plants usually need waterings only during drought.

• Many groundcovers and ornamental grasses get nutrients from decomposing mulches. However, a light spring feeding may benefit them.

• Aphid presence can be ignored unless populations are high. Skip the sprays if beneficial insects are present. Other pests this month are mites, mealybugs, scale, and powdery mildew.

MARCH

• If you have bare spots where turf won't grow, consider adding a groundcover.

• Very few grasses like shade. Once you have the right spot, planting is easy. With only a plant or two, just open the hole, loosen the surrounding soil, then add the plant. When planting a large area, loosen the entire area and add lots of organic matter.

• Some groundcovers need trimming to keep them off walkways and other plants. Trim them back 6 inches to a foot or more to avoid frequent pruning.

• The dry season is coming. Make sure new plantings have adequate moisture. The first month or two is usually the critical period. Older established plants only need water during drought or when plants wilt.

• If you missed the spring feeding, make a fertilizer application.

• Mites are often a problem during drier months. Other pests becoming active include aphids, caterpillars, powdery mildew, and scales.

APRIL

• Adding groundcovers and ornamental grasses can continue throughout the year, though it's best to buy creeping groundcovers early in the season. They can become entangled while waiting at the nursery. If entangled, trim to remove the problem portions.

• You can also divide groundcovers. Dig the entire plant or just a portion to divide. Set the portions in the new site at the same depth they were in the garden. Add mulch and water thoroughly. Begin feeding in two or three weeks. Full pots from the nursery can also be divided.

• Established plantings can often go a week or two without irrigation. Make sure new plantings have adequate moisture.

• No fertilizer is needed for groundcovers and grasses at this time. If you want to push growth, give plants a light feeding. Plants in containers should be fed monthly.

• Some insects are becoming active. Check for grasshoppers, mealybugs, mites, powdery mildew, and scale.

MAY

• Continue planting any groundcovers and ornamental grasses you might like. You don't have to give special soil preparation, but in large beds the addition of organic matter helps stretch the time between waterings.

• Your plants and the weeds will grow well. Reduce weeds before planting by controlling the perennial type with a nonselective herbicide that permits rapid replanting. Once your new plants are in the ground, weed control is up to you. Add a layer of mulch, use landscape fabric, apply preemergence weed control product, carefully spot-kill weeds with non-selective herbicide, and remember that hoeing and pulling are still good ways to control weeds.

• We have one more month of dry weather. Keep up regular watering of newly planted groundcovers and ornamental grasses. Once established, make periodic checks.

• Delay all feedings until summer.

• Caterpillars and aphids may be the worst pests at this time of year. Where needed, use a soap spray.

JUNE

• Continue plantings as needed.

• Check groundcovers that may be growing out of control. The start of the rainy season is when you can expect a flush of new shoots. Keep plants off walkways. Some groundcovers can climb trunks and should be trimmed back from the base a foot or more. Continue to control weeds.

• Most plantings make good growth as the rainy season returns. You may not have to do any watering. However, continue to check the soil of recently added plants.

• Fertilize now or next month. If plants are making normal green growth or you want to limit shoot development, skip this feeding. New plantings should probably receive the fertilizer. Apply only to plants with adequate soil moisture.

• With the summer rains comes the chance of rot problems. Leaf spots may also be a problem but are often minor and can be ignored. Summer pests include aphids, caterpillars, grasshoppers, and scales.

JULY

• If you don't have a lot of room but still want to enjoy groundcovers and grasses, use a small area or plant in containers. Keep up with the growth of your groundcovers. There is always trimming to do to keep them in-bounds. Many ornamental grasses begin flowering during early summer months. The inflorescence is the attractive portion and should be left on plants until it turns brown. Many gardeners like to cut and dry the flowering portions for arrangements.

• Mother Nature is probably helping with waterings. Continue to check the more recent plantings for water needs. Few established plants need special watering now.

• If you delayed or missed a planned feeding for summer, apply fertilizer now. For container gardens, apply slow-release fertilizer at planting then note on the calendar when the next will be needed.

• Most plantings can tolerate some defoliation from the caterpillars and grasshoppers. Scale may also be active.

AUGUST

• Now is the perfect time to pick groundcovers to fill small spaces. They may be little areas between the building and sidewalk, or between the pool and the grass.

• Don't let the hot summer keep you from adding plants. Just be sure you have a well-prepared site before planting. Add organic material to help hold moisture. After planting, thoroughly moisten and add a mulch layer.

• Groundcovers that bloom during spring should get their last trimming of the year.

• Regular rains should provide lots of water, but continue to check new plantings to make sure they are moist.

• Most plantings have adequate fertilizer to get them through the summer season. The next scheduled feeding for in-ground plantings is September. Continue to feed container plantings with liquid fertilizer or slow-release fertilizer when scheduled.

• Mealybugs may be found on tropical plants. Other pests and problems include caterpillars, grasshoppers, leaf spots, scale, and root rot.

SEPTEMBER

• The weather is becoming a little cooler, and it's easier to spend time outdoors. Garden centers are restocking plants for fall. Groundcovers and ornamental grasses can be planted now. Use good planting techniques.

• Try to perform the trimming of groundcovers so much of the new growth will mature before severe winter weather in central and northern portions of the state.

• As the rainy season comes to an end, you may have to take over the waterings. The only plants that usually need special watering are new plantings and container plants.

• It's time for the last feeding of the year, if needed to maintain growth and green leaves. Many plants receive adequate nutrients from feedings of surrounding plants. If they are growing vigorously, you might skip this feeding.

• Caterpillars are often heavy in fall. Where needed, handpick or apply product with *Bacillus thuringiensis*. Other active pests include grasshoppers, mites, leaf spots, and scales.

OCTOBER

• This is the perfect time to get outdoors and enjoy the landscape, and it's ideal for making new plantings.

• Complete all needed trimming this month. Many ornamental grasses will be making their fall display. If you wish, cut some of the long inflorescence to dry or use in fall displays. When the flower stalks fade, many turn brown and can be cut from the plants as needed.

• Check new plantings regularly for needed moisture.

• If you missed or delayed the September feeding, there is still time to supply nutrients.

• Gardeners may begin noticing many leaf spots on deciduous groundcovers during fall. Some are getting ready for winter and leaf spotting as the leaves begin to drop is normal. Even some evergreen types, including Mandevilla, are not as vigorous during fall and may develop brown to yellow patches. This is normal. Pests you might be concerned about are caterpillars, grasshoppers, mites, and scale insects.

NOVEMBER

• It continues to be a good time for planting. Where possible, till up planting sites to add a number of groundcovers or grasses. However if only adding one or two plants, soil preparation is not needed.

• Most plant growth is slowing because of cool weather and shorter days. Your job is to remove groundcover growths that may be overgrown or affecting other plantings. Continue to control weeds.

• Cool weather means slower growth and less waterings. As always, continue to check new plantings to make sure soil is moist. Well-established plants seldom need watering, except in containers.

• Feeding is over for the year, except in containers. Continue fertilizing monthly with liquid or apply slow-release fertilizer as scheduled.

• Mites can remain a pest during fall. Luckily groundcovers are fairly resistant. Mealybugs may develop, especially in shady spots. Soap sprays are used for both mites and mealybugs. Caterpillars and grasshoppers may still be around.

DECEMBER

• Shop your garden center early because they often reduce stock in December for holiday plants. You can keep plants in containers for a while if the time is not right for planting.

• Little care is needed. If you don't like the meadow look of browning flower stems on grasses, cut them back.

PERENNIALS
for Florida

J ust about every landscape should have a flower garden, but you have to decide how much work yours is going to entail. Perennials help make your planning easy by producing new growth and flowers for more than just a few months.

During the 1970s and much of the 1980s, annual flowers ruled, and there was just a sprinkling of perennials at garden centers. Perhaps it was because Florida had so many great annuals, or maybe everyone just forgot about the many flowers that last more than a year—but perennials almost became "extinct." Then all of a sudden, during the early to mid-1990s, perennials were rediscovered. It was almost a plant revolution when gardeners decided they were tired of changing the flower beds every three or four months. They wanted something permanent, and they turned back to perennials.

You are not going to find here many perennial gardens that resemble those of the Northern states, whose gardens are planted along paths or by rocks on the side of a hill with flowers that come into bloom during the early spring months. Florida's perennials are in bloom most of the year and may be intermingled with annuals, trees, and shrubs. (You can add the rocks and a berm or two.)

There is a lot of variety among Florida perennials. Some are quite traditional and grow for years with normal care. Others are treated as long-living annuals, since they may need more cold than Florida can provide. Many are tropical and produce almost continuous bloom for years. Every now and then in North and Central Florida some tropical perennials are severely damaged by cold, but they usually grow back from buds near the ground.

The definition of a perennial is not precise—you probably know it as a plant that lives for more than two years. In this chapter a perennial is broadly defined as a long-living herbaceous plant. We may add a woody plant or two that fits in this category, but we are going to exclude the bulbs, shrubs, roses, and groundcovers presented in other chapters.

PLANNING

Use perennials to help make your planning easier. They produce new growth and flowers for more than just a few months. This means you can count on an attractive planting for a year or two before major bed renovation is needed.

Decide on where you need color in the landscape and then see where perennials might help. Remember, perennials come in all heights and widths, so they can squeeze into small spaces or be clustered together to fill an entire bed. Here are a few ways to use perennials in the Florida landscape:

- Plant a garden devoted only to perennials.
- Mix perennials and annuals in a garden.
- Add perennials to shrubby borders.
- Edge your walkways with bushy perennials.

- Create small spots of color with just one species along walkways.
- Use the plants to accent water features.
- Fill planters and hanging baskets with perennials, or use them in combination with annuals.
- Add color to shady spots in the landscape.

One thing to keep in mind is that perennials normally give the best displays when clustered together. Try planting groups of three, five, seven, or more of the same type in any one flower bed. Use the taller perennials in the back or center of the bed, and the short or creeping types along the edges.

Here is another thought: Why not use perennials as the base planting for your garden and fill in small areas with annual color throughout the year? This mixes the best of the two plant groups and gives extra seasonal color.

PLANTING

Perhaps you are planting perennials simply because you like the flowers. Many gardeners also add them to the landscape to eliminate having to constantly till and replant flower beds. Whatever your reasons for growing perennials, it makes sense to give the planting site your best care from the beginning.

First check the perennial list on pages 212 and 213. Find a site with the proper light level for the plants you would like to grow. It's important to put the right plant in the right place.

Select a site without a lot of competition: if there are impermeable tree roots in the ground or a runaway hedge nearby, your perennials are probably not going to do well. You need a garden site that can provide years of good growing conditions. Here are the steps to good soil preparation:

1. Control all weeds with a nonselective herbicide that permits replanting. Many weeds can also be dug out, but just a few left-behind sprigs can quickly start a new infestation.
2. Till the soil deeply to disperse weed seeds and pest problems into the ground.
3. Work lots of organic matter into sandy and clay soils. This helps ensure good root growth, some water retention, available nutrients for plant growth, and good drainage to promote attractive perennials. Use peat moss, compost, and similar materials.
4. Many gardeners like to add composted manure or a light scattering of fertilizer before planting.

Florida perennials can be planted year-round. You can pick them out in bloom at garden centers, use plants shared with neighbors, or grow them from seed. In most cases, it's best to start seeds in containers and move them to the garden when they are an appropriate size.

After planting, most perennials like a mulch to control weeds and maintain a moist soil at a uniform temperature. Keep the mulch back from the base of the plants.

WATERING

Keeping a moist soil is especially important during the establishment period. New garden perennials have a limited root system that needs time to grow out into the surrounding soil. It's best to water daily for the first week or two. After that, the perennial garden can be placed on an as-needed watering schedule.

- Water when the surface soil begins to feel dry to the touch.
- Use the plants as a guide. If they wilt, a good watering is probably needed.
- Get to know the type of plants you are growing. Some, like blanket flower, butterfly weed, and lantana, are very drought tolerant. Others, including hosta and violets, like a moist soil.

- Maintain a 2- to 3-inch layer of mulch over the soil surface. Some good mulch materials are old hay, pine needles, barks, and coarse compost.
- When water is needed, apply ½ to ¾ inch.
- Use soaker hoses and micro sprinklers where possible.

FERTILIZING

Most perennials are not heavy feeders. You can use a general fertilizer, following a schedule, or give the plants a feeding when either growth slows or leaf color begins to fade. Many perennials would rather have frequent feedings at first, then have the diet reduced as they reach maturity. You can also use slow-release fertilizer products to take some of the work out of feeding the plants. Several brands are available at local garden centers.

- When growth is desired, apply a general fertilizer every six to eight weeks, March through November. Use slow-release products according to label directions.
- Place mature plantings on a maintenance schedule of feedings in March, June, and September.
- Scatter the fertilizer over the surface of the soil or mulch, and water-in.
- Do not remove the mulch layer to feed the plants.

PEST CONTROL

Perennials are usually very tough and durable. You may experience aphids, leafminers, whiteflies, and/or grasshoppers as noted on other garden plantings. A spray may be needed, or simply learn to tolerate a few insects. Some plants have scale problems; these are more serious and need immediate control. Get to know your plants, then treat major pest problems as noted.

- Handpick as many pests as possible and destroy them.
- You may have to remove some plant portions to control major infestations.
- Control aphids and whiteflies with insecticidal soaps available at garden centers.
- Control scale with oil sprays available at garden centers.
- Control caterpillar infestations with natural *Bacillus thuringiensis* sprays.
- Use synthetic sprays for insects, mites, and diseases only as a last resort and according to label directions.

BEEBALM
Monarda didyma

HARDINESS
Zones 8–9

COLOR(S)
Red, white, pink, pastel flowers

PEAK SEASON
Blooms mid- to late-summer

MATURE SIZE
2 to 3 feet x 1 to 2 feet

WATER NEEDS
Prefers moist soil, but do not overwater.

CARE
Easy to grow when provided with rich well-drained soil.

PROBLEMS
Leaves often affected by mildew. Provide adequate air circulation and distance between plants to avoid it. Newer cultivars may be resistant.

USES AND SELECTIONS
Beebalm's big showy flower heads are irresistible to hummingbirds, and bees and butterflies also visit. Plant in wildflower and butterfly gardens. The leaves are aromatic, like its cousin the mint. Common names include Oswego Tea and Bergamont. Flowers of the species are red. Horse Mint (*M. punctata*) is a good native for North and Central Florida. New, improved cultivars have bigger flowers and sturdier growth. There are also shorter varieties suitable for smaller gardens. Good selections are 'Aquarius', 'Cambridge Scarlet', 'Petite Wonder', and 'Snow Queen'.

BEGONIA
Begonia spp.

HARDINESS
Zones 9b–11

COLOR(S)
Foliage all shapes, textures, colors, often boldly patterned; pink, red, white flowers

PEAK SEASON
Blooms spring and summer, year-round in warm areas; year-round foliage

MATURE SIZE
10 inches to 4 feet x 10 inches to 4 feet

WATER NEEDS
Likes constant moisture with excellent drainage. Keep well watered.

CARE
Beds must drain perfectly, yet retain water. Add sand, pea rock, limestone, or orchid mix to potting soil. Don't overload with organic matter. Mulch. Use slow-release fertilizer. Grow in protected areas in North and Central Florida. Cover in cold weather or grow in containers and bring inside. May come back after damaged by cold. Tuberous Begonias do not do well in South Florida.

PROBLEMS
Handpick snails

USES AND SELECTIONS
Tuberous, Angel-wing, Rex, and Rhizomatous are some Begonia classes. Use in raised beds, containers, as understory plantings in shade, or around a pond. They make excellent companions for Ferns, Bromeliads, or Aroids.

BLANKET FLOWER
Gaillardia x grandiflora

HARDINESS
Zones 8–9

COLOR(S)
Yellow, red and combination flowers

PEAK SEASON
Blooms summer and fall

MATURE SIZE
2 to 3 feet x 1 to 2 feet

WATER NEEDS
Drought tolerant

CARE
Plant forms tidy clumps of somewhat fuzzy foliage. Once established it is carefree. This rugged plant is tolerant of poor soil, drought, and heat.

PROBLEMS
Trouble-free foliage

USES AND SELECTIONS
Use cheerful Blanket Flower for low-maintenance borders with other bright colors, including yellow daisies or coreopsis, or red Salvia. Solid color versions are also available. Some of the best are wine-red 'Burgundy', which combines beautifully with blue perennials and the new 'Mesa Yellow', a prolific, shorter cultivar that is a 2010 All-America Selection. Use in xeriscape plantings, wildflower beds, butterfly gardens, in the front of borders, in container displays, or along walkways. 'Goblin' is a dwarf cultivar.

BLUE PHLOX
Phlox divaricata

HARDINESS
Zones 8–9

COLOR(S)
Light blue, lavender, pink flowers

PEAK SEASON
Blooms late spring through summer

MATURE SIZE
1 to 1½ feet x 1 foot

WATER NEEDS
Prefers moist conditions

CARE
Needs humus-rich, well-drained soil and mulch to protect shallow root system. Too much sun may cause the plant to slow its growth. Feed in spring with rose fertilizer if soil isn't rich enough.

PROBLEMS
With too much moisture and humidity, it may develop mildew. Provide plenty of air circulation, good drainage, and space between plants to help prevent it.

USES AND SELECTIONS
Blue Phlox is perfect for the front of a shade border, wildflower garden, or as a woodland groundcover. The numerous little flowers are scented, explaining one of its common names, Wild Sweet William. Another name is Wild Blue Phlox. Several varieties are available. 'Chattahooche' is lavender-blue with dark-purple centers, and the prolific white-flowered 'Fuller's White'.

BUSH DAISY
Gamolepis chrysanthemoides

HARDINESS
Zones 8b–11. If frozen, regrows from base each spring.

COLOR(S)
Yellow flowers

PEAK SEASON
Blooms year-round in South and much of Central Florida

MATURE SIZE
2 to 4 feet x 3 to 4 feet

WATER NEEDS
Somewhat drought tolerant. However, flowers best with regular waterings.

CARE
Plant in any soil. Requires little care. Growth habit is loose, so trim occasionally to encourage dense growth.

PROBLEMS
Only nematodes are serious concern.

USES AND SELECTIONS
Also called African Bush Daisy and Daisy Bush. Use this rounded plant as a tall colorful groundcover, small shrub, or perennial border. The delicate leaves are fern-like. Bush Daisy also makes a nice specimen or foundation planting. It can be used in xeriscape and butterfly gardens, or in front of a fence where its loose growth is not important. A similar plant, *Euryops pectinatus*, is sometimes used instead of Bush Daisy because it is more compact and blooms better.

BUTTERFLY WEED
Asclepias spp.

HARDINESS
Zones 8–11. If freezes back, usually returns in spring.

COLOR(S)
Red, orange, and yellow flowers

PEAK SEASON
Blooms spring to fall

MATURE SIZE
1 to 4 feet x 1 to 3 feet

WATER NEEDS
Drought tolerant once established. Many species also tolerate moist and sometimes wet soils.

CARE
Plant in any soil. The *Asclepias* family is easy to grow, with more than twenty species native to Florida. Plants may be grown as perennials or annuals. Feed occasionally to encourage flowering.

PROBLEMS
Aphids may infest the leaves. Butterfly Weed readily self seeds. *Asclepias* are poisonous if ingested.

USES AND SELECTIONS
Plant Butterfly Weed (also called Milkweed) in perennial borders, wildflower gardens, and for naturalizing. This exceptional butterfly plant is important as a nectar source and larval food. It is a foundation plant for most butterfly gardens. The unusual pods are used in dried arrangements. *A. tuberose* is a non-native species often sold in the trade.

CAST IRON PLANT
Aspidistra elatior

HARDINESS
Zones 8–11. Leaves are cold sensitive. Prune off any freeze-damaged leaves before spring growth begins.

COLOR(S)
Large dark green leaves

PEAK SEASON
Foliage year-round

MATURE SIZE
2 to 3 feet x 2 feet

WATER NEEDS
Drought tolerant but makes best growth in moist soils. During severe drought, water weekly.

CARE
Space about 12 to 18 inches apart. Provide the first feeding four to six weeks after planting. Thereafter, fertilize in spring, summer, and early fall. Cast Iron Plant is slow growing, requiring almost no maintenance.

PROBLEMS
Prefers well-drained soil. Resistant to most pests. Protect from cold winter winds.

USES AND SELECTIONS
It is very durable, takes most soil conditions, and even tolerates deep shade. Dense tropical leaves make good backdrop for smaller plants or as a groundcover. Use near patios, along walkways, in containers, or wherever greenery is desired. There are varieties with variegated, striped, and spotted leaves.

CHRYSANTHEMUM
Chrysanthemum hybrids

HARDINESS
Zones 8–9

COLOR(S)
Red, pink, gold, yellow, rust flowers

PEAK SEASON
Blooms late summer, fall, and sometimes spring. Often used as a fall annual.

MATURE SIZE
2 to 3 feet x 2 to 3 feet

WATER NEEDS
Prefer moist soil, but tolerate some dryness. However, keep moist during the heat of summers, especially in containers.

CARE
Plants early so their roots get established for a long healthy season. In summer, pinch back or remove buds to encourage larger flowers in fall.

PROBLEMS
Relatively pest and disease free. In dry conditions spider mites may occur.

USES AND SELECTIONS
Chrysanthemums (commonly called Mums) come in an incredibly wide range of colors and shapes. There are hundreds of cultivars, with new selections being developed frequently. Plant in groups for best impact. They also work well in containers, for cut flowers, and especially in small gardens. They never seem to give the good displays of northern gardens.

CONEFLOWER

Echinacea purpurea

HARDINESS
Zones 8–10

COLOR(S)
Lavender flowers

PEAK SEASON
Blooms spring to fall

MATURE SIZE
2 to 4 feet x 1 to 2 feet

WATER NEEDS
Somewhat drought tolerant in partial shade

CARE
Plant in well-drained soil. This low care Florida native has excellent heat tolerance. Cut back in early summer to encourage bushier growth and more flowers. Tends to be a short-lived perennial that needs replanting.

PROBLEMS
Old blossom heads should be removed to ensure a long flowering period.

USES AND SELECTIONS
Interest in Coneflowers has grown dramatically as interest in low-maintenance, drought-tolerant plants has increased. Use Coneflowers along walkways, in borders, in mixed beds, in wildflower gardens, for naturalizing, containers, butterfly gardens, and xeriscape landscapes. They make excellent cut flowers. New varieties are regularly introduced with larger bloom size, more compact growth, and increased fragrance. 'Sunrise', 'Sunset', and 'Sundown' are orange, gold, and red. There is even an unusual multi-petalled selection called 'Doubledecker'.

COREOPSIS

Coreopsis spp.

HARDINESS
Zones 8–10

COLOR(S)
Yellow flowers

PEAK SEASON
Blooms summer

MATURE SIZE
1 to 3 feet x 2 to 3 feet

WATER NEEDS
Drought tolerant

CARE
This carefree plant withstands intense heat and low soil fertility. It doesn't even mind salt and wind. It keeps providing masses of flowers for months on end.

PROBLEMS
Problem free

USES AND SELECTIONS
Interest in Coreopsis (also called Tickseed) has increased as interest in native and drought-tolerant plants has grown. They fit in and among all sorts of other perennials, creating an appealing look that is lush and casual. In addition, their sunny yellows complement other garden colors very well. Use them along walkways as well as in borders, mixed beds, wildflower gardens, containers, butterfly gardens, and xeriscape landscapes. Coreopsis is the Florida State Wildflower, with thirteen native species. New varieties are regularly introduced with varying petals shapes, different growth habits, and more intense colors.

CROSSANDRA

Crossandra infundibuliformis
(synonym: *C. undulifolia*)

☀️ ☀️ ☀️ 🦋 🐦 🌿 🪴 🌴

HARDINESS
Zones 9–11

COLOR(S)
White, orange, red, salmon, yellow flowers

PEAK SEASON
Blooms summer through fall

MATURE SIZE
To 3 feet x to 3 feet

WATER NEEDS
Somewhat drought tolerant, but blooms best with regular moisture

CARE
Plant in well-drained, enriched soil. It loves rain, heat, and humidity. Fertilize monthly with balanced fertilizer from March to October. Grow as a small shrub or trim regularly to be bushy and compact.

PROBLEMS
The species produces seeds that readily self-sow and can become weedy. Pull up all the seedlings or use a sterile cultivar like 'Orange Marmalade'.

USES AND SELECTIONS
The brilliant Crossandra flowers stand out against their glossy, dark-green foliage. They also attract butterflies. Crossandra is one of several plants with the common name of Firecracker Plant or Firecracker Flower. Use this showy plant in borders, as a groundcover, or in containers and planters. Cultivars include 'Orange Marmalade', 'Tropic Flame', and 'Florida Sunset'.

FIRESPIKE

Odontonema cuspidatum
(synonyms: *O. strictum* and *O. tubiforme*)

☀️ ☀️ ☀️ 🦋 🐦 🌿 💧

HARDINESS
Zones 8–11. In colder regions dies back in winter and resprouts in spring.

COLOR(S)
Crimson flowers on spikes

PEAK SEASON
Blooms midsummer through winter

MATURE SIZE
To 6 feet x 6 feet or more

WATER NEEDS
Tolerates short periods of drought. Grows best with weekly watering during dry times. Blooms best with more regular moisture.

CARE
Plant in well-drained, enriched soil. This prolific bloomer does well even in partial shade. It spreads by underground root suckers, forming clumps. Stems also root when they fall to the ground. These thickets can be controlled by pruning. Pruning can also be used to encourage denser growth on the sparse stems.

PROBLEMS
Usually trouble free

USES AND SELECTIONS
Use Firespike as an accent, in mixed borders, and as background planting. Other common names are Cardinal's Guard and Scarlet Flame. Ideal for butterfly gardens and locations to enjoy hummingbirds attracted by the red tubular flowers.

FOUR O'CLOCK
Mirabilis jalapa

HARDINESS
Zones 8–11. Mulch in colder areas for winter frost protection.

COLOR(S)
Red, magenta, pink, yellow, white, and bicolor flowers

PEAK SEASON
Blooms summer

MATURE SIZE
2 to 3 feet x 2 to 3 feet

WATER NEEDS
Regular moisture during growing season. Reduce watering in winter.

CARE
Plant in any soil. Do best in full sun. These fast-growing, tough perennials may last long after other plants. They develop deep tubers.

PROBLEMS
Essentially trouble free. Four O'Clock readily self-sows and if not controlled when seedlings are young, tubers are difficult to remove. Plants are poisonous if ingested.

USES AND SELECTIONS
The easy-to-grow Four O'Clock has a long southern gardening tradition. Use in beds and borders. The sweetly scented flowers last from evening (not four o'clock) until the next morning. They are still colorful when not open. Use in gardens around patios or entryways, where the fragrance and flowers can be appreciated after hours.

GERBERA DAISY
Gerbera jamesonii

HARDINESS
Zones 9–11

COLOR(S)
White, cream, pink, red flowers

PEAK SEASON
Blooms summer through fall

MATURE SIZE
To 18 inches x 12 inches

WATER NEEDS
Allow to dry out between waterings. Avoid being soggy.

CARE
Plant in deep, well-drained, enriched soil. Prefers full sun. Feed monthly throughout summer or use time-release fertilizer. Use fertilizer containing iron and magnesium.

PROBLEMS
Treat as an annual in areas with prolonged freezes or plant in containers and provide winter protection. The plant can rot (newer varieties have most problem) when watered too much or planted too deep. Handpick caterpillars and cutworms.

USES AND SELECTIONS
Use as a border plant, in containers, or anywhere bright color is needed. Plant a bed with a single color or mix-n-match. Also called Transvaal Daisy, Gerberas make long-lasting cut flowers. There are single and double flower forms, with blooms reaching 7 inches across. Select old garden varieties for best growth and in-ground planting.

GOLDENROD
Solidago cultivars

HARDINESS
Zones 8–11

COLOR(S)
Yellow flowers

PEAK SEASON
Blooms summer to fall

MATURE SIZE
1 to 6 feet, depending on species and cultivar

WATER NEEDS
Tolerates moist to dry conditions

CARE
Plant in any well-drained soil; even poor soils produce bountiful spires of golden flowers. These perennials are easy to care for and tough enough for roadside plantings.

PROBLEMS
Erroneously blamed for causing hay fever

USES AND SELECTIONS
Goldenrod is a glorious sight and the sunny color complements other mid- and late-season bloomers. It's especially beautiful with blue flowers. Besides nineteen native Florida species, there are some terrific cultivars. The best ones are well behaved and stay in-bounds for perennial borders. Plant Goldenrod in mixed or single species wildflower gardens and in native plant gardens. 'Fireworks' is a compact, clump-forming plant, 3 to 4 feet tall. 'Golden Fleece' is a dwarf selection, less than 2 feet tall, that's ideal for smaller garden spaces.

HOSTA
Hosta cultivars

HARDINESS
Zones 8–9a

COLOR(S)
Green, blue-green, chartreuse, variegated foliage; lavender, white flowers

PEAK SEASON
Bloom period varies by species and cultivar

MATURE SIZE
1 to 2 feet x 1 to 5 feet

WATER NEEDS
Requires constant moisture, especially during summer

CARE
Plant in enriched soil. Hosta only grows in northern Florida since it doesn't tolerate extended heat and humidity. Check for the cultivars that grow well in your area.

PROBLEMS
Slugs and snails are common pests. Use baits to control them.

USES AND SELECTIONS
Plant Hosta (also called Plantain Lily) in shady borders, mass plantings, containers, and along walkways. Use where their broad leaves contrast or complement other plants. With hundreds of Hosta cultivars available, they can even be used to provide an unusual accent of blue-green or lime-green foliage in mass plantings. Hosta hybridizers continually create remarkable new patterns. Sometimes the flowers, which appear on an upright spike, are fragrant.

IMPATIENS
Impatiens walleriana

HARDINESS
Grow well throughout Florida for most of the year. North and Central Florida gardeners may need to provide winter protection, but cold-affected Impatiens may grow back.

COLOR(S)
All color flowers

PEAK SEASON
Blooms year-round

MATURE SIZE
10 to 24 inches tall

WATER NEEDS
Space 12 to 14 inches apart in thoroughly moistened soil. Once established, water when soil feels dry. Container-grown plants may need more frequent watering.

CARE
If Impatiens become tall and lanky, prune back to within 1 foot of the ground.

PROBLEMS
May have caterpillars, slugs, and mites. Hand-pick or use approved pesticide. Nematodes may also be a pest. There is no easy control, so replace soil in infested beds or grow plants in containers.

USES AND SELECTIONS
Impatiens provide color in areas where other plants refuse to bloom. Using Impatiens is an economical way to fill large areas with color. Can be planted in ground beds, containers, and hanging baskets.

LEATHER FERN
Acrostichum danaeifolium

HARDINESS
Zones 9–11

COLOR(S)
Dark-green foliage

PEAK SEASON
Year-round foliage

MATURE SIZE
4 to 10 feet x 3-plus feet

WATER NEEDS
Keep moist.

CARE
Although nutritional requirements are low, a small amount of slow-release or organic fertilizer is beneficial. All Ferns like occasional fish emulsion. If grown in containers, submerge in a pond or caulk the drainage holes to keep growing medium wet to moist.

PROBLEMS
May get scale. Wipe off with alcohol soaked cotton. Handpick any snails. Protect from freezing.

USES AND SELECTIONS
The beefiest and largest native Fern in the United States. The fronds are wide and stiff, not delicate. These large Ferns look good at a natural pool's edge, a canal bank, a lakefront, or other low-lying area where its feet stay wet. For streamside, they are made to order. Use in native plant gardens with moist zones. A single clump at a pond's edge makes a bold statement.

PENTAS
Pentas lanceolata

HARDINESS
Zones 9–11. Use as annual in colder locations.

COLOR(S)
Pink, white, lilac, red blooms

PEAK SEASON
Spring through summer

MATURE SIZE
To 30 inches x 18 inches

WATER NEEDS
Water new plantings daily for a week or two. Taper off to water once or twice weekly.

CARE
These rapid, easy-care growers need good drainage. Use slow-release fertilizer at planting time, and again every three or four months in South Florida. Cut back in early spring to rejuvenate. They get woody and leggy after three or four years. Take cuttings to replace old plants with new. Cover during freezes for protection in Central Florida.

PROBLEMS
Control spider mites with water spray or horticultural oil.

USES AND SELECTIONS
Mix with other butterfly plants. Use a wave of single color for best effect and to attract butterflies. Plant in a meadow with other wildflowers. Come in regular and dwarf sizes, so use as background shrubs or foreground flowers.

PERIWINKLE
Catharanthus roseus

HARDINESS
Zones 9–11

COLOR(S)
Pink, white, rose, purple flowers

PEAK SEASON
Year-round blooms

MATURE SIZE
To 24 inches x 12 inches or more

WATER NEEDS
Keep new plantings moist for first month or so, then gradually taper off watering. Don't water too much.

CARE
Prefers dry, sandy soil. Don't pamper. Relatively drought resistant when established and very heat tolerant. A teaspoon of slow-release fertilizer at planting is sufficient. When small, they look best for neat gardens. When larger, they sprawl and look less tidy. Cut back when too straggly.

PROBLEMS
Poisonous if ingested or smoked. Newer selections less susceptible to rot problems.

USES AND SELECTIONS
Plant in beds, containers, and window boxes. Use as edging, groundcover, or camouflage for leggy shrubs. White Periwinkles are also visible at night. There are many beautiful selections with different colors and growth habits. These beautiful, rugged plants were among the first flowering plants traded by South Florida pioneers.

PLUMBAGO
Plumbago auriculata

HARDINESS
Zones 9–11. Prune freeze damage after spring growth begins.

COLOR(S)
Cobalt-blue flowers

PEAK SEASON
Blooms spring through summer

MATURE SIZE
3 to 4 feet x 8 feet

WATER NEEDS
Moderately drought tolerant when established. Water during dry season.

CARE
Plumbago blooms best with fertilizer. Apply three times per year. The plant falls over and roots, so prune to keep in-bounds. Or, tie to a support such as arbors or gates for a dramatic effect. Prune back hard at the end of winter.

PROBLEMS
Provide good air movement to avoid summer leaf and stem diseases.

USES AND SELECTIONS
Use as a short shrub or giant groundcover. The color complements magenta Bougainvillea or yellow flowers. Because Plumbago is low and sprawls, it can serve as an underplanting to disguise legginess of taller shrubs. The mounding shape also works well at an entry gate or in containers and planters. Red and white varieties are available.

POINSETTIA
Euphorbia pulcherrima

HARDINESS
Zones 9–11. Frosts and freezes damage stems and foliage.

COLOR(S)
Red, white, pink bracts that look like flowers

PEAK SEASON
Winter

MATURE SIZE
Varies

WATER NEEDS
Keep moderately moist, but never wet

CARE
Move holiday Poinsettias outdoors when the weather warms. Before planting in full sun, gradually accustom it to increasing light levels. Plant in enriched, well-drained soil. Prune to within 12 to 18 inches of the ground in early spring after blooming is over and frost danger has passed. Fertilize monthly during growing season. Prune until early September to get a compact plant. Pinch back all new growth to have only four leaves.

PROBLEMS
Do not plant near night lights, which affect the bud formation. Some people are sensitive to the sap of Poinsettias.

USES AND SELECTIONS
The species grows to 10 feet and has less showy bracts (often thought to be the flowers). Holiday plants are cultivars that can be grown outdoors.

RUDBECKIA
Rudbeckia spp.

HARDINESS
Zones 8–9

COLOR(S)
Yellow, orange, and black flowers

PEAK SEASON
Blooms summer and fall

MATURE SIZE
2 to 3 feet x 2 feet

WATER NEEDS
Drought tolerant but also tolerates higher moisture levels

CARE
Needs well-drained soil. Salt tolerant. Require little care. Blooms on many varieties don't require staking. Tends to be a short-lived perennial that needs replanting.

PROBLEMS
Pests and diseases aren't usually a problem on most varieties, especially natives.

USES AND SELECTIONS
Rudbeckias (also called Black-Eyed Susans) are long blooming with numerous bright flowers. Plant as a border, for cut flowers, or as a mixer in perennial displays with plants like Beebalm, Daylilies, Ornamental Grasses, and Lavender. Also good for wildflower and native plant gardens. There are numerous variations, including the PPA Plant of the Year for 1999, *R. fulgida* var. *sullivantii* 'Goldsturm', which has larger flowers. *R. hirta* is one of several species native to Florida.

SALVIA
Salvia splendens

HARDINESS
Zones 8–10. Provides almost year-round color throughout Florida. In Southern regions Salvia grows as a perennial. In Central Florida cover during cold weather, and in Northern areas it is likely to be damaged by frosts and freezes.

COLOR(S)
Bright red, salmon, pink, purple, white flowers

PEAK SEASON
Blooms year-round

MATURE SIZE
8 to 18 inches tall

WATER NEEDS
Space 10 to 16 inches apart in thoroughly moistened soil. Once established, wait until soil surface feels dry, then soak.

CARE
When buying, avoid potbound plants. Keep plants attractive and encourage new shoots by periodically removing old flower heads and extra-long stems. May reseed.

PROBLEMS
Handpick caterpillars, mites, and slugs

USES AND SELECTIONS
Also called Scarlet Sage, it can be planted in ground beds and containers. Beds of different types and colors display well, as do plantings with Dusty Miller, Marigold, and Petunia. The red-flowered native Tropical Sage (*S. coccinea*) grows well in landscapes.

SHASTA DAISY
Leucanthemum x superbum

☀ ☀ ☀ 🌱 🌿 💧 🏆

HARDINESS
Zones 8–9

COLOR(S)
White flowers with orange centers

PEAK SEASON
Blooms spring and summer

MATURE SIZE
1 to 3½ feet x 2 to 3 feet

WATER NEEDS
Drought tolerant

CARE
Plant in enriched, well-drained soil. Easy to grow well.

PROBLEMS
Performs better in cooler summers, so provide afternoon shade and water during summer. Grow as an annual in southern Florida.

USES AND SELECTIONS
There are many excellent cultivars to choose from. 'Becky' is long blooming and stands up to heat and humidity. It won the 2003 PPA Award. Shorter varieties, like 'Esther Read', are also available. The long-blooming 'Aglaia' is fringed, for a totally different look. Use for long-lasting cut flowers, mass plantings, and in butterfly gardens. Shasta Daisy's white blooms also make beautiful additions to night gardens and those using only white flowers. Find a locally adapted selection for best growth in your area of Florida.

SOCIETY GARLIC
Tulbaghia violacea

☀ ☀ 🍐 🌿 💧

HARDINESS
Zones 9–11

COLOR(S)
Lilac, pink, white flowers

PEAK SEASON
Peak blooms spring and summer

MATURE SIZE
1 to 2 feet x equal spread

WATER NEEDS
Keep moist to get started. Water less in winter.

CARE
Plant close to surface, in bed with good drainage and organic matter. Add a little bonemeal in bottom of the hole. Use slow-release fertilizer in spring, summer, and fall. The plant forms clumps, and tubers can be separated in winter.

PROBLEMS
If overwatered or kept in shade, can succumb to fungus. Also attracts aphids and whiteflies.

USES AND SELECTIONS
These tropical bulbs are better in groups. Use to line a walkway, add a medium-level backdrop to smaller-growing plants, as potted plants in water gardens, or en masse in front of shrubs. Try Society Garlic among culinary herbs. This relative of the Onion family was thought to be less offensive than true Garlic, hence the name.

SPANISH BAYONET
Yucca aloifolia

☼ ☀ 🦋 🐝 💧 🌀

HARDINESS
Zones 8–11

COLOR(S)
White flowers

PEAK SEASON
Everygreen foliage; spring blooms

MATURE SIZE
8 to 12 feet x 4 feet

WATER NEEDS
Drought tolerant

CARE
Requires excellent drainage. Use water-soluble or time-release fertilizer recommended for foliage plants. If planted in containers, add extra sand to potting mix and shards to make sure drainage holes won't clog. It will become top heavy, so cover soil with rocks to add weight.

PROBLEMS
The memorably sharp leaf tips make an effective home-protection system when planted along property lines. Avoid planting in areas where children play or visitors may walk.

USES AND SELECTIONS
Salt and drought tolerant, group Spanish Bayonet with other plants that don't need much water, in seaside gardens, or in beds with plenty of sand. They are interesting for vertical elements, as background plants, or at fence corners. Low-growing Shore Juniper can be used to accent a clump of these growing on sand dunes.

SPINELESS CENTURY PLANT
Agave attenuata

☼ ☀ 💧 🌀

HARDINESS
Zones 9–11

COLOR(S)
Yellow flowers; foliage light bluish-green

PEAK SEASON
One-time blooms; year-round foliage

MATURE SIZE
2 to 4 feet x 3 feet

WATER NEEDS
Water when young. Very drought tolerant when established.

CARE
Requires good drainage. To improve drainage add sand to planting material or use succulent potting soil with additional sand or perlite. Plant at any time except while flowering. Little care is needed. It tolerates heat, drought, and some salt exposure. Use liquid fertilizer two or three times a year.

PROBLEMS
Much smaller and safer than the Century Plant, which has sharp spines.

USES AND SELECTIONS
Use as specimen or grouped together. Plant in sandy beds, rock gardens, or areas without irrigation. Agaves are excellent choices for the rocky Florida Keys. The plant flowers after about 10 years, not 100. The tall flower spike can reach several feet, and flowers form around it, hence the name Foxtail Agave.

STOKES' ASTER

Stokesia laevis

HARDINESS
Zones 8–10

COLOR(S)
Blue, lavender, yellow, white flowers

PEAK SEASON
Blooms late spring and summer

MATURE SIZE
1 to 2 feet x 1 to 2 feet

WATER NEEDS
Prefers moist soil

CARE
Does best in enriched soil. Requires little care. Remove faded flower heads to ensure longer flowering.

PROBLEMS
Untroubled by pests

USES AND SELECTIONS
The large flowers are up to 4 inches across, plus very full and fluffy. This effect is created by many thin petals and a flurry of stamens in the middle. Plant in mixed wildflower and butterfly gardens as well as containers and cutting gardens. Besides the Florida native species, there are several cultivars. Two of the best cultivars are lavender-blue 'Blue Danube' and powder blue 'Klaus Jelitto'. 'Alba' is white and 'Mary Gregory' is yellow. There are also dwarf varieties with compact growth.

SWAMP FERN

Blechnum serrulatum

HARDINESS
Zones 8–10. Protect from freezing with southern exposure or other protection.

COLOR(S)
Shiny-green leaves with new growth a coppery color

PEAK SEASON
Evergreen foliage

MATURE SIZE
To 5 feet x various

WATER NEEDS
Needs constant moisture

CARE
Plant in spring or warm months. Keep rhizome fairly close to soil surface. Swamp Fern loves shade and damp muck. It's best to plant in mulch, letting their roots travel just below the surface. Foliage fertilizer or fish emulsion can be added every two weeks in summer, monthly in winter. After winter, remove old and damaged fronds. If necessary, trim back any growth extending beyond the desired planting area.

PROBLEMS
May sometimes get scale or mealybugs. Unless severe, may not need treatment. Ferns may be susceptible to damage from oils and insecticides.

USES AND SELECTIONS
The Florida native Swamp Fern (also called Toothed Fern) is an excellent groundcover for large, moist areas, like the edge of ponds, swamps, or marshes.

VARIEGATED FLAX LILY

Dianella tasmanica 'Variegata'

HARDINESS
Zones 8–11

COLOR(S)
White and green foliage

PEAK SEASON
Evergreen

MATURE SIZE
To 3 feet x to 3 feet

WATER NEEDS
Very drought tolerant

CARE
Plant in any well-drained soil. Dianella is somewhat salt tolerant and tough enough for street plantings. It will grow in most light levels.

PROBLEMS
If scale becomes a problem, use oil spray or other recommended treatment. Parts may be poisonous if eaten.

USES AND SELECTIONS
This relatively new introduction from New Zealand has become very popular as interest in low-maintenance and environmentally friendly gardening has increased. It is grown for its foliage; the small blue flowers are insignificant. The brightly colored leaves complement both flowering and foliage plantings. It can also lighten a dark tropical shade garden. Use Variegated Flax Lily as groundcover, edging, or background planting for shorter annuals or perennials. It is suitable for containers as well as xeriscape gardens.

VERONICA

Veronica spicata

HARDINESS
Zones 8–9

COLOR(S)
Blue-purple, red flowers

PEAK SEASON
Blooms summer

MATURE SIZE
1 to 2 feet x 1 to 2 feet

WATER NEEDS
Prefers average moisture levels, neither too wet nor too dry.

CARE
Plant in average soil. This carefree perennial does well when growing in the northern parts of the state.

PROBLEMS
Doesn't do well in the extended heat and humidity of some central areas and southern Florida. Pests and diseases are not a problem.

USES AND SELECTIONS
With its full, showy flower spike, Veronica is a terrific choice for sunny or partially sunny perennial displays. Its long, dense flower spikes appear throughout the summer. Use with other mid-border perennials. One of its most sensational editions is the 18- to 20-inch-high 'Sunny Border Blue', which won top PPA honors in 1993 and continues to be popular. Other attractive species form 8-inch compact dwarf mounds or have silvery-gray leaves.

WILD PETUNIA
Ruellia caroliniensis

HARDINESS
Zones 8–11. May freeze to ground but will regrow from roots.

COLOR(S)
Blue-lavender flowers

PEAK SEASON
Summer blooms

MATURE SIZE
20 inches x various

WATER NEEDS
Water daily for a week, then gradually taper off. Drought tolerant once established. Do not keep too wet.

CARE
Little care is required after it is established. Not fussy about soil. Can reseed themselves, given right conditions.

PROBLEMS
This is a Florida native. It is less compact and bushy than numerous invasive nonnative Ruellias sold at nurseries, including Mexican Bluebell, 'Chi Chi', and other cultivars. These common varieties readily reseed themselves and have become nuisance plants throughout the state. Consider this when selecting plants for your garden.

USES AND SELECTIONS
The popularity of butterfly gardens and native plants, coupled with water conservation concerns contributed to Ruellia's popularity. Recommended for xeriscape and butterfly gardens. Use in low-maintenance planting with Necklace Pod or Butterfly Bush to attract butterflies.

YARROW
Achillea millefolium

HARDINESS
Zones 8–9

COLOR(S)
Yellow, white, red, rose, pink, salmon, or mixed flowers

PEAK SEASON
Summer blooms

MATURE SIZE
2 to 3 feet x 2 to 3 feet

WATER NEEDS
Drought tolerant once established

CARE
Once established, the plants are self-sufficient. The flat-topped blossoms, usually up to 5 inches across, are actually tight clusters of myriad tiny flowers.

PROBLEMS
In the warmer parts of the state, Yarrow may not be as reliable as a flower. However, it can be used for its bright green, delicate foliage.

USES AND SELECTIONS
Ideal in locations with plenty of sun and average soil. Yarrow provides lots of color all summer long. They look great in sweeps, clumps, or interspersed throughout a perennials bed—anywhere you want dependable color. They make good cut flowers, fresh or dried. The ferny foliage at the base of the plants makes an attractive, gray-green, off-season groundcover.

PERENNIALS

Name	Area of Florida	Common Height (Inches)	Common Width (Inches)	Flower Color/ Season	Light Needed
African Iris	Throughout	24	24	White, blue, yellow/ Year-round	Sun–light shade
Angelonia	Throughout	18	12	White, purple/ Year-round	Sun
Beebalm	NC	36	30	Reddish/April–June	Sun
Bird of Paradise	CS	36	36	Orange, blue/ Year-round	Sun–light shade
Blanket Flower	Throughout	18	18	Yellow, orange, red/ Mar.–Nov.	Sun
Blue Daze	Throughout	12	18	Blue/Year-round	Sun
Blue Ginger	CS	36	24	Blue/May–Oct.	Light shade
Blue Phlox	N	12	12	Blue/Mar.–April	Light shade
Blue Sage	CS	60	30	Blue/Dec.–Mar.	Light shade
Bush Daisy	Throughout	24	24	Yellow/Year-round	Sun–light shade
Butterfly Weed	Throughout	36	36	Yellow, orange/ Year-round	Sun–light shade
Cardinal's Guard	CS	72	48	Scarlet/ May–Oct.	Light shade
Cat's Whiskers	CS	36	30	White, lavender/ Mar.–Nov.	Sun–light shade
Chrysanthemum	NC	18	24	Varied/Sept.–May	Sun–light shade
Coneflower	NC	30	12	White, purple/ April–August	Sun
Coreopsis	Throughout	18	18	Yellow/April–Oct.	Sun
Crossandra	Throughout	12	12	Orange/May–Oct.	Sun–shade
False Dragon Head	Throughout	24	24	White, pink, lavender/Sept.–Oct.	Sun–shade
Firespike	Throughout	72	36	Red/ year-round	Sun–light shade
Four O'Clock	Throughout	36	36	White, yellow, red/ April–Oct.	Sun–light shade
Gaura	NC	24	18	White, pink/ year-round	Sun
Gerbera Daisy	Throughout	18	18	Varied/Year-round	Sun–light shade
Goldenrod	NC	36	24	Yellow/May–Oct.	Sun
Heliconia	CS	60	24	Yellow, orange, red/ Year-round	Sun–light shade
Hosta	NC	18	18	White, lavender/ June–Aug.	Shade

PERENNIALS

Name	Area of Florida	Common Height (Inches)	Common Width (Inches)	Flower Color/ Season	Light Needed
Jacobinia	CS	48	36	White, pink/ Year-round	Shade
Lantana	Throughout	24	24	Cream, yellow, red, lavender/ Year-round	Sun
Lion's Ear	Throughout	48	18	Orange/Oct.–April	Sun
Mexican Heather	Throughout	18	18	White, purple/ Year-round	Sun–light shade
Pentas	Throughout	48	36	White, pink, red, lavender/ Year-round	Sun–light shade
Philippine Violet	Throughout	48	36	White, lavender/ Sept.–April	Sun–light shade
Poinsettia	CS	72	72	White, pink, red bracts/Dec.–Mar.	Sun–light shade
Rudbeckia	NC	30	18	Yellow/ May–Oct.	Sun
Ruellia	Throughout	36	24	Blue, violet, pink/ April–Nov.	Sun–light shade
Salvia	Throughout	48	48	Blue, red, pink, white, yellow/ Year-round	Sun
Shasta Daisy	NC	24	12	White/May–June	Sun
Shrimp Plant	Throughout	60	48	Reddish-brown/ March–Oct.	Sun–light shade
Stokes' Aster	Throughout	12	12	White, blue/ May–July	Sun–light shade
Veronica	NC	18	18	Blue, white/ May–July	Sun–light shade
Violet	NC	10	12	White, blue/ Mar.–June	Light shade
Yarrow	NC	18	18	Yellow, rose, white/May–June	Sun
Yellow Alder	CS	24	24	Yellow/Year-round	Sun

N = North Florida   C = Central Florida   S = South Florida

BE FRUITFUL AND MULTIPLY

Perennials continue to grow from year to year. However, you may want to increase the number of plants to expand your garden or to give to a friend. Here are some ways to propagate your perennials from plants you already have.

START NEW PLANTS FROM OLD

From May through early summer is the best time to start new plants to fill in the landscape with favorite perennials. Use tip cuttings taken early in the morning from perennials that have just-matured new growth. Some that root very easily are Blue Daze, Bush Daisy, Butterfly Weed, Chrysanthemum, Firespike, and Pentas.

• Cut stems 4 to 6 inches long from the tip portions, then remove flowers.
• Stick the cut ends 1 to 2 inches deep in a pot or tray of vermiculite to root.
• Keep the cuttings and vermiculite moist, and enclose the containers of cuttings in a clear plastic bag.
• Leave the top open just a little and use a few dowels to hold the plastic off the foliage.
• Set in bright light but out of direct sun. Most perennial cuttings root in eight to ten weeks. When the cuttings root, transplant them to small containers.

SAVING SEEDS FOR SOWING

Many perennials can be started from seeds saved from one season to another, including Salvias, Violets, Gerbera Daisy, Butterfly Weed, and Blanket Flower. Let seeds dry on the plants. When pods begin to open, it's time to harvest. Try gathering the seeds on a dry day.

Bring seeds indoors and let them dry a little longer on a screen or cheesecloth. After a few days, add each type to a plastic bag or a jar and label with the plant name and date. They are then ready for storage.

Keep the seeds in a vegetable storage section of the refrigerator, not the freezer.

If you wish, a paper towel containing a handful of dry milk can be added to each bag as a drying agent.

Use the seeds within a year to get the best germination.

KEEPING MUMS ANOTHER YEAR

Don't expect the Chrysanthemum, which gives great displays in Northern gardens, to work as well in Florida landscapes. It can be done, but with considerable effort. Florida Chrysanthemums are known as garden mums. They are planted throughout the year, but mainly when in bloom during late summer through fall. Mums in Florida are a bit strange, as our climate, with its warmish winter weather, encourages extra blooms. Here are some mum care tips:

• Select mums you like when in bloom and add them to the garden.
• Keep the soil moist and feed lightly every six to eight weeks year-round.
• Prune off faded flower heads as they develop.
• Divide plants in spring to form new beds.
• Plants make good growth during the long days of summer. Give them needed trimmings so they will remain compact. Root the trimmings if needed to start more plants.
• Give the plants a final trimming in mid-August, as they start to form flower buds for fall.
• Chrysanthemums often develop leaf diseases during the summer's hot, rainy weather. A fungicide may be needed to prevent major leaf decline.

SAVE A PLANT

Sometimes winters are nasty in Florida, catching gardeners off guard. It may not be possible to save an entire plant, but you may save a portion by first taking cuttings before the plant freezes. Then follow the steps from "Start New Plants from Old."

JANUARY

• Protect cold-sensitive plants. It only takes a little effort to prevent damage. Move containers to warmer area. Cover plantings to the ground with blankets or cloths. (Plastic provides little protection.) Turn trashcans or cardboard boxes over plants. Use outdoor-approved electric lights under covers for a little heat.

• Use perennials for bouquet material. Some provide only greenery this month, but many have flowers. A little pruning can also be done now.

• Most plantings need minimal amounts of moisture. Give good soakings when watering is required. Keep new plantings extra-moist for first few weeks. Then gradually reduce waterings to an as-needed basis.

• Very little fertilizer is needed this month. Yellowing plants in southern regions can receive a light feeding as needed.

• Cut away winter damage to prevent rot problems and improve appearance. A few mealybugs, slugs, and snails might still be a problem.

FEBRUARY

• February can be quite cold, with frosts and freezes in Central and North Florida. By month's end, most areas enjoy consistently warm weather.

• Cold-hardy perennials can be planted now. Keep less hardy plants in their containers until after the average last frost date.

• As winter finishes up, there is a need for some pruning. Don't rush to prune out dead or declining portions, as some cold may linger. When winter is over, take out brown plant portions and do any reshaping. Some perennials, like Chrysanthemums and African Iris, may be getting ready to produce spring flowers, so trim off only what is needed.

• It won't hurt to get a little jump on spring with fertilizing.

• Bugs and diseases start to become more active, mostly in South Florida. Look for aphids, mealybugs, slugs, snails, and powdery mildew.

MARCH

• Even though there is a frost chance until mid-month, all Florida gardeners can begin perennial plantings. Most grow well during the warmish days and cool nights ahead.

• Now is the time to direct plant growth. Prune to correct lopsided growth and nip out tips of developing shoots to encourage fuller plants. Avoid trimming shoots that are starting to flower.

• Separate plantings into heavy- and low-water use areas so irrigation systems can be run only as needed. Keep plants on a low-water usage program. It helps them develop a deeper root system, discourages many pests, and saves watering dollars.

• If you missed feeding last month, apply the first feeding of the year. Give new plants extra half doses of fertilizer to encourage growth.

• Welcome beneficial insects such as lady beetles, lacewings, and praying mantis. Try not to spray when good bugs are present. But watch for the bad ones: aphids, mealybugs, slugs, and snails.

APRIL

• If large plants are overgrowing their neighbors, either prune them or transplant the smaller plant.

• Remove fading flower heads. Groom if needed to reshape these plants. Prune lanky limbs.

• Keeping soil moist. Once perennials establish a good root system, they will draw moisture stored in the ground. Improve sandy soil to hold extra moisture.

• Check your feeding calendar, then look at plant growth. If the soil is rich and plants are not using all the nutrients, a feeding can be skipped. If foliage is bright green, wait a few more weeks; if yellow-green, apply more fertilizer.

• A white form of scale insect is common on Bird of Paradise and similar plants with thick, persistent foliage. It can be rubbed off with your finger or toothbrush, or controlled with soap or oil spray. Garden fleahoppers are becoming noticeable. Control with a general insecticide. Other April garden pests are aphids, mealybugs, slugs, snails, and powdery mildew.

MAY

• Alkaline soil may keep azaleas and similar acid-loving plants from doing well close to exterior walls. Overhangs can keep spots either very dry or very wet. If you've had plant failures around your walls, consider soil preparation before replanting. Check for and correct drainage problems. Check acidity and adjust if needed. Consider a raised bed. Improve sandy soils and install a microsprinkler.

• Some perennials are not fully awakened from dormancy. Make sure each has room to grow. Label all perennials so they aren't forgotten during the dormant season.

• If you fed plants earlier in the spring, no fertilizer application is needed yet. But if it's been six to eight weeks since feeding or the plants are yellowish, apply fertilizer. Fewer feedings are needed with slow-release fertilizers.

• Leaves damaged by leafminers can be removed or ignored. For serious problems, use a garden spray. Control leaf spot with fungicide. Aphids, mealybugs, slugs, and snails could be present.

JUNE

• Perennials are not fussy and can be dug and divided almost any time of year. During hot summer months you have choices when dividing: move them to a new bed, grow them in containers, or give them to friends. Keeping them in containers for a few months or longer has two advantages: they can be stored until a new bed is prepared and the plants get off to a vigorous start with controlled conditions.

• The daily rains should do most of the watering this month.

• Most perennial plantings get a second feeding as the rains return. Even if you use a slow-release fertilizer, check your calendar for the next feeding time.

• Many perennials have toughened up after spring growth so bugs don't find them as tasty. New pests may include grasshoppers and katydids. Handpick or use insecticide. Aphids on new growth may be controlled by lady beetles. Slugs and snails also love summer weather.

JULY

• Plan other perennial gardens, such as problem turf areas or old annual beds that would require less work.

• If purchasing perennials now, either add during a cooler time of day or keep them in their pots until fall. Just trim back overgrown portions and keep them well fed.

• Pruning now spruces up the gardens and saves work for later on. Trim off dead or infected portions and old flower heads. Cut back stems overhanging walks and pinch out tips of lanky plants to encourage denser growth.

• Summer rains still provide most water needs Check container plantings daily. They dry very quickly.

• The rains encourage rapid growth and wash away nutrients. Check your calendar—it may be time for another feeding.

• Some pests are sure to be feeding. Many can be tolerated if only a few plant portions are affected. Handpick when possible. If pests are more numerous, you may need an insecticide.

AUGUST

• If you started rooting cuttings a month or so ago, they may be ready for containers. If you tug a little and they resist, roots are forming. Lift out gently. When the rootball is about the size of a quarter, it's ready for a pot. Most transplants should then grow rapidly and be ready for the garden in six to eight weeks. This is the last month to count on the rainy season to make watering new plantings easier.

• Enjoy the last full month of the rainy season. Container gardens still need your attention, as do recent transplants.

• Most gardens are still growing with nutrients from previous feedings. Transplants and container gardens need regular fertilizer applications, unless fed with slow-release.

• Correcting poor drainage can prevent root rot. Aphids, garden fleahopppers, grasshoppers, slugs, and snails are active and may need control.

SEPTEMBER

• It's out with the old and in with the new. A long, hot summer is hard on plants, and many spots may need renovation. If you have some replacements from cuttings, divisions, or seeds, you will be ready.

• Lots of pruning is in order. Cut back to a branch angle or bud, or to the ground. If you want a plant to fill in from the base, cut about a foot above where new branches should begin. A good pruning now prepares plantings for growth in milder fall weather.

• Be prepared to water more often as the rainy season fades away.

• All perennials should be ready for a fall feeding. Try to schedule it just as the rainy season ends, around mid- to late September. If it doesn't rain, water after feeding.

• With drier weather, mites increase. Pests that continue their activity through fall are aphids, garden fleahoppers, grasshoppers, slugs, and snails.

OCTOBER

• Prepare beds for fall planting. With new plants be conscious of water needs, because this season is dry. Consider using perennials in large pots of varying sizes. Container gardens can last for months, but gradually the plants run out of room. When this happens, remove the perennials and add them to the landscape.

• Poinsettias form their flower buds this month if they have no nighttime light. Note where yours are growing. Move containers to darker area, resist turning on outdoor lights near Poinsettias, or cover plants near streetlights from before sundown until sunrise.

• If you skipped September's feeding, now is the time to complete fertilizer applications for in-ground plantings. Container plantings should continue with their liquid fertilizer feeding every other week.

• Some pests will fade. However, stay alert to the presence of aphids, garden fleahoppers, mites, slugs, and snails.

NOVEMBER

• This is a pleasurable time to add perennials to the landscape. Consider keeping new cold-sensitive ones in containers in northern areas until spring.

• Mulches can be very important during fall and winter. Besides retaining moisture, loose mulch near plants can provide cold protection. Keep a bale or two of weed-free hay or pine needles handy for protection when cold is predicted.

• Edging makes perennial beds look more attractive and can be done any time. However, it is a lot easier during these cooler months.

• Perennials don't need much water during cooler months and can exist for a week or more without a sprinkling. Water only when necessary.

• Feeding time is over in North Florida. Gardeners in Central Florida should hurry to complete their fertilizing. South Florida gardeners can continue their regular schedule, but stretch the time a little between applications.

DECEMBER

• Perennials can be planted at any time. Most garden centers are clearing their shelves, so look for good buys and keep warm until spring. More perennials will become dormant with cooler temperatures.

• Beware of freezing temperatures by month's end. Keep cold protection ready for sensitive perennials. Although South Florida gardeners can often ignore this cold talk, they must stay alert to surprise freezes.

• Most plants need minimal watering during this dry, cool time of year. Most can last a week or more without a watering if they are mulched. Only pots in plants should be of real concern and checked daily.

• Feeding time is over, with very few plants making growth in northern and central parts of the state. In southern areas continue normal feedings.

• Cold weather in Florida slows insect pests down. Plants in protected locations and in warmer areas of the state may find some aphids, mites, slugs, and snails still active.

ROSES &
SHRUBS
for Florida

Often growing between groundcovers and trees, shrubs build unity in the landscape design with repeating foliage color and leaf shape. Shrubs may bear attractive flowers, colorful berries, and unique leaf shapes. Some only offer seasonal interest; when the show is over, they fade into the background with other landscape plantings. Others are on display year-round. These are often permanent accents given a prominent spot where they are sure to be noticed by visitors.

There are so many ways to use shrubs:

- Tall shrubs make good view barriers. Select denser-growing varieties if you want complete blockage.
- Use shrubs to exclude sounds. A thick, small-leafed sound barrier can silence busy streets or active neighbors.
- Plant shrubs to form hedges, large or small, natural or formal in growth habit.
- Shrubs can be used to form a backdrop for other garden features. Flower gardens, sundials, birdbaths, and statuary look great displayed against the greenery.
- Use shrubs as foundation plantings. They can hide ugly home features and soften architecture.
- Cluster shrubs together to create seasonal color.
- Plant a shrub just because you like it. Try to work it into an accent spot or cluster several together for a color backdrop.

You can probably think of many other reasons to plant shrubs in your landscape.

PLANNING

Shrubs are fairly permanent plantings. They can be dug up and moved, but it's not a fun job and you will lose all the growth that has occurred developing your design. For this reason, you should try to make as many firm decisions about your shrub plantings as possible.

The state of Florida is long and quite varied in the climatic conditions that affect plant growth. In our shrub tables (pages 245 to 247), we have tried to make the selection of shrubs easy by noting the best regions for each. Check with your local garden center, your Extension Service, or even a gardening friend to determine whether or not a shrub is suited to your area.

Think about what types of shrubs you would like in the landscape, and have a purpose in mind for each. Should they be tall or small? Do you want flowers? Here are a few more factors to consider when planning shrub plantings:

- How many shrubs do you need? It is usually best to plant a cluster, using odd numbers to avoid symmetrical designs. Use the eventual width of the plants as a guide when deciding how many to plant in a space (half to three-quarters the width is the best between-plant spacing).

- Arrange plants according to light requirements. Don't allow tall plants to hide smaller shrubs. Make sure that plants preferring lower light levels have a shady spot.
- Place shrubs with year-round interest in key spots. Use them near entrances and patios, and along walkways. Plant larger shrubs at the endpoint of a view, creating a focal point.
- Check your soil. Some shrubs, like azaleas, need an acidic soil, but most like a pH in the 6.5 to 7.0 range, which is slightly acid to neutral.
- Select hardy shrubs most often. If you want a few that are more cold sensitive, realize that they may be frozen back to the ground or completely killed during a severe winter.

PLANTING

Most shrubs grow well in sandy soil, but you can make care a lot easier by enriching these sites (and clay sites) with organic matter. Till the entire bed and work in peat moss, compost, and composted manure. Check the soil pH and adjust before planting if needed.

Make sure the ground has good drainage. If in doubt, mound up the planting site a bit to help extra moisture move away from the root system. In some wet locations, consider using more formal raised beds, or developing swales to move moisture to other areas of the landscape. To prevent soil from washing away, avoid planting shrubs near the dripline of a roof. In these spots you may consider guttering.

- Open up a hole that is at least twice as wide as the rootball, but no deeper.
- Ease the new plant from the pot. If the root system is tightly woven together, gently pry some of the roots loose.
- Position the plant at the same depth it was growing in the container, or with the top of the rootball 1 to 2 inches above the ground.
- Fill in around the new shrub with soil removed from the hole. If possible, add water to the hole as the soil is added. This is especially important with larger shrubs.
- Form a 4- to 6-inch berm of soil around the edge of the rootball to hold water and direct it down through the rootball. Thoroughly moisten the shrub.
- Add a 3- to 4-inch mulch layer. Keep the mulch back a few inches from the base of the shrub.

CARE

Part of caring for shrubs is taking periodic walks through the landscape to notice how well they are growing. If growth is normal, just pass on by. If you notice wilting foliage, yellow leaves, or pests, however, immediate attention is needed.

Shrubs also need direction, whether a light pruning to keep limbs from reaching over paths, or a full seasonal pruning to renew vigor. Make sure you prune the plants at the best time so as not to remove flower buds from the more colorful types.

WATERING

Newly planted shrubs need regular attention. How long this period of scrutiny lasts depends on the time it takes the plants to develop roots in the surrounding soil. Some, like azaleas, may not be able to live on their own for a year or two.

Maintaining a moist soil is critical. Hand watering is best. Fill the berm with water so it thoroughly wets the rootball and moves out into the surrounding soil. Hand water for at least several weeks until the plants begin to adjust and grow in their new site. Reduce the waterings to an as-needed schedule, then follow these tips:

- Water when the surface soil below the mulch begins to feel dry. For drought-tolerant shrubs, allow several additional days between waterings. Some, once established, may not need special waterings at all.
- Apply ½ to ¾ inch water at each irrigation.
- Water in the early morning.
- Install soaker hoses or microsprinklers, which put the water directly where it is needed.

FERTILIZING

One way to promote growth is by using fertilizer. During good growing weather, shrubs can quickly convert nutrients into new stems and foliage. You may want to feed newer shrub plantings a little more often to help them fill in.

Commercial fertilizers are applied in liquid or granular form.

Some gardeners like to use natural products. Composted manure can be applied to the surface of soils or over mulches. Fresh manure should be tilled into the soil 90 to 120 days before planting. Composted manures can also be made into teas for drenching the ground. Some natural products are being formulated into granular fertilizers for surface applications.

Here are some options to use when feeding shrub plantings:

- NEW PLANTINGS: Feed lightly every six to eight weeks, March through October, with either liquid or granular general garden fertilizers.
- ESTABLISHED PLANTINGS: Feed two to four times a year. Apply a feeding in March and one in September to maintain growth and good plant color. If needed, additional feedings may take place in June and August. Use a general garden fertilizer or a 16-4-8 product at label rates. Water thoroughly. There is no need to remove mulch— watering moves the nutrients off the granules and into the ground. You may notice some carrier portions of the fertilizer staying behind. Slow-release fertilizers can be used to feed the plants over an extended period of time.

PEST CONTROL

All shrubs have pests, some more than others. Often you do not know you have a problem until the plant starts to decline. Maybe you'll notice some yellow foliage, then find scale insects on the underside of leaves. With other shrubs, you may only notice a declining limb as the first indication of a fungal infection.

Some insect damage is very noticeable in the early stages. You cannot miss azalea leaf caterpillars or large grasshoppers. Handpick them. Following are a few pests you might find:

APHIDS: Small pear-shaped insects of varying colors, aphids live in new growths. Control as needed with a soap or oil spray following the label instructions.

CATERPILLARS: The immature stage of moths or butterflies chew plant foliage, stems, or flowers. Handpick and destroy them, or the plants can be treated with a *Bacillus thuringiensis*-containing natural insecticide.

LEAF SPOTS: Various shaped yellow to brown spots caused by fungal activity on leaves, many leaf spots are normal and can be ignored. Where new, healthy leaves are infected or the fungus is affecting the quality of the plant, a fungicide should be applied according to label instructions.

SCALE INSECTS: Insects covered with a wax-like coating may range from pinhead to dime size. Where needed, control with an oil spray, following label instructions.

AMERICAN BEAUTYBERRY
Callicarpa americana

HARDINESS
Grows throughout Florida

COLOR(S)
Pink blooms; purple fruits; green foliage

PEAK SEASON
Spring blooms, year-round in South Florida

MATURE SIZE
6 x 8 feet

WATER NEEDS
Very drought tolerant, but also grows in moist soils

CARE
This Florida native grows where other shrubs do not, requiring minimal care or fertilizer. If additional growth is desired, feed in March, May, and August. It grows quite lanky and should be pruned in late winter by cutting back to a few feet below desired height.

PROBLEMS
Caterpillars and grasshoppers are seldom a problem and can be handpicked.

USES AND SELECTIONS
Beautyberry's main beauty is during fall and winter when fruit clusters turn purplish. It becomes a wonderful accent plant in naturalistic areas and along walkways. It makes a good space divider and view barrier since it remains semi-evergreen during winter. Plant in clusters of three or more for best fall display. Use with other drought-tolerant plants.

AZALEA
Rhododendron spp.

HARDINESS
Zones 8–9; Native Azaleas only in colder areas; a few hybrids will grow in South Florida

COLOR(S)
Pink, red, white, purple blooms; green foliage

PEAK SEASON
Spring blooms

MATURE SIZE
2 to 6 feet x 2 to 6 feet

WATER NEEDS
Does best with adequate water

CARE
Once established, grow well with minimal care. Azaleas may take two years to develop and benefit from feeding in March, May, and September. Water regularly, especially during drought. Every three to five years give rejuvenation pruning.

PROBLEMS
Too much shade gives poor flowers but good foliage. Caterpillars, lace bugs, and mites may be problems.

USES AND SELECTIONS
Most plantings bloom for three to four weeks, then fade into the background as a backdrop, space divider, or transition plant. Use lower-growing Azaleas as groundcovers and small hedges along walkways. Plant in clusters for best color. Florida is home to four native Azaleas, medium to large shrubs.

BUTTERFLY BUSH
Buddleia officinalis

☀️ 🦋 ⚘ 🌿 🐝

HARDINESS
Zones 8–10

COLOR(S)
Lilac, pink, red, white, purple flowers

PEAK SEASON
Blooms spring to fall

MATURE SIZE
4 to 8 feet

WATER NEEDS
Has moderate drought tolerance when established. Keep roots moist until established, then water during drought.

CARE
Once established, they require minimal care. Some die back during winter. Remove old growth so new flowering shoots will appear. Feed once in March, May, and September. Water heavily from August through October.

PROBLEMS
Caterpillars and grasshoppers can be ignored to keep from harming desirable insects.

USES AND SELECTIONS
With numerous long flower clusters, Butterfly Bush does an excellent job of attracting butterflies and bees. Use near a patio where they can be observed or in a butterfly garden with full sun. Does best in mass plantings or with other plants to keep it from falling over. Can also be planted in a container when given enough water and pruned into small tree.

CAMELLIA
Camellia japonica

☀️ ☀️ ☀️ 🌱 🌿 🪴

HARDINESS
Zones 8–9

COLOR(S)
Flowers in shades of pink, red, white; green foliage

PEAK SEASON
Blooms late November through March

MATURE SIZE
10 to 12 feet x 6 to 8 feet

WATER NEEDS
Keep moist, especially new plantings. Once established, tolerates short periods of drought if well mulched.

CARE
Prefers lightly shaded locations, planted in acidic, well-drained soil. Feed in March, June, and August. Trim immediately after flowering, before the end of April, when the next year's buds are formed.

PROBLEMS
Dry rootballs on new plantings kill many Camellias. Tea scale is common. It can be controlled with oil spray, which also treats mites.

USES AND SELECTIONS
Blossoms up to 5 inches across put on a major display when few other shrubs are flowering. Use for accent plantings, view barriers, and backdrops. Plant with shrubs that prefer filtered sun and acidic soil, like Azaleas, Hydrangeas, and Gardenias. Also use with beds of shade-loving perennials.

CHENILLE PLANT
Acalypha hispida

HARDINESS
Zones 10b–11; protect from cold in Central and North Florida

COLOR(S)
Crimson flowers; green foliage

PEAK SEASON
Blooms spring through fall

MATURE SIZE
8 to 10 feet x 6 feet

WATER NEEDS
Don't let the shrub go for weeks without water, especially if summer rains dry up.

CARE
Does best and becomes readily established in rich, well-drained soil. Fertilize 2 or 3 times a year. Prune after flowering to keep it in-bounds.

PROBLEMS
Aphids may appear on new growth. Also check for scale and mealybugs. Use insecticidal soap or recommended pesticide.

USES AND SELECTIONS
Plant where Chenille Plant's unusual and showy flower is highlighted. Use in a mixed greenery planting of shrubs and Lady Palms, along a property line, or next to a path. Blend carefully with Crotons, Hibiscus, Snowbush, and Alocasia for a tropical screen. There are several varieties in other colors, including copper or mottled foliage and white flower spikes.

CHINESE FRINGE BUSH
Loropetalum chinense

HARDINESS
Zones 8–10a

COLOR(S)
White to deep pink flowers; green foliage, new varieties with reddish leaves

PEAK SEASON
Main blooms February through April

MATURE SIZE
8 feet x 6 feet

WATER NEEDS
New plants need adequate water. Drought tolerant once established.

CARE
Apply first feeding after four or six weeks, then fertilize every other month for first two years. Thereafter feed in March, June, and September. New plants grow vigorously, forming long shoots. Periodically tip out the shoots for a more compact plant. After spring blooming prune overgrown plants.

PROBLEMS
Decline has been reported with some varieties. Check with your local Extension Agent.

USES AND SELECTIONS
Also called Chinese Witchhazel, use for foundation plantings, stand-alone accents, hedges, or as view barriers. Take advantage of its drought tolerance by planting with similar shrubs. Use with annuals and perennials as a backdrop or in containers. New varieties have reddish foliage and pink flower forms.

COCCULUS
Cocculus laurifolius

HARDINESS
Zones 9–11

COLOR(S)
Insignificant yellow flowers; shiny bright-green foliage

PEAK SEASON
Blooms spring and summer

MATURE SIZE
12 feet x 12 feet

WATER NEEDS
Relatively drought tolerant once established. Water weekly to encourage growth and during drought.

CARE
Grows best in poor, but well-drained, soils. Once established, grows well with minimal care. Feed in March, May, and September. Prune to keep compact and full. In late winter, trim back any cold- damaged portions in North Florida plantings.

PROBLEMS
May be poisonous. Scale may affect Cocculus. Apply recommended pesticide.

USES AND SELECTIONS
Called the Seed Snail because its seeds resemble a snail shell. (Does not fruit in Florida.) Makes a great evergreen hedge or border for sun or shade. Can also be used as a contrasting backdrop with perennials of Bird-of-Paradise, Heliconias, Gingers, and Bananas. The foliage is used to make wreaths and is added to arrangements. The Carolina Snail Seed is native to North Florida.

COCOPLUM
Chrysobalanus icaco

HARDINESS
Zones 9–11

COLOR(S)
Green foliage

PEAK SEASON
Evergreen

MATURE SIZE
3 to 20 feet x 15 feet

WATER NEEDS
Drought tolerant once established

CARE
Has low nutritional requirement but new plants benefit from feeding twice a year. In native garden, substitute aged compost or composted manure for fertilizer. Pinch to keep it at a particular size. Once established, grows well with minimal care.

PROBLEMS
Pest free

USES AND SELECTIONS
This South Florida native is a useful medium to large shrub. The coastal salt-tolerant form is low and sprawling. The inland red-tipped variety grows larger but is not as salt tolerant. Cocoplum is ideal for bringing a Florida feel to a landscape that might include Cabbage Palms, Fakahatchee Grass, and Wax Myrtle. Use as formal or informal hedge, as a background planting, or as a screen. The fruit is eaten by birds, wildlife, and people, so Cocoplum is used when creating a wildlife habitat.

CRAPEMYRTLE
Laegerstromia indica

☀ 🐝 🍃 💧

HARDINESS
Zones 7–10

COLOR(S)
Red, pink, lavender, coral, white flowers; green foliage

PEAK SEASON
Blooms summer and fall

MATURE SIZE
20 feet x 20 feet

WATER NEEDS
Drought tolerant and does well in many soils but not standing water. Mulch to retain moisture.

CARE
Fertilize in March, June, and August. Prune lightly in late winter before new growth begins. If too many twigs grow out, thin to shape. If suckers develop from base, remove stems less than pencil-size diameter.

PROBLEMS
Older varieties susceptible to powdery mildew. Newer cultivars are disease resistant.

USES AND SELECTIONS
Use this reliable bloomer in mixed informal planting or as specimen. Let Crapemyrtle grow into a small tree and, during the summer flowering period, shine above other foliage, such as Plumbago, Philodendrons, and small Heliconias. After a few years the bark peels and becomes quite attractive. The leaves turn yellow then orange-red before falling in midwinter.

FATSIA
Fatsia japonica

☀ ☀ 🌿 🌴

HARDINESS
Zones 8–10

COLOR(S)
White flowers

PEAK SEASON
Blooms in fall

MATURE SIZE
8 feet x 4 feet

WATER NEEDS
Keep moist. Will also tolerate wet soils.

CARE
Prefers slightly acidic, enriched soil. Feed regularly to maintain lush foliage. The plant may become leggy looking as older leaves fall off. Either cut back or stake for support. Fatsia is also salt tolerant.

PROBLEMS
Pests or diseases are usually not a problem.

USES AND SELECTIONS
Fatsia, also called Japanese Aralia, is grown for its deeply lobed, bold leaves, which are very striking. Use Fatsia as a patio plant in the ground or in containers. It also works well if carefully mixed with other plants that aren't overwhelmed by the huge leaves. Usually Japanese Aralia is best when used against a fence or other background that does not compete for attention, or perhaps to complement a fountain or statue. Plant with other low-maintenance shade-loving plants.

FIREBUSH
Hamelia patens

HARDINESS
Zones 10–11. Prune out cold-damaged areas each spring.

COLOR(S)
Scarlet flowers; green foliage with occasional reddish cast

PEAK SEASON
Year-round blooms

MATURE SIZE
15 feet or more x 6 feet

WATER NEEDS
Firebush is a Florida native, very drought resistant once established. Keep moist until established and use mulch to retain moisture.

CARE
This fast-growing shrub is very tolerant of Florida heat. Prune lightly to keep Firebush in control, or hard to keep it small.

PROBLEMS
Caterpillars and aphids may appear but are not usually a big problem.

USES AND SELECTIONS
Incorporate into a butterfly garden or use several near a patio where butterfly and hummingbird activity can easily be seen. Also can be planted in a mixed border with Wax Myrtle, Wild Coffee, Necklace Pod, Beautyberry, and Cocoplum. Use them along with native trees to create a wildlife habitat or where you do not irrigate in water-conserving landscape design.

FIRECRACKER PLANT
Russelia equisetiformis

HARDINESS
Zones 9–11

COLOR(S)
Red, yellow, coral flowers

PEAK SEASON
Evergreen foliage and almost year-round blooms

MATURE SIZE
4 feet x 4 feet

WATER NEEDS
Somewhat drought tolerant once established. Does best with regular waterings.

CARE
Plant in well-drained enriched soil. Fertilize regularly. The fast-growing Firecracker Plant does not require much care and is even tolerant of salt spray.

PROBLEMS
None

USES AND SELECTIONS
Firecracker Plant (also called Coral Plant) is very unique looking. It has countless thin, rushlike stems that erupt upward then cascade down to form gentle arches. There are no leaves to speak of, but the stems are filled with clusters of tubular flowers that attract butterflies and hummingbirds. (They can be dried for use in arrangements.) Plant as an accent to fill planter boxes or containers. The weeping habit can also be used to overflow a wall, hide a raised bed, or cover a bank.

FLORIBUNDA ROSE
Rosa hybrids

HARDINESS
Grow throughout Florida. Prune North Florida winter damage before spring growth begins.

COLOR(S)
Flowers in all colors except blue; foliage green

PEAK SEASON
Spring and summer blooms

MATURE SIZE
To 4 feet x 4 feet

WATER NEEDS
Keep soil moist. Use enriched soil and mulch.

CARE
Once established, feed and treat for pests monthly. In North and Central Florida reduce feedings during late fall and winter. Groom regularly and prune back one third to one half in late winter, keeping to three to seven main stems. Some very bushy plants may need staking.

PROBLEMS
Common pests include blackspot and mites. Yellow Roses may have greater pest resistance.

USES AND SELECTIONS
Most buds are pointed to slightly rounded and have the Hybrid Tea Rose look. They are considered very hardy and generally pest resistant. Floribundas are suited for smaller gardens or planting in clusters with perennials. The smallest of these multipurpose hybrids are miniatures.

FLORIDA PRIVET
Forestiera segregata

HARDINESS
Zones 8–11

COLOR(S)
Yellow flowers

PEAK SEASON
Blooms winter and spring; leaves usually evergreen

MATURE SIZE
10 to 15 feet x 5 to 10 feet

WATER NEEDS
Very drought tolerant but also does well in moist soils.

CARE
Does well in almost any soil or moisture level. Florida Privet is a tough native that even withstands brief flooding and is salt tolerant. It commonly grows in coastal areas. Prune this moderate grower if using as a hedge or espalier.

PROBLEMS
No serious pests or diseases

USES AND SELECTIONS
Also called Wild Olive, this native has small leaves with dense growth. It makes excellent hedges, screens, and espaliers. Also useful as a specimen planting, in wildlife gardens, for slope erosion, and seaside landscapes. Hedges can easily be maintained at most heights or Florida Privet can be left completely natural as a small tree. Birds and bees are attracted to the flowers and abundant berries.

233

GARDENIA

Gardenia jasminoides

☼ ☼ ☼ 🌢 🌱

HARDINESS
Zones 8b -11

COLOR(S)
White flowers; dark-green foliage

PEAK SEASON
Blooms spring, sporadic flowers throughout summer; foliage evergreen

MATURE SIZE
12 x 3 or 4 feet

WATER NEEDS
Keep moist. Fluctuating soil moisture leads to yellowing leaves.

CARE
Prefers acidic soil. Gardenias are heavy feeders and in alkaline soils thrive on high-nitrogen, acid-forming fertilizer. Use small amounts every 2 or 3 months. A lack of micronutrients causes yellow leaves; use a foliar micronutrient spray. For iron deficiency, use an annual iron drench. Prune lightly after major flowering to keep shrub compact. Prune any cold damage after new spring growth appears.

PROBLEMS
Thrips affect flowers. Use beneficial lacewings, oil spray, or insecticide.

USES AND SELECTIONS
Use this slow-growing evergreen as a specimen plant, or blend with foliage plants that are colorful in the non-blooming months. 'Miami Supreme' is the biggest selling cultivar in Florida, with large, extremely fragrant flowers. 'Radicans' is a dwarf. Obtain on nematode resistant rootstocks.

GRANDIFLORA ROSE

Rosa hybrids

☼ 🦋 🍐 🌢 🌰 🌷 🌿

HARDINESS
Grow throughout Florida. In cooler areas prune winter damage before spring growth begins.

COLOR(S)
All color flowers except blue; foliage green

PEAK SEASON
Blooms spring and summer

MATURE SIZE
8 feet x 5 feet

WATER NEEDS
Keep soil moist. Use enriched soil and mulch.

CARE
Feed monthly and treat for pests. In North and Central Florida reduce feedings during winter. Since plants grow tall and wide, prune annually in January or February. Cut back one third to one half, remove small twigs, and reduce main canes to three to seven in number. Add a stake or two to prevent wind damage.

PROBLEMS
Blackspot and mites can cause major decline

USES AND SELECTIONS
Grandiflora have taller bushes than Hybrid Tea Roses, with the full clusters of Floribundas. Plant just a bed or create clusters among perennials, annuals, and accent shrubs. Plant with Salvias, Marigolds, Pentas, Lantana, and Heliconia. The first Floribunda, 'Queen Elizabath', is still a favorite.

HIBISCUS
Hibiscus rosa-sinensis

HARDINESS
Zones 9b -11

COLOR(S)
All color flowers except blue; green foliage

PEAK SEASON
Blooms spring through summer; evergreen foliage

MATURE SIZE
20 feet or more x 15 feet

WATER NEEDS
Fairly drought tolerant once established. May need water in dry season. Don't let roots stand in water.

CARE
Use slow-release fertilizer with 3-1-3 ratio. In alkaline soils use micronutrient spray three times a year to prevent deficiencies. In cooler regions, grow in protected garden areas, in containers, or as annuals. Prune off cold damage in spring.

PROBLEMS
Control whiteflies and aphids with insecticidal soap or soap spray. Prune off areas infected with armored scale. Mites and midges can cause bud drop.

USES AND SELECTIONS
Although Hibiscus blooms last only a day, they flower prolifically. Palm plantings can be bordered or interplanted with big, flashy Hibiscus for a true tropical picture. Or plant with Heliconias and Bananas for a similar feel. Don't mix lots of colors.

HYBRID TEA ROSE
Rosa hybrids

HARDINESS
Grows throughout Florida

COLOR(S)
All color flowers except blue; foliage green

PEAK SEASON
Blooms spring and summer

MATURE SIZE
5 to 6 feet x 5 feet

WATER NEEDS
Keep soil moist. Use enriched soil and mulch to retain moisture.

CARE
Feed monthly and treat for pests. In North and Central Florida reduce feedings during winter. In January or February prune back one third to one half. Remove weak stems and limit bushes to seven strong stems.

PROBLEMS
Blackspot may require weekly fungicide sprays in hot, rainy weather. During dry weather, mites can be a major problem. Other pests include thrips, powdery mildew, aphids, caterpillars, and stem cankers.

USES AND SELECTIONS
Tea Roses are bushy and produce stems of single blossoms. Plant in a Rose bed or a few clusters. Make sure they have adequate spacing, leaving room for annuals and perennials around the edges including Ageratum, Alyssum, Periwinkle, and Lantana.

HYDRANGEA
Hydrangea macrophylla

HARDINESS
Zones 8–9. Requires some cold weather to do well.

COLOR(S)
Pink, blue, white flowers

PEAK SEASON
Blooms spring through summer

MATURE SIZE
5 feet x 5 feet

WATER NEEDS
Need lots of water and will wilt from moisture stress. Check frequently during hot weather and drought.

CARE
Does best with well-drained, enriched soil that retains moisture. Feed once in March, May, and September. Prune any freeze damage in early spring and prune again after flowering in summer. Remove older flower heads and reshape plant.

PROBLEMS
Handpick caterpillars or treat with recommended pesticide

USES AND SELECTIONS
Grows well in containers for porches, patios, and along walkways. Display in-ground with filtered sun lovers like Allamanda, Indian Hawthorn, Azaleas, and Camellias. Best used in mass plantings of three or more plants, as background shrubs, hedges, or accents. Hybridizers are always coming up with new varieties of this popular plant, including dwarf forms.

INDIAN HAWTHORN
Rhaphiolepis indica

HARDINESS
Zones 8–11

COLOR(S)
White, pink flowers; dark-green foliage

PEAK SEASON
Blooms spring; foliage evergreen

MATURE SIZE
3 to 5 feet x 3 feet

WATER NEEDS
Drought tolerant once established

CARE
Needs well-drained soil. Indian Hawthorn is a tough plant that doesn't require much care. It has compact growth and unlike most other shrubs, doesn't need pruning to be kept as a low hedge or border. It also is somewhat salt tolerant.

PROBLEMS
Indian Hawthorn is very strong and resists most problems. Leaf spot and scale may occasionally occur.

USES AND SELECTIONS
This compact, slow-growing plant is excellent for low-maintenance plantings. It may be used as foundation plants, low hedges, or borders. A measure of its toughness is that it is planted commercially in parking lots and highway medians. The lightly fragrant flowers provide berries for winter birds, making Indian Hawthorn useful in wildlife gardens.

IXORA

Ixora coccinea

☀ ☀ 🌿 🪴 🌊

HARDINESS
Zones 9–11

COLOR(S)
Red, orange, pink, yellow, salmon flowers; green foliage

PEAK SEASON
Blooms spring through summer; evergreen foliage

MATURE SIZE
2½ to 6 feet x 6 feet

WATER NEEDS
Requires good drainage. Water regularly.

CARE
Ixora likes fertilizer to keep producing big balls of flowers, called umbels. They prefer acidic soil, so they benefit from mulch and high-nitrogen fertilizers. Treat micronutrient deficiencies in alkaline soils with epsom salts when fertilizing, an annual iron drench, occasional manganese sulfate applications, and a micronutrient spray. Lightly prune to shape; Ixora performs best when not sheared. Wait until spring before pruning freeze damage.

PROBLEMS
Some new cultivars require less shaping, are more tolerant of rocky soils, and are resistant to nematodes.

USES AND SELECTIONS
Combine Ixora with Crotons, Palms, Bromeliads, or bulbs for easy-care plantings that are colorful but not confusing. New cultivars come in dwarf forms, as well as sizes growing to 12 feet.

LADY-OF-THE-NIGHT

Brunfelsia americana

☀ 🧴

HARDINESS
9b–11

COLOR(S)
White flowers

PEAK SEASON
Blooms summer

MATURE SIZE
10 to 15 feet x 5 to 10 feet

WATER NEEDS
Water every few days in dry season

CARE
Feed three times a year using fertilizer with micronutrients. Reduce nitrogen amount for fall feeding. When spraying liquid fertilizer on orchids, spray *Brunfelsia*, too. Lady-of-the-Night may get cold damage in Central Florida. Prune off damage after new spring growth begins. Prune to shape this naturally sprawling shrub.

PROBLEMS
Plant parts are poisonous if ingested

USES AND SELECTIONS
Plant *Brunfelsia* where the rich evening perfume can be appreciated. When placed on the southeast corner of the house, the clovelike fragrance will float on the prevailing breeze. This shrub is incredibly showy when flowering; it blooms profusely all at once. Allow it to sprawl amid groupings of Alocasiasm Gingers, and Lady Palms. Other *Brunfelsia* species come in different colors and bloom at other times of the year.

LIGUSTRUM
Ligustrum japonicum

HARDINESS
Zones 8–10

COLOR(S)
White flowers

PEAK SEASON
Blooms spring; foliage evergreen

MATURE SIZE
12 feet x 8 feet

WATER NEEDS
Drought tolerant. For best growth, water weekly, especially during drought.

CARE
Prefers any well-drained soil. Feed once in March, May, and September. Formal hedges may need pruning several times during grow-ing season. Tree forms need periodic pruning to keep open growth habit and remove sprouts along trunk.

PROBLEMS
May get caterpillars, grasshoppers, and scales. Handpick or treat with recommended pesti-cide. Good care overcomes fungal spots.

USES AND SELECTIONS
Ligustrum japonicum, also called Japanese Privet, is planted as a hedge, view barrier, accent plant, and tree. It can be pruned or permitted to grow naturally. It is often used as a small tree in smaller gardens and near patios. This is one of numerous *Ligustrum* species in the landscape industry. Two others (Chinese and Glossy Privet) are invasive and should not be planted.

NATAL PLUM
Carissa spp.

HARDINESS
Zones 9b–11

COLOR(S)
White flowers; red fruit; glossy dark-green leaves

PEAK SEASON
Blooms summer; evergreen foliage

MATURE SIZE
Varies

WATER NEEDS
Drought tolerant. Do not overwater.

CARE
Does best in sandy, well-drained soil. Tolerant of salty spray and soil. Grows in partial shade but flowers more in full sun. Only requires light pruning to keep as a hedge.

PROBLEMS
Plant back from walkways so that spines do not interfere with people. All parts of the plant are poisonous, except for ripe fruit.

USES AND SELECTIONS
Carissas are sweetly fragrant, especially at night, with edible fruit used for preserves. The glossy, dense foliage makes them excellent hedges, groundcovers, or screens. They can be used in containers, planters, and as accent or founda-tion plants. Carissas are superb plants for seashore landscapes. There are numerous species and cultivars with very diverse growth habits and heights, from dwarf groundcovers to small trees.

NECKLACE POD
Sophora tomentosa

HARDINESS
Zones 9b–11

COLOR(S)
Yellow flowers; silvery green foliage

PEAK SEASON
Blooms winter and spring

MATURE SIZE
6 to 10 feet x 10 feet

WATER NEEDS
Water well until established, then stand aside. Very drought tolerant.

CARE
This durable shrub is salt tolerant and beautiful. Flowering is most plentiful in winter and spring, but may continue throughout the year. Necklace Pod produces long, segmented pea pods, like the small pearls of a necklace. Prune in spring to keep long branches in check. In Central Florida, grow in protected area. Prune away cold damage after new spring growth emerges.

PROBLEMS
Handpick occasional caterpillars or ignore

USES AND SELECTIONS
A freestanding Necklace Pod is pretty, but when placed among a border of butterfly shrubs it takes on a useful function as well. It is perfect for pineland plantings. Use with Palmettos, Firebush, American Beautyberry, and other native shrubs.

NIGHT-BLOOMING JESSAMINE
Cestrum nocturnum

HARDINESS
Zones 9–11

COLOR(S)
White flowers; glossy green leaves

PEAK SEASON
Blooms spring, summer; evergreen foliage

MATURE SIZE
12 feet x 12 feet

WATER NEEDS
Can tolerate short periods of drought but makes best growth if watered weekly, especially during drought. Do not let roots get waterlogged.

CARE
Prefers any well-drained soil. Feed once in March, May, and September. The Night-Blooming Jessamine is a sprawling shrub with long, vinelike stems and frequent pruning may be needed. Plantings in Central Florida may be affected by freezing weather and need spring pruning to remove damage. Grows in full or partial sun, but blooms better in full sun.

PROBLEMS
Caterpillars and grasshoppers can be handpicked or treated with recommended pesticide. Plants are poisonous if ingested.

USES AND SELECTIONS
The small flowers pack a powerful, sweet fragrance, most noticeable at night. Use as a specimen, in mixed plantings, or as a border. It provides larval food for butterflies.

OLD GARDEN ROSE
Rosa hybrids

HARDINESS
Grows throughout Florida

COLOR(S)
All color flowers except blue

PEAK SEASON
Blooms spring and summer

MATURE SIZE
To 6 feet x 8 feet

WATER NEEDS
Keep soil moist. Use enriched soil and mulch.

CARE
Based on the plant size and shape, check spacing and need for a support. Fertilize monthly. Reduce feedings during winter in North Florida. In January or February prune back bush types by one third to one half, thinning if needed. Leave climbers to grow, with renewal pruning every two or three years.

PROBLEMS
Many older varieties show resistance to Rose pests. Watch for blackspot and mites.

USES AND SELECTIONS
Old Garden Roses are varieties planted before 1867, which includes tall bush types, Climbers, and miniature forms. They travelled from Europe to New World settlers' homesteads. They are more fragrant than modern hybrids and may be more vigorous. Fill a bed, use as shrubs, or create a backdrop for annual and perennial plants.

OLEANDER
Nerium oleander

HARDINESS
Zones 8–11. In cold areas, it may freeze to the ground but grows back from its base.

COLOR(S)
White, pink, red, salmon flowers

PEAK SEASON
Blooms spring through fall

MATURE SIZE
12 feet x 12 feet

WATER NEEDS
Very drought tolerant. Water during severe drought or to encourage growth.

CARE
Thrives in sand or well-drained soil. Exist with feedings given to nearby plants. For extra growth, feed in March, May, and September. Southern plantings require regular pruning.

PROBLEMS
All parts are very poisonous. Caterpillars, aphids, and scale may appear. Handpick or use recommended pesticide.

USES AND SELECTIONS
This showy, sometimes fragrant, shrub can be planted as a hedge, space divider, view barrier, or small tree. Plant in clusters for more color. Use large Oleanders at the rear of the landscape for distant color. Also can be used as backdrop for lower-growing flowers, shrubs, and ornamental grasses. Use dwarf types can in foundation plantings and around patios.

JAPANESE PITTOSPORUM
Pittosporum tobira

☀ ☼ ☼ 🦋 🜂 💧 🌊

HARDINESS
Zones 8–10

COLOR(S)
White flowers; green, variegated leaves

PEAK SEASON
Blooms spring; evergreen foliage

MATURE SIZE
8 to 12 feet x 8 to 12 feet

WATER NEEDS
Drought tolerant once established. Grows best with moderate moisture.

CARE
Not particular about soil. Can be grown as a shrub or small tree, depending upon amount of pruning. It grows faster when fertilized. In alkaline soils provide annual micronutrient spray.

PROBLEMS
Undersides of leaves affected by aphids and scale. Avoid wet soils which lead to leaf spot and root rot.

USES AND SELECTIONS
Japanese Pittosporum makes good informal hedges or can be pruned for a formal look. It also can be used in containers or as small patio trees, where the citrusy flower fragrance will be appreciated. Pittosporum is tough enough to be used regularly in commercial plantings and seaside landscapes. A dwarf variety grows only 2 feet high and another popular cultivar is variegated.

PLUMBAGO
Plumbago auriculata

☀ 🦋 🌱 💧 🌊

HARDINESS
Zones 9–11. Prune freeze damage after spring growth begins.

COLOR(S)
Cobalt-blue flowers

PEAK SEASON
Blooms spring through summer

MATURE SIZE
3 to 4 feet x 8 feet

WATER NEEDS
Moderately drought tolerant when established. Water during dry season.

CARE
Blooms best with fertilizer. Apply three times per year. The plant tends to fall over and root, so prune to keep in-bounds. (Flowers trimmed off will be quickly replaced.) Or, tie to a support such as an arbor or gate for a dramatic effect. Prune back hard at the end of winter.

PROBLEMS
None

USES AND SELECTIONS
Serves as a short shrub or giant groundcover. The color nicely complements magenta Bougainvillea or yellow flowers. Because Plumbago is low and sprawls, it can serve as an underplanting to disguise legginess of taller shrubs. The mounding shape also works well at an entry gate or in containers and planters. Red and white varieties are available.

WAX MYRTLE
Myrica cerifera

HARDINESS
Zones 8–11

COLOR(S)
Greenish to greenish-yellow flowers

PEAK SEASON
Blooms in spring; evergreen leaves

MATURE SIZE
15 to 25 feet

WATER NEEDS
Can flourish under moist or dry conditions. Keep roots moist during first season.

CARE
Once established, requires very little care, except for occasional pruning plus spring and fall feedings. It suckers from the roots, which helps Wax Myrtle grow into clumps. They may be left alone, shaped, or removed.

PROBLEMS
None reported

USES AND SELECTIONS
This supremely versatile native plant grows from the Everglades to the pinelands. Wax Myrtle is excellent for xeriscape, low-maintenance, and native landscapes. Use it for a screen or background plant, or with other native shrubs. It can also be shaped into hedges, but grows too large for use close to the home. Male and female flowers are on separate plants. In winter, the female's waxy fruits are appreciated by wildlife and birds.

WILD COFFEE
Pschotria nervosa

HARDINESS
Zones 9b (if protected)–11

COLOR(S)
Insignificant white flowers; glossy deep-green leaves; red berries

PEAK SEASON
Blooms spring and summer; late summer and fall berries

MATURE SIZE
6 to 15 feet x 5 to 6 feet

WATER NEEDS
Keep roots moist until established, then water during drought. Plants wilt when thirsty.

CARE
Fertilize two or three times a year for plants to look their best. Prune in spring for fuller shrub and after summer's renewal growth for shaping.

PROBLEMS
None reported

USES AND SELECTIONS
This native Florida shrub makes a beautiful hedge in semi-shade. Plant beneath Palms or Gumbo Limbo trees that will provide shade and sun. The leaf texture and shine makes Wild Coffee especially useful in native gardens. Although the flowers are very small, butterflies like them. The shrub stretches out and becomes lanky in shade, but stays compact in partial to full sun. High or partial shade is ideal.

SHRUBS

Name	Average Size H. (ft.)	W. (ft.)	Area of Florida	Flower Color	Season	Light Needs
Abelia	4–6	4–6	NC	White	Summer	Sun, light shade
Allamanda, Bush	4–6	4–6	CS	Yellow	Year-round	Sun, light shade
Anise	8–10	6–8	NCS	*		Sun, shade
Aucuba	5–6	2–3	N	*		Shade
Azalea, Indian	6–8	4–6	NC	Varied	Spring	Light shade
Azalea, Kurume	3–4	2–3	NC	Varied	Spring	Light shade
Azalea, Native	5–6	4–6	N	Varied	Spring	Light shade
Banana Shrub	10–12	6–8	NC	Yellow	Spring	Sun, light shade
Barberry, Japanese	5–6	3–4	N	Yellow	Spring	Sun, light shade
Barberry, Wintergreen	5–6	3–4	N	Yellow	Spring	Sun, light shade
Beautyberry	5–6	4–5	NC	Lilac	Spring	Sun, light shade
Bottlebrush	8–10	8–10	NCS	Red	Spring	Sun
Brunfelsia	6–8	4–6	CS	Purple	Spring	Sun, light shade
Butterfly Bush	4–6	4–6	NC	Varied	Spring-fall	Sun
Camellia, Japonica	10–12	6–8	NC	Varied	Winter	Sun, light shade
Camellia, Sasanqua	10–12	6–8	NC	Varied	Winter	Sun
Cape Jasmine	6–8	6–8	CS	White	Spring-summer	Sun, light shade
Cassia	6–8	6–8	CS	Yellow	Fall	Sun
Chaste Tree	10–12	10–12	NC	Blue	Summer	Sun
Cleyera, Japanese	8–10	4–6	NCS	Yellow	Spring	Shade
Cocculus	10–12	6–8	CS	*		Sun, light shade
Cocoplum	10–15	10–15	S	White	Year-round	Sun, light shade
Crapemyrtle	6–15	8–10	NC	Varied	Summer	Sun
Crapemyrtle, Dwarf	2–4	3–4	NC	Varied	Summer	Sun
Croton	6–8	4–6	CS	*		Sun, light shade
Euonymus, Creeping	1–2	3–4	N	*		Sun, shade
Euonymus, Japanese	6–8	4–6	N	*		Sun, light shade
Fatsia	5–6	2–3	NCS	*		Light shade
Feijoa	8–10	6–8	NCS	White, red	Spring	Sun, light shade
Firebush	6–8	6–8	CS	Red	Year-round	Sun, light shade

* = Inconspicuous Flower Color   N = North Florida   C = Central Florida   S = South Florida

SHRUBS

Name	Average Size H. (ft.)	W. (ft.)	Area of Florida	Flower Color	Season	Light Needs
Firecracker Plant	4–5	3–4	CS	Red	Year-round	Sun, light shade
Florida Privet	8–10	6–8	CS	White	Spring	Sun
Florida Yew	8–10	8–10	NC	*		Light shade
Fortune's Mahonia	3–4	2–3	N	Yellow	Spring	Light shade
Gardenia	6–8	4–6	NCS	White	Spring	Sun, light shade
Hibiscus	8–10	6–8	CS	Varied	Year-round	Sun, light shade
Holly, Chinese	10–12	6–8	NC	White	Spring	Sun, light shade
Holly, Dwarf Burford	5–6	4–5	NC	*		Sun, light shade
Holly, Dwarf Yaupon	3–4	3–4	NCS	*		Sun, shade
Holly, Japanese	2–4	2–3	N	*		Sun, light shade
Holly Malpighia	1–2	1–2	CS	Pink	Spring-summer	Shade
Hydrangea, French	5–6	4–5	NC	Blue-Pink	Spring-summer	Light shade
Hydrangea, Oakleaf	5–6	4–5	NC	White	Summer	Light shade
Indian Hawthorn	3–4	3–4	NCS	White, pink	Spring	Sun, light shade
Ixora	4–6	3–4	CS	Red, yellow	Year-round	Sun, light shade
Japanese Boxwood	3–4	2–3	NC	*		Sun, shade
Jasmine, Arabian	4–5	3–4	S	White	Summer-fall	Sun, light shade
Jasmine, Downy	5–6	4–6	CS	White	Spring-fall	Sun, light shade
Jasmine, Primrose	5–6	5–6	NC	Yellow	Spring-summer	Sun
Jasmine, Shining	4–5	4–5	CS	White	Spring-summer	Sun, light shade
Juniper, Chinese	4–6	4–6	NC	*		Sun
Juniper, Shore	1–2	4–6	NCS	*		Sun
Juniper, Spreading	1	3–4	N	*		Sun
King's Mantle	4–6	4–6	CS	*	Summer	Sun, light shade
Ligustrum, Japanese	10–12	6–10	NCS	White	Spring	Sun, light shade
Ligustrum, Sinense	6–8	4–6	NCS	White	Spring	Sun, light shade
Loropetalum	6–8	4–6	NC	White, pink	Spring	Sun, light shade
Natal Plum	6–8	4–6	CS	White	Spring	Sun, shade

* = Inconspicuous Flower Color   N = North Florida   C = Central Florida   S = South Florida

SHRUBS

Name	Average Size H. (ft.)	Average Size W. (ft.)	Area of Florida	Flower Color	Season	Light Needs
Oleander	10–12	6–8	NCS	Varied	Year-round	Sun
Orange Jessamine	10–12	6–8	CS	White	Spring-fall	Sun, light shade
Philodendron, Selloum	6–10	8–10	CS	*		Sun, shade
Pittosporum	8–10	8–10	NCS	White	Spring	Sun, light shade
Plumbago	4–6	4–6	CS	Blue	Year-round	Sun, light shade
Podocarpus, Yew	20–25	8–10	NCS	*		Sun, light shade
Powder Puff	8–10	8–10	CS	Red	Winter	Sun, light shade
Pyracantha	8–10	6–8	NC	White	Spring	Sun
Red-tip Photinia	6–8	5–6	NC	White	Spring	Sun
Reeves Spirea	5–6	4–5	NC	White	Spring	Sun
Rose of Sharon	8–10	6–8	NC	Varied	Summer	Sun, light shade
Sea Grape	12–20	10–12	CS	*		Sun, light shade
Serissa	1–2	1–2	NCS	White	Spring-summer	Sun, light shade
Silverthorn	10–12	8–10	NC	Tan	Winter	Sun
Simpson Stopper	10–12	6–8	CS	White	Spring	Sun
Snowbush	4–6	4–5	CS	White	Summer	Sun, light shade
Surinam Cherry	10–12	8–10	CS	White	Spring	Sun, light shade
Sweet Osmanthus	10–12	6–8	NC	White	Winter	Light shade
Texas Sage	5–6	4–5	NCS	Lavender	Spring-fall	Sun, light shade
Thryallis	5–6	4–6	CS	Yellow	Summer	Sun, light shade
Ti Plant	4–6	3–4	CS	White, pink	Fall	
Tibouchina	8–10	6–8	CS	Purple	Summer	Sun
Viburnum, Black Haw	6–8	5–6	NCS	White	Spring	Sun
Viburnum, Laurestinis	6–8	4–5	NC	White, pink	Winter	Sun
Viburnum, Sandankwa	5–6	4–5	NCS	White	Spring	Sun, light shade
Viburnum, Sweet	10–12	6–8	NCS	White	Spring	Sun
Wax Myrtle	10–12	6–8	NCS	*		Sun, light shade

* = Inconspicuous Flower Color   N = North Florida   C = Central Florida   S = South Florida

JANUARY

• Winter is great for planting shrubs. If beds are not ready, keep plants in containers and water often. This is also a good time to move plants in your landscape. Roses can be planted year-round when container grown, but bare-root specimens are best planted this month or next.

• Summer-blooming shrubs are ready for winter pruning. Give Roses (except climbing types) their annual pruning. Cut back $1/3$ to $1/2$, keeping 3 to 7 main stems.

• Most shrubs are not heavy water users. All, however, need water in order to become established and produce growth. Even drought-tolerant plants look their best only when provided with adequate water. Keep new rose plantings moist.

• Wait about another month to feed shrubs. In North and Central Florida feed roses every six to eight weeks, until spring. Keep South Florida roses on a monthly fertilizing schedule.

• Check plantings for scale and sooty mold. Aphids and mealybugs may appear during warmer winter days.

FEBRUARY

• Leave cold damaged plants alone for a few weeks to see what is alive or dead. Water as needed, but do not apply fertilizer until growth begins. If plants are frozen to the ground, wait until late spring before replacing. They might recover.

• Container-grown roses can be planted year-round. This is the last month to plant bare-root roses.

• As plants send out new shoots, direct growth by trimming stems back to buds pointed in the right direction. If plants need denser growth, pinch out shoot tips.

• As plants start growing, cool weather reduces moisture needs. Wait until plants tell you they need water. Keep the rootballs of new plantings moist. Use mulch and a soaker hose or microsprinklers.

• In North and Central Florida feed roses every 6 to 8 weeks, until spring. In South Florida maintain the monthly schedule.

• Aphids, mealybugs, leaf spot, and scale may start showing up on new shrub growth.

MARCH

• Spring and fall are the best times to plant roses.

• Complete winter pruning of shrubs. Cut out declining portions and reshape winter-damaged shrubs and roses. Winter-flowering shrubs can be trimmed as they finish blooming, but before new growth appears. Prune any winter damage from Roses before spring growth begins.

• Warmer weather signals increased water needs. Most shrubs are drought tolerant so check if the upper inch of soil is dry before watering. New shrub and rose plantings should be kept moist.

• If you fell a little behind fertilizing, feed shrubs now. Use a general fertilizer (ideally, with micronutrients added) or a specialized blend for Azaleas, Hibiscus, or Gardenias. Apply monthly feeding to roses. Use 12-4-8 or similar Rose fertilizer.

• A few pests you may want to control are aphids, mealybugs, leaf spots, and scale. The fungus on Azalea flowers is usually ignored. Roses are susceptible to mites and blackspot.

APRIL

• Plant Roses in spring or fall. Shrubs can be kept in containers until ready for the landscape. Keep the soil moist and apply liquid fertilizer every other week. Just before planting cut off any extra-long roots growing through the holes.

• Weeds can be pulled and spot-killed with nonselective herbicide for use with growing plants. Prevent them with refreshed mulch layers, a pre-emergence herbicide, landscape fabric, and periodically raking or hoeing the soil.

• During this hot, dry time of year, frequently check for shrubs that may need water. It does not hurt to wilt a little. Keep new roses moist. Groom roses throughout the growing season.

• Fertilizer is optional this time of year for shrubs, unless making up for missed feeding. Continue regular monthly feeding for roses.

• Thrips may spoil Gardenia flowers. Control with insecticidal spray before the buds open. Look for aphids, caterpillars, mealybugs, leaf spots, and scale.

MAY

• Continue planting individual shrubs and container-grown roses, or complete beds. Work in lots of organic matter with sands and clays. Moving plants at this time of year is difficult. Wait until cooler weather.

• After spring growth, some shrubs will need trimming. Up to one-third of the old wood can be removed during any spring pruning. Groom roses throughout the growing season.

• Check plants regularly for water needs during this hot, dry month.

• Apply monthly rose feeding, but wait to feed shrubs. The rainy season is just ahead and you will get better use of fertilizer with natural rainfall. However, if you notice some plants on the yellow side, then a feeding is needed.

• Plant pests love summerlike weather. Many grasshoppers have recently hatched and can be chewing holes in foliage. Try handpicking these difficult-to-control pests, or use an insecticide. More summer shrub pests are aphids, caterpillars, mealybugs, and scale.

JUNE

• In Florida we add landscape plantings year-round, but it's a lot more stressful for you during summer. Try working during the cooler morning and early evening hours. Work in shady garden areas during midday. Drink lots of water, wear a hat, and use sunscreen.

• Hurry to complete Azalea, Camellia, and Gardenia pruning as they form buds for next year. Delay pruning plants that flower during summer. Groom roses throughout the growing season.

• Summer rains may be doing most of your watering. But check often and when a few days pass without rain, it may be your turn to provide the moisture.

• A second feeding of fertilizer can be provided to encourage additional growth or maintain shrub color. Continue with regular monthly rose fertilizer applications.

• Keep your eye out for summer pests. Aphids, caterpillars, grasshoppers, leaf spot, and scale can occur. Blackspot may affect Roses now.

JULY

• Nothing is keeping you from planting except the heat. If you are adding tropical plants, they won't mind it a bit as long as you follow good planting techniques. Nature is providing much of the required irrigation.

• Hydrangeas are in bloom and will soon be reading for trimming. Remove old flower heads and trim to reshape the plants. Complete all azalea and gardenia pruning early this month. It's probably too late for additional pruning of camellias without affecting some flowering. Groom roses throughout the growing season.

• Keep up with weeding and preventive measures.

• You probably won't have to do a lot of watering thanks to frequent summer rains.

• If you missed June's shrub feeding, apply it during summer months. Give roses their monthly fertilizer.

• The rainy season helps control some pests, like mites, but encourages others. Look for aphids, lacebugs, caterpillars, grasshoppers, and leaf spots. Blackspot may affect Roses now.

AUGUST

• Continue regular hedge pruning, allowing new shoots to grow 6 or more inches before shearing. Cut them back to within an inch or two of previous cuts. Every few years major prunings to reduce height and width are needed. Groom roses throughout the growing season.

• This is the last full month of rainy season, so you probably won't have lots of watering.

• Gardeners wanting the most from their shrubs may give a third feeding. Apply granular fertilizers under the plants' spread, use liquid fertilizers as a spray or drench over the plants (washing off foliage if applied during heat of the day), or apply composted manure as a topdressing. Give monthly rose fertilizer application.

• Use pesticides only when destructive insects are out of control. Many beneficial insects are in the landscape, including ladybugs, lacewings, and mantids. Pests you may have to control are caterpillars, grasshoppers, lacebugs, and leaf spots. Blackspot may affect Roses now.

SEPTEMBER

• Adding new shrubs and Roses should get easier as weather becomes cooler. By late September, the moderating temperatures might coax you outdoors to begin planting. At least you can get the soil ready. Test the pH of the soil and make adjustments as needed. Enrich sandy soils with organic matter. Till in peat moss, compost, or composted manure.

• Do some fall shrub pruning. Groom roses throughout the growing season.

• Watch the weather to know when to pick up on watering.

• You could begin shrub feedings during September, but most gardeners wait a little longer, unless plants show signs of deficiencies. Give roses their monthly feeding.

• Many bugs develop large populations during summer that keep feeding into fall. You may find aphids, caterpillars, grasshoppers, leaf spots, and mites. Blackspot may affect Roses now. Develop a pest-control strategy for fall.

OCTOBER

• Fall is a great time to add new roses and shrubs. Milder weather allows root systems to grow with little stress on foliage. New plantings need moisture daily for first few weeks. Add layer of mulch. Thereafter, use soil moisture as a guide. Water when top inch of soil starts to dry.

• Complete all fall shrub pruning in Central and North Florida. Continue grooming roses as needed.

• You are on watering duty for the next seven or so months.

• This is feeding time for all shrubs, the last feeding of the year. Give roses their monthly fertilizer application.

• Most gardeners will be fighting some pests for a month or two longer before cooler weather slows their growth. Mites may increase because of the drier weather on both shrubs and roses. Check plantings for caterpillars, grasshoppers, lace bugs, and leaf spots.

NOVEMBER

• Adding plants is enjoyable during November. There is less stress on you and the shrubs.

• Pruning time is over for all shrubs in Central and North Florida, where trimming done now will encourage growth that might be damaged by cold. South Florida shrubs can be trimmed as needed.

• This is a dry but cooler month. Water only when needed. Most shrubs (except heavy water users) can last a week or more between irrigation or are very drought tolerant.

• Hurry to complete any last-minute fertilizer applications for shrubs. Allow them adequate time to mature the foliage before winter weather arrives. South Florida gardeners can continue to feed plantings as needed. In North and Central Florida reduce rose feedings to every six to eight weeks, until spring.

• Pest activity starts to slow down in November, but continue regular checks on the landscape. Aphids, caterpillars, grasshoppers, leaf spots, and mites stay active on warm days.

DECEMBER

• Winter arrives this month and it's a great time to add shrubs. If you have some in the wrong place, it's also a good time to relocate them. When moving plants, make sure the soil is moist and try to get a large intact rootball.

• Be prepared for cold weather, with protection available for sensitive shrubs when freeze warnings are sounded.

• Feeding time is over for most shrub plantings. If you missed a fertilizer application, it is probably best to wait until late-winter or spring. Only shrubs producing growth or exhibiting deficiencies should be fed this month. In North and Central Florida reduce rose feedings to every 6 to 8 weeks, until spring.

• Only in the warmer locations are pests on shrubs usually active. Look for leaf spots and scale on warm days. During the drier months, mites may attack Roses. Spray undersides of leaves with water as first defense.

TREES &
PALMS
for Florida

Perhaps there is nothing more sacred in the landscape than trees. Maybe it's because you can relate to them. They can be hugged and climbed and you watch them grow. Many gardeners planted trees when they were young and still go back to check on their progress.

Deciding where to plant a tree takes careful consideration. Once the tree is in the ground, it's not easily moved. Here are just a few considerations:

1. Should the tree be evergreen or deciduous?
2. Do you want a flowering tree?
3. How tall do you want the tree to grow?
4. Will fruits be of benefit or a problem?

Use our table (pages 278 to 280) to select a favorite or two, then check it out at local garden centers and botanical gardens.

Florida gardeners love their palms, which add a tropical look. Check the palm chart (pages 280 to 281). Find some ways to use palms:

- Cluster several tall palms to provide a lightly shaded area.
- Use groups as tree substitutes to frame a home.
- Add an interesting palm planting near the patio as an accent.
- Plant palms as replacements for street trees.
- Plant small palms in containers on patios or near entrances.

PLANNING

Take a look at your yard and decide where you want shade. Should it be light shade or filtered? If it is too dense, you may not be able to grow grass—and it may be a problem for growing flowers and vegetables. But this is only the beginning. Trees have numerous uses in the landscape. Here are a few:

- Plant trees to block objectionable views. It may take some time, but most trees grow faster than you think, so you don't always have to start with large trees.
- Add interest to the landscape. Some trees have attractive flowers and others have colorful fruits. A few also offer fall color, attractive bark, or have unusual foliage.
- Frame a home or view. If there is a distant view such as a lake or a garden, it can be enhanced by framing with trees. Large trees are best kept to the sides of the home and back of the property.
- Keep the wind out of your yard. A barrier of trees on the northwest side of the yard can keep out some cold winter winds. Trees also help to keep down dust and other debris.

PLANTING

Adding a tree is not difficult, but make sure you have the right spot before you dig. Keep large trees 15 to 20 feet from the home. You don't need roots approaching the foundation to cause cracks or many limbs overhanging the roof.

Also keep trees away from septic systems and drainage pipes. Roots grow best where the soil is moist. Any drain field or leaking pipe provides an ideal water source where roots can grow and affect drainage.

Another concern is overhead wires. Use only small trees under utility lines, or make sure larger trees are well to the side of the wires.

As you locate the tree, make sure it is not in the middle of the yard. A tree can block a clear view of the home for police and emergency personnel.

Underground utilities should be located. Calls to electric, telephone, and cable TV companies are all it takes to have the lines marked so you won't cut wires and interrupt service.

Unlike shrubs, trees do not require a big, prepared planting site. In most cases, it is only necessary to dig a hole two or more times wider than the rootball and no deeper. Then follow these steps to complete the planting:

1. Position the tree in the hole at the same depth it was in the container or slightly higher out of the ground.
2. Begin filling the hole with water and soil at the same time. We normally do not recommend improving the fill soil unless you want to.
3. When the hole is filled with soil, create a 4- to 6-inch berm of soil around the outer edge of the rootball to catch and direct water down through the root system.
4. Add a 3- to 4-inch mulch layer starting at the outer edge of the rootball and water.
5. If a tree might be affected by winds, it should be staked.

Palms are planted in a manner very similar to trees, with the exception that the rootballs are often much smaller. And the best planting time for dug palms is March through August. Palms make the best root and top growth when the weather is warm. If container grown, plant at any time. Tall palms will need staking.

Unlike trees, palms dug from the ground should have about half the older leaves removed at planting time. The remaining leaves are usually drawn up above the bud and tied in place (for about sixty days) to retard water loss. Cabbage palms often have all leaves removed during transplanting. Palms transplanted from containers do not need special pruning.

CARE

New plantings need different care from the care received by older, well-established trees. You want new trees to quickly root into the surrounding soil to become well anchored.

WATERING

New trees and palms need plenty of water. Fill the berm daily for the first month or more. Some horticulturists suggest daily waterings of larger trees for more than four months. They also recommend keeping palm plantings moist for a similar period.

After that, water every other day for several additional months. You have to judge the root growth and determine when the tree can grow on its own. Here are a few watering thoughts:

- Some trees are slow to become established. Dogwoods and magnolias appear to be two of the worst. Most trees are established after a year.
- Small trees (6 to 8 feet) are on their own more quickly than taller and older trees. Be ready to give older trees more care during drier weather for well over a year.
- Fill the basin formed from the berm full of water. Make sure enough water is applied to wet the rootball at each irrigation.
- Don't count on the irrigation system. Hand watering is best during the establishment period.
- Keep a 3- to 4-inch mulch layer over the soil outside the rootball area to keep the ground moist.
- Once the trees and palms are established, very few need frequent watering.

FERTILIZING

Most gardeners are surprised to learn that shade and flowering trees need fertilizer only during the establishment period. This is when they form new roots and make rapid stem and leaf growth. Three to five years after planting, most special feedings can be discontinued. The first limited feeding is normally applied four to six weeks after planting. Just a light scattering over the surface of general garden fertilizer is usually sufficient.

There are many fertilizers available for trees. Studies show those high in nitrogen give the best results. Try a 12-4-8, 16-4-8, or similar product. The fertilizer rate is to supply one pound of nitrogen over each 1,000 square feet of soil surface under the limbs and out past the dripline. Here are some feeding suggestions:

1. Feed once in the spring and once in fall. Gardeners who want to promote extra growth add an early-summer feeding.
2. Apply fertilizer at 1 pound of nitrogen per 1,000 square feet. For 12-4-8, use 8 pounds; for 16-4-8, use 6 pounds. Usually this is the lawn rate shown on the bag.
3. Use a handheld or push spreader to apply fertilizer under the trees. Tossing by hand may not give good distribution. Appy to the soil surface or over mulch; it is no longer placed in the ground.
4. Water the fertilized area to begin moving nutrients into the soil.
5. Continue feedings on a regular schedule for three to five years. Thereafter, most trees obtain adequate nutrients from nearby feedings.

If for any reason a tree declines or becomes injured, regular feedings can be resumed for short periods.

Feed Palms on a regular schedule for their lifespan. Current recommendations call for feeding three to four times a year with slow-release palm fertilizer. If a slow-release product is not utilized, a regular palm fertilizer should be applied lightly but monthly during the growing season. A suggested rate is 1 to 2 pounds of a standard palm fertilizer for each 100 square feet of area under the palm spread.

PEST CONTROL

Trees and palms do have pests, but most established plantings are resistant and can withstand some holes and defoliation. The real concern is associated with new plantings. A pesticide may be applied where insects, mites, or diseases appear to be causing major damage. Because of their size, very few large established trees or palms are sprayed.

Check your young trees and palms during walks in the yard for pest problems. If noted, many can be hand picked from the plants and destroyed. See pages 349 to 352 for descriptions and controls.

ARECA PALM
Dypsis lutescens

HARDINESS
Zones 10–11

PEAK SEASON
Evergreen; spring flowers

MATURE SIZE
To about 20 feet x 15-plus feet

WATER NEEDS
Keep roots moist the first year, then irrigate once or twice a week during hot and dry months.

CARE
Tolerant of many soils. Feed with palm fertilizer with high potassium plus micronutrients. Arecas are susceptible to potassium deficiency, when older leaves get yellow spots. Some nursery Arecas are adapted to shade and must gradually be acclimated to sun.

PROBLEMS
Remove suckers from clump interior to allow circulation, reducing vulnerability to fungus, scale, and mealybugs.

USES AND SELECTIONS
Graceful Arecas are one of South Florida's most used Palms. Arching fronds are feather-like with golden bases. Arecas form thick clumps and are widely used for screening, hedging, or background plantings. When kept pruned, they're beautiful specimen plants. Arecas are compatible with many flowering shrubs, serving as a backdrop to display blooms. Use as container plants in cooler locations.

BALD CYPRESS
Taxodium distichum

HARDINESS
Zones 8–11

COLOR(S)
Bright green leaves in summer, turn coppery in fall before dropping

MATURE SIZE
100 feet x 30 feet

WATER NEEDS
Typically grows in water or at water's edge, where it does best. However, this Florida native can grow in dry soils. Keep roots moist, but not waterlogged, until established. Once established, only needs water during severe drought.

CARE
If planted out of water, feed in March and June for first two or three years. Trees in water need no special feedings. Prune during winter to keep straight trunk and even branching.

PROBLEMS
Use *Bacillus thuringiensis* for any caterpillars

USES AND SELECTIONS
One of Florida's few trees that grow in wet or dry soils. Best used lakeside with one or two trees and other wet root plantings. Cypress roots develop short protrusions above ground called "knees" that help stabilize the tree or perhaps exchange gases. The needle-like leaves have feathery appearance.

259

BISMARCK PALM
Bismarckia nobilis

☼ ☀ ◊ 🌴

HARDINESS
Zones 9b–11

MATURE SIZE
40 to 70 feet x 15 to 20 feet

WATER NEEDS
Water daily for first few weeks, then reduce waterings but keep root zone moist for first growing season. Plant at beginning of rainy season to reduce irrigation. Established Palms are very drought tolerant.

CARE
Plant in well-drained soil. Prefers full sun. When young, use palm fertilizer in March, June, and October. Mature Palms usually get along on their own. Bismarck Palm doesn't exhibit nutritional deficiencies like other Palms and is somewhat salt tolerant.

PROBLEMS
Bismarck Palms recover from occasional light freeze damage.

USES AND SELECTIONS
Bismarck Palms are massive and striking. Their huge trunks with light blue-green fronds (to 4 feet across) are beautiful and command attention, even from a distance. They make excellent specimens in large gardens and can be planted along driveways or paths for a spectacular entrance. For maximum impact, plant in front of dark-green vegetation.

BLACK OLIVE
Bucida buceras

☼ ◯ ◊ 🌊

HARDINESS
Zones 10–11

COLOR(S)
Tiny white flowers

PEAK SEASON
Blooms April; evergreen foliage

MATURE SIZE
40 to 50 feet x 30 feet

WATER NEEDS
Keep rootball moist until established. Mature trees have high drought tolerance.

CARE
Fertilize three months after planting. Feed young trees three times a year in spring, summer, and fall. Prune dead wood, crossing branches, and water sprouts. Once mature, Black Olive needs little attention.

PROBLEMS
Outside southern Florida, plant in protected area or southern exposure since Black Olive can be cold sensitive.

USES AND SELECTIONS
This large shade tree requires a big space. Use in large yards or as a street tree. It is moderately fast-growing, resistant to wind, and tolerant of salt breezes. Also grows well on rocky soil. The leaves drop and are replaced throughout the year. When mature, it can be underplanted with Bird's Nest Anthuriums, big-leafed Philodendrons, and Bromeliads.

BOTTLEBRUSH
Callistemon rigidus

☼ 🌺 🌼 🐝 💧

HARDINESS
Zones 9–11

COLOR(S)
Red flowers

PEAK SEASON
Major blooms late winter through spring; evergreen foliage

MATURE SIZE
15 feet

WATER NEEDS
Keep rootball moist until established. Established trees need water only during severe drought.

CARE
Does best in well-drained sandy soils. Fertilize four to six weeks after planting. Feed in March and June for first two or three years. Prune any cold damage (in Central Florida) before spring growth begins. May need pruning to encourage even branching. Prune during late spring, after major bloom.

PROBLEMS
None reported

USES AND SELECTIONS
Bottlebrush adds a tropical look with flower clusters along the stem ends. Good accent plant for an area near entrance or patio. Use as stand-alone tree, an unclipped hedge, or cluster several together as a view barrier. Use with shrubs that flower at alternate times including Thryallis, Plumbago, Hydrangeas, and Jasmine. Some varieties have weeping growth habit or deeper red colors.

BUTIA PALM
Butia capitata

☼ ☼ ☼ ☼ 🦋 🍐 🐿 🥚 💧 🌴 〰

HARDINESS
Zones 8–10

COLOR(S)
Blue-green fronds

PEAK SEASON
Spring flowers

MATURE SIZE
15 feet x 15 feet

WATER NEEDS
Keep new plantings moist and do not allow to dry out for several growing seasons. Once established is very drought tolerant.

CARE
Add container plants at any time. Plant field-dug palms during spring and summer. Usually obtain nutrients from feedings of nearby plants. To encourage growth and maintain best color, fertilize once in March, June, and October with palm fertilizer. Somewhat salt tolerant.

PROBLEMS
Susceptible to leaf spots and trunk rots

USES AND SELECTIONS
Butia Palm is one of Florida's finest landscape plants. It is often planted as a focal point or to line streets. There is plenty of room for ground-cover plantings beneath this large palm. Use ornamentals that repeat the needle-like look, including Junipers, Liriope, and African Iris. The slow-growing Palm (also called Pindo or Jelly Palm) can be planted under most utility wires.

CABBAGE PALM
Sabal palmetto

HARDINESS
Zones 8–11

PEAK SEASON
Evergreen; blooms summer

MATURE SIZE
40 feet x 10 feet

WATER NEEDS
Until roots begin growing out from new plantings, thoroughly wet the rootball. Make sure soil does not dry out for several growing seasons. Established Cabbage Palms only need watering during extreme drought. However, they also tolerate moist soils.

CARE
Transplant in late spring to midsummer, with all fronds removed. Mulch to retain moisture. Fertilize in March, June, and October with palm fertilizer.

PROBLEMS
Brace newly planted larger specimens to prevent wind damage.

USES AND SELECTIONS
This is the official state tree of Florida. The palm has been used for hats, baskets, Native American roofs, and food. After older fronds drop, the remaining bases add interest to the trunk. Use as single specimen but looks best in clusters of three or more. The native Dwarf Palmetto is found throughout Florida as understory plant to 6 feet tall.

CEDAR
Juniperus virginiana

HARDINESS
Zones 8–10

COLOR(S)
Green leaves; blue-green fruits

MATURE SIZE
40 to 50 feet x 10 to 20 feet

WATER NEEDS
Water until established, then forget about it. Very drought tolerant. Does not like soggy roots.

CARE
Thrives in any well-drained soil. Carefree. Lower branches are sometimes pruned when they droop.

PROBLEMS
No serious pests

USES AND SELECTIONS
Once the most common tree in the eastern United States, it's also called Southern Red Cedar and Red Cedar. Florida was once filled with these tough, long-lived trees. Cedar Key was named for them and its port shipped fragrant cedar lumber to northern factories to make pencils and hope chests. Plant them as specimens, screens, and windbreaks. They also are suitable as bonsai, Christmas trees, and in wildlife gardens. The bark and trunk on mature trees have a showy, aged appearance. Some specimens take on a picturesque windswept look. Birds relish the blue-green fruit.

CHINESE ELM
Ulmus parvifolia

HARDINESS
Zones 8–9

COLOR(S)
Flowers not showy

PEAK SEASON
Late-summer flowers; semi-evergreen foliage

MATURE SIZE
35 to 40 feet

WATER NEEDS
Keep soil moist for first year or two. Thereafter, they are quite drought tolerant.

CARE
Plant at least 15 feet from buildings. Needs more staking than other trees. Keep stakes for up to a year. Feed lightly in March and June during first three years only. Maintain central leader until 6 to 8 feet tall, then allow branching for a weeping look. Prune periodically to keep limbs above sidewalks and patios.

PROBLEMS
Usually pest free

USES AND SELECTIONS
Grow as specimen tree to showcase the interesting peeling bark. Also suitable for patio, street, and general landscape use. Plant with other drought-tolerant selections. Use shade-tolerant underplantings including Bromeliads, Ivy, and Asiatic Jasmine. Several varieties include the wide-spreading, weeping 'Drake Elm' (more susceptible to wind damage) plus native Elm species.

CHINESE FAN PALM
Livistona chinensis

HARDINESS
Zones 9b–11

PEAK SEASON
Evergreen foliage

MATURE SIZE
20 to 30 feet x 15 feet; fronds 3 to 6 feet wide

WATER NEEDS
Established trees need little more than occasional irrigation in dry season.

CARE
The tough Chinese Fan Palm is not fussy and doesn't require babying. When fertilized a couple times a year, it does nicely. If removing brown fronds, wait until leaf stems are brown. The Palm can utilize needed potassium from the old leaves as they age.

PROBLEMS
Keep area around base open for air circulation, which helps prevents fungal disease. Susceptible to palm leaf skeletonizer.

USES AND SELECTIONS
Grow in containers in areas where freezing temperatures are likely. Older (taller) Chinese fan Palms allow the use of Bromeliads planted beneath or around them. Seeds are deep blue-green and pretty, ripening summer through fall. The drooping frond ends are divided so they seem to be hung with split ribbons.

CRAPEMYRTLE

Laegerstromia indica

HARDINESS
Zones 8–10

COLOR(S)
Red, pink, lavender, coral, white flowers; green foliage

PEAK SEASON
Blooms summer and fall

MATURE SIZE
20 feet x 20 feet

WATER NEEDS
Drought tolerant and does well in many soils but not standing water. Mulch to retain moisture.

CARE
Fertilize in March, June, and August. Prune lightly in late winter before new growth begins. If too many twigs grow out, thin to shape. If suckers develop from base, remove stems less than pencil-size diameter.

PROBLEMS
Older varieties susceptible to powdery mildew. Newer cultivars are disease resistant.

USES AND SELECTIONS
Use this reliable bloomer in mixed informal planting or as specimen. Let Crapemyrtle grow into a small tree and, during the summer flowering period, shine above other foliage, such as Plumbago, Philodendrons, and small Heliconias. After a few years the bark peels and becomes quite attractive. The leaves turn yellow then orange-red before falling in midwinter.

DOGWOOD

Cornus florida

HARDINESS
Zones 8–9

COLOR(S)
White flowers

PEAK SEASON
Blooms early spring; foliage deciduous

MATURE SIZE
20 to 35 feet x 25 to 35 feet

WATER NEEDS
Needs moist soil for best growth, especially in sandy soil. Mulch heavily. Do not let roots get soggy.

CARE
Plant in enriched, well-drained soil. Hard to establish in sandy soils. Prune to either one or several trunks. Leaves turn red and purple in autumn, more vividly in northern areas.

PROBLEMS
Susceptible to several diseases plus aphids and scale

USES AND SELECTIONS
Plant as specimen, background, or framing tree. Its size is ideal near patios and in smaller gardens for shade. It also does well beneath large oaks or pines. Numerous selections have different bract (flower) and tree forms. They include pink (do not thrive in Florida), dwarf, and weeping types. Red berries ripen in fall, remain into winter, and are relished by birds and wildlife. Native to Florida.

FLORIDA SILVER PALM
Coccothrinax argentata

HARDINESS
Zones 10b–11

MATURE SIZE
20 feet x 5 feet

WATER NEEDS
Water daily for first few weeks, then reduce waterings but keep root zone moist for first growing season. Plant at beginning of rainy season to reduce irrigation. When established, are very drought tolerant.

CARE
When young, use palm fertilizer in March, June, and October. Mature Palms get along on their own, unless leaves become off-color. Then apply nutrients. Grow in containers and protect from freezing in Central and North Florida.

PROBLEMS
Overwatering or wet feet can cause disease.

USES AND SELECTIONS
This very slow-growing small native has drooping fronds with silvery undersides. The fragile-looking Silver Palm is extraordinarily tough, being highly salt and drought tolerant. It is good for seaside homes plus xeriscape and native landscapes. It is suitable for patio and townhouse gardens with limited space. It looks good in groups of three to five or combined with other plants.

GEIGER TREE
Cordia sebestena

HARDINESS
Zones 10–11

COLOR(S)
Orange flowers

PEAK SEASON
Blooms year-round

MATURE SIZE
25 feet x 15 feet

WATER NEEDS
Established trees need little more than occasional irrigation in dry season.

CARE
Fertilize in spring and fall only. This tough little tree is salt and drought tolerant, but not cold tolerant. Leaves will turn brown when temperatures hit the low 40s to upper 30s. In a freeze, it dies to the ground but resprouts from the roots.

PROBLEMS
To treat the geiger beetle, use Sevin® or Rotenone on the larvae.

USES AND SELECTIONS
Plant with Sea Grape for a natural coastal setting, or give it a place of its own. Hummingbirds are attracted to the bright flowers. Use as a background for a butterfly garden. Plant with other native trees on perimeter of yard where irrigation does not reach. The Texas Wild Olive is a cold-tolerant, white-flowering relative. The fruits are edible but not tasty.

GUMBO LIMBO

Bursera simaruba

HARDINESS
Zones 10–11

COLOR(S)
Red to silver-red peeling bark

PEAK SEASON
Loses then regrows leaves in late winter and early spring. Dark red fruit takes a year to ripen.

MATURE SIZE
30 to 40-plus feet x 20-plus feet

WATER NEEDS
Water established trees during drought; keep mulched.

CARE
Once established, the fast-growing Gumbo Limbo needs little care. Trees can be started from branch cuttings. Keep root zone and branch watered.

PROBLEMS
The occasional aphids and caterpillars are not a problem.

USES AND SELECTIONS
This native is often found in river and coastal areas of the warmer parts of Florida. For light, high shade a mature tree makes a beautiful specimen, especially older trees with a large girth. Low underplantings of ferns and bromeliads show off the almost sculptural trunks. When planted on the south side of a home, this deciduous tree allows winter sun to come through the branches for energy-conscious plantings.

HOLLY

Ilex spp.

HARDINESS
Zones 8–10

COLOR(S)
Red berries; green leaves

PEAK SEASON
Fall and winter berries

MATURE SIZE
20 to 40 feet x 15 to 25 feet

WATER NEEDS
Most Hollies like well-drained acid soils and are drought tolerant once established. Water during droughts. A few, including Dahoon species, grow in damp sites.

CARE
Feed once in March and June for first three years. Give minimal trimming so limbs can develop berries.

PROBLEMS
The leaf drop in late winter signals the coming new growth and is not a problem. Witch's Broom disease may become a problem.

USES AND SELECTIONS
The adaptable Holly is good for shade, view barriers, hedges, and accents. Hollies have upright growth habit so they can be spaced within 10 to 20 feet of other trees and buildings. Plant with other small trees and large shrubs. Attractive with acid-loving plants like Azaleas, Camellias, and Gardenias. 'East Palatka' Holly has many berries, which attract wildlife.

LADY PALM
Rhapsis spp.

☀️ ☀️ 🌱 🥥 💧 💐 🌴

HARDINESS
Zones 9b–11

MATURE SIZE
6 to 15 feet x 15 feet

WATER NEEDS
Water daily for a few weeks, then gradually irrigate less often, keeping rootball moist. After the first growing season, Lady Palms can withstand fairly dry conditions. Reduce watering to a minimum except in drought.

CARE
Use palm fertilizer a couple times a year. Grow in protected areas of Central Florida; in colder areas grow in containers.

PROBLEMS
When hungry or in full sun, the leaves turn yellow.

USES AND SELECTIONS
The pliable and forgiving Lady Palm brings a sense of grace to landscapes. It beautifully serves as a screen and hedge when grown as a middle layer between a ground cover and taller Palms. It is also used in containers. Two species work well in Florida. *Rhapis excelsa* slowly grows to 12 or 14 feet. *R. humilis* is taller, with more drooping leaves, and it takes more cold.

LICUALA PALM
Licuala grandis

☀️ ☀️ ☀️ 🐝 🪴 🌴

HARDINESS
Zones 10–11

MATURE SIZE
To 9 feet x 5- to 6-foot crown

WATER NEEDS
This rainforest Palm likes plenty of moisture. Water thoroughly, twice weekly in dry season, to encourage roots to penetrate deep soil. Mulch well.

CARE
Licualas can be set back dramatically by transplanting, so place carefully. A low area with a humid microclimate protected from winds and hot sun is best. Shrubs, trellises, or other garden devices can be used for protection. Growth is slow, but leaves stay on a long time. Use standard fertilizer.

PROBLEMS
Falling fruit or branches from overhead may damage the large leaves

USES AND SELECTIONS
The round, pleated leaves of Licuala Palms are so different and attractive that even non-Palm fanciers admire them. The Palms look good in groups. Because they are slow growing, these Palms can be planted in containers, using a saucer to catch water and keep the rootball wet.

267

LIGNUM VITAE

Guaiacum sanctum

☼ ☀ Ⓝ ❀ ◌ 〰

HARDINESS
Zones 10b–11

COLOR(S)
Blue-violet flowers; golden pods

PEAK SEASON
Bloom spring to summer; evergreen leaves

MATURE SIZE
15 to 20 feet x 10 to 15 feet

WATER NEEDS
Keep rootball moist after planting. Once established is drought tolerant.

CARE
Needs excellent drainage. Use half-strength fertilizer weekly for new seedlings and slow-release fertilizer every three to four months for larger trees.

PROBLEMS
It takes several years for the tree to produce the incomparable blue flowers.

USES AND SELECTIONS
Plant this very slow-growing tree where small flowers can be seen near patio, home entrance, or in a mega-container. Use Lignum Vitae as a specimen tree. The tree has extremely heavy hard wood and black heartwood, which will not float. Now prized for wood turners, it was once used for boat and submarine construction. The United States Navy harvested trees from the Florida Keys, where it occurs naturally. The few left today are endangered.

LIVE OAK

Quercus virginiana

☼ ❀ Ⓝ ◕ ◌ 〰

HARDINESS
Zones 8–10

PEAK SEASON
Leaves drop in spring before new growth

MATURE SIZE
50 or more feet x 80 feet

WATER NEEDS
Drought tolerant once established

CARE
Take a wide range of soils. Mulch or plant with shallow-rooted ground cover. Although once thought to be slow growing, fertilizer, water, and mulch bring faster growth. Once established, little care is necessary.

PROBLEMS
Select locations with room for limbs which naturally grow low and horizontal. Hanging Spanish Moss may appear. It adds character and isn't harmful.

USES AND SELECTIONS
Whether grouped with other trees or alone, this strong and long-lived tree is ruggedly handsome. It is highly prized as a shade or street tree. Orchids grow wonderfully in it, as do Bromeliads. Use Ferns and Bromeliads beneath. In Florida there are specimen Live Oaks that are hundreds of years old. Some mark Indian burial spots. The Sand Live Oak is smaller and suitable for smaller landscapes.

MAHOGANY
Swietenia mahagoni

HARDINESS
Zones 10–11. Use only in frost- and freeze-free locations.

PEAK SEASON
Leaves drop in spring before new growth begins.

MATURE SIZE
45 feet x 40 feet

WATER NEEDS
Water new plantings, gradually tapering off watering. Established trees are drought tolerant. Irrigate during severe drought.

CARE
Feed four to six weeks after planting. Fertilize once in March and June for two or three years. Prune in winter to keep straight trunk and develop even branching.

PROBLEMS
Pests include caterpillars and borers. Use *Bacillus thuringiensis* and other recommended controls.

USES AND SELECTIONS
A great tree to combine with other small trees and greenery. Suitable for shade, to plant streetside, or to frame the home. Lawn will grow in dappled shade beneath it. The strong wood, salt tolerance, and wind resistance make Mahogany suitable for coastal landscapes. Add the tropical look with Bamboo, Hibiscus, Oleander, Bird-of-Paradise, and Bananas. The Mahogany's Central and American relative is used for timber.

PIGEON PLUM
Coccoloba diversifolia

HARDINESS
Zones 9–11

COLOR(S)
White flowers; fallen leaves turn golden

PEAK SEASON
Blooms around March; evergreen foliage

MATURE SIZE
30 to 50 feet x 15 to 20 feet

WATER NEEDS
Water young trees. Once established, they take drought well.

CARE
Fertilize consistently for first few years. If growing in a group, it grows tall and narrow; it grows shorter and fatter in sun.

PROBLEMS
None

USES AND SELECTIONS
Pigeon Plum is plentiful in coastal hammocks from the center of Florida to the Keys. It has dense upright growth and pretty bark, which make it useful for street planting or house framing, in formal or informal designs. Use in coastal plantings, along a wall, in large planters, or a native habitat. This versatile tree can blend with Wild Coffee, Ligustrum, Beautyberry, and other coastal woodland plants. It is used to harsh conditions, taking wind and salt spray well. Female trees have somewhat edible berries, which attract wildlife.

PLUMERIA

Plumeria spp.

☀ ☀ ☀ 🪴 🌱 💧 🌴🌊

HARDINESS
Zones 10–11 and warmer areas of 9b

COLOR(S)
Red, white, yellow, pink, multihued flowers

PEAK SEASON
Blooms summer through fall; deciduous foliage

MATURE SIZE
20 to 25 feet

WATER NEEDS
Very drought tolerant. Do not allow standing water.

CARE
Requires well-drained soil. Feed monthly during growing season using fertilizer with micronutrients. Long narrow leaves grow only at ends of stubby branches, which can be pruned for multiple trunks. Has some salt tolerance.

PROBLEMS
Branches susceptible to breaking. Poor drainage can cause root rot. Must be protected from freezing. Control of rust fungus may be needed.

USES AND SELECTIONS
Use Plumeria (also called Frangipani) where its beauty and fragrance can be appreciated—near decks, patios, and entryways. Plant for a tropical look. This showy specimen tree can also be planted close to a home, to benefit from the building's warmth. There are countless species and cultivars. Grows well in containers in cooler locations.

PYGMY DATE PALM

Phoenix roebelenii

☀ ☀ ☀ 🐝 🌴

HARDINESS
Zones 10–11 and warmer areas of 9b

MATURE SIZE
10 feet x 8-plus feet

WATER NEEDS
Keep the root zone of newly planted Date Palms moist during the first growing season. This has more need for water than other Palms.

CARE
Use palm fertilizer with micronutrients to prevent deficiencies in March, June, and October. May show potassium deficiencies and need additional applications of potassium sulfate with manganese sulfate. Protect from cold in Central and North Florida. Pygmy Date Palm is small enough to grow in large containers.

PROBLEMS
The spines at the base of Phoenix Palm fronds warrant care when trimming and handling.

USES AND SELECTIONS
The versatile shorter Pygmy Date is easiest to prune and useful for entrances, small accent trees, and containers for the pool and patio areas. Multi-trunked specimens are especially attractive. A group of two or three makes a nice vignette at an entry or in a small garden.

RED MAPLE

Acer rubrum

HARDINESS
Zones 8–10

COLOR(S)
Small red flowers; green leaves turn red and orange in fall before dropping

PEAK SEASON
Spring blooms are followed by new leaves

MATURE SIZE
40 to 50 or more feet x 30 feet

WATER NEEDS
Tolerates some extended flooding but prefers slightly drier areas or periodically wet, acidic soils.

CARE
Get trees with a single leader to prevent future splitting. Avoid dry, sandy soils. Once established, little care is required if properly located.

PROBLEMS
Not the same as the Red Norway Maple of northern climates. Borers may be a problem.

USES AND SELECTIONS
This big handsome tree is adapted to wet areas, such as a lakefront. The beauty of changing fall leaves is possible with this Florida native. Red Maples can be used to frame a house or garden, or as shade or specimen trees. Plant with Cabbage Palms, Sweet Bay Magnolia, Dahoon Holly, Wax Myrtle, and Leather Ferns.

REDBERRY STOPPER

Eugenia confusa

HARDINESS
Zones 10–11

COLOR(S)
White flowers; glossy dark-green foliage

PEAK SEASON
Blooms spring

MATURE SIZE
20 feet x 10 feet

WATER NEEDS
Drought tolerant once established

CARE
Plant from beginning of rainy season through midsummer. Mulch to retain moisture. Adapted to rocky soil. Fertilize in moderate amounts. The leaves will complain when the tree is hungry, by turning a little yellow. Once established, needs little care.

PROBLEMS
None

USES AND SELECTIONS
This slow-growing native is a durable and dependable small tree that should be planted more often. Use in small gardens and patios, or with a group of natives. This beautiful little tree can be useful for townhouse and zero lot line landscapes where space is tight. Its columnar growth habit suits entryway plantings. Three other Stopper species are also native to Florida: Red Stopper (one of Florida's rarest native trees), Spanish Stopper (salt tolerant), and White Stopper (salt tolerant).

REDBUD
Cercis canadensis

 ☀ Ⓝ 🍃 💧

HARDINESS
Zones 8–9

COLOR(S)
Purple-pink flowers

PEAK SEASON
Blooms spring before foliage; foliage deciduous

MATURE SIZE
20 to 30 feet x 15 to 25 feet

WATER NEEDS
Drought tolerant, although it grows best with some moisture and tolerates brief periods of standing water.

CARE
Plant in enriched soil. Transplant spring or fall. Plant containerized trees any time. Tends to grow multiple trunks, with drooping outer branches. If desired, can be pruned to have single trunk.

PROBLEMS
Branches susceptible to breakage. Scale can be controlled with horticultural oil sprays. Borers and webworms may also occur.

USES AND SELECTIONS
Plant Redbud as a shade tree or use near a patio. This flowering tree makes a beautiful specimen and works well when planted as a shrub border. The leaves turn yellow before falling in winter. Combine with Dogwood for beautiful colors in both spring and fall. There are numerous cultivars. However, this Florida native is the one predominantly planted.

ROYAL PALM
Roystonea elata

☀ Ⓝ 🐝 🌴

HARDINESS
Zones 10–11

MATURE SIZE
50 feet x 30 feet

WATER NEEDS
Newly planted Royal Palms should be kept moist until roots begin to grow out. Make sure soil does not thoroughly dry out for several growing seasons. Mulch new plantings to retain moisture. Once established, water weekly or whenever soil begins to dry, especially during drought.

CARE
Looks and grows best when fertilized once in March, June, and October with palm fertilizer. Periodically remove older leaves to keep attractive specimen.

PROBLEMS
Brace new plantings to prevent wind damage. In some soils they can exhibit nutrient deficiencies. Apply fertilizer with adequate potassium and micronutrients.

USES AND SELECTIONS
Plant these tall, fast-growing Palms alone or in clusters of three or more. Use as accents or in rows along wide streets. The long area of smooth green trunk at the top catches attention. Add ornamentals that complete the tropical look, including Bougainvillea, Crotons, Allamanda, Gingers, and Philodendrons.

ROYAL POINCIANA
Delonix regia

HARDINESS
Zones 10b–11

COLOR(S)
Cerise, scarlet, and yellow flowers

PEAK SEASON
Blooms pring to summer; often but not always deciduous

MATURE SIZE
25 to 40 feet x 40 feet

WATER NEEDS
After planting, keep root zone moist throughout first growing season. While young, water in dry season. Drought tolerant when established.

CARE
Plant in large, open space; it requires a big landscape. Apply fertilizer in early spring. Prune out deadwood.

PROBLEMS
This tree is too large for a small yard. Roots can uplift asphalt. Aggressive roots and long pods create a grass cutter's nightmare.

USES AND SELECTIONS
The cascading canopy of brilliant color makes a flowering Royal Poinciana stop traffic. After the enormous initial showing in spring, flowers linger throughout summer. The doubly compound leaves have a ferny look and provide dappled shade. Goldfcourses, parks, and wide boulevards are best for this large, spreading tree.

SATINLEAF
Chrysophyllum oliviforme

HARDINESS
Zones 10–11. Will freeze back if unprotected.

COLOR(S)
White flowers; green leaves with coppery backs

PEAK SEASON
Blooms spring

MATURE SIZE
30 to 40 feet x 15 feet

WATER NEEDS
Keep roots moist throughout first growing season. Fairly drought tolerant when established.

CARE
Fertilize until plant becomes established. Seedlings may proliferate and can be dug at any time.

PROBLEMS
Caterpillars may occasionally chew the leaves.

USES AND SELECTIONS
Few other trees have leaves as beautiful as the native Satinleaf. Group several trees along a drive or property line for a beautiful statement of dark green and copper. As a specimen tree, the copper undersides are clearly visible when wind blows or when you're beneath it. The dark purple fruits attract birds. If landscaping for wildlife, use with Wild Coffee, Pigeon Plum, Sea Grape, and other fruit-bearing natives that offer birds and small animals food and shelter. The flowers are sweetly scented.

SAW PALMETTO
Serenoa repens

HARDINESS
Zones 8–11

PEAK SEASON
Spring and summer flowers

MATURE SIZE
6 feet x 6 feet

WATER NEEDS
Keep new plantings moist until roots start growing out. Mulch heavily. Do not let soil dry out for several growing seasons. Once established is very drought tolerant.

CARE
Plant in any soil. Allow plenty of space for these clump-forming, low-maintenance palms, which grow as wide as tall. Prune back as needed. Usually fertilizing surrounding plants is enough feeding. Has high salt tolerance.

PROBLEMS
May be affected by palmetto weevils and palm leaf skeletonizers

USES AND SELECTIONS
Use Saw Palmettos as view barriers and space dividers. Most attractive in clusters of three, it can be used as an accent plant near patios and along walkways. Add to natural Florida settings with other natives including Hollies, Pines, ornamental grasses, and Coreopsis. Fruit is eaten by wildlife and extracts from it are used to treat benign prostate problems.

SLASH PINE
Pinus elliottii

HARDINESS
Zones 8–10

PEAK SEASON
Evergreen

MATURE SIZE
To 100 feet x 50 feet

WATER NEEDS
Water daily for first few weeks, then gradually taper off. Drought tolerant when established.

CARE
Plant in well-drained soil. Feed four to six weeks after planting. Continue fertilizing once in March and June for two or three years. Once established, grows quite rapidly. Too frequent watering and fertilizing of established trees can cause decline.

PROBLEMS
Driving over pine roots may damage them. Pests include caterpillars and borers. Use recommended control for caterpillars. Keep construction equipment away from trees to prevent borer damage.

USES AND SELECTIONS
Underplant with acid-loving Azaleas, Camellias, and Hydrangeas. Can also be clustered as a backdrop for home sites and in wildlife areas. Other Pines may be considered for Florida landscapes, depending upon the region, including the Sand Pine, Spruce Pine, Longleaf Pine, Loblolly Pine, Japanese Black Pine, and Virginia Pine.

SOUTHERN MAGNOLIA
Magnolia grandiflora

HARDINESS
Zones 8–10

COLOR(S)
White flowers; glossy green leaves

PEAK SEASON
Blooms May through July; Evergreen but sheds most leaves in late winter and spring, before new growth begins.

MATURE SIZE
80 to 90 feet x 30 to 40 feet

WATER NEEDS
New plantings very moisture sensitive. Keep soil moist with frequent waterings. Apply mulch. Once established is drought tolerant in enriched soils.

CARE
Feed in March and June for first three years.

PROBLEMS
Scale and black sooty mold can be ignored or controlled with oil spray.

USES AND SELECTIONS
Magnolias represent the South. They're ideal to frame a home, for shade, or to serve as backdrop. It's often difficult to find plants to grow under Magnolias. Use Bromeliads, Begonias, Ivy, and Impatiens. Request by variety to obtain desired flowering or leaf characteristics. Some take too long to flower and grow too tall. 'Little Gem' is smaller and an early bloomer, with extended flowering.

SWEETBAY MAGNOLIA
Magnolia virginiana

HARDINESS
Zones 8–10

COLOR(S)
White flowers; green leaves

PEAK SEASON
Blooms summer; evergreen to semi-evergreen foliage

MATURE SIZE
50 feet x 20 feet

WATER NEEDS
Tolerates wet soil with poorer drainage. Grows best in moist, fertile soils. Grows in sandy soils if provided adequate water. Water new plantings daily for first few weeks, then gradually taper off. Established trees should not be allowed to dry. Water whenever soil feels dry.

CARE
Fertilize four to six weeks after planting. Continue feeding in March and June for first two or three years only. Prune older trees in late winter to keep trunk straight and develop even branching.

PROBLEMS
Control scales with oil spray. Use borer spray or recommended method to control borers.

USES AND SELECTIONS
Plant this great shade and accent tree in damp areas and for naturalistic plantings. Use with other moisture-loving trees and shrubs, such as Bald Cypress and Wax Myrtle.

SWEET GUM
Liquidambar styraciflua

HARDINESS
Zones 8–10A

COLOR(S)
Fall foliage colorful before leaves drop

MATURE SIZE
50 feet x 20 feet

WATER NEEDS
Water daily for first few weeks, then gradually taper off. Established trees are drought tolerant.

CARE
Feed four to six weeks after planting, then once in March and June for two or three years. Established trees do not need additional feedings. Prune in late winter for a straight trunk and even branching.

PROBLEMS
Use *Bacillus thuringiensis*, oil spray, or other recommended controls for caterpillars and thrips. Older limbs often produce a corky ridge. This is a normal growth.

USES AND SELECTIONS
The Sweet Gum is a truly reliable native tree with a good shape that won't get too tall for average landscapes. It is upright and pyramidal in habit. The lobed leaves have a starlike appearance and are great for fall color. Mature trees produce a prickly seed ball that can hurt bare feet.

TABEBUIA
Tabebuia caraiba

HARDINESS
Zones 10–11

COLOR(S)
Golden yellow flowers

PEAK SEASON
Leaves drop just before flowers appear in spring.

MATURE SIZE
25 to 40 feet x 40 feet

WATER NEEDS
Water daily for first few weeks, then gradually taper off. Established trees are drought tolerant. Water during severe drought.

CARE
Feed four to six weeks after planting. Continue fertilizing once in March and June for only two or three years. Prune crossed or dead limbs after flowering. In mid-Central Florida plant in warmest landscape location. Areas near a lake are best. Frozen trees grow back but need training to keep central trunk.

PROBLEMS
None

USES AND SELECTIONS
Also called Trumpet Tree, its bloom is spectacular and it makes an excellent small specimen tree. Its showstopper display lasts for up to a month and fallen blossoms produce a yellow carpet. Also prized for its gnarled-looking trunks. Other yellow species grow in warmer parts of zone 9b.

TABEBUIA IPE
Tabebuia impetiginosa

HARDINESS
Zones 9b–11

COLOR(S)
Pink flowers

PEAK SEASON
Blooms spring

MATURE SIZE
25 feet x 25 feet

WATER NEEDS
Water daily for first few weeks. Gradually taper off to watering as needed. Drought tolerant once established.

CARE
Plant in well-drained enriched soil. Feed four to six weeks after planting. Continue feedings in March and June for two or three years. Prune to remove deadwood and keep one central trunk.

PROBLEMS
During cold the flowers may be damaged, but limbs unaffected.

USES AND SELECTIONS
Also called Pink Trumpet Tree or Ipe. It is a great stand-alone accent tree to view at a distance or combined with other small trees. Use with underplantings of seasonal flowers. After the leaves drop in late winter, the pink blossoms make their month-long display. They then fade and drop to the ground creating a carpet of color. Other pink-flowering Tabebuias are found in Central and South Florida.

TEXAS WILD OLIVE
Cordia boissieri

HARDINESS
Zones 8b–11

COLOR(S)
White flowers

PEAK SEASON
Blooms and foliage year-round

MATURE SIZE
About 20 feet x 10 to 15 feet

WATER NEEDS
Keep root zone moist for first growing season and gradually allow nature to take over. Is drought tolerant.

CARE
Takes wide range of soils. Fertilize with Palm fertilizer. These little trees require little care and may flower at an early age, even at one foot high.

PROBLEMS
Avoid areas that flood or are near sprinklers. No major pruning is necessary. Remove dead wood, rubbing, or diseased branches in late winter or early spring.

USES AND SELECTIONS
This little flowering tree is also called White Olive and White Geiger. Its good behavior and blooms are suitable in a front yard, near an entryway, or as a specimen tree. Plant with other drought-tolerant plants, like Trailing Lantana, Liriope, or Kalanchoe. Not sensitive to cold like its cousin, the Geiger Tree.

TREES

Name	Area of Florida	H/W (Feet)	Soil Type	Flowers/Season	Fruits	Best Uses
African Tuliptree	S	50/50	Average	Orange, yellow/Winter, spring	Not showy	Accent, shade
American Holly	NC	40/20	Average	White/Spring	Red/Fall	Accent, street, shade
Attenuate Holly	NC	30/15	Average	White/Spring	Red/Fall	Street, shade
Bald Cypress	NCS	80/30	Wet or dry	Inconspicuous	Green/Summer	Street, shade
Black Olive	S	40/40	Average	Inconspicuous	Black/Fall	Shade, street
Bottlebrush	CS	15/15	Average	Red/Spring	Not showy	Accent, street
Cattley Guava	S	20/15	Average	White/Spring	Red/Summer	Accent, shade, street
Cedar	NCS	50/20	Average	Inconspicuous	Not showy	Accent, hedge
Cherry Laurel	NC	35/30	Average	White/Spring	Black/Fall	Shade, street
Chickasaw Plum	NC	20/20	Average	White/Spring	Reddish/Summer	Accent, shade, street
Chinese Elm	NC	35/40	Average	Greenish/Fall	Not showy	Shade, street
Chinese Pistache	NC	25/25	Average	Greenish/Spring	Orange/Fall	Shade, street
Crapemyrtle	NC	20/20	Average	Various/Summer	Brown/Fall	Accent, shade, street
Dahoon Holly	NCS	25/10	Moist	White/Spring	Red/Fall	Accent
Dogwood	NC	30/20	Moist	White/Spring	Red/Fall	Accent, shade
Fringe Tree	NC	12/10	Average	White/Spring	Not showy	Accent, under story
Geiger Tree	S	25/25	Average	Orange/Spring	Not showy	Accent, shade, street
Golden Rain Tree	NC	30/30	Average	Yellow/Fall	Pink pod/Fall	Accent, shade, street
Golden Shower Tree	S	40/40	Average	Yellow/Summer	Pod/Fall	Accent, shade, street
Italian Cypress	NCS	30/10	Average	Inconspicuous	Not showy	Accent, hedge
Jacaranda	CS	40/50	Average	Purple/Spring	Not showy	Accent, shade
Jerusalem Thorn	NCS	20/20	Average	Yellow/Summer	Not showy	Accent

N = North Florida   C = Central Florida   S = South Florida

TREES

Name	Area of Florida	H/W (Feet)	Soil Type	Flowers/ Season	Fruits	Best Uses
Laurel Oak	NCS	60/50	Average	Inconspicuous	Acorn/Fall	Shade, street
Lignum Vitae	S	15/10	Average	Blue/ Year-round	Yellow/ Year-round	Accent
Ligustrum	NCS	15/15	Average	White/Spring	Black/Fall	Accent, shade
Live Oak	NCS	60/100	Average	Inconspicuous	Acorn/Fall	Shade, street
Loblolly Bay	NC	40/15	Moist	White/Summer	Not showy	Accent, shade
Loquat	NCS	25/20	Average	White/Fall	Orange/Fall, winter	Shade, fruit
Mahogany	S	50/50	Average	Green/Spring	Brown/Fall	Shade, street
Pigeon Plum	S	30/20	Average	White/Spring	Red/Fall	Accent, shade, street
Plumeria	S	20/20	Average	White,pink/ Summer	Not showy	Accent, street
Queen's Crape Myrtle	S	30/30	Average	Purple/ Summer	Not showy	Accent, shade, street
Redbud	NC	25/20	Average	Pink/Spring	Not showy	Accent, shade, street
Red Maple	NCS	40/30	Moist	Red/Winter	Reddish/ Spring	Shade, street
River Birch	NC	40/30	Moist or dry	Inconspicuous	Not showy	Accent, shade, street
Royal Poinciana	S	40/50	Average	Orange, red/ Summer	Not showy	Accent, shade, street
Saucer Magnolia	NC	25/20	Average	Pink/Spring	Not showy	Accent
Sea Grape	CS	20/12	Average	White/Spring	Purple/ Summer	Accent, shade, street
Shumard Oak	NC	60/60	Average	Inconspicuous	Acorn/Fall	Shade, street
Silk Tree	NC	30/30	Average	Pink/Spring	Not showy	Accent, shade
Silver Buttonwood	S	15/15	Average	Inconspicuous	Not showy	Accent, shade, street
Slash Pine	NCS	60/40	Average	Inconspicuous	Cone	Shade
Southern Magnolia	NCS	80/40	Moist or dry	White/Summer	Green pod/ Summer	Accent, shade, street
Southern Juniper	NCS	30/30	Average	Inconspicuous	Blue/Fall	Shade, street, hedge
Sugarberry	NC	50/50	Moist	Inconspicuous	Red/Fall	Shade, street

TREES

Name	Area of Florida	H/W (Feet)	Soil Type	Flowers/ Season	Fruits	Best Uses
Sweet Acacia	CS	15/20	Average	Yellow/ Year-round	Brown/ Year-round	Accent, street
Sweetbay Magnolia	NCS	40/20	Moist	White/Spring	Not showy	Shade
Sweet Gum	NC	60/30	Moist or dry	Inconspicuous	Brown/Fall	Shade, street
Sycamore	NC	80/60	Average	Inconpicuous	Brown/Fall	Shade, street
Tabebuia	CS	25/25	Average	Yellow, pink/ Spring	Not showy	Accent, shade
Tuliptree	NC	80/30	Average	Yellowish/ Spring	Not showy	Shade, street
Water Oak	NCS	50/60	Average	Inconspicuous	Acorn/Fall	Shade, street
Wax Myrtle	NCS	15/20	Moist or dry	Inconspicuous	Blue/Fall	Accent, street
Weeping Fig	S	50/70	Average	Inconspicuous	Not showy	Shade
Winged Elm	NC	30/25	Average	Inconspicuous	Not showy	Shade, street
Yaupon Holly	NC	20/15	Average	White/Spring	Red/Fall	Accent, street
Yellow Poinciana	CS	50/50	Average	Yellow/ Summer	Not showy	Accent, shade
Yew Podocarpus	NCS	40/20	Average	Cream/Spring	Purple/ Summer	Accent, hedge

PALMS

Name	Area of Florida	Height (Feet)	Light Needs	Growth Habit	Best Uses
Areca	S	10–20	Sun, filtered sun	Multistemmed	Accent, patios
Australian Fan	CS	40–50	Sun	Single trunk	Clusters
Bismarck	CS	40–70	Sun	Single trunk	Accent, street
Butia	NCS	10–20	Sun	Single trunk	Accent, patios
Cabbage	NCS	30–40	Sun	Single trunk	Clusters, streets
California Washington	NCS	50–60	Sun	Single trunk	Clusters, streets
Canary Island Date	NCS	30–40	Sun	Single trunk	Accent, streets
Chinese Fan	CS	20–30	Sun	Single trunk	Clusters, patios

PALMS

Name	Area of Florida	Height (Feet)	Light Needs	Growth Habit	Best Uses
Date	NCS	40–50	Sun	Single trunk	Accent, streets
Dwarf Palmetto	NCS	3–6	Sun	Single trunk	Accent, natural areas
European Fan	NCS	6–8	Sun, filtered sun	Multistemmed	Accent, patios
Florida Silver	S	15–20	Sun, filtered sun	Single trunk	Accent, patios
Gru-Gru	S	30–40	Sun	Single trunk	Clusters, streets
Jamaica Thatch	S	10–20	Sun	Single trunk	Clusters
Lady	CS	8–10	Filtered sun	Multistemmed	Foundations, patios
Licuala	S	6–8	Filtered sun	Single trunk	Accent, patios
MacArthur	S	20–25	Sun, filtered sun	Multistemmed	Accent, patios
Malayan Dwarf Coconut	S	40–60	Sun	Single trunk	Clusters, street
Mexican Washington	NCS	80–90	Sun	Single trunk	Streets
Needle	NCS	4–5	Light shade	Multistemmed	Accent, natural areas
Paurotis	CS	15–20	Sun, light shade	Multistemmed	Accent, patios
Puerto Rico Hat	CS	40–50	Sun	Single trunk	Clusters
Pygmy Date	S	8–10	Sun, filtered sun	Single trunk	Accent, patios
Queen	CS	25–30	Sun	Single trunk	Clusters, streets
Royal Palm	S	80–90	Sun	Single trunk	Clusters, streets
Saw Palmetto	NCS	4–6	Sun, filtered sun	Multistemmed	Accent, natural areas
Senegal Date	S	20–25	Sun	Multistemmed	Accent, patios
Solitaire	S	15–20	Sun, filtered sun	Single trunk	Accent, patios
Windmill	NC	10–15	Sun, filtered sun	Single trunk	Accent, patios

N = North Florida   C = Central Florida   S = South Florida

JANUARY

• Trees can be planted now, but Palm plantings should wait until warmer weather. Plant dormant bare-root trees shortly after receipt and keep soil moist.

• Start pruning shade trees. Don't perform major pruning of fruiting or spring flowering trees, or Crapemyrtle. But just about any tree can have dead limbs removed, suckers and lanky growths trimmed, and crisscrossed limbs controlled. Trim old seed stalks and declining fronds from Palms.

• Few established trees and Palms need special waterings. However, most new plantings should be watered daily for first few months. The larger the tree, the longer watering is needed before the tree is left on its own.

• Shade and flowering trees are often fertilized for the first three to five years. Thereafter, root systems can remove nutrients from ground. Palm feedings should be delayed until warmer weather.

FEBRUARY

• When purchasing trees, look for disease-free ones with straight trunks and good branching. Avoid twin trunks and branches with sharp "V" angles. Rootbound trees have been in containers too long and may take extra time to become established. A small compact tree may root faster than a larger one. Transport new trees carefully or arrange for delivery.

• Maintain a 3- to 4-inch mulch layer around trees and Palms, beginning 6 or more inches from the trunk.

• Keep soil of new trees thoroughly moist for several months.

• Feed trees (not Palms) for their first three to five years. Apply fertilizer either now or next month. Apply fertilizer over the ground with a spreader or use tree spikes, liquid fertilizer, or composted manure.

• Caterpillars may start appearing. Most can be ignored, but if infestation is heavy it can be pruned or sprayed. Also look for aphids, scales, and thrips. Seldom are controls applied except in small trees.

MARCH

• Buy container-grown trees and Palms with good root system. If container soil is dry, soak it well. Cut off roots growing out of holes to make removal easier. If winds are a concern, stake the tree.

• Make sure younger trees maintain a straight trunk. Remove all limbs that may compete with central leader. Once shade trees are above head high, branching is allowed to develop a rounded tree. Palms need little guidance. Keep buds of nursery-dug plants covered with leaves for about 60 days.

• Keep up water schedule for new plantings since March is a dry month.

• If you missed the February feeding, do it now. Spread the fertilizer, then water thoroughly. For Palms apply "palm special" under the fronds' spread. Where possible, use slow-release product. Unlike trees, Palms need regular annual feedings.

• Stressed trees may be susceptible to borers. Palms may be affected by the palmetto weevil. Contact local Extension Service for control recommendations.

APRIL

• The time for planting bare-root trees is over, but you can still add balled-and-burlapped and container-grown trees. Most balled-and-burlapped trees and palms are planted by nurserymen these days. Homeowners usually plant container specimens. Be sure to stake trees against wind damage.

• Check new trees regularly for possible problems. Provide pruning or other care as needed.

• Don't forget regular waterings for new plantings. Older trees and palms can exist with seasonal rains.

• Feeding time is over for most trees. If you forgot the spring feeding, there is still time. The next feeding for new trees is scheduled in June. Continue feeding palms as needed during spring.

• Treehoppers may appear in some trees but damage is usually minimal. Caterpillars may be extra heavy this month but most can be ignored or treated with natural spray. The oak leaf blister is caused by a fungus, which must be controlled before infection occurs, in winter or early spring.

MAY

• There is still plenty of planting time. Nursery inventory will be reduced for summer. If you get trees home but can't plant them yet, keep them at landscape light levels. Check daily for water needs. If stored for long time, feed liquid fertilizer every other week or apply slow-release fertilizer. Now is the ideal time to add Palms.

• Continue grooming all trees and palms. Remove limbs and fronds that interfere with landscape maintenance. Adjust ties on staked trees so they don't cut into trunks.

• Keep watering on regular schedule.

• Wait until June to fertilize trees. Feed Palms slow-release fertilizer or use light feeding of regular fertilizer.

• Powdery mildew fungus loves spring months. It will not cause major decline, but causes contorted and smaller leaves. Treat young trees with fungicide. Other active pests are borers, caterpillars, thrips, palm leaf skeletonizers, and scale. It is normal for Magnolias to drop their leaves during spring.

JUNE

• Prevent potential damage from storms and hurricanes. Check for weak or insect-damaged branches. Consider older trees that could affect buildings or neighboring property. Although Palms are very wind-resistant, remove declining fronds and coconuts.

• Planting never stops. Add container-grown trees or palms. All Palm plantings are best done at this time.

• With a little luck, Mother Nature will help with watering. Provide daily soaking of new plantings if necessary. New trees, or those needing a boost, can receive a special feeding this month. If you missed palm feeding last month, provide a slow-release fertilizer feeding or a light application of regular fertilizer.

• Pests may be noticed in many trees. But their damage is minimal and seldom are sprays needed. Look for aphids, borers, mites, oak leaf blister, powdery mildew, and scale. In palms, check for skeletonizers and leaf spots.

JULY

• Summer pruning can be made on trees that flower during winter. But don't delay much longer since buds are formed during summer. Don't forget to remove dead or declining limbs.

• To keep crapemyrtles blooming, remove seed-heads. Cut limbs back to a point about the size of your finger to stimulate new growth and blooms. With good pruning you can keep them flowering through September.

• Check Palm fronds and remove older leaves but not too many green ones, which are needed for food production.

• Summer rains should do most of the watering. Make sure new plantings stay thoroughly watered.

• Forget tree feedings for another month or two unless you are a little behind. If on the monthly Palm feeding schedule, remember that a light application is all you need.

• Lacewings and thrips are summer tree pests that are usually tolerated. Other insects feeding in summer include aphids, caterpillars, and scales.

AUGUST

• Continue adding container-grown trees and palms. Rains make planting easier and provide some waterings. Decide now where you need additional Palms or shade trees.

• Continue summer pruning of unwanted or damaged limbs, competing shoots, out-of-bounds branches, and old palm fronds and seed stalks. Do not apply paints or wound coverings.

• With a little luck, summer rains will provide some waterings for at least another month. Make sure rootballs of new plantings get completely wet.

• No tree feeding is needed for another month or two. Give Palms another slow-release feeding or a light feeding of standard palm fertilizer, followed by a watering.

• Grasshopper, katydids, or beetles may chew tree leaves. Unless trees are small, the damage is minimal and will not affect their growth. Hand pick on young trees or apply insecticide. On trees, look for aphids, lacebugs, thrips, scale, and whiteflies. Palms may have skeletonizers and leaf spots.

SEPTEMBER

• Tree and Palm planting can continue with container-grown material. Provide good care while transporting home. If you cannot move them properly, ask for delivery.

• Eliminate competition from weeds, grass, and shrubs around the tree base. Coverings can encourage foot rot and give insects a hiding place. Use weed trimmers carefully so they don't damage the trunk.

• In most years the rainy season ends by mid-month. If you have new trees and palms, keep up daily waterings.

• Give fall feeding for new trees this month or next. Palm feedings of slow-release fertilizer should be delayed another month. If using standard palm fertilizer, apply the light monthly feeding.

• Damage from tree borers is usually ignored. Where possible, prune them from trees to eradicate the population. Twigs dropped from twig girdler activity should be destroyed. Some active insects are caterpillars, scales, and whiteflies.

OCTOBER

• Planting gets easier during cooler weather. Add several stakes for support if affected by winds. Allow the trunk a little freedom to move.

• Tree and Palm care begins to wind down in fall. Continue checking for storm-damaged limbs and fronds, and declining portions. These can be removed anytime. In colder parts of the state try to complete major pruning. Where possible, the planting should be dormant or growth slowed.

• You do not need to be as conscientious about watering new trees and palms this month, but it's best if they remain moist until established.

• If you missed the September tree feeding, there is still time. Scatter fertilizer (without a weed-killer) under the trees' spread then water in. This is the last palm feeding of the year if you are using either slow-release or standard fertilizers.

• Pests slow their feeding habits with cooler weather and damage is generally ignored. Pests include caterpillars, lacebugs, and twig girdlers.

NOVEMBER

• Adding trees to the landscape never stops in Florida, thanks to container production. As weather turns cooler, it becomes easier to move balled-and-burlapped and bare-root trees. Planting techniques are about the same. Late fall and winter are not the best time to add Palms to the landscape. If necessary, container-grown palms can be added in warmer areas.

• Taller trees and those with large canopies should be staked for up to a year. Don't stake a tree if it's not needed. The natural movement of the trunk produces a sturdier tree.

• It's drier but cooler so watering is not quite as necessary as during hotter weather. Do make sure the soil stays moist with newer trees.

• Feeding is over for trees and palms until next February or March. If container plants are growing, give a light feeding.

• Spanish and ball moss, lichens, and peeling bark on trees are normal and seldom need attention.

DECEMBER

• Delay all palm plantings until warmer weather, March through midsummer. If transplanting a tree, make sure the soil is moist when digging.

• Make sure the area under trees and palms remain weed-free. Even though winter arrives this month, Florida has winter weeds. Pull weeds by hand or spot-kill with a nonselective herbicide that permits use around growing plants. Renew mulches as needed to maintain a moist soil and help control weeds.

• Feeding time is over for the rest of the year. Most trees and palms are dormant and have received all the nutrients needed for growth. The next feeding time for trees up to three to five years of age is February or March. Palm feeding time begins in March. Make sure all leftover fertilizer is stored in a sealed bag to keep it from clumping and becoming difficult to spread.

• Most pests are not very active at this time of year.

TROPICAL
PLANTS
for Florida

Long ago we called the tropics "The Torrid Zone." Perhaps we should go back to that name to once again bring a sense of urgency to what we now discuss so dispassionately, given the wholesale destruction under way there. If we knew more about the tropics, this sense of danger to the tropical natural world might be more real to us. Because so much of life exists in the tropics, our concern needs to manifest itself before all life is threatened.

If we look closely at tropical plants, we can allow them to serve as gateways to our understanding of larger tropical ecosystems. They will lead us not to one vast, oppressively hot place, but to a whole galaxy of niches, from the tops of enormous, 200-foot trees to the diminutive and mostly unknown world of fungi. The stories of tropical plants are tales of adaptation, exploitation, temptation, seduction, and unlikely triumph in a climate that promotes ceaseless competition for life itself.

A STORY TO TELL

Start with the story of a vine that begins its life on the forest floor, where it seeks not light at germination but darkness. For darkness means shadow, and shadow in all likelihood means a tree trunk. Once there, a small leaf emerges and flattens itself against the damp bark of the buttressing root, itself an architectural wonder. The next leaf is thrust over the top of the first, slightly higher on the tree, until eventually, the vine has worked its way into the upper canopy. There, it can quit making these tiny, clinging-for-dear-life leaves. There, it can detect more light and more air, and so it begins growing bigger leaves, better able to take in the sun, to bask in the rain, to reach out from the trunk and wobble in the wind, vigorous and, yes, victorious.

Orchids, on the other hand, do not attack their hosts, but coexist with them. Dust-like seeds find the fungus-rich compost that collects on a tree branch, and they germinate, uniting with the fungus in a relationship that provides food for the seed and a home for the fungus. Then, residing in a peculiar elevation, the plant has figured out a way to signal pollinators to find it. One of them creates flowers with the exact scent that a male euglossine bee uses to attract a female bee, and it disperses the scent, molecule by molecule, to bring in the bee. Once there, the bee wedges himself inside the flower to secure packets of the perfume for himself, and in the process he triggers the latch of the pollinia (the tiny golden orbs of male pollen produced by the flower); they stick to him as he backs out to fly away. Greedy for more, the bee visits another flower. Only this time, the pollinia become attached to the sticky female stigma, and the Orchid is pollinated.

Other Orchids create bee look-alike flowers, so the male bees believe they have spotted a female bee. The disguise works.

These stories are endlessly intriguing. They turn the tropics from abstract forests to living organisms, flirting, tempting, copulating, repro-

ducing, and communicating in ways that are stunning to behold—once you have the Rosetta stone of understanding.

Additionally, these plants are super resourceful because of the competition with other plants for space, light, air, water, and reproductive success. They have devised all kinds of strategies for surviving: they climb; they soar; they perch; they strangle; they jump into the light at the first opportunity. You would, too, if your life depended on it. And in the process, they have become glorious garden specimens.

The Orchid and the vine are just two examples of plants useful in Florida gardens. Add to them Gingers, which attract their pollinators with flower spikes of brilliant color; Bromeliads that store water in their vase-like rosettes; herbaceous low-lying plants that have lens-shaped leaf cells to catch light or special coloring to better utilize the light available or holes to keep from tearing or drip tips to let the rain run off . . . these plants are the dressing for subtropical gardens, the pin on the lapel, the brooch at the throat.

WORTH THE EFFORT

Many require extra care, particularly from the center of Florida northward. Like human Floridians, they get cold quickly and need protection in what is inclement to them. Like human Floridians, they may be sensitive to light, and so prefer the protection of shade. Like human Floridians, they like their daily shower but don't want to sit in a bath for long or they'll wrinkle. It just takes common sense, when you think about it.

Most of the plants in this section thrive best in South Florida gardens. Many will also do well outside in other areas of Florida during the summer. In pots, they can easily be moved back and forth, provided there is adequate humidity indoors.

Don't be afraid to try them. They bring wonderful foliage patterns and colors, beautiful flowers, and an intriguing way of life with them. And they tell stories that you can repeat to your friends.

Tropical plants have very different appearances and growth habits. However, here are some tips to help them grow best:

- Most tropical plants prefer well-drained, enriched soil with plenty of moisture. Like many rainforest plants, they like water but also good drainage.
- Dig a hole a little larger than the size of the container in which you buy the plant.
- Add compost or some organic matter.
- Carefully remove the pot from the rootball.
- Place the plant, keeping it at the same level in the ground as it was growing in the container.
- Water in the backfill and add mulch to mediate moisture.
- Slow-release fertilizer is practical in order to keep a flow of nutrients available throughout the growing season.

- If foliage yellows, apply periodic foliar sprays of micronutrients or add fish emulsion to keep tropical plants performing well.
- Keep tropical plants that prefer moist soil together with other water-thirsty plants to avoid over-watering the entire landscape just to water them.
- Areas in wind and sun will require more frequent waterings.
- Pests that may occur include mealybugs, scale, thrips, and spider mites.

THE MANY FACES OF ORCHIDS

The splendor of Orchids is almost impossible to resist if you live in a climate where they can be grown easily. They are among the most romantic of flowers and comprise the largest plant family known, with more than 20,000 species and untold numbers of manmade hybrids.

Orchids have become hugely popular in the last decade, with Phalaenopsis Orchids topping the charts. One reason is the long-lasting spray of flowers, which can remain pretty for two months. Commercial Orchid growers have developed highly colored Phalaenopsis blooms, with stripes, spots, and splotches vying for attention in colors ranging from tangerine to deep mahogany. Cattleya flowers and plants have been hybridized as windowsill plants, shrinking in size but also becoming more colorful. And Vanda Orchids and relatives are able to produce flowers three or four times a year, rather than once, with smaller but more boldly colored flowers.

Enticing perfume is a characteristic of many Orchids. Cattleyas and Oncidiums, for example, may give off rich chocolate or vanilla aromas. Some Orchid growers sell Orchids advertised for their fragrance.

HOW ORCHIDS GROW

Many Orchids, such as Cattleyas, are air plants, or epiphytes (epi means "upon"; phyte means "plant"). They grow on other plants, most often tree branches, expanding into clumps by means of a rhizome, or a stem from which roots grow downward and shoots grow up. They are not parasites—they take no nutrients away from the tree on which they grow.

To germinate in nature, Orchid seeds have to be infected with a fungus, a fact not known until the turn of the century. It would be years before Orchid scientist L. Knudson would discover how to create an artificial medium in agar on which to germinate seed. After that happened, these once priceless flowers began to soar in popularity. Today, Orchids are grown by people in every walk of life.

The epiphytic Orchids most easily grown in South Florida are the Cattleyas and relatives and hybrids, Vandas and several relatives and hybrids, Oncidiums, Phalaenopsis, and Dendrobiums. Cattleyas are sympodial, meaning new growth arises at the base of a parent after the parent has flowered, forming a series of stems. Vandas, Phalaenopsis, and other Orchids are monopodial, meaning they grow on a single stem. Growing in trees, epiphytic Orchids have developed special roots that are photosynthetic, yet covered with a silver-gray coating of cells that absorbs water and protects against desiccation. These roots cling tightly to tree bark or clay pots. Pseudobulbs are water-storage organs. Orchids with pseudobulbs, such as Cattleyas and Oncidiums, require less water than do those without. (More Orchids die from over-watering than under-watering.)

AGLAONEMA
Aglaonema spp.

HARDINESS
Zones 10–11

COLOR(S)
Small white flowers; green foliage with patterns of ivory, red, pink, and more

PEAK SEASON
Summer blooms

MATURE SIZE
2 to 3 feet x 1 to 4 feet

WATER NEEDS
After established, let soil become medium-dry between watering.

CARE
They prefer shade, although morning sun is fine, particularly for silvery leaves. Aglaonemas thrive in well-drained soil. Use 20-20-20 soluble fertilizer at half strength every two weeks or a slow-release foliage formula. Protect plants from cold.

PROBLEMS
In dry weather, mites may appear. Mealybugs may occur if brought indoors for winter. Wipe with rubbing alcohol.

USES AND SELECTIONS
Display Aglaonema (Chinese Evergreen) next to paths or in raised beds as ground covers. In containers can beautify patio and townhouse gardens. Give vitality to the "floor" of shade gardens, with groups of complementary colors. Try Diffenbachias, Begonias, and Ferns to add color and texture. New varieties from Thailand come in myriad colors and patterns.

ALOE
Aloe vera

HARDINESS
Zones 9b–11

COLOR(S)
Gray-green leaves; reddish inflorescence on flower stalk

PEAK SEASON
Bloom in late spring to early summer

MATURE SIZE
1 to 2 feet x 2 to 3 feet

WATER NEEDS
Very drought tolerant but needs well-drained soil

CARE
This succulent is easy to grow and requires very low maintenance. Aloe grows slowly, forming clumps.

PROBLEMS
Do not overwater. The thick leaves are edged with short spines.

USES AND SELECTIONS
Aloe's clear gel-like sap helps burns and other wounds heal faster. It was once grown close to the home for quick access to leaves for medicinal purposes. Today it is an ingredient in everything from first aid cream to shampoo. This drought-tolerant plant can be used for xeriscape and rock gardens, as well as in planters, as a ground cover, or in mass plantings. It is also used as a small accent or as a border planting. Grow in containers in colder locations.

ANGEL'S TRUMPET
Brugmansia spp.

☀ ☀ ☀ 🌿 💧 🌴

HARDINESS
Zones 9b–11

COLOR(S)
Orange, white, yellow, pink, or two-toned

PEAK SEASON
Blooms most of year; foliage evergreen

MATURE SIZE
To 15 feet x 15 feet

WATER NEEDS
Water well to establish, then can tolerate some drought. Flowers best with water during dry periods.

CARE
Fast-growing *Brugmansia* can be left untrimmed with branches drooping to the ground. Or it can be pruned into an upright tree or overhead canopy to better display flowers. Frost kills them back to roots but they come back.

PROBLEMS
Shield from winds to protect blooms. All parts are poisonous or narcotic when eaten.

USES AND SELECTIONS
The abundant hanging flowers, up to 12 inches long, create a dramatic and exotic effect. For maximum impact, plant as a free-standing specimen to show off blooms without crowding from other plants. Can also be used as a border or in containers. Use near decks or patios to enjoy the fragrance. Formerly called *Datura*.

ANTHURIUM
Anthurium spp.

☀ ☀ 🌱 🌿 🪴

HARDINESS
Zones 10–11

COLOR(S)
Generally grown for foliage

PEAK SEASON
Evergreen foliage

MATURE SIZE
Varies with species

WATER NEEDS
Plants in terra cotta pots or mounted in trees dry faster, especially in windy weather. Check moisture levels closely and water daily if necessary. Once established, rain will be sufficient except in dry seasons.

CARE
Plant terrestrial Anthuriums in shady beds with other tropicals, in pots, or as specimens throughout the garden. Good drainage is the key. Epiphytic ones can be attached and grown in trees. Anthuriums do well with slow-release fertilizer, supplemented with occasional foliar sprays. Feed those in trees with mesh bags filled with slow-release fertilizer.

PROBLEMS
None

USES AND SELECTIONS
Anthuriums have dramatic foliage and some have unique spathes (flowers). They add distinction to a tree trunk, garden path, or bed, and complement Bromeliads, Ferns, and even boulders. Anthuriums may be used as summer flowers in Central or North Florida, or grown in containers.

AUSTRALIAN TREE FERN
Sphaeropteris cooperi

☼ ☼ 🪴 🌴

HARDINESS
Zones 9b–11

COLOR(S)
Green foliage on russet trunk

PEAK SEASON
Evergreen

MATURE SIZE
12 to 18 feet x 8 to 15 feet

WATER NEEDS
Requires regular moisture

CARE
This slow growing fern prefers fertile, well-drained soils. Plant in area protected from wind. Fertilize lightly regularly during growing season. Do not apply fertilizer to plant that is stressed by lack of water.

PROBLEMS
Do not allow to completely dry out. The hair on the trunk and undersides of fronds can be irritating; handle with gloves.

USES AND SELECTIONS
Ideal as a specimen along shady entryways and around patios or pools. Underplant with small ferns or other low-growing tropicals. For an exotic look, attach orchids to the trunk. Although this fern provides a soothing tropical feel, it is hardier than it looks. It can briefly take freezing weather and still come back. When provided with plenty of moisture, can withstand almost full fun.

BIRD-OF-PARADISE
Strelitzia reginae

☼ ☼ 🪴 🌱 🌴

HARDINESS
Zones 9–11

COLOR(S)
Flowers orange and white with blue

PEAK SEASON
Most blooms in summer and fall

MATURE SIZE
3 to 4 feet x 4 feet

WATER NEEDS
Water well then let dry

CARE
Bird-of-Paradise forms clumps and has tuberous roots, which should be set just at soil surface. Although slow growing, feed monthly with balanced fertilizer or slow-release fertilizer. Reduce frequency of feeding as plants near flowering size. Remove dying leaves to allow light into center of clump.

PROBLEMS
Use recommended pesticide to treat scale. Over-crowded, unfertilized plants will not produce flowers.

USES AND SELECTIONS
Plant as an eye-catching accent, in front of hedges, or in foundation plantings. Bird-of-Paradise can also be used with relatives, including Traveler's Palms and Heliconias, at the back of the garden. This plant can be arresting, providing color outside and cut flowers for inside. There are several selections, including Giant Bird-of-Paradise, which grows to 30 feet.

BIRD'S NEST FERN
Asplenium nidus

HARDINESS
Zones 9b–11

COLOR(S)
Apple-green foliage

MATURE SIZE
To 4 feet

WATER NEEDS
Does best with regular moisture. Only allow to dry slightly between waterings.

CARE
Provide them with well-drained soil plus an area protected from drying winds and cold temperatures. Feed monthly with diluted fertilizer or fish emulsion. The Fern is slow growing and does not require much care if the basics are provided. This epiphytic fern naturally grows in jungle trees.

PROBLEMS
Handpick any snails.

USES AND SELECTIONS
This showy vase-shaped fern has thick, undivided fronds, unlike other ferns. It is an excellent specimen plant that quickly captures attention. It has a strong tropical flavor and can be used as an accent or in clusters as ground covers in shady gardens, perhaps under a tree fern. Also suitable for containers. Group with other plants requiring high humidity and frequent waterings. There are cultivars with ruffled edges.

BROMELIAD
Aechmea, Billbergia, Guzmania, Neoregelia, Tillandsia spp.

HARDINESS
Zones 9b–11

COLOR(S)
Varies with genus and species

PEAK SEASON
Varies

MATURE SIZE
Few inches to several feet

WATER NEEDS
Keep Bromeliad cups filled with water

CARE
Fertilize ¼ strength monthly. Off-shoots can be removed and planted. Bromeliads grown outdoors in Central and North Florida must be removed or covered during freezing weather.

PROBLEMS
If water in cup stagnates, mosquito larvae will grow. Flush every few days, use horticultural oil, or add *Bacillus thuringiensis* formulated to kill the larvae. When working with spiny Bromeliads, use bee-keepers or rose gloves. Scale may appear in overcrowded conditions.

USES AND SELECTIONS
Bromeliads are all around performers. They can be selected for almost anything from ground covers to specimens and from Pineapples to Spanish Moss. Some genera grow in trees, others under them. Use as accents or mass plantings. Their often brilliant colors have tropical flare, plus some produce inflorescences lasting many months.

CALATHEA
Calathea spp.

HARDINESS
Zones 10–11

COLOR(S)
Foliage in shades of green, white, pink, silver, and combinations

MATURE SIZE
Varies with species, to 5 feet tall x 4 feet wide

WATER NEEDS
Keep moist

CARE
Plant in beds enriched with organic material. Use slow-release fertilizer. Does well with early morning or late afternoon, but not midday sun. Some *Calathea* species can tolerate cold snaps if well watered and growing under trees. Use as houseplant in Central and North Florida to protect from cold.

PROBLEMS
Handpick any snails.

USES AND SELECTIONS
Calatheas (Peacock or Rattlesnake Plant) are among the most ornate plants, with beautifully patterned leaves on short stems. Markings usually follow the central vein, with endless combinations. The undersides are frequently red or wine colored. Inconspicuous flowers are produced inside bracts. Calatheas are wonderful in beds beneath canopy trees, such as Oaks, with Palms and Aroids, or Ferns. Also does well in containers on shady patio or deck.

CATTLEYA
Cattleya spp.

HARDINESS
Zones 10b–11. Takes low-40s temperatures for short periods.

COLOR(S)
White, lavender, purple

PEAK SEASON
Varies

MATURE SIZE
20 to 40 inches

WATER NEEDS
Water every two or three days, allowing medium to become almost dry. Like high relative humidity.

CARE
Plant in February or March. Use quick draining orchid-growing mix. Position four or five "back" bulbs with new growth toward pot's center. Anchor with pot clip. Use balanced fertilizer every week or two until October. Until March, monthly use fertilizer like 10-30-20 to promote blooms.

PROBLEMS
Plants that don't bloom usually need more light. To prevent fungus, don't overcrowd.

USES AND SELECTIONS
This queen of orchids is extraordinarily tough and makes good beginner plant. Tie or wire to trees with rough bark in 50 percent light. Or plant in pots to bring inside when flowers are glorious. North and Central Florida gardeners can keep Orchids outdoors in trees or shade houses in warmer months.

COPPERLEAF
Acalypha wilkesiana

☼ ☼ ☼ ◊ 🌴

HARDINESS
Zones 9 -11

COLOR(S)
Coppery leaves mottled in bronze, green, purple, red, pink

PEAK SEASON
Evergreen foliage

MATURE SIZE
8 to 12 feet x 6 to 8 feet

WATER NEEDS
Somewhat drought tolerant. Prefers regular watering during drought.

CARE
Plant in any well-drained soil. Does best with enriched soil. This fast-growing shrub may need occasional trimming to look tidy and to cut off any drooping side branches. A late winter pruning can remove portions affected by freezes.

PROBLEMS
Aphids, miles, and scale may be problems. Use recommended pesticides.

USES AND SELECTIONS
This colorful shrub with large leaves can steal attention from other plants, so place it carefully. However, it makes a wonderful specimen with showy year-round color. Copperleaf comes in different multi-hued cultivars that provide a rainbow of colors, which explains its other common name, Joseph's Coat. It looks best planted amid mixed-green-foliage plants. Plant it as a hedge, view barrier, border, or accent.

COSTUS
Costus spp.

☼ ☼ 🌿 🪴 🌴

HARDINESS
Zones 10b–11

COLOR(S)
Yellow, orange, white blooms

PEAK SEASON
Summer blooms

MATURE SIZE
4 to 8 feet x 4 to 5 feet

WATER NEEDS
Keep moist, with less water in winter.

CARE
Locate in high, light shade where shallow-rooted Costus can clump and spread. Mulch and use acid-forming fertilizer. Once stems have flowered and bracts faded, cut out parent stem. Every few years Costus benefits from digging and refreshing the beds with organic material. Grow in protected areas or containers in cold sensitive areas.

PROBLEMS
Costus tends to look haggard in winter.

USES AND SELECTIONS
Use Costus as an accent, in containers, or as mass plantings. Also called Spiral Ginger, try Costus beneath Oaks with stands of red and pink Gingers. *Costus speciosus* is 8 or 9 feet tall with white flowers from red bracts. Use as a screen. There is a Costus with variegated leaves.

CROTON
Codiaeum variegatum

HARDINESS
Zones 9b–11. In colder areas plant in containers and protect from frosts and freezing.

COLOR(S)
Green, pink, yellow, red foliage

PEAK SEASON
Year-round foliage

MATURE SIZE
3 to 8 feet x 3 feet

WATER NEEDS
Relatively drought resistant. Water during periods of extended drought.

CARE
Does well in sandy soils and with feedings given to nearby plants. Does better with fertilizer, applied in March, May, and September. Look best when protected from midday sun. For compact plants with colorful shoots prune periodically.

PROBLEMS
Scale, thrips, and mites may occur. Apply recommended pesticide.

USES AND SELECTIONS
These relatively narrow plants are ideal for cramped gardens and small spots between house and sidewalk. Also good for hedges and screens. Great accent plant for containers or beds. Best used with surroundings of greenery. A rainbow of color combinations is available, in a wide range of leaf shapes. Some selections tolerate lower light, although colors may be subdued.

CROWN OF THORNS
Euphorbia milii

HARDINESS
Zones 9b–11. Damaged by freezes.

COLOR(S)
Pink, red, orange, salmon, yellow, and bi-colors

PEAK SEASON
Year-round blooms

MATURE SIZE
1 to 3 feet

WATER NEEDS
Very drought tolerant

CARE
This tough, slow-growing plant requires little maintenance, blooming year-round in heat, sun, drought, and seaside conditions that would kill other plants. Requires well-drained soil. Too much shade or overfertilization will reduce the number of blooms. Although the flower is actually small, it is surrounded by colorful showy bracts.

PROBLEMS
Do not overwater. Milky sap may cause skin irritation or be poisonous if eaten.

USES AND SELECTIONS
Recent interest in the tough but thorny Crown of Thorns has resulted in many new hybrids. This exotic-looking succulent now comes in numerous colors and dwarf sizes. It is ideal for xeriscape or rock gardens. Also use as a hedge. Plant the dwarf varieties, which have more attractive foliage, as ground covers and bedding plants.

CYCADS
Cycas and *Zamia* spp.

HARDINESS
Zones 9–11

COLOR(S)
Green

MATURE SIZE
From 18 inches to 12 feet x 4 to 8 feet wide

WATER NEEDS
Drought tolerant

CARE
Requires well-drained soil. Feed this tough, slow grower with Palm or slow-release fertilizer. Yellowing leaves signal nutrient deficiencies.

PROBLEMS
Mealybugs and scale can be a problem. Combat with insecticidal soap or systemic insecticide, used alternately with light horticultural oil. The popular Queen and King Sagos (*Cycas circinalis* and *C. rumphii*) may have deadly scale infestations.

USES AND SELECTIONS
The rosette form and stiff leaves make Cycads living sculptures. They can be used as specimens and accents. They are also stunning when collected in beds or artfully set on a mound or in a container. Two are small enough to be ground covers, including Coontie, the only Florida native (*Zamia pumila*), which is both drought and salt tolerant. Cycads go with Palms and Aloes, but are exquisite when planted by themselves.

DENDROBIUM
Dendrobium spp.

HARDINESS
Zones 10–11

COLOR(S)
White, yellow, lavender, rose, maroon

PEAK SEASON
Blooms fall, spring, summer

MATURE SIZE
6 inches to 4 feet

WATER NEEDS
Water generously during spring. During winter allow plant to dry out between waterings.

CARE
Plant in spring on cork pieces, in pots with quick-draining medium, or on trees. Attach to cork or trees with florist's tape or wire. Prefers 50 to 70 percent shade. In pots, put oldest growth against sides. Feed every week or two in spring with balanced fertilizer. Liquid fertilizers with a drop or two of dish detergent get absorbed more quickly by roots and leaves. Reduce fertilizer in winter.

PROBLEMS
When overwatered, offshoots may be produced, which can be cut off and potted.

USES AND SELECTIONS
Dendrobiums are diverse, including miniatures. North and Central Florida growers can keep them in trees or shade houses during warm months, but protection is needed when temperatures drop below 50°F.

DRACAENA
Dracaena spp.

☀ ☀ 💧 🪴 🌴

HARDINESS
Zones 10b–11. Some species tolerate more cold.

COLOR(S)
Leaves solid green or striped with ivory, yellow, or red

MATURE SIZE
Varies by species

WATER NEEDS
Need good drainage. Can stay fairly dry for long periods.

CARE
Not fussy and does well despite neglect. However, it prefers acidic soil and fertilizer to stay rich green. Fertilize with other landscape plants in spring, summer, and fall. When top of branch is cut off, new buds and heads of leaves form. Tops can be rooted for new plants.

PROBLEMS
None

USES AND SELECTIONS
Use Dracaena when narrow, vertical elements are needed. It is useful as an accent or for screening. Clusters with plants of differing heights are especially effective. In Central and North Florida grow in containers and protect from temperatures below 40°F. There are approximately 150 *Dracaena* species, many used as interior plants because they tolerate low light and stay same size for years.

ELEPHANT EAR
Alocasia spp.

☀ ☀ ☀ 🪴 🌴

HARDINESS
Zones 9–11. Damaged by cold in northern regions and during prolonged cold in South Florida.

COLOR(S)
Green and dark green, often with colored veins

PEAK SEASON
Year-round foliage

MATURE SIZE
2 to 12 feet x 8 feet

WATER NEEDS
Provide plenty of water in spring. Water twice weekly if it doesn't rain.

CARE
Use slow-release fertilizer two or three times a year, once in spring if in pots. Supplement with foliar spray to bolster nutrients. If leaves yellow, use micronutrient spray or fish emulsion. Prune away cold-damaged leaves in early spring.

PROBLEMS
May bleach out when in sun all day

USES AND SELECTIONS
The enormous Elephant Ear leaves proclaim tropical in gardens. Use in the center, a corner, or toward the back for dramatic effects. Also attractive in pots and ponds. Varieties come in all sizes and veination patterns. Some take more sun than others. Often confused with Taro, also called Elephant Ear.

FERN
Many genera, species, and varieties

HARDINESS
Zones 8–11

COLOR(S)
Green foliage, some with reddish or iridescent tints

MATURE SIZE
6 inches to 3 feet x various

WATER NEEDS
A few ferns can tolerate some drought, but most require regular watering. Some, like the native Leather Fern, need constant moisture.

CARE
Terrestrial types need good drainage. Planting in mulch is ideal. Those attached to trees, like the Staghorn, can be packed with sphagnum moss. Tender roots of Ferns can be burned easily by pellet or granular fertilizer. An 8-8-8 or fish emulsion is best. Fertilize monthly or every two weeks or use diluted water-soluble fertilizer whenever watering.

PROBLEMS
Many ferns require protection from cold temperatures and cold drying wind.

USES AND SELECTIONS
In subtropical and tropical gardens, Ferns are all-purpose plants. They can hover by walkways, serve as ground covers, fill hanging baskets, creep on trees, encircle Palms, and act as accents. They bring grace to everything they do.

FICUS
Ficus spp.

HARDINESS
Zones 9b–11. Damaged by freezes.

COLOR(S)
Foliage green with occasional red or variegation

PEAK SEASON
Evergreen

MATURE SIZE
Few inches to 40 feet

WATER NEEDS
Drought tolerant once established. Need regular watering in containers.

CARE
Usually fast growing without any fertilizer. If used as hedges, need frequent pruning to maintain shape.

PROBLEMS
Ficus roots are strong and may grow above the soil. Consider surrounding sidewalks and structures when locating a Ficus.

USES AND SELECTIONS
This diverse class ranges from the small Creeping Fig to the enormous Banyan Tree, with many shrubs and trees in between. Ficus are grouped together because they bear fig-like fruit. Their glossy green leaves and ability to tolerate a wide range of conditions (except hard freezes) makes them ubiquitous in South Florida and common in Central Florida. They are vigorous growers and can quickly provide dense view barriers or shade. Use in containers, as patio plants, borders, hedges, and shade trees.

GINGER
Alipinia spp.

HARDINESS
Zones 9–11

COLOR(S)
Red, pink, purple, white

PEAK SEASON
Summer blooms; foliage evergreen

MATURE SIZE
3 to 15 feet x various

WATER NEEDS
Requires good soil moisture

CARE
Locate in high shade, allowing room to grow. Gingers are fast growers and prefer to be well fertilized. They will spread and form big clumps. Maintain by cleaning out old, brown stems. In Central and North Florida, use in containers, protected from chilling winds.

PROBLEMS
Too much light causes yellowing

USES AND SELECTIONS
This useful plant says welcome to the tropics. There are about 1,000 species, with new ones being discovered all the time. The flowers are lovely amid the broad tropical foliage. A popular Pink Ginger contrasts nicely with the Red. Use mass plantings of dwarf and variegated forms in understory beds and as ground covers. The true Ginger, *Zingiber officinale*, can be grown in partial sun and is fragrant.

GINGER LILY
Hedychium coronarium

HARDINESS
Zones 8–11

COLOR(S)
White flowers

PEAK SEASON
Blooms summer

MATURE SIZE
2 to 4 feet x various

WATER NEEDS
Loves moist soil. Mulch is essential.

CARE
Allow enough space, especially in shaded locations, for this assertive grower. Like other Gingers, its rhizome grows close to the surface. Slow-release fertilizer provides nutrients throughout the season. Fewer flowers are produced in deep shade.

PROBLEMS
Freezing weather kills them back, but they may resprout from rhizomes.

USES AND SELECTIONS
Plant groups of Ginger Lilies (commonly called Butterfly Ginger) near entryways and patios to enjoy their lovely aroma. Grow in containers on patios and around pools. Also use as fillers around waterfalls and ponds. They're tall enough to be visible over Lilies, Coleus, Begonias, and other low-lying shrubs. Group with other water-thirsty plants to avoid overwatering the entire landscape. There are about 50 *Hedychium* species in many colors, some of which may flower for up to six weeks.

HELICONIA
Heliconia spp.

☼ ☼ ☼ 🌱 🌾 🍃 🪴 🌴

HARDINESS
Zones 10b–11 and warmer areas of Central Florida.

COLOR(S)
Yellow, orange, scarlet flowers

PEAK SEASON
Blooms spring and summer

MATURE SIZE
2 to 15 feet x various

WATER NEEDS
Once established, may need watering twice weekly if it doesn't rain. If sunny or windy water more often.

CARE
Requires good drainage and some protection from cold and wind. Leaves get yellow on hungry plants. To feed their big appetites use slow-release fertilizer combined with periodic micronutrient sprays and compost. Stake any stems that lean so flowers will show.

PROBLEMS
Handpick snails. Use fungicide to control root and stem rot.

USES AND SELECTIONS
These fascinating plants, also called Lobster Claw, have become important tropical plants in Florida. Use at garden's edges, as specimen plants, along walls, and behind Shrimp Plants. Plant for accents or in mass plantings. Use dwarf varieties in containers, especially in colder areas. Cultivars and color forms number in the hundreds.

MONSTERA
Monstera deliciosa

☼ ☼ 🍃 🌴

HARDINESS
Zones 9b–11

COLOR(S)
Green foliage; white spathe

PEAK SEASON
Evergreen foliage

MATURE SIZE
To 50 feet x 2 foot leaf width

WATER NEEDS
Requires regular watering

CARE
This plant grows quickly in almost any soil, although it prefers well-drained, enriched soil. It will clamber over rocks or up trees. Little care is required. To speed growth, feed with a balanced fertilizer.

PROBLEMS
Usually pest free, although in dry seasons the lubber grasshopper may consume leaves. All parts of the plant except for the ripe fruit can be poisonous.

USES AND SELECTIONS
The instantly recognizable Monstera leaf often symbolizes tropical plants. Use the vine to climb trees or a pergola. It also makes a good shrubby ground cover, both growing over rocks or in soil. Sometimes called the Swiss cheese or Ceriman Plant, this vine produces an edible fruit that requires about a year to ripen and is said to taste like fruit salad.

MUSSAENDA
Mussaenda philippica

☼ ☼ 🌿 🌴

HARDINESS
Zones 9–11

COLOR(S)
Pink, white, yellow

PEAK SEASON
Year-round blooms with more in summer

MATURE SIZE
9 to 10 feet x 6 feet

WATER NEEDS
Keep soil moist

CARE
Plant in full sun for best color. Fertilize with an acid-forming or Gardenia fertilizer. Flowers and showy bracts form on branch ends, so spring pruning will encourage more branches. Prune after bracts fade to encourage more flowering in same season. If shrubs grow too large or leggy, cut back quite hard. Grow in containers in Central and North Florida because it is vulnerable to damage below 45°F.

PROBLEMS
Fungal leaf spot can affect some plants.

USES AND SELECTIONS
Plant in mixed border so shorter shrubs conceal leggy trunks. Plant with purple foliage plants to complement the pink varieties. Mussaenda is not for the everyday duty of planting along a fence. Its lusciousness is best in smaller doses.

NIGHT BLOOMING CEREUS
Hylocereus undatus

☼ ☼ ☼ 🌿 🌺 🌸 💧 🌴 🌀

HARDINESS
Zones 9b–11

COLOR(S)
White blooms

PEAK SEASON
Blooms summer; evergreen foliage

MATURE SIZE
Climbs to 30 feet; stems are triangular about 3 inches across

WATER NEEDS
This Cactus is drought tolerant once established. Water more frequently in summer.

CARE
Attach with florist's tape to start the vine, until plant starts producing its own aerial roots. Grows quickly, branching frequently. Fertilize monthly during summer for maximum blooms.

PROBLEMS
Handle stems with care to avoid spines

USES AND SELECTIONS
Climbs burlap-covered poles, masonry walls, palm trunks, and up onto tree branches. It has fragrant nocturnal blooms up to 12 inches long and across. Some varieties are grown for edible fruit, which is prized in Thailand and called Dragon Fruit or Pitaya. Dragon Fruit is widely grown in Dade County. This unusual plant is salt tolerant and can be found growing wild in South and Central coastal Florida. Several cacti have the same common name.

305

ONCIDIUM
Oncidium spp.

☀☀🧴🌱🌿🪴🌴

HARDINESS
Zones 10–11

COLOR(S)
Yellow with brown, maroon, or olive

PEAK SEASON
Spring blooms

MATURE SIZE
3 inches to 2 feet

WATER NEEDS
Keep evenly moist, except for miniatures, which like to dry between watering.

CARE
Attach with florist's tape, wire, or pantyhose to tree limbs or trunks of trees and palms. In pots, use a fast-draining mix. During warm growing season fertilize frequently with diluted water-soluble fertilizer every week or two. Consistency is key. Bloom-booster fertilizer can be substituted three or four times in fall. Oncidiums can be acclimated to tolerate sun. North and Central Florida growers must bring them in or provide protection when temperatures drop below 50°F.

USES AND SELECTIONS
Oncidiums are star performers and consistently provide cascades of flowers with little care, tolerating all kinds of awful weather, except freezes. Numerous varieties come in all the spots, stripes, and bright color you could want, plus fragrance variety, too.

PEACE LILY
Spathiphyllum spp.

☀☀🌱🌿🌴

HARDINESS
Zones 10–11

COLOR(S)
White flowers; deep-green, shiny foliage

PEAK SEASON
Blooms summer

MATURE SIZE
12 inches to 4 or more feet

WATER NEEDS
Likes moisture in regular amounts, with good drainage. Don't overwater.

CARE
Choose shady location with some protection against cold. In too much shade, the plants will grow but not flower. Use foliage or general-purpose fertilizer three or four times a year.

PROBLEMS
Testing in the 1990s showed that the Peace Lily was a top performer in removing indoor air pollutants and alleviating sick building syndrome.

USES AND SELECTIONS
Peace Lily sizes go from petite to huge. They make wonderful potted specimens for both indoors and out. As entryway plants they are show-offs, especially the large cultivars. Consider them for shady patios and pair with Begonias. Combine with Tree Ferns for interesting texture contrast. Use as a temporary summer ground cover in Central and North Florida.

PEPEROMIA
Peperomia spp.

HARDINESS
Zones 10–11

COLOR(S)
Green, or variegated foliage with cream or burgundy

MATURE SIZE
12 to 18 inches x 4 inches

WATER NEEDS
Requires well-drained soil. Mulch to keep evenly moist.

CARE
Fertilize two or three times a year; less often if mulched or surrounding plants are fertilized. Some plants clump up or mound slightly. Cuttings can be easily rooted or planted directly in the ground.

PROBLEMS
Handpick snails.

USES AND SELECTIONS
Often seen as houseplants. In your garden Peperomias can easily serve as ground covers, potted plants for patio or waterfalls, fillers among shady rocks around ponds, or roamers in your natural shade garden. Also make a pretty hanging basket, particularly those with variegated leaves. Use tree stumps left in the garden or decorative logs as a place to get them started. Too tender for widespread use in Central and North Florida, unless grown in containers. South Florida is home to native species.

PERSIAN SHIELD
Strobilanthes dyerianus

HARDINESS
Zones 9b–11

COLOR(S)
Leaves iridescent dark-green with silvery purple on top and purple underneath

PEAK SEASON
Evergreen

MATURE SIZE
3 to 4 feet x 2 to 3 feet

WATER NEEDS
During growing season prefers moisture. With enriched soil and mulch, it has slight drought tolerance. In dormant season, reduce watering.

CARE
Grows best with morning sun and afternoon shade. In colder areas it dies back to roots with frost. However, it may return in spring even in Zone 8.

PROBLEMS
To prevent it from getting too tall, pinch back to stimulate branching.

USES AND SELECTIONS
Persian Shield's textured showy leaves add drama, even though the winter flowers aren't attractive. It provides unique color in shady gardens where flowering plants don't thrive. Use it as an accent, in mass plantings, and among flowering plants in bedding areas. In containers, place it in the back or middle so it doesn't steal all the attention.

PHALAENOPSIS
Phalaenopsis spp.

☀️ ☀️ 🌱 🌿 💐 🌴

HARDINESS
Zones 10–11

COLOR(S)
White, yellow, pink, peach, bronze, orange, and spots

PEAK SEASON
Blooms winter to spring

MATURE SIZE
8 to 16 inches

WATER NEEDS
Prefer to have roots moist but not wet. They like to dry slowly, although never completely dried out.

CARE
Keep in shadowy area of shade house, between 70 to 50 percent shade. Pot in loose-draining mix with sphagnum to retain moisture. Use soluble 20-20-20 fertilizer every week or two during growing season. Toward the end of October switch to bloom-booster fertilizer and add 1 tablespoon of epson salts to strengthen flower spike. In North and Central Florida keep outside in shade houses during warm months, but protect when temperatures drop below 55°F.

PROBLEMS
Don't let water remain in crown, which can lead to crown rot.

USES AND SELECTIONS
For grace, sophistication, and elegance, the popular Phalaenopsis (Moth Orchid) is the best. Flowers can stay unblemished for weeks and ...ies come in all colors.

PONYTAIL
Beaucarnea recurvata

☀️ ☀️ ☀️ 💧 💐 🌴 🌀

HARDINESS
Zones 9b–11

COLOR(S)
Green foliage, whitish flower

PEAK SEASON
Blooms in spring; evergreen leaves

MATURE SIZE
12 to 18 feet x 10 to 15 feet

WATER NEEDS
Very drought tolerant. Water deeply, then allow to dry out.

CARE
This slow grower requires little care, although indoor plants must be gradually acclimated to the garden. Provide room to grow up and out. Mature plants may withstand freezing temperatures and are somewhat salt tolerant. Large plants may flower.

PROBLEMS
To prevent root rot use well-drained soil and don't mulch close to base.

USES AND SELECTIONS
Sometimes called Ponytail Palm, this is not a Palm but a succulent related to Yucca. It looks like a Dr. Seuss character or contemporary sculpture. Its spindly branches rise from a swollen base and are topped with tufts of long droopy leaves. Use this unique plant as an attention-getter. It does well in containers, xeriscape plantings, and low-maintenance or rock gardens.

SANSEVIERIA
Sansevieria spp.

HARDINESS
Zones 9b–11

COLOR(S)
Green, silver, yellow-edged, or patterned like snake skins

PEAK SEASON
Evergreen

MATURE SIZE
6 inches to 5 feet x to 8 feet

WATER NEEDS
Very drought tolerant. Water only when needed.

CARE
Requires well-drained soil. Spreads firmly but slowly. Fertilize lightly twice a year, if at all.

PROBLEMS
Do not overwater. Mature clumps may need to be restrained. *S. hyacinthoides* is considered invasive.

USES AND SELECTIONS
There are about sixty *Sansevieria*, also called Snake Plant and Mother-in-Law's Tongue. There are tall thin varieties, dwarf forms, and ones with short, broad, silvery-green leaves. The irregular flowers are light green or white, sometimes fragrant. This is a very tough plant, able to withstand drought, neglect, high and low light levels, and some salt exposure. It may even survive freezing weather. Use this multipurpose plant as a ground cover, edging, in pots, in rock gardens, in beds, and even as an accent plant.

SHRIMP PLANT
Justicia brandegeana

HARDINESS
Zones 9–11

COLOR(S)
White flowers within overlapping copper, red, yellow, lime green bracts

PEAK SEASON
Blooms almost year-round; foliage evergreen

MATURE SIZE
3 to 6 feet x 3 feet

WATER NEEDS
Keep soil moist, especially during hot weather

CARE
Likes fertile, well-drained soil. It is adaptable and easy to grow. Feed monthly during growing season or apply slow-release fertilizer in spring. It's killed to ground by hard frosts but comes back with warm weather. Can also be grown as an annual in northern range.

PROBLEMS
Branches sometimes get spindly. Keep tip pruned to increase bushiness and promote flowering.

USES AND SELECTIONS
This exotic sprawling shrub can be used wherever color masses are needed. Group together in mass plantings or plant in mixed perennial beds and borders. Since the 6-inch-long showy flower spikes attract butterflies and hummingbirds, use in wildlife gardens. Varieties come in several flower colors and one with white foliage variegation.

STAGHORN FERN
Platycerium spp.

☀ ☀ 💧 🌴

HARDINESS
Zones 9b–11

COLOR(S)
Both green and brown fronds

MATURE SIZE
2 to 6 feet across

WATER NEEDS
Water thoroughly, then allow to dry out. Do not overwater or place where constantly wet.

CARE
There are both basal fronds and antler-shaped (fertile) foliage fronds. Once established, Staghorns need minimal care. Feed monthly during summer with liquid fertilizer. Provide good air circulation. Can be mounted onto a board or tree, with sphagnum moss behind the fern. Attach with florist's tape or pantyhose, which new shield fronds will cover.

PROBLEMS
Beginners often overwater Staghorns. If in doubt, wait until the green fronds become limp before watering. The fuzzy brown growth on the back of fronds are spores and are normal.

USES AND SELECTIONS
This unusual epiphytic Fern is striking as a wall decoration, mounted on trees, or when hanging from branches. *Platycerium bifurcatum* is the easiest to grow and handles temperatures down to 25°F.

TARO
Colocasia esculenta cultivars

☀ ☀ ☀ 🪴 🌴

HARDINESS
Zones 8–11

COLOR(S)
Green, black, violet, patterned foliage; green, red, purple stalks

MATURE SIZE
To 6 feet tall x 5 feet

WATER NEEDS
Likes moist or wet soil. Will tolerate full sun with plenty of water.

CARE
This fast-growing plant needs lots of food to look its best. Fertilizer monthly during summer.

PROBLEMS
The wild taro, *C. esculenta*, is invasive in Florida. Although Taro is used for food and poi, unless properly prepared, it can cause stomach problems.

USES AND SELECTIONS
Taro's huge velvety leaves are bold and make a tropical statement. It can be used for accents, background plantings, and in containers. Taro also does well in ponds and along streams. There are more than 200 cultivars for ornamental or food use, with new hybrids being introduced often. The most distinctive have almost black or highly patterned leaves with contrasting colored stems. Often confused with Alocasia, which is also called Elephant Ear.

TI PLANT
Cordyline terminalis

HARDINESS
Zones 10b–11

COLOR(S)
Green foliage, or green, cream, red combinations

MATURE SIZE
6 feet x 20 inches

WATER NEEDS
Keep moist for summer, let dry slightly in fall and winter

CARE
Plant in high shade with bright, indirect light. Their best color comes in fall and winter. Too much light or fertilizer can bleach the foliage. Do not over fertilize *Cordyline* growing in shade. Organic fertilizer, such as compost or fish emulsion, is gentle, and slow-release is fine. Tip cuttings easily develop roots. These tender plants are suitable for container culture in Central and North Florida, especially miniature hybrids.

PROBLEMS
Watch for mealybugs, scale, and thrips, plus spider mites in winter.

USES AND SELECTIONS
Use colorful Ti Plants between billowy shrubs for flair, contrast a group of dark burgundy ones with variegated Ginger, and use the tricolor for bringing color to Palm and Aroid plantings. They are exclamation points.

TRAVELER'S TREE
Ravenala madagascariensis

HARDINESS
Zones 10–11

COLOR(S)
White flowers

PEAK SEASON
Blooms summer

MATURE SIZE
40 feet x 25 feet

WATER NEEDS
Likes plenty of water during summer, less in winter

CARE
Plant in area large enough to accommodate large head of leaves. Use a slow-release fertilizer in summer until plant reaches fair size. Then feed three times yearly. As natives of high altitudes they take more cold than most tropicals. In smaller gardens remove suckers from the base.

PROBLEMS
For best appearance, remove wind-tattered leaves.

USES AND SELECTIONS
These handsome wonders of botanical geometry are attention-getters when pruned so their fan shows off, especially when young and closer to eye level. A mature Traveler's Tree can be a stunning sculptural element where low plants suddenly give way to exuberance. When inappropriately used, these impressive specimens can overpower the rest of the garden. The bases of the 10- to 12-foot leaves fill with water, handy for travelers.

JANUARY

• Cut some Anthuriums or other tropical flowers for indoor winter beauty.

• January and February are the coldest months. If you have cold-sensitive tropical plants in northern or central parts of Florida, protect them from north winds and low temperatures. Move container plantings to a safe location and cover in-ground tropical plants with cloths or blankets. Do not use plastic, which provides no cold protection and can cook plants if not removed during the day. Be sure covers reach to the ground to trap warmth of surrounding soil. Pay close attention to plants with large or thin leaves, like Elephant Ear and Taro.

• In South Florida tropical plants can be planted most times of the year. However, the cold and dry months are the worst times to make new plantings.

• Tropicals have slowed their growth and need less moisture. Water when needed.

• Mites may appear with the drier weather. Mealybugs may also be a problem.

FEBRUARY

• February is often the coldest month of the year. Be prepared for any unusually low temperatures, even in the warmer areas of the state. Cover sensitive tropicals or move them to sheltered parts of the landscape. For cold sensitive ground covers that cannot be moved, thoroughly wet the soil before the freeze. Cold winds can damage delicate ferns. Move at-risk ferns and other hanging baskets to protected locations or cover carefully with blankets.

• Some tropical plants that are damaged by cold will regrow once warmer weather returns. Cut off any unsightly dead leaves, but wait until spring for trimming.

• Water when needed.

• Mites may continue to be a problem with the drier weather. Scale may also be more noticeable · this time of year as plant growth remains slow. Both insects can be controlled with oil spray, if applied when temperatures are above 40 degrees. Insects and sooty mold slowly flake off after a month or more.

MARCH

• Some tropical plants can be propagated from now until summer.

• Separate or cut off a clump of Anthuriums.

• As plants start to grow, they will need more moisture. Water regularly and renew the layer of mulch to retain moisture. Begin watering Orchids more frequently now.

• Prune cold-damaged tropical plants.

• Begin this season's fertilizing of most tropical plants now. Using slow-release fertilizer makes sense for these hungry plants, which have a long growing season. After you make the first application, note the next scheduled feeding on your calendar. Some plants, like Ferns, need low-dose feedings more regularly. They grow well with fish emulsion monthly or every two weeks. Orchids do best with a special fertilizer blend and now is the time to start applying it. Some prefer to use a low dose with every watering. Make sure to soak all the leaves and roots.

• Aphids may start to appear on new growth.

APRIL

• This is a good month to plant many tropicals, when the coming spring rains will provide natural irrigation. The weather outside is still cool so planting is stress-free.

• Move container tropical plants back outside in colder parts of the state.

• Bring a pot of blooming Phalaenopsis Orchids inside for a month or more of display. Place in a bright spot and do not overwater while indoors.

• Prune cold- and wind-damaged foliage to make room for new growth.

• Many tropical plants prefer to dry out between waterings. They cannot tolerate constantly wet roots and must have good drainage. Check any plantings that may be a problem when the rains return. Move those plants to a better location, build raised beds with good drainage, or plant in containers.

• Apply monthly feedings of Ferns and Orchids. Fertilize other tropical plants, unless using slow-release fertilizer.

• As new growth appears, pests may become more active.

MAY

• As the rainy season approaches, this is the best time to plant most tropicals. In-ground plantings can be made, as well as those that require attaching to trees, like Orchids or some Ferns and Bromeliads. Plants on branches or trunks can even be tied on with florist tape (Orchids) or glued on with construction adhesive (Bromeliads).

• Remove suckers from the base of Traveler's Tree when they're still small. Also begin watching fast-growing tropical plants, like Gingers, for overgrowth that may need to be trimmed.

• Until the rainy season arrives at the end of the month, water regularly, especially new plantings.

• Feed Orchids and Ferns. Also fertilize other tropical plants, especially flowering varieties. Using slow-release fertilizer with micronutrients is an excellent way to provide a steady supply of nutrients to these heavy feeders. After the first application, note on your calendar the next scheduled feeding time.

• Mealybugs and scale may occur.

JUNE

• During the rainy season is the best time to add new tropical plants. They grow best when organic material is added to the soil and plantings are topped with a mulch layer to retain moisture. Group tropicals together so the entire landscape does not need to be watered whenever they need moisture.

• Cuttings and divisions may be made now, while the plants are making fast growth and nature is providing the irrigation.

• Mother Nature is probably doing the watering. However, continue to monitor new plantings for moisture levels and provide any waterings that are needed, especially if the rains fail.

• Tropical plants are in full growth mode now and using nutrients at a rapid rate. Keep up regular feedings. If leaves yellow, apply a micronutrient foliar spray.

JULY

• Tropical plants are the source of many exotic flowers in arrangements. Periodically, cut a few blooms and bring them indoors. As an example, Bird-of-Paradise blossoms are even more beautiful when displayed close up.

• Keep shrub-like tropical plants, including Croton and Copperleaf, trimmed so they stay full and bushy. Some that may become leggy, like Mussaenda, may need hard pruning.

• Watering should not be necessary this month, but continue to check new plantings to make sure they have enough moisture.

• Fertilize most tropical plants now, unless using slow-release fertilizer. If leaves are yellow, apply a micronutrient foliar spray. Orchids and Ferns should get their regular feedings.

• Snails and slugs are very active, as well as caterpillars and grasshoppers. If plant foliage is too wet and air circulation poor, fungal leaf spots may occur.

AUGUST

• Be prepared to move or protect wind-sensitive tropical plants if a hurricane or storm approaches. Pruning damaged plants may be required afterwards.

• As tropicals make lots of growth, they may need pruning to allow for flowers and new growth. Plants like Dracaena can be topped to force new leaf heads. Others like the Gingers can have old stems removed.

• Make sure summer rains aren't flooding any tropicals, keeping their roots in standing water.

• Fertilize most tropical plants now, unless using slow-release fertilizer. Orchids and Ferns should get their regular feedings.

• Check that Bromeliad cups are regularly flushed to keep out mosquitoes. Or treat with a *Bacillus thuringiensis* product formulated to kill their larvae.

• Snails and slugs are very active, as well as caterpillars and grasshoppers.

SEPTEMBER

• Cut off any Bromeliad pups once they are about a third the size of the parent plant, then plant. They may appear at any time of the year. Wear long rose gloves to protect your arms from spiny varieties. Other tropicals can still be planted. Once the rains subside, you will need to provide the waterings. Start checking all plants regularly for moisture levels, especially new plantings.

• September and October are usually the height of hurricane season. Be prepared to move or protect wind-sensitive tropical plants if a hurricane or storm approaches. Pruning damaged plants may be required after it passes.

• Prune excessive growth as needed to control and to shape tropical plants.

• Continue to fertilize tropicals. Plant growth will start to slow down, especially in Central and Northern Florida.

• Snails and slugs are very active, as well as caterpillars and grasshoppers. As the weather begins to dry, mites may make an appearance.

OCTOBER

• Tropical plants can still be added to the landscape. However, tropicals will now need your on-going attention so they stay moist.

• September and October are usually the height of the hurricane season. Be prepared to move or protect wind-sensitive tropical plants if a hurricane or storm approaches. Pruning damaged plants may be required after it passes.

• Tropical plant growth continues to slow down. As the days get shorter and temperatures cooler, plants will be using less water and fewer nutrients. Continue to monitor for moisture levels, especially of new plantings. Renew mulch layers. Use soaker hoses or microsprinklers wherever possible.

• Continue Fern and Orchids feedings. In the northern part of the state, this may be the season's last feeding to make certain new growth can mature before the damaging cold weather. Container plantings can still be fed.

• Snails and slugs are very active, as well as caterpillars and grasshoppers. Mites occur as the weather is drier.

NOVEMBER

• Tropical plants can still be added, although this is not a good time to become established before cold weather arrives. Keep new plantings moist and be prepared to protect them against cold in the coming months.

• Although the weather is cooler and plant growth has slowed, continue to monitor the water needs of all tropical plants, especially new plantings. Spray foliage regularly to discourage pests and to make up for lack of rainfall. Make sure your irrigation system is working and doesn't have any bare spots.

• Bring blooming Orchids indoors for maximum enjoyment. Don't overwater.

• Except for a light fertilizer application in South Florida, don't feed in other parts of the state.

• As weather turns dry, watch for mites, mealybugs, or other pests, especially on leaf undersides.

DECEMBER

• Be prepared to cover sensitive tropicals if you are unable to move them. A sheet or blanket is the best material to use if draped directly on top of the plants. If growing in containers, move tropicals indoors when first frost or freeze is forecast.

• Make sure tropical plants are pest free before bringing inside. Carefully and thoroughly wash all leaves, especially nooks and crannies. Use alcohol to wipe away lingering insects.

• Many low light tropical plants can beautify patios and rooms with good light.

• In South Florida a light fertilize application can be made if plants are still growing. Do not fertilize until spring in other parts of the state.

• Scale may be more noticeable this time of year as plant growth remains slow. Scale and mites can be controlled with oil spray, if applied when temperatures are above 40°F. Insects and sooty mold slowly flake off after a month or more.

VINES
for Florida

My, how they get around, these vines. Shameless climbers, stealthy twiners, exuberant clingers, superlative sprawlers, midnight ramblers . . . cling to me like a vine, we say, and mean every word at the time.

The vining lifestyle must be the envy of the plant world. After all, everyone else stays put. Only the vines scramble hither and yon, scampering up trees and across fences, under guard rails and around poles. Look at Morning Glories. Look at Passion Vines. But look fast, or you'll miss them going by. Yes, we exaggerate—but only slightly.

THE POSSIBILITIES OF VINES

The ability to camouflage may be a vine's most useful characteristic. Vines have many possibilities. Some can hide a concrete block wall in just one or two seasons. Other vines that have clusters of hanging flowers, such as the Jade Vine or Bleeding Heart, make a beautiful trellis plant. Pergolas and trellises can be used to create outdoor rooms or walkways, with vines adding colorful, natural decoration. Grow Philodendrons on a tree or stump, Flame Vine on a lamppost, or Bridal Wreath on porch lattice . . . your garden will benefit from their unique qualities.

PLANNING

Nature gave vines the ability to reach for the sun. Very few really like the shade, and all love sunny sites. In fact, all vines grow best when given some support, usually a trellis or a wire or wood support. They can be trained to be freestanding or attached to a wall. Vines tend to grow very quickly during the warmer months.

Put vines to use hiding a wall or fence. Green plants are much easier to look at than wire, wood, or concrete.

Many vines produce colorful flowers. Some can be in bloom just about year-round, while others are seasonal.

Use vines trained to a trellis or fence to separate areas of the landscape. Create the rooms of the landscape with vines.

Plant vines as accent features. Use the flowers and fruits to attract attention. Use them at the end of a view or to create a focal point.

Vines are ideal where you have limited space but need some height. They can grow in a container and still climb a wall or trellis.

Use vines to create overhead cover on an arbor or similar structure.

PLANTING

Vines aren't very particular about planting sites. Most do like a well-drained soil, but it can be sandy, clay, or peaty. Care is made a lot easier if the soil is enriched with organic matter, but in fact you can pop these plants in the ground just about anywhere. When their roots systems become established, many are drought tolerant. Here are just a few tips to give the soil the best preparation for your new plantings:

- Spot-kill weeds with a non-selective herbicide that permits replanting.
- Till compost, peat moss, and composted manure into sandy or clay sites.
- Check the soil acidity and adjust to a slightly acid pH.
- Level the planting site . . . and you are ready to plant.

It is important to learn a little about the plant to be added to the landscape. If you are going to use more than one vine, give them adequate room to grow. Make sure you learn which is going to spread out and will need more room. Most of this information is found on plant labels or can be obtained from garden center employees. Now you can put the plants in the ground:

- Open a hole big enough to hold the root system plus some growing room.
- Position the plant so the rootball is even with the surface of the soil.
- Fill in around the rootball with water and soil.
- Add a 2- to 3-inch layer of mulch to conserve water and prevent weeds.
- Keep the planting site moist with frequent waterings.

CARE

Primary care involves guiding the growth of the new plants and keeping older plants in-bounds. Periodically check the new growths from beginning vines to make sure they are filling the trellis. If needed, pinch back ends to cause branching and new growth. Vines may need periodic trimming to stay in-bounds. Some seem to want to invade other plants or climb trees. You will need to check these plantings monthly for errant growth during warm weather. Cut them back hard after flowering or in early spring before they shoot out.

WATERING

Vines are a hardy bunch. Once established, most can exist primarily with seasonal rains. After planting, however, you should give each enough water to establish a root system and begin growth out into the surrounding soils.

- Hand water individual plants to maintain a moist rootball and surrounding soil. In water-resistant soil, it may be necessary to build small berms around the plants to catch and hold water.
- Apply ½ to ¾ inch water at each irrigation.
- Water daily for the first few weeks. Then reduce the waterings to every other day for a few more weeks.

- Gradually reduce the waterings to an as-needed schedule.
- Maintain a 2- to 3-inch mulch layer over the root system.
- Water during the early-morning hours.
- When the plants begin growth and roots can be found in the surrounding soil, watering can be reduced to an as-needed schedule. Too much water can cause many vines to develop root rot problems. Feel the soil, and if it's dry in the upper inch, it may need watering. Reapply ½ to ¾ inch of water.

FERTILIZING

Feeding is needed only to encourage growth, usually during the establishment period. After the vines fill a trellis, little fertilizer is needed. All can be fed lightly about three times a year to help the plantings produce new shoots, leaves, and flowers.

- Apply a 6-6-6, 10-10-10, or 16-4-8 fertilizer at the general rate for garden use once in March, July, and September if needed to encourage growth.
- Scatter the fertilizer over the surface of the soil or mulch in the planted area.
- Do not place the fertilizer near the stems.
- Water after feeding to move the nutrients into the soil.
- Feedings can be continued on a yearly schedule as needed to maintain growth. If the plantings are making adequate growth, feedings can be skipped. Many vine plantings are never fertilized. They obtain nutrients from decomposing mulches and fertilizer applied to nearby plantings.

PEST CONTROL

Many vines grow pest free. Seldom do you have to spray, as they can tolerate the few leaf spots and holes made by pests. Sometimes a few get out of control, and these hot spots can be spotted during walks in the landscape. Handpick from the plants or treat with natural sprays.

APHIDS: Small pear-shaped insects of numerous colors usually feeding in new growths and flower buds. They may be associated with ants that feed on their excreta. Small populations can be tolerated and may be controlled by beneficial insects. Where needed, control with a soap spray following the label instructions.

GRASSHOPPERS: Large brown to green insects with big legs that hop or fly between plants. They chew large holes in leaves or entire plant portions. Best controlled by handpicking or use of synthetic insecticides.

LEAF SPOTS: Yellow to brown spots forming on plant foliage, usually caused by a fungus. Often prevalent on weakened plants and at leaf drop time. Can usually be ignored. If needed, control with a natural copper-containing fungicide or a synthetic fungicide following label instructions.

MEALYBUGS: White to gray scale-related insects to 1/8 inch long. Often associated with sooty mold. The insects reduce plant vigor and cause decline. Control with a soap or oil spray as needed, following label instructions.

MITES: Small pinpoint-size arachnids that suck juices from foliage. May be clear or of tan to reddish color. They cause leaves to yellow and drop. Control with a soap or oil spray as needed.

POWDERY MILDEW: A white fungal growth on the surface of plant foliage. Most prevalent during the spring season. Can cause yellowing and leaf drop. Usually ignored unless excessive and plant damage is noted. If needed, control with a natural copper-containing fungicide or a synthetic fungicide, following the label instructions.

SCALE INSECTS: Brown to white specks to dime-size bumps on leaf surfaces and stems. Many are associated with the dark sooty mold fungus living on excreta from the insects. If minor, they can be removed by hand, but most need an oil or synthetic insecticidal treatment to obtain control.

ALLAMANDA
Allamanda cathartica

☼ ❀ ◗ ❦

HARDINESS
Zones 9–10

COLOR(S)
Yellow flowers

PEAK SEASON
Spring, summer, fall blooms; foliage evergreen

MATURE SIZE
5 feet; vining

WATER NEEDS
Once established are fairly drought tolerant, but need weekly watering in dry season.

CARE
Grows vigorously in enriched soil and loves fertilizer. Apply fertilizer with micronutrients in spring and fall. Or use slow-release fertilizer twice a year. Cut back hard in early spring to remove intertwined stems. In Central Florida, prune after warm weather returns.

PROBLEMS
The milky white sap is toxic. Few insects bother Allamanda, except aphids in spring. Use ladybugs or horticultural oil spray.

USES AND SELECTIONS
Allamanda doesn't have tendrils to cling, but sprawls and reaches with gusto, needing a strong support. Use to wrap chain-link fences in large yellow flowers and glossy leaves. Tie against a wooden privacy fence and allow shoots to cascade down. Or lean it on a picket fence. There are purple, pink, and bronze cultivars.

BLEEDING HEART
Clerodendrum thomsoniae

☼ ❀

HARDINESS
Zones 9–11

COLOR(S)
White with red flowers

PEAK SEASON
Blooms summer; evergreen foliage

MATURE SIZE
To 15 feet

WATER NEEDS
Prefers moist, but not soggy, soil

CARE
This vine grows by twining. Unlike most vines, Bleeding Heart can be pruned into a shrub. When provided with support, it can be grown as a somewhat restrained vine. It is slightly salt tolerant.

PROBLEMS
In colder areas, plant Bleeding Heart in a container so it can be protected when temperatures drop below 45°F.

USES AND SELECTIONS
Since Bleeding Heart is a much less vigorous vine than others, it is best planted in limited areas like a trellis or a garden arch. Save the more spirited vines for covering fences and arbors. The beautiful and unusual flower clusters have interior crimson petals. After they fall, the surrounding showy white calyces remain. It is also called Bleeding Heart Vine, Glorybower, and Bleeding Glory Bower.

BOUGAINVILLEA
Bougainvillea spp.

☀ ❀ 💧 ❦ 🌴

HARDINESS
Zones 9–11

COLOR(S)
Small white flowers surrounded by bracts in all colors

PEAK SEASON
Spring through fall blooms; foliage evergreen

MATURE SIZE
6 to 20 feet

WATER NEEDS
Once established, irrigate then allow to dry before watering. Will not flower well if receives too much regular water.

CARE
Not fussy about soil but likes steady fertilizer. Use balanced fertilizer in summer and bloom-booster in fall. Tolerant of cold; comes back from ground if frozen. Prune and shape in September.

PROBLEMS
Small moth caterpillars may attack the leaves. Let the cycle run its course or use recommended pesticide. Be careful of thorns, more prominent on young plants.

USES AND SELECTIONS
The stunning color of the papery bracts is dazzling. A good fence plant. Supremely beautiful when colors are mixed. Can be grown in large containers. The semi-thornless varieties are good container plants for patios or balconies. The purple *B. spectabilis* is more cold tolerant than others.

BRIDAL WREATH
Stephanotis floribunda

☀ ❀ 💧 ❦ ❦

HARDINESS
Zones 10–11

COLOR(S)
White flowers; glossy dark-green leaves

PEAK SEASON
Blooms summer; evergreen foliage

MATURE SIZE
To 15 feet

WATER NEEDS
Prefers to be moist, but not wet. Let dry a little between waterings.

CARE
Plant in sun or part shade in enriched, well-drained soil. *Stephanotis* climbs by means of twining. Train over trellises and keep pruned. Feed lightly with balanced fertilizer to encourage maximum flowering.

PROBLEMS
Grow in containers in frost-prone areas to move indoors for protection against cold.

USES AND SELECTIONS
The clusters of long-lasting white flowers are often used for wedding bouquets, which explains some of its many common names: Madagascar Jasmine, Bridal Bouquet, Hawaiian Wedding Flower, Stephanotis, and Wax Flower. Plant in areas where the strong fragrance can be appreciated, over mail boxes, near patios, and by entryways. While the white variety is considered very attractive against the thick dark-green leaves, a variegated form is also available.

CALICO FLOWER
Aristolochia spp.

☀ ☀ 🦋 🌴

HARDINESS
Zones 8–11

COLOR(S)
Purple flowers

PEAK SEASON
Blooms summer; evergreen foliage except in northern areas

MATURE SIZE
15 or 20 feet

WATER NEEDS
Water daily until established. Then water regularly.

CARE
Plant in partial shade in enriched soil, with a support. Leaves wilt if too dry, so some midday shade is best. Use a slow-release fertilizer plus a bloom-booster fertilizer at the beginning of summer. Grows quickly.

PROBLEMS
These robust vines can escape. Prune whenever needed and pull out volunteer seedlings. *A. littoralis* (syn. *elegans*) has invasive potential in Florida. Poisonous even though sometimes used as herb.

USES AND SELECTIONS
Aristolochia is also called Dutchman's Pipe and Pipe Vine. Their dense twining foliage makes good screens, even on chain-link fences. The large, unusual flowers are showy. These plants lure butterflies and provide food for butterfly larva. Construct a trellis for the vine in a large container with commercial potting mix.

CAPE HONEYSUCKLE
Tecoma capensis

☀ ☀ 🐦 💧 🌊

HARDINESS
Zones 9–11

COLOR(S)
Bright orange-red flowers

PEAK SEASON
Blooms spring through winter; evergreen foliage

MATURE SIZE
To 10 feet x 5 feet as shrub; to 25 feet long as vine

WATER NEEDS
Moderately drought tolerant once established

CARE
Plant in any well-drained soil. Blooms best in full sun, but tolerates light shade. This vine is more like a sprawling shrub that likes to wander. To use as a vine, it must be tied in place. Prune regularly to train as a shrub or hedge. It is salt tolerant.

PROBLEMS
Cape Honeysuckle takes root where branches droop down to contact the ground.

USES AND SELECTIONS
Use Cape Honeysuckle as a shrub, hedge, view barrier, or climbing vine. This tough plant is especially useful in seaside conditions where it stands up to heat, wind, and salt. The clusters of tubular flowers attract hummingbirds. A yellow cultivar and a more compact cultivar with orange flowers are available.

CAROLINA YELLOW JESSAMINE

Gelsemium sempervirens

HARDINESS
Zones 8–9

COLOR(S)
Yellow flowers

PEAK SEASON
Blooms early winter

MATURE SIZE
20 feet; climbing

WATER NEEDS
Water daily for first few weeks; gradually taper off to as needed. Drought tolerant but prefers weekly waterings.

CARE
Grows well in sandy soils. Makes lots of growth, so allow adequate room. Apply light fertilizer four to six weeks after planting. Repeat feedings for established vines during March, May, and September. Prune when plants begin to grow out of bounds. Every few years prune in early spring after flowering.

PROBLEMS
No major pests affect this native vine. All portions are poisonous if eaten.

USES AND SELECTIONS
Plant as a space divider or backdrop for a patio or garden opening. Stage other flowers in front, including Pentas, Salvia, Gaillardia, and Caladiums. Use to hide fences or cover walls. Although shoots can grow over 20 feet long, this vine does not normally get way out of control.

CLEMATIS

Clematis x jackmanii

HARDINESS
Zones 8–9

COLOR(S)
A rainbow of flower colors

PEAK SEASON
Blooms summer, fall; deciduous foliage

MATURE SIZE
15 feet or more

WATER NEEDS
Needs regular waterings

CARE
Plant in well-drained soil. Grow best when plant is in sun or partial shade, but root zone is cool. Use mulch or overplant the roots. Feed every two weeks for best flowers.

PROBLEMS
The stems are somewhat fragile and can be easily broken.

USES AND SELECTIONS
The Jackman group of clematis hybrids has large flowers, single or double, up to 7 inches across. The vines are better behaved and produce flowers later than *Clematis ternifolia*, which is becoming invasive in Florida. Grow Jackman Clematis on fences, walls, and trellises. The plant also looks good winding its way up lamp post, where its twining stems can cling and show off the beautiful flowers. The Jackman Clematis won an award from the Royal Horticultural Society.

CONFEDERATE JASMINE

Trachelospermum jasminoides

☼ ☼ ☼ ☼ 🌱 🌿 🪹 💧

HARDINESS
Zones 8–10

COLOR(S)
White flowers

PEAK SEASON
Blooms early winter; foliage evergreen

MATURE SIZE
6 feet; climbing

WATER NEEDS
Water daily for first few weeks. Gradually taper off to watering as needed. Drought tolerant but for best growth, water weekly.

CARE
Grows well in sandy Florida soils. Lightly scatter 6-6-6 under vine's spread four to six weeks after planting. Repeat for established vines during March, May, and September. Prune when it begins to grow out of bounds. To renew growth, every few years prune in spring after flowering.

PROBLEMS
Control scale with oil-containing insecticide or other recommended pesticide.

USES AND SELECTIONS
A great plant for trellises under Oak, Pine, and similar trees. With just a little support it forms a dense view barrier or attractive vertical accent. Fragrant flowering lasts a month. It's an ideal wall covering for small gardens or a turf substitute in hard-to-mow areas. 'Variegatum' has green-and-cream-colored foliage.

CORAL HONEYSUCKLE

Lonicera sempervirens

☼ 🦋 🌿 🌱 Ⓝ 🪹 💧

HARDINESS
Zones 8–10

COLOR(S)
Reddish orange and yellow blooms; red berries

PEAK SEASON
Spring through summer blooms; evergreen foliage

MATURE SIZE
20 feet or more; climbing

WATER NEEDS
Water daily for first few weeks after planting. Gradually taper off to an as-needed schedule. Vines are drought tolerant—but when growth is desired, water weekly.

CARE
Feed four to six weeks after planting with light fertilizer scattering under vine's spread. Repeat for established vines during March, May, and August. Prune when grows out of bounds. Give renewal pruning in late spring every three or four years. Grows best where plants receive some chilling winter weather.

PROBLEMS
Usually pest-free

USES AND SELECTIONS
A Florida native for fences, masonry walls, and trellises. Use as a space divider and view barrier, keeping its foliage near the ground. Look especially good with other natives, ornamental grasses, Palms, and most perennials. Selections come in yellow and red.

FLAME VINE
Pyrostegia venusta

☼ ◐ 🌴

HARDINESS
Zones 9–11

COLOR(S)
Bright orange flowers

PEAK SEASON
Winter blooms

MATURE SIZE
Indeterminate

WATER NEEDS
Drought tolerant once established

CARE
Plant on a fence or trellis in full sun, in enriched soil to keep it vigorous. Fertilize once a year in the spring; further fertilization is not necessary. After the blooms have dropped, cut the vine back hard. Flowers grow at the terminals of new shoots, so creating new shoots for the following year by pruning will earn you more flowers. Flame Vine is fairly cold tolerant. If temperatures hit 32°F, the vine will grow back rapidly. Take "semi-hardwood" cuttings in summer for rooting. These cuttings are neither totally green, nor with stems totally brown and stiff. Apply a little growth hormone on the ends and keep them moist.

PROBLEMS
None

USES AND SELECTIONS
It can be dazzling with little care. Use to cover fences and trellises.

GARLIC VINE
Cydista aequinoctialis

☼ ☀ 🌢

HARDINESS
Zones 9–11

COLOR(S)
Flowers start purple then fade to almost white

PEAK SEASON
Blooms spring, fall

MATURE SIZE
To 12 feet

WATER NEEDS
Needs average water. Mulch to retain moisture.

CARE
Plant in well-drained soil. Unlike many other vines, Garlic Vine has only a moderate growth rate. Prune the plant after flowers are gone, since buds form on new growth. Can be planted in containers to move indoors for protection against freezing temperatures.

PROBLEMS
The leaves smell like garlic, but only when crushed. They can be used as a garlic substitute in cooking.

USES AND SELECTIONS
When flowering, Garlic Vine has a very unusual look. The clusters of funnel-shaped flowers have several different colors, from purple to almost white. Attractive for hiding a chain-link or other fence or planted on a trellis. This plant has numerous synonyms for its botanical name, but luckily all are commonly called Garlic Vine.

JADE VINE
Stronglyodon marcobotrys

☼ ☼ ☼ 🌴

HARDINESS
Zones 10b–11

COLOR(S)
Blue-green flowers

PEAK SEASON
Blooms winter and spring

MATURE SIZE
Indeterminate

WATER NEEDS
Keep roots well irrigated to get established. Drought tolerant once flourishing.

CARE
Plant at the base of a support, where it can immediately begin climbing. Apply slow-release fertilizer three times a year. In late fall use low-nitrogen formula to help flower development. Jade Vine needs a pergola or an arbor that is as burly as this strong vine. Pinch off stray sprouts. This is an aggressive vine, which can get a stranglehold on whatever it clutches—including trees and electrical wires. It may need "hacking" instead of pruning. Do not be afraid to take a machete to it.

PROBLEMS
Cold sensitive. Sometimes considered a temperamental grower.

USES AND SELECTIONS
The aquamarine flowers grow on chains up to 3 feet long. The exotic color is very memorable and only found in shallow tropical seas or rare bird feathers.

MANDEVILLA
Mandevilla spp. and hybrids

☼ ☼ 🌿 🌴 🌊

HARDINESS
Zones 9–11. In Zone 8, it regrows after cold damage.

COLOR(S)
Pink, yellow, white, red flowers

PEAK SEASON
Blooms summer; foliage evergreen

MATURE SIZE
To 10 feet

WATER NEEDS
Withstands brief droughts. Do not overwater.

CARE
Plant in enriched, well-drained soil. Grow in full sun, preferably with midday shade. Fertilize during summer for maximum blooms. With regular trimming, this twining vine can be kept bushy. Has moderate salt tolerance. Plant in containers and bring indoors for cold protection.

PROBLEMS
Stressed plants may get mealybugs, scale, or whiteflies.

USES AND SELECTIONS
Use showy Mandevilla near entryways and patios to enjoy the large flowers. Use over arbors, trellises, or mailbox posts. It makes colorful screens to hide unsightly fences or sheds. Once called Pink Allamanda because it only came in pink. Now there are yellow, white, and red selections. The pink hybrid 'Alice du Pont' is still popular. (Mandevilla was once known as *Dipladenia splendens*.)

MONSTERA (CERIMAN)

Monstera deliciosa

☀ ☀ 🌱🌴

HARDINESS
Zones 10–11

COLOR(S)
Green foliage; white spathe

PEAK SEASON
Evergreen foliage

MATURE SIZE
To 50 feet x 2 foot leaf width

WATER NEEDS
Requires regular watering

CARE
This plant grows quickly in almost any soil, although it prefers well-drained, enriched soil. It will clamber over rocks or up trees. Little care is required. To speed growth, feed with a balanced fertilizer.

PROBLEMS
Usually pest free, although in dry seasons the lubber grasshopper may consume leaves. All parts of the plant except for the ripe fruit can be poisonous.

USES AND SELECTIONS
The instantly recognizable Monstera leaf often symbolizes tropical plants. Use the vine to climb trees or a pergola. It also makes a good shrubby groundcover, both growing over rocks or in soil. Sometimes called the Swiss cheese or Ceriman Plant, this vine produces an edible fruit that requires about a year to ripen and is said to taste like fruit salad.

ORNAMENTAL SWEET POTATO

Ipomoea batatas

☀ ☀ ☀ 💧🪴

HARDINESS
Zones 9–11

COLOR(S)
Foliage chartreuse, dark purple, multi-hued

PEAK SEASON
Year-round foliage; summer blossoms

MATURE SIZE
2 to 4 feet

WATER NEEDS
Once established, underground tubers retain some moisture.

CARE
Plant in well-drained soil. Keep pruned to control the vigorous vines and to encourage branching. Grows well in full sun, but does better with some shade.

PROBLEMS
Beetles may eat holes in the leaves, but may be ignored in this fast-growing plant. Control with insecticide. Keep the plant within bounds.

USES AND SELECTIONS
Varieties of this fast-growing vine come in several colors and are often planting together for maximum visual impact. Ornamental Sweet Potato makes a colorful groundcover in both sun and in partial shade. It also does well around the rocks and sides of water gardens. Use it to make a bold statement in container plantings, especially when cascading over the edges.

PAINTED TRUMPET

Clytostoma callistegioides
(Synonyms: *C. lindelyana* and
Bignonia callistegioides)

☼ ☼ ◌

HARDINESS
Zones 8–11

COLOR(S)
Pale lavender flowers; dark-green foliage

PEAK SEASON
Blooms spring; evergreen foliage

MATURE SIZE
20 feet or more

WATER NEEDS
Is drought tolerant. When given plenty of moisture it grows more aggressively.

CARE
Will grow in any well-drained soil, although it's more compact and less rampant in sandy soils. This robust and carefree grower climbs using tendrils that tightly grab things in its path. Painted Trumpet is fast growing.

PROBLEMS
Virtually pest free. The vine may need to be restrained. Seeds pods are large and prickly.

USES AND SELECTIONS
The showy flowers put on a large, beautiful display in spring and may continue into summer. Use this fast grower where there is plenty of room to spread. It is not suitable for smaller gardens. Plant on arbors, over pergolas, and as screens to block unwanted views. Other common names are Violet Trumpet Vine and Argentine Trumpet Vine.

PANDOREA

Pandorea jasminoides

☼ 🌴

HARDINESS
Zones 10–11

COLOR(S)
White-pink flowers

PEAK SEASON
Spring and summer

MATURE SIZE
To 6 feet

WATER NEEDS
Water daily for first few weeks. Gradually taper off to an as-needed schedule. Pandorea (Bower Vine) is drought tolerant. However, when growth is desired, water weekly. Feed four to six weeks after planting, applying a light scattering of balanced fertilizer under the spread of the vine. Repeat single feedings for established vines during March, May, and August.

CARE
Tolerates sandy soils but grows best in enriched soil. Prune when begins to grow out of bounds. After years of growth, may need renewal pruning during late winter. Freezing will cause major damage. Remove damaged sections before spring growth begins. Mulch well to protect the basal buds during winter months.

PROBLEMS
Pest problems are few

USES AND SELECTIONS
Also called Bower Vine, can be used on trellises, fences, or similar supports.

PASSION VINE

Passiflora spp.

HARDINESS
Zones 9–11. Killed to ground by severe frost, but grows back.

COLOR(S)
Blue, purple, white, red, crimson flowers

PEAK SEASON
Blooms spring and summer

MATURE SIZE
20 feet or more

WATER NEEDS
Somewhat drought tolerant once established, but blooms better with regular waterings

CARE
Plant in any well-drained soil. Easy to grow.

PROBLEMS
Passion Vine is rampant and can get out of control. If necessary, prune severely to reign it back in-bounds. The two-flowered variety (*P. bicolor*) is invasive in Florida.

USES AND SELECTIONS
Grow these natural climbers on fences, arbors, walls, or trellises. Can be used to cover up unsightly features, like chain-link fences. Ornamental Passion Vine hybrids and species do not bear fruit. However, they do attract lots of butterflies. The vines provide both nectar and larval food. For maximum benefit in butterfly gardens, do not use insecticides. There are a few native Florida Passion Vines.

PHILODENDRON

Philodendron spp.

HARDINESS
Zones 10b–11

COLOR(S)
White spathe; foliage green

PEAK SEASON
Intermittent blooms; foliage evergreen

MATURE SIZE
To top of tree, and then down again

WATER NEEDS
Water daily until vine produces new leaves and roots, then gradually reduce watering.

CARE
Feed with organic or Palm fertilizer. Philodendrons, like other Aroids, are sensitive to cold. Many Philodendrons survive cold and drought unscathed by growing beneath trees. They may withstand cold, but not freezes. Mix liquid silicon into soluble fertilizer to strengthen cell walls, reducing vulnerability to cold, heat, and drought. Prune vigorous climbers.

PROBLEMS
Handpick snails

USES AND SELECTIONS
Philodendrons are extremely agile at surviving in their native rain forests. They can survive in the dim areas or climb for the light. This makes them suitable for gardens and easier to contain than some other vines. In fact, some are even suitable for containers. There are several cold-tolerant species.

QUEEN'S WREATH
Petrea volubilis

☼

HARDINESS
Zones 10b–11

COLOR(S)
Blue-purple flowers

PEAK SEASON
Spring blooms

MATURE SIZE
To 35 feet

WATER NEEDS
Water two or three times a week in summer, twice weekly in winter.

CARE
This vigorous vine must be supported by a pergola or arbor. Without tendrils, the vine twines and does best on craggy surfaces. Fertilize in spring, summer, and fall. Cut back hard after flowering or in late winter. In Central Florida, plant this tender vine in a sunny area.

PROBLEMS
Has few pests, although spider mites can be a problem in dry weather. Give the affected areas a hard spray of water.

USES AND SELECTIONS
Because it is so strongly seasonal, the vine shows off when it finally does flower. Using it at an arching front gate, or on a pergola or trellis of some sort is ideal. Give it a place to show off. With age, the vine develops a thick trunk.

RANGOON CREEPER
Quisqualis indica

☼ ☼ ☼ 🜄 🌱 🌀

HARDINESS
Zones 10–11

COLOR(S)
Flowers start white, then change to pink, then red

PEAK SEASON
Blooms summer; evergreen foliage

MATURE SIZE
Over 40 feet

WATER NEEDS
Water regularly during growing season, less during winter.

CARE
Plant in well-drained soil. Rangoon Creeper starts as a bush and then becomes an energetic vine, using its spiny stems to hold as it twines. It grows lush quickly.

PROBLEMS
Handle with care because of the thorny stems. Keep an eye on this vine so that it doesn't get out of control. Prune when necessary.

USES AND SELECTIONS
Rangoon Creeper can appear to be different plants. A cluster of flowers will have several colors at once as individual blossoms age. Its appropriate botanical name means "who" (*quis*) and "what" (*qualis*).This rampant grower needs a strong support to hold the long, glossy leaves and to showcase the drooping fragrant flowers. Plant on arbors, trellises, arches, sturdy fences, and pergolas.

TRUMPET CREEPER
Campsis radicans

HARDINESS
Zones 8–9

COLOR(S)
Orange flowers

PEAK SEASON
Blooms summer; foliage evergreen

MATURE SIZE
30 or more feet

WATER NEEDS
Water daily for first few weeks after planting. Gradually taper off to an as-needed schedule. Vines are quite drought tolerant and only need weekly watering during drought. This native also adapts to moist conditions.

CARE
Grows in most Florida soils, but does best in enriched soil. Feed four to six weeks after planting, applying a light scattering of balanced fertilizer under the vine's spread. Repeat feedings for established vines are normally not needed. Needs a trellis, fence, or similar support.

PROBLEMS
None

USES AND SELECTIONS
The large blooms are borne in clusters and attract hummingbirds. Plant this native to hide a sunny wall or fill a trellis. Use with other natives—ornamental grasses, shrubs, and Saw Palmettos. Suitable as a space divider or backdrop for other plantings. There is a yellow selection.

WISTERIA
Wisteria sinensis

HARDINESS
Zones 8–9

COLOR(S)
Lavender flowers

PEAK SEASON
Spring blooms; deciduous foliage

MATURE SIZE
To 24 feet

WATER NEEDS
Water daily for first few weeks after planting. Gradually taper off to an as-needed schedule. Drought tolerant and only needs watering during drought. For extra growth, water weekly.

CARE
Needs strong trellis, fence, or similar support. Tolerant of sandy soils, but makes best growth in enriched soil. Feed four to six weeks after planting, scattering balanced fertilizer under vine's spread. Repeat for established vines during March, May, and September for first year or two, then reduce feedings to once or twice annually. Supplying too much care may result in reluctant bloomers.

PROBLEMS
Apply a soap, oil, or other recommended pesticide for any mites or thrips.

USES AND SELECTIONS
Train to a trellis against a wall as an accent or space divider. Add contrasting perennials and bulbs. Flowers of some vines are fragrant. 'Alba' has white blossoms.

VINES

Name	Area of Florida	Climbing Height (ft.)	Foliage Type	Flowers Color/Season	Light Needed
Allamanda, Purple	CS	Variable	Evergreen	Purple/Summer-fall	Sun
Allamanda, Yellow	CS	Variable	Evergreen	Yellow/Year-round	Sun, light shade
Bengal Clock Vine	CS	20–30	Evergreen	White, blue/Summer	Sun
Bleeding Heart	CS	12–15	Evergreen	White & red/Spring-fall	Sun, light shade
Bougainvillea	CS	10–20	Evergreen	Numerous/Year-round	Sun
Bower Vine	CS	15–20	Evergreen	White & pink/Spring	Sun, light shade
Bridal Wreath	S	10–15	Evergreen	White/Summer	Sun, light shade
Calico Flower	CS	12–15	Evergreen	White & brown/Summer	Sun, light shade
Cape Honeysuckle	CS	6–10	Evergreen	Orange/Summer-fall	Sun
Cat's Claw Vine	NCS	20–30	Evergreen	Yellow/Spring	Sun, light shade
Chinese Wisteria	NC	20–30	Deciduous	Lavender/Spring	Sun
Confederate Jasmine	NCS	15–20	Evergreen	White/Spring	Sun, shade
Coral Vine	CS	30–40	Evergreen	Pink/Spring-fall	Sun
Flame Vine	CS	30–40	Evergreen	Orange/Winter	Sun
Garlic Vine	CS	20–30	Evergreen	Lavender, pink, White/Spring-fall	Sun, light shade
Japanese Clematis	NC	10–15	Evergreen	White/Summer	Sun
Mandevilla	CS	15–20	Evergreen	Pink/Spring-fall	Sun
Mexican Flame Vine	CS	15–20	Evergreen	Orange/Spring-summer	Sun, light shade
Monstera	CS	15–20	Evergreen	Green/Summer	Light shade, shade
Ornamental Sweet Potato	CS	2–6	Evergreen	Inconspicuous	Sun, light shade
Painted Trumpet	NCS	15–20	Evergreen	Lavender/Spring	Sun
Passion Flower, Red	CS	15–20	Evergreen	Red/Spring-summer	Sun
Pothos	CS	20–30	Evergreen	Inconspicuous	Shade
Queen's Wreath	S	20–30	Evergreen	Purple/Spring-summer	Sun, light shade
Rangoon Creeper	CS	15–25	Evergreen	White, red/Summer	Sun, light shade
Showy Combretum	CS	15–20	Evergreen	Red/Fall-spring	Sun
Trumpet Creeper	NC	20–30	Deciduous	Orange/Summer	Sun
Trumpet Honeysuckle	NC	15–25	Evergreen	Orange, yellow/Spring-summer	Sun
Yellow Jessamine, Carolina	NC	20–30	Evergreen	Yellow/Winter	Sun, light shade

N = North Florida   C = Central Florida   S = South Florida

JANUARY

• When planting vines, it's not necessary to dig up a large area when just a small spot will do. Choose a site near a support. Determine the maximum width and space plants so shoots grow together at maturity.

• Vines may need grooming. Trim dead and declining plant portions. Remove extra-long shoots growing out of bounds. Plants that flower during late winter or early spring usually have pruning delayed until after blossoms fade.

• In South Florida, plants may begin growth and spring feedings can begin. Feed only if you want to encourage growth. In Central and North Florida wait until February or March to fertilize.

• Most insects do not become active until growth begins. However, scale can appear at any time. Control with oil spray, if temperatures are above 40 degrees. Insects and sooty mold slowly flake off after a month or more.

FEBRUARY

• This is the most stress-free planting time of year. The weather is warming and garden centers are filling. Most vines are tough and need very little site preparation. However, results are more certain with good planting procedures.

• Water new plantings daily for a week or two. For the next few weeks, water every few days. Hand water to make sure moisture runs through the root system. Use soaker hoses or microsprinklers where possible. Except during drought, established plants usually do not need waterings.

• Keep vines off trees, where they compete for light. Give them their own spots—trellises, arbors, or walls.

• Many vines get nutrients from decomposing mulches. However, a light spring feeding may benefit them.

• Some aphid presence can be ignored on new growth. When populations are high, apply insecticidal soap or synthetic insecticide. Skip the sprays if beneficial insects are present. Other pests this month are mites, mealybugs, scale, and powdery mildew.

MARCH

• If you are only planting one vine, open the hole, loosen surrounding soil, then add the plant. When you are planting a large area, it's best to loosen the entire area and add lots of organic matter.

• Vines need guidance as they begin growing. Direct them onto a trellis so they can form a complete wall covering or create a solid view barrier. Some may need regular trimming to keep them in-bounds. Pinching back the vines just above buds will cause branching and produce additional shoots.

• The dry season is coming. Make sure new plantings have adequate moisture. The first month or two is usually the critical period. Established plants only need water during drought or when plants wilt.

• If you missed the spring feeding, make a fertilizer application.

• Mites are often a problem during drier months. Other pests becoming active include aphids, caterpillars, powdery mildew, and scale.

APRIL

• Adding vines can continue throughout the year, though it's best to buy vines early in the season. They can become entangled while waiting at the nursery. If you do obtain a vine later in the season, try to find one on a trellis so the shoots can be easily switched to your growing area. Where plants are entangled, trim away the problem portions.

• Check vines to make sure they are filling the trellis or climbing the wall properly. Position or tie shoots if necessary. Trim back shoots that are too vigorous.

• Established plantings can often go a week or two without irrigation. Make sure new plantings have adequate moisture.

• No fertilizer is needed for vines at this time. If you want to push growth, give plants a light feeding. Plants in containers should be fed monthly.

• Some insects are becoming active. Check for grasshoppers, mealybugs, mites, powdery mildew, and scale.

MAY

• Continue planting any vines you might like. You don't have to give special soil preparation, but in large beds the addition of organic matter helps stretch the time between waterings.

• Your plants and the weeds will grow well. Reduce the weeds before planting by controlling the perennial type with a nonselective herbicide that permits rapid replanting. Once the new vines are in the ground, weed control is up to you. Add a layer of mulch, use landscape fabric, apply a pre-emergence weed-control product, carefully spot-kill weeds with non-selective herbicide, and remember that hoeing and pulling are still good ways to control weeds.

• We have one more month or dry weather. Keep up regular watering of newly planted vines. Once established, make periodic checks for moisture adequate levels.

• Delay all feedings until summer.

• Caterpillars and aphids may be the worst pests at this time of year. Where needed, use a soap spray.

JUNE

• Check vines that may be growing out of control. The start of the rainy season is when you can expect a flush of new shoots. Keep plants off nearby shrubs and out of trees. Continue to control weeds.

• Most plantings make good growth as the rainy season returns. You may not have to do any waterings of even newly established plantings. However, continue to check the moisture levels of recently added plants.

• It's now or next month for feeding. If plantings are making normal green growth or you want to limit shoot development, skip this fertilizing. New plantings should probably receive the feeding. Apply only to plants with adequate soil moisture and dry foliage. Water afterwards.

• With the summer rains comes the chance of rot problems. Leaf spots may also be a problem but are often minor and can be ignored. Summer pests include aphids, caterpillars, grasshoppers, and scale.

JULY

• If you don't have a lot of room but still want to enjoy vines, use a small area or plant in containers. Vines are especially useful in containers on patios, balconies, or over the edges of walls. They can even make nice stand-alone displays.

• Keep up with the growth of vines. There is always trimming to do to keep them in-bounds.

• Mother Nature is probably helping with the watering. Continue to check the more recent plantings for water needs or possible overwatering. Very few established plants need special watering at this time.

• If you delayed or missed a planned feeding for summer, now is the time to apply fertilizer. For container gardens, apply slow-release fertilizer at planting then note on the calendar when the next will be needed. They may be fed monthly with liquid fertilizer.

• Most plantings can tolerate some defoliation from the grasshoppers and caterpillars. Scale may also be active.

AUGUST

• Don't let the hot summer months keep you from adding plants. Just be sure you have a well-prepared site before planting. Add organic material to help hold moisture. After planting, thoroughly moisten and add a mulch layer.

• This is the last pruning time for Bougainvillea. Trim to keep them in-bounds and then let them form buds for winter bloom. Other vines that bloom during spring should get their last trimming of the year.

• Regular rains should provide lots of water, but continue to check new plantings to make sure they are moist.

• Most plantings have adequate fertilizer to get them through the summer season. The next scheduled feeding for in-ground plantings is September. Continue to feed container plantings with liquid fertilizer or slow-release fertilizer when scheduled.

• Mealybugs may be found on tropical plants. Other pests and problems include grasshoppers, caterpillars, scale, leaf spots, and root rot.

SEPTEMBER

• With cooler weather it's easier to work outdoors. Any vines can be planted now.

• Sometimes vines get completely out of control and need major pruning. The best time for rejuvenation pruning is after they flower, but you can actually trim any time the plants are making growth. Heavy pruning may delay flowering for a year. Try to trim so the new growth will reach maturity before severe winter weather in central and northern portions of the state.

• As the rainy season ends, you must provide water for new plantings and container plants.

• It's time for the last feeding of the year, if needed to maintain growth and green leaves. Many plants receive adequate nutrients from feedings of surrounding plants. If they are growing vigorously, you might skip this feeding.

• Caterpillars are often heavy in fall. Handpick or apply product containing *Bacillus thuringiensis*. Other active pests include grasshoppers, leaf spots, mites, and scales.

OCTOBER

• There is no excuse not to get outdoors and enjoy the landscape, and it's an ideal time to make needed plantings. You may have divided some plants earlier and added them to containers, or made a few purchases and just left them in pots. Use this cooler time to add them to the landscape.

• Complete all needed trimming this month.

• Check new plantings regularly for needed moisture. Make sure the water is wetting the rootballs.

• If you missed or delayed the September feeding, there is still time to supply nutrients.

• Gardeners may begin noticing many leaf spots on deciduous vines during fall. Some are getting ready for winter, and leaf spotting as the leaves begin to drop is normal. Even some evergreen types, including Mandevilla, are not as vigorous during fall and may develop brown to yellow patches. This is normal. Pests you might be concerned about are caterpillars, grasshoppers, mites, and scale insects.

NOVEMBER

• It continues to be a good time for planting. Where possible, till up a planting site to add a number of vines. However, if only adding one or two plants, the soil preparation is not needed.

• Most landscape plant growth is slowing. If it's not the cool weather, it's the shorter days that reduce growth. Your job is to remove vine growth that may be interfering with landscape movement or affecting other plantings. Continue to control weeds.

• Cool weather means slower growth and less waterings. As always, continue to check new plantings to make sure soil is moist. Well-established plants seldom need watering, except in containers.

• Feeding is over for the year, except in containers. Continue fertilizing monthly with liquid or apply slow-release fertilizer as scheduled.

• Mites can remain a pest during fall. Luckily vines are fairly resistant. Mealybugs may develop, especially in shady spots. Soap sprays are used for both mites and mealybugs. Caterpillars and grasshoppers may still be around.

DECEMBER

• Little care is needed this month. Very little pruning is needed except for vines that may blow off a trellis or arbor.

• Continue to check all plantings for adequate water. Water as needed to maintain moist soil for new plantings. Older plantings can usually go weeks between waterings. Container plantings can usually skip a day or two. This is also a good time to check the irrigation system.

• Don't feed in-ground plantings. If you have container plantings, stretch the feedings to four to six weeks. Skip feedings if plants are dormant.

• Scale insects might be quite evident. Cooler months are good to control with oil spray, as long as the temperatures are above 40 degrees. Coat all portions of the plant. In warmer location of the state where plants continue to grow, check for aphids, mealybugs, and mites that may need control.

APPENDIX

CONSERVING WATER IN THE GARDEN

If we weren't the Sunshine State, Florida might well be called the Aquatic State. We have almost 1,200 miles of coastline, more than 4,000 lakes, 11,000 miles of waterways, the second largest lake in the United States, and the world's largest concentration of first magnitude springs. We are directly tied to our aquatic resources.

Unfortunately for gardeners, as these limited water resources becomes more precious because of drought and development, outdoor usage has been restricted by local agencies and water management districts. The time of day and frequency that water can be used on lawns and plantings is limited, depending upon the time of year and size of the current reserves. Some counties now have year-round restrictions. Others make reclaimed water available.

Some experts estimate that more than 50 percent of landscape water use is wasted due to evaporation, runoff, and unnecessary watering. Unnecessary watering is especially common in Florida, since sandy soils are unable to retain water. Gardeners in the state are learning as much as they can to help conserve water.

WATER DEEPLY AND LESS OFTEN

In many ways, plants are like some people. They don't work any harder than they have to. Consequently, if all moisture needed is right near the surface, plants won't use extra energy and nutrients to grow roots deeper into the soil where moisture levels are consistently higher.

This is why the key is to water infrequently but deeply. *Reducing* the overall amount of water to plants (and especially lawns) keeps them growing stronger. Deep watering encourages deep roots, and roots that are encouraged to explore farther into the soil to find sustenance have better access to moisture when the area closer to the surface dries out. This upper layer always dries out first because soil at or near the surface warms faster and is subject to evaporation and the drying effects of wind.

When a gardener waters every day but only for brief periods, water rarely soaks deeply enough into the soil to encourage roots to grow there. In order for roots that are growing only near the surface to stay healthy and alive, continued frequent watering is *required* to provide them with sufficient moisture. The "pampered" plants never have to develop an extensive root system reaching farther down to find water.

Now, deep watering doesn't mean turning on the sprinkler and leaving it on while you go play golf. Once the surface layer of most soils becomes saturated, all the water applied from that point on runs off and is wasted, or in the case of sandy soils, filters through and is wasted.

WATER AT THE RIGHT TIME OF DAY

The hotter it is, the more water is lost to evaporation. Add wind to the equation and even more water is vaporized in the atmosphere before it ever reaches the ground. Depending on your irrigation system and the timing of when you water, as much as half the water can be lost to drift and evaporation.

If you water at night or very early in the morning, temperatures are cooler and winds are calmer. These are also the best times to use soaker hoses or microsprinklers. The coolness and darkness, along with calm skies, allows soil to soak up the maximum amount of water.

PROGRAM YOUR IRRIGATION SYSTEM

How much water is enough to keep our lawns and landscapes looking great without overdoing it? Experts tell us that lawns need an average of one inch of water per week from all sources. This includes rainfall and supplemental irrigation to make up the deficiency. That's true for lawns and most plants.

To find out how much water your sprinklers (automatic or manual) are delivering, place tuna or cat food cans around the yard and check how long it takes to get an inch of water. Also note if your irrigation system needs to have some heads adjusted. Your goal is to have it deliver even coverage to the desired areas. Watering driveways and streets is a big waste of water.

Include a rain sensor in your automatic system. Studies have shown that installing a rain sensing device in areas with frequent rains can reduce water usage by as much as 30 percent.

Program your irrigation system for seasonal needs. As plants and lawns go from active growth into dormancy and back again, their need for water changes. Plants use approximately 40 percent less water in the slower growth seasons when compared to the peak demands. If your irrigation system doesn't have this kind of programming, mark your calendar to makes the necessary changes throughout the year.

CONVERT TO SOAKER HOSES AND MICROSPRINKLERS

Watering directly at the soil level is the most efficient way to irrigate, for two reasons. First, it cuts down on wasted water tremendously. Water is delivered directly to the soil. Because water is not shot into the air before falling back to earth, all is right where the plant needs it most—at the roots. There is no drift or evaporation. Furthermore, the water isn't deflected away or suspended on the foliage where it is exposed to wind and sun, culprits of rapid evaporation. Second, by watering at the soil level, the foliage stays dry. Keeping foliage dry is an important step in minimizing plant diseases.

Microsprinkler systems are also called drip irrigation, micro-irrigation, and trickle irrigation. Modern technology has improved the original design used since ancient times when buried clay pots were filled with water, which gradually seeped into the soil. The systems available now are readily available as kits or individual components. Drip irrigation is easy to install.

MULCH, MULCH, MULCH

Mulch is one of the most versatile additions to any garden. It has many uses, with one of the most important being to conserve water. A layer of mulch up to 4 inches thick will provide an insulating blanket that reduces evaporation, slows runoff, moderates soil temperature on hot days, and lowers the moisture requirements of the plants. It also dramatically cuts down on weed production, lowering the demand and competition for nutrients and water.

Mulch can be organic, such as leaves, straw, compost, bark, or wood chips. It can even be gravel or plastic. In all cases, the mulch holds the moisture in place, in the ground, right where it is needed most. (Using mulch can reduce water usage by 5 to 10 percent, saving up to 4,400 gallons of water a year.)

XERISCAPE™: USE THE RIGHT PLANT IN THE RIGHT PLACE

Xeriscape™ (pronounced zera-scape) was originated as a way to conserve water. The word comes from *xeros*, meaning dry, with *landscape*. The concept is used to describe gardening with plants whose natural requirements are appropriate to the local climate and reduce the need for water, maintenance, and other resources. It does not mean using plants that live without water. More simply, it means grouping plants according to their water needs and using plants that are better adapted to the local area—specifically choosing native plants whenever possible. In addition to helping conserve water, using xeriscape™ practices has another crucial water-related benefit for Florida. It reduces the amount of pollutants (fertilizers and pesticides) that contaminate our water supply and other water bodies.

Florida's extended growing season means that as much as half our household water is used outdoors, mostly for lawn and garden irrigation. Ninety percent of the state's public water supply comes from underground sources, primarily our aquifer. Unfortunately, these sources are not large enough to support all the needs of our population during rainy years, and in dry times they are depleted even faster. The results of over pumping to fill the public water requirements are lowered lake levels, sinkhole formations, and saltwater intrusion into some regions of the state's aquifer.

As an outcome of these problems, Florida's five regional water management districts were charged with preserving and protecting the state's water resources. They support xeriscape principles as an important way to help conserve the state's unique aquatic resources. The districts produce numerous resources (printed and electronic) to help gardeners understand and implement gardens that work for both them and for nature. An excellent website with an interactive section to help you select the best plants for your landscape is www.Floridayards.org. The following are summaries of xeriscape™ gardening's seven principles.

PLAN AND DESIGN

This is the first step whether you are creating a new garden or updating your current land-scape. Start with your property plat to create a master drawing. It may help to make lots of copies and use tracing or graph paper. There are also several landscape software programs available. Some even provide 3-D views of the designs. Identify your current plants, topography, and structures (house, garage, shed). Be sure to also include all the hardscape (driveways, patios, pools, fences, paths). Inventory specific growing conditions, such as shade, sun, drainage, flooding, and wind direction. Check for any municipal codes, easements, deed restrictions, and utilities.

Decide how you and your family want to use the yard. Plan which spaces should be private and which should be public. Decide where you want sun and where would you like to create a shady area. Consider surrounding views to block (such as nearby houses and roofs) or ones you would like to incorporate into your design (such as an ocean view or adjacent park). Be sure to plan for the full year, since plants and your needs change season by season. Another important thing to do is to design with both the young and full-grown plants in mind, especially for trees and larger plants.

OBTAIN A SOIL ANALYSIS

Florida soils obviously sustain an enormous range of plant life. However the typical Florida "soil" is not the dark topsoil common in other parts of the country. In fact, our official state soil isn't dirt, it is Myakka fine sand. The first step to understanding the soil in your yard is to determine its composition, from sand to clay. Then test the pH of several samples around your yard to determine how acidic or alkaline they are. Test kits are available at most garden centers and assistance may be available at your local Extension Service.

Most plants prefer neutral or slightly acidic soil. However some prefer either alkaline soils or more acidic levels. Amendments like peat or compost can be added to adjust pH levels, although they do not permanently alter the pH. If you have acidic soil you can choose plants like gardenias, azaleas, blueberries, and camellias. Some fertilizers are adjusted for low pH conditions to maximize release of specific nutrients for acid-loving plants.

CHOOSE PROPER PLANTS

It is important to select plants that match the conditions in various spots around your yard. Consider the plant's mature height and width, how much sun or shade it needs, what soil it prefers, its cold tolerance, and of course, its water needs. Whenever possible preserve native vegetation. Those trees and shrubs have learned how to successfully grow in the conditions you have, without extensive water, fertilizer, or maintenance. Native plants are important components to xeriscape gardens because of those characteristics. When you add plants to your landscape, consider using natives since they require less resources and maintenance, which often fits in well with today's lifestyles.

You are not restricted to native plants or those that use very little water. A key concept of xeriscape™ gardens is to group plants according to their water needs. So if you want to have lush tropical plants, vegetables, or specialty flowers, group them each into areas according to how much moisture they require. Design in a smart way, to keep moisture-loving plants together. This concept is central to the effectiveness and popularity of xeriscaping™ and is often summarized by the phrase "right plant in the right place."

USE TURF WISELY

Over the past few decades the percentage of turf in Florida landscapes has steadily been shrinking. New home landscaping now makes greater use of groundcovers and mulch. It's not unheard of to see homes without any grass at all in the front yard. Reducing turf area results in a dramatic savings of water usage, while greatly reducing the amount of time and expense that homeowners have to spend cutting, edging, fertilizing, weed killing, and preventing pests. If your lawn is large, consider reducing its size. Start by enlarging the beds that surround it. Additional strategies are to replace turf with walkways or mulched areas and to use groundcovers as an alternative for at least part of the current lawn.

Two of the easiest and most beneficial ways to use turf wisely are to reduce fertilizing and to schedule it carefully. The less the grass grows, the less water is needed and the fewer times it has to be mowed. Follow the suggested tips in Chapter 5, as well as the procedures for when and how much to water, as well as when to fertilize. By adhering to these recommendations you will accomplish several goals—reduce water usage, improve the health of Florida's aquifer and water-ways, save time and money, and reduce noise pollution in your neighborhood. Also be certain to adhere to any irrigation restrictions that may be in effect in your municipality.

IRRIGATE EFFICIENTLY

Efficiency comes down to not wasting water. This is best accomplished by grouping plants based on their water needs. Put moisture-loving plants together, separated from groupings of drier plants. Sprinklers and microsprinklers can then be tailored to each of the areas and auto-mated systems can be scheduled accordingly. They will apply water only when and where the individual plants really need it.

Make sure your irrigation system has a rain sensor and that it is working correctly to shut off your automatic sprinkler when it has rained. Florida Law requires that they be present on irriga-tion systems installed after 1991. The sensors have been shown to save from 25 to 40 percent of outdoor water use. Some municipalities provide them for free.

Install a rain barrel to collect water from your roof. The barrels are especially practical for watering patio and other plants that require hand watering. They are now available in decorator styles. Some municipalities make them available to residents for a very low cost.

In some parts of the state reclaimed water is available for outdoor irrigation. This reused water comes from domestic wastewater that has been treated and disinfected. Using reclaimed water helps conserve the state's valuable (and rapidly dwindling) water supply. Florida leads the nation in implementing reclaimed water usage. Learn if it is available in your community and how to get it.

USE MULCHES

Besides conserving water, mulch helps moderate temperature, slow erosion, reduce weeds, and may produce small amounts of slowly released nutrients. Organic mulches produce the most benefits, although inorganic mulches like gravel or stone still provide some benefits.

PERFORM PROPER MAINTENANCE

Maintaining healthy plants involves fertilizing and trimming plants when necessary, remov-ing weeds that compete for nutrients and water, and eliminating pests before they become a major problem. Fertilize lightly and only when necessary. Over-fertilizing is costly, stimulates excessive growth, can aggravate pest problems, and requires more watering. The resulting runoff carries nutrients into the aquifer and waterways, where they become pollutants which degrade the water quality. When plants are correctly placed and given enough room, there is less need to prune, which is less stressful to the plant. Prune carefully, only when needed. Use mulch to dra-matically reduce the need for weeding. Regularly check your plants for any pests. Catching pests early, while their numbers are few, allows for treatment with the least toxic method possible.

ATTRACTING WILDLIFE

Florida is a state with some of the most diverse wildlife populations in the United States. However, as its natural wildlife habitat gets replaced by human development, the environment suitable for animals and birds decreases in size and diversity. With careful planning, it is possible to provide a landscape that is attractive to both wildlife and people, as well as help to replace habitat that has disappeared.

To attract butterflies, birds, and animals to your yard, three essential features must be provided for them—food, water, and cover. The more diversity you can provide, the more types of wildlife will visit your property. So while a large, neatly mowed lawn might appear attractive on the surface, it contains only a single kind of plant with lots of herbicides and pesticides. That isn't very appealing to wildlife since it doesn't provide food or cover for most species.

FOOD

Food can be provided in any of several forms, including those that bear seeds, produce nectar, or provide food for caterpillars. When deciding what to plant in your landscape, choose plants that will be a food source for the type of wildlife you would like to attract—birds, butterflies, or other wildlife.

WATER

Water can be as simple as a birdbath that is kept full or something more elaborate like a creek or ornamental pond. To prevent mosquitoes from breeding, standing water must be kept fresh, contain fish which will eat the larva, or be treated with products that kill the larva. The sound of moving water is like a beacon for wildlife and also sounds wonderful in the yard.

COVER

Cover for wildlife means areas in which they feel safe to nest, hide, sleep, eat, and travel. Sometimes the same plants that provide food can also provide shelter. Birds prefer planted areas with a foliage canopy.

It is simple to make your landscape friendlier to wildlife without adding any digging. While it may sound obvious, house pets that run loose in the yard are one of the biggest deterrents. Reduce using insecticides to treat your garden or lawn, which also kill many beneficial insects that may be food sources for birds or grow up to be butterflies. Provide a consistent and protected place for wildlife to drink and eat. Provide bird houses to encourage them to nest.

If you want to create a real wildlife refuge, many plants can be added to make your yard attractive to them. Use plants targeted to appeal to the kinds of wildlife you want as visitors. Butterflies need both sources of nectar as well as food supplies for caterpillars after eggs hatch. You must be willing to overlook less-than-perfect foliage as they dine.

Birds may be year-round residents, migrants, or winter visitors. Check the type of food and preferred nesting sites that various birds like and plant accordingly. Hummingbirds favor nectar-rich plants with bright orange or red flowers into which they can insert their long beaks. The blossoms generally need to be at least two feet above the ground. They may also visit feeders designed specifically for them.

NATIVE FLORIDA PLANTS

There are many reasons to use native Florida plants, which come is all sizes, shapes, and colors. When selected for the right location, natives in the landscape require less maintenance, water, fertilizer, and pesticide. They are easier on the gardener, the pocketbook, and the environment. Planting natives is also a good way to help restore natural communities that have been greatly reduced by decades of development in the state.

Natives with similar growing requirements should be grouped together to make maintenance easier. This also allows watering to be done only when they need it without watering the entire landscape. Florida has an incredibly diverse number of plants, with over 2,500 considered native. Below is a list of the ones profiled in this book, arranged by chapter.

Other excellent resources are available when planning your landscape or converting a garden. The Florida Native Plant Society has an excellent website that helps you choose the right native for your region of the state, as well as your growing preferences. Visit them at www.fnps.org to use their interactive tool for plant selection. Another excellent website is hosted by the Florida Yards and Neighborhoods Program, www.FloridaYards.org. It is also filled with information and interactive options to choose exactly the right plant for your needs.

ANNUAL
Sunflower
Viola

BULBS
Blue Flag Iris
Canna
Swamp Lily

CITRUS, NUTS, AND OTHER FRUITS
Passion Fruit
Persimmons
Sea Grape

ORNAMENTAL GRASSES AND GROUND COVERS
Broad Sword Fern
Florida Gamma Grass
Lopsided Indian Grass
Muhly Grass
Purple Lovegrass
Sand Cordgrass
Wiregrass

PERENNIALS
Blue Phlox
Butterfly Weed
Coneflower
Coreopsis

Goldenrod
Leather Fern
Rudbeckia
Stokes' Aster
Swamp Fern
Wild Petunia

ROSES AND SHRUBS
American Beautybush
Azalea
Cocculus
Cocoplum
Firebush
Florida Privet
Necklace Pod
Oleander
Sea Grape
Sweet Viburnum
Wax Myrtle
Wild Coffee

TREES AND PALMS
Bald Cypress
Cabbage Palm
Cedar
Dogwood
Florida Silver Palm
Geiger Tree
Gumbo Limbo
Holly
Lignum Vitae
Like Oak

Mahogany
Pigeon Plum
Red Maple
Redberry Stopper
Redbud
Royal Palm
Satinleaf
Slash Pine
Southern Magnolia
Sweetbay Magnolia
Sweet Gum

TROPICAL PLANTS
Bromeliad
Cycad
Fern
Peperomia

VINES
Carolina Yellow Jasmine
Passionvine
Trumpet Creeper

INVASIVE PLANTS IN FLORIDA

Most gardeners know the story of how Kudzu was innocently introduced into the South in the late 1800s. But soon it started running wild, taking over gardens, trees, and just about anything that stood still long enough. Kudzu is the poster child for invasive plants.

Unfortunately, since Florida does not have extremely cold weather, many plants have moved in and don't want to leave. These exotics have become invasive, unlike the well-behaved exotic plants that fill our gardens and farms. They have rapidly, and sometimes uncontrollably, reproduced. Seeds may be spread by the wind, by birds, by water, or by other wildlife. Others extend their reach with very aggressive runners.

Control of these invasive plants is important for several reasons. Invasives often choke out or displace native plants. They also interfere with plant and animal life in bodies of water, as well as impede navigation and flood control. The control of invasive exotics is very expensive in Florida. Progress is being made in public natural areas, but the work is never ending.

As gardeners, we can each do our part. Whenever possible we should avoid planting any of the invasive exotics on the federal, state, or regional lists. There are countless native and non-invasive exotics that can be used in their place. If you have any questions about what should or should not be planted, check with your local Extension Service. The Florida Exotic Plant Pest Council (www.fleppc.org) maintains a list of plants that have adverse affects on Florida's biodiversity and plant communities. It is updated every two years and also includes plants on the Federal and State of Florida lists.

FLORIDA PEST CONTROL

APHIDS are small pear-shaped insects, variously colored, that feed only on new growth. Look for them in buds and new leaves. They often produce lots of sap and excreta that attract ants and encourage growth of black sooty mold fungus. A soap spray is usually all that is needed for control. If lady beetles are present, a control may not be needed.

BLACKSPOT produces dark spots, often with a yellow halo, on roses; affected leaves drop and plant vigor is affected. You can help keep this disease under control by watering only during early-morning hours to allow foliage to dry during the day. Control with fungicides as needed, especially during rainy weather.

BORERS are insects or insect larvae that feed in the woody parts of plants. Borers may be an indication of more severe problems. Check for sap or sawdust around the trunks of trees and dying branches. If only minor, the damage from borers can be ignored—the plant may have the problem under control. When borer activity appears severe, some control can be achieved with sprays. Follow label instructions. Look for major causes of plant stress and correct while controlling the borer attacks. If borers persist, have the plants checked by a specialist. Severe damage or infections may make plant removal necessary.

BROWN PATCH is a turf disease caused by a fungus living in most soils. The fungus is active during warmish late-fall and early-spring weather in moist soils and locations with poor air movement. The disease causes large, brown, somewhat circular areas to develop. Control with a fungicide if severe.

CATERPILLARS are the immature stages of moths or butterflies. They chew plant foliage, stems, or flowers, and are of varying sizes and colors. They are best handpicked and destroyed, or the plants can be treated with a *Bacillus thuringiensis*-containing natural insecticide or a synthetic product, following label directions. Some gardeners allow caterpillars to feed on their plants, as many turn into attractive moths or butterflies.

CHINCH BUGS, common in St. Augustinegrass, cause yellow spots in the lawn that gradually enlarge. Adults are $1/5$ inch long, and black with white crossed wings. Immature stages are red and the size of a pinpoint. Check sunny warm areas for small yellowing patches that start to turn brown and enlarge. Look for the chinch bugs at the edge of a yellow-and-green area. They overwinter in all areas of Florida and begin mounting large populations in spring. When the insects are damaging the turf, treat just the affected areas and a few feet around them with a lawn insecticide labeled for chinch bugs. The damage usually continues for two weeks after the pests are under control due to toxins placed in the runners by the bugs. Replace severely damaged turf.

CUTWORMS are the larvae of various moths. They feed on and destroy a wide variety of plants, often chewing through stems near the ground as if cutting them off. Check for cutworms when preparing new beds. If present, handpick from the beds or treat the soil with a general insecticide labeled for preplant application. A paper or cardboard collar placed at the plant base around the stem can also help control cutworms.

DOLLAR SPOT is a fungal disease that can attack any lawn but is often seen in Bermudagrass. It's often an indication of weak turf affected by drought or pest problems. Usually a fertilizer application helps the grass outgrow the fungus.

GARDEN FLEAHOPPERS are $1/16$-inch-long black insects that suck juices from Marigold, Verbena, and similar flowers, plus some vegetables and herbs. The damage resembles mite injury, so look for the little black bugs. Use a general garden insecticide for piercing-and-sucking-type insects labeled for your plants.

GRASSHOPPERS are large-legged brown to bright-green insects up to 2 inches long that chew plant foliage. Some damage can be ignored. Otherwise, handpick them or apply a synthetic insecticide labeled for chewing insects.

GRUBS are the immature stage of beetles and damage some turf. The grubs are white with a brown head and three pairs of legs at the front of the body. They live underground feeding on roots. Look for grass that is yellowing in patches. Dig up a layer of sod an inch or two below the surface. Sometimes the sod just rolls back when affected. Look for the grubs. If two or more are present per square foot of turf, you need a control. Apply a granular or liquid insecticide labeled for grubs. Products generally have to be watered into the soil to be effective . . . but follow the label instructions.

LAWN CATERPILLARS chew grass blades, making a lawn look closely mowed. Several types might be active. The three most common are the sod webworm, army worm, and grass looper. Check the grass blades—if they appear to be chewed, you most likely have a lawn caterpillar. Army worms and grass loopers feed on the blades during the day and sod webworms at night. During the day, sod webworms hide in the grass near the ground. When caterpillars are at work, try a natural control containing the *Bacillus thuringiensis* organism. Synthetic pesticides for lawn caterpillar control are also available. Treat only the infested area and a few feet around it. Keep damaged areas moist and the grass will usually grow back.

LEAF SPOTS are various-shaped yellow to brown spots caused by fungal activity on leaves. Many are normal and can be ignored, as the fungus may attack older foliage as it declines and drops. Where new and healthy leaves are infected and the fungus is affecting the quality of the plant, control with a copper-containing fungicide or synthetic fungicide according to label directions for your plants. Ligustrums and Pittosporums are notorious for having fungal problems. Some have to be tolerated, as just about all these plantings seem to have a little of the fungus present.

LEAFMINERS are the immature stages of a moth or fly that tunnel between the leaves of plants. Some damage should be tolerated. Some control can be obtained by hanging sticky boards near plantings in flower, vegetable, or herb gardens. Where needed, apply a properly labeled synthetic insecticide.

MEALYBUGS are white insects about ⅛ inch or smaller, often found in buds and leaf angles of plants. They suck juices from plants and encourage growth of sooty mold. Look for a general decline in plant vigor. Wash off with a soap solution, daub with rubbing alcohol, or treat with a natural insecticidal soap product. You may also control with an oil or synthetic insecticide, following label instructions.

MITES are small pinpoint-sized arachnids that are prevalent during warm, dry weather or on plants kept inside. They suck juices from plant foliage. Damage is often first noted as a yellowing to browning of foliage. You need a hand lens to see these pests but can often spot transparent skins on leaves with the unaided eye. Check for mites under leaves. They are often found near the veins of the leaves at first and then they spread out. They may be clear or orange in color; some make webs. Control with a strong stream of water, soapy solution, or soap spray. Horticultural oil and synthetic sprays may also be used on some plants, following label instructions.

MOLE CRICKETS are often found in all lawns but are especially damaging to Bahiagrass and Bermudagrass. The adult mole crickets lay eggs that start hatching in May. When the ground begins to feel soft under the grass, it's the first hint the insects may be present. Monitor the populations in your lawn with a soap flush starting in May. Mix 1½ tablespoons of a mild dish detergent in 2 gallons of water, and sprinkle over 4 square feet of turf. If young crickets are present, they will scramble to the soil surface in a matter of minutes. When two or more mole crickets are spotted in a square foot of lawn, it's time to apply a control. Apply a mole cricket bait or liquid control, following label instructions. They should be applied in late afternoon after any rains. The mole crickets come to the surface of the soil at night to feed. Sprays are also available. Follow label instructions for effective control. Note that some sprays should be watered into the soil but others are left on the surface.

MUSHROOMS AND TOADSTOOLS may produce fruiting bodies on the surface of the soil during damp weather. Don't worry too much when you see them. They cause no harm and can be picked from a lawn and garden or knocked over to shrivel. Some are poisonous so it's best to remove them when children or pets might be in the area.

PALMETTO WEEVIL is a large beetle-like insect that usually attacks transplanted Cabbage and some other palm species, causing death. They can also attack any stressed palm due to poor growing conditions or other pests. Contact your local Extension Service office to obtain the latest control recommendations.

POWDERY MILDEW is a common disease of many landscape plants that can be seen as a white covering on the surface of foliage and buds. The disease affects the appearance of the plants, reduces vigor, and can distort growth. Most plants are susceptible to this powdery-looking fungus, but only a few including Roses, Gerbera and some Crapemyrtles, have a real problem.

When it becomes severe, try a copper fungicide or one of the synthetic fungicides available at local garden centers, following label instructions.

ROOT KNOT NEMATODES are microscopic roundworms that feed on plant roots. Nematodes reduce plant vigor and cause the plants to decline. Many vegetables and annual flowers are affected. Try planting nematode-resistant varieties or practicing soil solarization during the summer. Check with your Extension Service for new nematode control products.

SCALES are yellow, green, or dark-colored insects that have a waxy coating and cluster on leaves and stems. They range in size from a pinhead to a dime. Most can be easily scraped off with a fingernail to reveal the insect under the covering. They are often hard to see and may be hidden under foliage. Some contribute to a black sooty mold. Wash off or control with a soap, horticultural oil, or synthetic insecticide spray. Follow label instructions to determine which plants can be treated with each product. When using oils, make sure you cover all portions of the plant and especially under the leaves. Winter is a good time to use oil sprays for scale insect control. The products are of low toxicity and are very effective at eliminating scale populations. Use oils when temperatures are above 40 degrees Fahrenheit and below 85. Oil sprays also remove the sooty mold that frequently accompanies scale infestations, but do not expect the scale or sooty mold to drop rapidly from the plants. Each is firmly attached and wears away with time.

SLIME MOLD is a fungus present on turf during damp periods, usually in late spring or early summer. It is scary looking, producing a gray covering over the surface of the leaves, but it is harmless. Just use a broom to sweep it off, or wash it away with water.

SLUGS and SNAILS are slimy pests that may or may not have a shell. They love leafy crops and come out during warm, moist weather to chew holes in plant leaves. Look for slime trails in the morning, then hunt for them at night. Handpick from the plants, lure into shallow containers of beer, or use a synthetic snail and slug bait, following label instructions.

SOOTY MOLD is a gray to black fungus associated with aphids, mealybugs, scale, and other piercing-sucking insects. Loosen with a soap spray or treat with a horticultural oil spray to control the pests associated with the sooty mold, following label instructions for your plant type.

STEM CANKERS appear on plant stems as gray to brown dead areas. Sometimes the bark is loose or cracked in the affected areas. This is where the fungus is living and causing the stem to decline. Prune out all canker portions, cutting back into healthy growth. Sterilize your pruning shears between cuts. Apply a fungicide made for your plant after pruning.

TAKE-ALL ROOT ROT is a fungus that affects stressed lawns. No fungicides have been found effective, and the disease may run rampant during the summer months. Lawns that receive too much water, are competing with other plants, have nematode problems, and have been under general stress are very susceptible. The best way to fight this disease is to mow the lawn at the proper length. This is normally the highest setting. If take-all root rot is diagnosed, apply light but frequent liquid fertilizer applications. When turf declines due to the disease, remove the old grass, till the soil deeply, and re-establish new sod. Try to eliminate any cultural problems that may weaken the turf.

THRIPS are very small insects, about the size of a thread, that attack flowers and some plant foliage. Your first hint of damage may be buds not opening properly and developing brown edges. Thrips are real spoilers of gardenias and roses. Remove a flower and pull it apart to see the very small clear to brownish thrips. Select an insecticide labeled for thrip control to treat the flower buds and foliage as needed.

WHITEFLIES are small fly-like insects, snow-white in color, that live among foliage. They have a yellowish immature stage that forms on the leaf undersides. Control with a soap or horticultural oil spray according to label instructions for your plants. Repeat sprays are usually needed.

GARDENS TO VISIT IN FLORIDA

American Orchid Society Visitor Center and
Botanical Garden - Delray Beach
www.aos.org

Arboretum of the University of Central Florida
– Orlando
www.arboretum.ucf.edu

Audubon House and Tropical Garden –
Key West
www.audubonhouse.com

Bok Tower Gardens – Lake Wales
www.boktowergardens.org

Busch Gardens – Tampa
www.buschgardens.com

Butterfly World – Coconut Creek
www.butterflyworld.com

Central Florida Zoo & Botanical Gardens –
Sanford
www.centralfloridazoo.org

Cummer Museum of Art & Gardens –
Jacksonville
www.cummer.org

Cypress Gardens – Winter Haven
www.cypressgardens.com

Deerfield Beach Arboretum – Deerfield Beach
www.deerfield-beach.com

ECHO Global Farm and Tropical Fruit Nursery
– Fort Myers
www.echonet.org

Edison and Ford Winter Estates – Fort Myers
www.efwefla.org

Eureka Springs Park – Tampa
www.hillsboroughcounty.org/parks/
parkservices/regionalparks.cfm

Fairchild Tropical Botanic Garden –
Coral Gables
www.fairchildgarden.org

Flamingo Gardens – Davie
www.flamingogardens.org

The Florida Botanical Gardens – Largo
www.flbg.org

Florida Citrus Arboretum – Winter Haven
www.doacs.state.fl.us/pi/budwood/arb.html

Florida Institute of Technology Botanical
Gardens – Melbourne
http://facilities.fit.edu/botanical_gardens.php

Four Arts Gardens – Palm Beach
www.fourarts.org/gardensabout

Fruit and Spice Park – Homestead
www.fruitandspicepark.org

John C. Gifford Arboretum, University of Miami
– Coral Gables
www.bio.miami.edu/arboretum

Heathcote Botanical Gardens – Fort Pierce
www.heathcotebotanicalgardens.org

The Kampong of the National Tropical
Botanical Garden – Miami
http://ntbg.org/gardens/kampong.php

Kanapaha Botanical Gardens – Gainesville
www.kanapaha.org

Key West Botanical Forest and Garden –
Key West
www.keywestbotanicalgarden.org

Harry P. Leu Gardens – Orlando
www.leugardens.org

Alfred B. Maclay State Gardens – Tallahassee
www.floridastateparks.org/maclaygardens

McKee Botanical Garden – Vero Beach
www.mckeegarden.org

Miami Beach Botanical Garden – Miami Beach
www.mbgarden.org

Montgomery Botanical Center – Coral Gables
www.montgomerybotanical.org

Morikami Museum and Japanese Gardens –
Delray Beach
www.morikami.org

Mounts Botanical Garden – West Palm Beach
www.mounts.org

Naples Botanical Garden – Naples
www.naplesgarden.org

Nature Coast Botanical Gardens –
Spring Hill
www.naturecoastbotanicalgardens.com

Ann Norton Sculpture Gardens –
West Palm Beach
www.ansg.org

Ormond Memorial Art Museum
and Gardens – Ormond Beach
www.ormondartmuseum.org

Palm and Cycad Arboretum, Florida State
College at Jacksonville   Jacksonville

Palma Sola Botanical Park – Bradenton
www.palmasolabp.org

Sarasota Jungle Gardens – Sarasota
www.sarasotajunglegardens.com

Marie Selby Botanical Gardens – Sarasota
www.selby.org

Sunken Gardens – St. Petersburg
www.stpete.org/sunken

Unbelievable Acres Botanic Gardens –
Palm Beach

University of South Florida Botanical Gardens
– Tampa
www.cas.usf.edu/garden

Vizcaya Museum and Gardens   Miami
www.vizcayamuseum.org

Parks and preserves abound throughout Florida at the local, state, and national levels. The award-winning Florida state park system is one of the largest in the country with 160 parks, spanning more than 700,000 acres. Parks offer visitors a bounty of beautiful outdoor scenery. They cover all types of ecosystems and gardens, from the Everglades to forests to demonstration butterfly gardens. Take advantage of these wonderful resources and visit often. The parks in Florida provide a storehouse of ideas and excellent examples of how many landscape plants look when in a mature state.

Florida's theme parks and tourist attractions are on the opposite end of the spectrum. However, they too can be excellent garden resources for landscape and plant ideas. While the Disney parks are the best known, there are many smaller attractions and zoos that are beautifully landscaped with native, ornamental, or tropical designs.

GLOSSARY

Acid soil: soil with a pH less than 7.0, sometimes called "sour" soil. Sulfur is typically added to the soil to make it more acidic.

Alkaline soil: soil with a pH greater than 7.0, often called "basic" or "sweet" soil. It lacks acidity, often because it has limestone in it. Lime is typically added to soil to make it more alkaline.

All-purpose fertilizer: powdered, liquid, or granular fertilizer with the three key nutrients—nitrogen (N), phosphorus (P), and potassium (K). It is suitable for maintenance nutrition for most plants. Many fertilizers now contain zero or little phosphorus, where this nutrient is adequate.

Amendment: components added to soil to improve fertility, water retention, or structure.

Annual: a plant that lives its entire life in one season. It is genetically determined to germinate, grow, flower, set seed, and die the same year. Some plants that are perennial in their native habitats, but not hardy in another region can also be used as annuals.

Balled and burlapped: describes a tree or shrub grown in the field whose soilball was wrapped with protective burlap and twine when the plant was dug up to be sold or transplanted.

Bare root: describes plants that have been packaged without any soil around their roots. (Often young shrubs and trees purchased through the mail arrive with their exposed roots covered with moist peat or sphagnum moss, sawdust, or similar material, and wrapped in plastic.)

Barrier plant: a plant that has intimidating thorns or spines and is sited purposely to block foot traffic or other access to the home or yard.

Beneficial insects: insects or their larvae that prey on pest organisms and their eggs. They may be flying insects, such as ladybugs, parasitic wasps, praying mantids, and soldier bugs, or soil dwellers such as predatory nematodes, spiders, and ants.

Berm: a narrow, raised ring of soil around a tree, used to hold water so it will be directed to the root zone.

Bract: a modified leaf structure on a plant stem near its flower, resembling a petal. Often it is more colorful and visible than the actual flower, as in Dogwood or Poinsettia.

Bt: abbreviation of *Bacillus thuringiensis*, an organism that attacks a certain stage in the life cycle of some pests. Forms of Bt can be created to target a particular species. Used as a natural pest control.

Bud union: the place where the top of a plant was grafted to the rootstock; usually refers to roses.

Canopy: the overhead branching area of a tree, usually referring to its extent including foliage.

Chlorotic: yellowing of leaves either from pest or nutrient problems.

Cold hardiness: the ability of a plant to survive the winter cold in a particular area.

Complete fertilizer: containing all three major components of fertilizers—nitrogen (N), phosphorus (P), and potassium (K), although not necessarily in equal proportions. An incomplete fertilizer does not contain all three elements.

Composite: a flower that is actually composed of many tiny flowers. Typically, they are flat clusters of tiny, tight florets, sometimes surrounded by wider-petaled florets. Composite flowers are highly attractive to bees and beneficial insects.

Compost: organic matter that has undergone progressive decomposition by microbialS and microbial activity until it is reduced to a spongy, fluffy texture. Added to soil of any type, it improves the soil's ability to hold air and water and to drain well.

Corm: the swollen, energy-storing structure, analogous to a bulb, under the soil at the base of the stem of plants such as crocus and gladiolus.

Crown: the base of a plant at, or just beneath, the surface of the soil where the roots meet the stems; the head of a Palm.

Cultivar: a CULTIvated VARiety. It is a naturally occurring form of a plant that has been identified as special or superior and is purposely selected for propagation and production.

Deadhead: a pruning technique that removes faded flower heads from plants to improve their appearances, abort seed production, and stimulate further flowering.

Deciduous plants: unlike evergreens, these trees and shrubs lose their leaves in the fall.

Desiccation: drying out of foliage tissues, usually due to drought or wind.

Division: the practice of splitting apart perennial plants to create several smaller-rooted segments. The practice is useful for controlling the plant's size and for acquiring more plants; it is also essential to the health and continued flowering of certain ones.

Dormancy or dormant period: time during which no growth occurs because of unfavorable environmental conditions. For some plants it is in winter, and for others summer. Many plants require this time as a resting period.

Drought tolerant: plants able to tolerate dry soil for varying periods of time. However, plants must first be well established before they are drought tolerant.

Established: the point at which a newly planted tree, shrub, flower, or grass begins to produce new growth, either foliage or stems. This is an indication that the roots have recovered from transplant shock and have begun to grow and spread.

Evergreen: perennial plants that do not lose their foliage annually with the onset of winter. Needled or broadleaf foliage will persist and continues to function on a plant through one or more winters, aging and dropping unobtrusively in cycles of three or four years or more.

Foliar: of or about foliage—usually refers to the practice of spraying foliage, as in fertilizing or treating with insecticide; leaf tissues absorb liquid directly for fast results, and the soil is not affected.

Floret: a tiny flower, usually one of many forming a cluster that comprises a single blossom.

Fungicide: a pesticide material for destroying or preventing fungus on plants.

Genus: a distinct botanical group within a family, typically containing several species. Plural form is "genera," referring to more than one genus.

Germinate: to sprout. Germination is a fertile seed's first stage of development.

Graft (union): the point on the stem of a woody plant with sturdier roots where a stem from a highly ornamental plant is inserted so that it will join with it. Roses are commonly grafted.

Hands: groups of female flowers on a banana; hands develop into bananas. A well-grown banana can produce about fifteen hands of bananas. The entire bunch is called a head.

Hardscape: the permanent, structural, non-plant part of a landscape, such as walls, sheds, pools, patios, arbors, and walkways.

Heat tolerance: the ability of a plant to withstand the summer heat in a particular area.

Herbaceous: plants having fleshy or soft stems; the opposite of woody.

Humus: partially decomposed organic matter.

Hybrid: a plant that is the result of intentional or natural cross-pollination between two or more plants of the same species or genus.

Invasive: when a plant has such a vigorous growth habit that it crowds out more desirable plants.

Low water demand: describes plants that tolerate dry soil for varying periods of time. Typically, they have succulent, hairy, or silvery-gray foliage and tuberous roots or taproots.

Micronutrients: elements needed in small quantities for plant growth. Sometimes called "minor elements." Sometimes a soil will be deficient in one or more of them and require a particular fertilizer formulation.

Mulch: a layer of material over bare soil to protect it from erosion and compaction by rain, to discourage weeds, to retain moisture, and for aesthetics. It may be inorganic (gravel, fabric) or organic (wood chips, bark, pine needles, chopped leaves).

Naturalize: (a) to plant seeds, bulbs, or plants in a random, informal pattern as they would appear in their natural habitats; (b) to adapt to and spread throughout adopted habitats (a tendency of some nonnative plants).

Nectar: the sweet fluid produced by glands on flowers that attract pollinators such as hummingbirds and honeybees, for whom it is a source of energy.

Node: structure on a stem from which leaves, roots, and branches arise.

Non-selective: herbicides that have the potential to kill or control any plant to which they are applied.

Organic material / matter: any material or debris that is derived from plants. It is carbon-based material capable of undergoing decomposition and decay.

Overseeding: distributing new grass seed on an established lawn to thicken the grass coverage or introduce another type of grass to extend the green season.

Partial shade: situation with filtered or dappled sunlight, or half a day of shade. In the South, part shade often refers to afternoon shade, when the sun is at its brightest and hottest.

Pathogen: the causal organism of a plant disease.

Peat moss: organic matter from peat sedges (United States) or sphagnum mosses (Canada), often used to improve soil texture. The acidity of sphagnum peat moss makes it ideal for boosting or maintaining soil acidity while also improving its drainage.

Perennial: a flowering plant that lives over two or more seasons. Many die back with frost, but their roots survive the winter and generate new shoots in the spring.

pH: a measurement of the relative acidity (low pH) or alkalinity (high pH) of soil or water based on a scale of 1 to 14, 7 being neutral. Individual plants require soil to be within a certain range so that nutrients can dissolve in moisture and be available to them.

Pinch: to remove tender stems and/or leaves by pressing them between thumb and forefinger. This pruning technique encourages branching, compactness, and flowering in plants, or it removes aphids clustered at growing tips.

Plug: piece of sod used in establishing a new lawn. Plugs can also be grown or purchased in small cells or pots within a flat, sometimes referred to as trays.

Pollen: the yellow, powdery grains in the center of a flower. A plant's male sex cells, they are transferred to the female plant parts by means of wind or animal pollinators to fertilize them and create seeds.

Pre-emergent: an herbicide applied to the soil surface to prevent weed seed from germinating.

Post-emergent: an herbicide applied to already germinated and actively growing weeds to kill or control them.

Raceme: an arrangement of single-stalked flowers along an elongated, unbranched axis.

Rhizome: a swollen energy-storing stem structure, similar to a bulb, that lies horizontally in the soil, with roots emerging from its lower surface and growth shoots from a growing point at or near its tip, as in Iris.

Rootbound (or potbound): the condition of a plant that has been confined in a container too long, its roots having been forced to wrap around themselves and even swell out of the container. Successful transplanting or repotting requires untangling and trimming away of some of the matted roots.

Root flare: the transition at the base of a tree trunk where the bark tissue begins to differentiate and roots begin to form just before entering the soil. This area should not be covered with soil when planting a tree.

Runoff: when water moves across the landscape without being absorbed, because of steep slopes, the water volume exceeds the soil's absorption capacity, the soil is compacted, or the surface is an impenetrable material. Runoff from areas with applied chemicals can cause problems in the waterbodies ultimately receiving the water.

Self-seeding: the tendency of some plants to sow their seeds freely around the yard. It creates many seedlings the following season that may or may not be welcome.

Selective: herbicides, and other pesticides, that target a particular type of weed or pest.

Self-seeding: the tendency of some plants to sow their seeds freely around the yard; can create many seedlings the following season that may or may not be welcome.

Semi-evergreen: tending to be evergreen in a mild climate but deciduous in a rigorous one.

Shearing: the pruning technique whereby plant stems and branches are cut uniformly with long-bladed pruning shears (hedge shears) or powered hedge trimmers. It is used when creating and maintaining hedges and topiary.

Slow-acting fertilizer: fertilizer that is water insoluble and therefore releases its nutrients gradually as a function of soil temperature, moisture, and related microbial activity. Typically granular, it may be organic or synthetic. Other names are slow-release, time release, and controlled-release fertilizers.

Species: a group of fundamentally identical plants within a genus.

Succulent growth: the sometimes undesirable production of fleshy, water-storing leaves or stems that results from overfertilization.

Sucker: a new-growing shoot. Underground plant roots produce suckers to form new stems and spread by means of these suckering roots to form large plantings, or colonies. Some plants produce root suckers or branch suckers as a result of pruning or wounding.

Thatch: layer of decaying grass found between the soil surface and the living grass blades.

Tuber: a type of underground storage structure in a plant stem, analogous to a bulb. It generates roots below and stems above ground (example: Dahlia).

Variegated: having various colors or color patterns. The term usually refers to plant foliage that is streaked, edged, blotched, or mottled with a contrasting color—often green with yellow, cream, or white.

Water-logged: soil that holds too much water for most plants to thrive, associated with poor aeration, inadequate drainage, or soil compaction.

White grubs: fat, off-white, wormlike larvae of some beetles. They reside in the soil and feed on plant (especially grass) roots until summer when they emerge as beetles to feed on plant foliage.

Wings: (a) the corky tissue that forms edges along the twigs of some woody plants such as Winged Euonymus; (b) the flat, dried extension of tissue on some seeds, such as Maple, that catch the wind and help them disseminate.

COUNTY EXTENSION OFFICES

ALACHUA COUNTY EXTENSION OFFICE
2800 N.E. 39th Avenue
Gainesville, FL 32609 -2658
(352) 955-2402
http://alachua.ifas.ufl.edu

BAKER COUNTY EXTENSION OFFICE
1025 West Macclenny Avenue
PO Box 1074b
MacClenny, FL 32063-9640
(904) 259-3520
http://baker.ifas.ufl.edu

BAY COUNTY EXTENSION OFFICE
2728 E. 14th Street
Panama City, FL 32401-5022
(850) 784-6105
http://bay.ifas.ufl.cdu

BRADFORD COUNTY EXTENSION OFFICE
2266 N. Temple Avenue
Starke, FL 32091-1028
(904) 966-6224
http://bradford.ifas.ufl.edu

BREVARD COUNTY EXTENSION OFFICE
3695 Lake Drive
Cocoa, FL 32926-8699
(321) 633-1702
http://brevard.ifas.ufl.edu

BROWARD COUNTY EXTENSION OFFICE
3245 College Avenue
Davie, FL 33314-7798
(954) 370-3725
http://broward.ifas.ufl.edu

CALHOUN COUNTY EXTENSION OFFICE
20816 Central Avenue E.
Suite 1
Blountstown, FL 32424
(904) 674-8323
http://calhoun.ifas.ufl.edu

CHARLOTTE COUNTY EXTENSION OFFICE
25550 Harbor View Road, Unit 3
Port Charlotte, FL 33980
(941) 764-4340
http://charlottc.ifas.ufl.cdu

CITRUS COUNTY EXTENSION OFFICE
3650 W. Sovereign Path, Suite 1
Lecanto, FL 34461
(352) 527-5700
http://citrus.ifas.ufl.edu

CLAY COUNTY EXTENSION OFFICE
2463 State Road 16 West, P.O. Box 278
Green Cove Springs, FL 32043-0278
(904) 284-6355
http://clay.ifas.ufl.edu

COLLIER COUNTY EXTENSION OFFICE
14700 Immokalee Road
Naples, FL 34120-1468
(239) 353-4244
http://collier.ifas.ufl.edu

COLUMBIA COUNTY EXTENSION OFFICE
164 S.W. Mary Ethel Lane
Lake City, FL 32025
(386) 752-5384
http://columbia.ifas.ufl.edu

DESOTO COUNTY EXTENSION OFFICE
2150 N.E. Roan Street
Arcadia, FL 34266-5025
(863) 993-4846
http://desoto.ifas.ufl.edu

DIXIE COUNTY EXTENSION OFFICE
99 N.E. 121st Street
Cross City, FL 32628
(352) 498-1237
http://dixie.ifas.ufl.edu

DUVAL COUNTY EXTENSION OFFICE
1010 N. McDuff Avenue
Jacksonville, FL 32254-2083
(904) 387-8850
http://duval.ifas.ufl.edu

ESCAMBIA COUNTY EXTENSION OFFICE
3740 Stefani Road
Cantonment, FL 32533-7792
(850) 475-5230
http://escambia.ifas.ufl.edu

FLAGLER COUNTY EXTENSION OFFICE
150 Sawgrass Road
Bunnell, FL 32110-9503
(386) 437-7464
http://flagler.ifas.ufl.edu

FRANKLIN COUNTY EXTENSION OFFICE
66 Fourth Street
Apalachicola, FL 32320-1775
(850) 653-9337
http://franklin.ifas.ufl.edu

GADSDEN COUNTY EXTENSION OFFICE
2140 West Jefferson Street
Quincy, FL 32351-1905
(850) 875-7255
http://gadsen.ifas.ufl.edu

GILCHRIST COUNTY EXTENSION OFFICE
125 E. Wade Street
Trenton, FL 32693
(352) 463-3174
http://gilchrist.ifas.ufl.edu

GLADES COUNTY EXTENSION OFFICE
900 US Hwy 27, S.W.
Moore Haven, FL 33471
(863) 946-0244
http://glades.ifas.ufl.edu

GULF COUNTY EXTENSION OFFICE
200 N. 2nd Street
Wewahitchka, FL 32465
(850) 639-3200
http://gulf.ifas.ufl.edu

HAMILTON COUNTY EXTENSION OFFICE
1143 N.W. US Hwy 41
Jasper, FL 32052-5856
(386) 792-1276
http://hamilton.ifas.ufl.edu

HARDEE COUNTY EXTENSION OFFICE
507 Civic Center Drive
Wauchula, FL 33873-9460
(863) 773-2164
http://hardee.ifas.ufl.edu

HENDRY COUNTY EXTENSION OFFICE
1085 Pratt Blvd., Dallas B Townsend Ag Center
Labelle, FL 33935
(863) 674-4092
http://hendry.ifas.ufl.edu

HERNANDO COUNTY EXTENSION OFFICE
19490 Oliver Street
Brooksville, FL 34601-6538
(352) 754-4433
www.co.hernando.fl.us/County-Extension

HIGHLANDS COUNTY EXTENSION OFFICE
4509 W. George Blvd.
Sebring, FL 33875-5837
(863) 402-6540
http://highlands.ifas.ufl.edu

HILLSBOROUGH COUNTY
EXTENSION OFFICE
5339 South County Road 579
Seffner, FL 33584-3334
(813) 744-5519
http://hillsborough.ifas.ufl.edu

HOLMES COUNTY EXTENSION OFFICE
1169 E. Hwy 90
Bonifay, FL 32425-6012
(850) 547-1108
http://holmes.ifas.ufl.edu

INDIAN RIVER COUNTY EXTENSION OFFICE
1028 20th Place, Suite D
Vero Beach, FL 32960-5360
(772) 770-5030
http://indian.ifas.ufl.edu

JACKSON COUNTY EXTENSION OFFICE
2741 Pennsylvania Ave., Suite 3
Marianna, FL 32448-4014
(850) 482-9620
http://jackson.ifas.ufl.edu

JEFFERSON COUNTY EXTENSION OFFICE
275 N. Mulberry Street
Monticello, FL 32344-2249
(850) 342-0187
http://jefferson.ifas.ufl.edu

LAFAYETTE COUNTY EXTENSION OFFICE
176 S.W. Community Circle
Suite D
Mayo, FL 32066-4000
(386) 294-1279
http://lafayette.ifas.ufl.edu

LAKE COUNTY EXTENSION OFFICE
1951 Woodlea Road
Tavares, FL 32778
(352) 343-4101
http://lake.ifas.ufl.edu

LEE COUNTY EXTENSION OFFICE
3406 Palm Beach Blvd.
Ft. Myers, FL 33916-3719
(239) 461-7510
http://lee.ifas.ufl.edu

LEON COUNTY EXTENSION OFFICE
615 Paul Russell Road
Tallahassee, FL 32301-7099
(850) 606-5200
http://leon.ifas.ufl.edu

LEVY COUNTY EXTENSION OFFICE
625 North Hathaway Avenue, Alt. 27
Bronson, FL 32621
(352) 486-5131
http://levy.ifas.ufl.edu

LIBERTY COUNTY EXTENSION OFFICE
P.O. Box 369
Bristol, FL 32321-0368
(850) 643-2229
http://liberty.ifas.ufl.edu

MADISON COUNTY EXTENSION OFFICE
184 College Loop
Madison, FL 32340-1426
(850) 973-4138
http://madison.ifas.ufl.edu

MANATEE COUNTY EXTENSION OFFICE
1303 17th Street West
Palmetto, FL 34221-2998
(941) 722-4524
http://manatee.ifas.ufl.edu

MARION COUNTY EXTENSION OFFICE
2232 N.E. Jacksonville Road
Ocala, FL 32470-3685
(352) 671-8400
http://marion.ifas.ufl.edu

MARTIN COUNTY EXTENSION OFFICE
2614 S.E. Dixie Highway
Stuart, FL 33494-4007
(772) 288-5654
http://martin.ifas.ufl.edu

MIAMI-DADE COUNTY EXTENSION OFFICE
18710 S.W. 288 Street
Homestead, FL 33030-2309
(305) 248-3311
http://miami-dade.ifas.ufl.edu

MONROE COUNTY EXTENSION OFFICE
1100 Simonton Street, #2-260
Key West, FL 33040
(305) 292-4501
http://monroe.ifas.ufl.edu

NASSAU COUNTY EXTENSION OFFICE
543350 US Hwy 1
Callahan, FL 32011-6486
(904) 879-1019
http://nassau.ifas.ufl.edu

OKALOOSA COUNTY EXTENSION OFFICE
5479 Old Bethel Road
Crestview, FL 32536
(850) 689-5850
http://okaloosa.ifas.ufl.edu

OKEECHOBEE COUNTY EXTENSION OFFICE
458 Highway 98 North
Okeechobee, FL 34972-2303
(863) 763-6469
http://okeechobee.ifas.ufl.edu

ORANGE COUNTY EXTENSION OFFICE
6021 South Conway Road
Orlando, FL 32812-3604
(407) 254-9200
http://ocextension.ifas.ufl.edu

OSCEOLA COUNTY EXTENSION OFFICE
1921 Kissimmee Valley Lane
Osceola Heritage Park
Kissimmee, FL 34744-6107
(321) 697-3000
http://osceola.ifas.ufl.edu

PALM BEACH COUNTY EXTENSION OFFICE
559 North Military Trail
West Palm Beach, FL 33415-1311
(561) 233-1700
www.pbcgov.com/coopext/home

PASCO COUNTY EXTENSION OFFICE
36702 State Road 52
Dade City, FL 33525-5198
(352) 521-4288
http://pasco.ifas.ufl.edu

PINELLAS COUNTY EXTENSION OFFICE
12520 Ulmerton Road
Largo, FL 33774
(727) 582-2100
http://pinellas.ifas.ufl.edu

POLK COUNTY EXTENSION OFFICE
1702 Hwy 17-98 South
Bartow, FL 33830
(863) 519-8677
http://polk.ifas.ufl.edu

PUTNAM COUNTY EXTENSION OFFICE
111 Yelvington Road, Suite 1
East Palatka, FL 32131-8892
(386) 329-0318
http://putnam.ifas.ufl.edu

SANTA ROSA COUNTY EXTENSION OFFICE
6263 Dogwood Drive
Milton, FL 32570-3500
(850) 623-3868
http://santarosa.ifas.ufl.edu

SARASOTA COUNTY EXTENSION OFFICE
6700 Clark Road
Twin Lakes Park
Sarasota, FL 34241-9328
(941) 861-5000
http://sarasota.ifas.ufl.edu

SEMINOLE COUNTY EXTENSION OFFICE
250 W. County Home Road
Sanford, FL 32773-6197
(407) 665-5551
www.seminolecountyfl.gov

ST. JOHNS COUNTY EXTENSION OFFICE
3125 Agricultural Center Drive
St. Augustine, FL 32092-0572
(904) 209-0430
http://stjohns.ifas.ufl.edu

ST. LUCIE COUNTY EXTENSION OFFICE
8400 Picos Road, Suite 101
Fort Pierce, FL 34945-3045
(772) 462-1660
http://stlucie.ifas.ufl.edu

SUMTER COUNTY EXTENSION OFFICE
7620 State Road 471, Suite 2
Bushnell, FL 33513-8716
(352) 793-2728
http://sumter.ifas.ufl.edu

SUWANNEE COUNTY EXTENSION OFFICE
1302 11th Street S.W.
Live Oak, FL 32064
(386) 362-2771
http://suwannee.ifas.ufl.edu

TAYLOR COUNTY EXTENSION OFFICE
203 Forest Park Drive
Perry, FL 32348-6340
(850) 838-3508
http://taylor.ifas.ufl.edu

UNION COUNTY EXTENSION OFFICE
25 N.E. 1st Street
Lake Butler, FL 32054-1701
(386) 496-2321
http://union.ifas.ufl.edu

VOLUSIA COUNTY EXTENSION OFFICE
3100 E. New York Avenue
DeLand, FL 32724-6497
(386) 822-5778
http://volusia.org/extension

WAKULLA COUNTY EXTENSION OFFICE
84 Cedar Avenue
Crawfordville, FL 32327-2063
(850) 926-3931
http://wakulla.ifas.ufl.edu

WALTON COUNTY EXTENSION OFFICE
732 N. 9th Street
DeFuniak Springs, FL 32433-3804
(850) 892-8172
http://walton.ifas.ufl.edu

WASHINGTON COUNTY EXTENSION OFFICE
1424 Jackson Avenue, Suite A
Chipley, FL 32428-1602
(850) 638-6180
http://washington.ifas.ufl.edu

FLORIDA WATER MANAGEMENT DISTRICTS

NORTHWEST FLORIDA
WATER MANAGEMENT DISTRICTS
81 Water Management Dr.
Havana, FL 32333-9700
(850) 539-5999
www.nwfwmd.state.fl.us

SOUTH FLORIDA
WATER MANAGEMENT DISTRICTS
3301 Gun Club Road
West Palm Beach, FL 33416-4680
(561) 686-8800
www.sfwmd.gov

SOUTHWEST FLORIDA
WATER MANAGEMENT DISTRICTS
2379 Broad Street
Brooksville, FL 34604-6899
(352)796-7211
www.swfwmd.fl.us

ST. JOHNS RIVER
WATER MANAGEMENT DISTRICTS
4049 Reid St.
Palatka, FL 32177
(386) 329-4500
http://sjr.state.fl.us

SUWANNEE RIVER
WATER MANAGEMENT DISTRICTS
9225 County Road 49
Live Oak, FL 32060
(386) 362-1001
www.srwmd.state.fl.us

BIBLIOGRAPHY

Bar-Zvi, David, Chief Horticulturist, and Elvin McDonald, series editor. *Tropical Gardening*. New York: Pantheon Books, Knopf Publishing Group, 1996.

Batchelor, Stephen R. *Your First Orchid*. West Palm Beach: American Orchid Society, 1996.

Bechtel, Helmut, Phillip Cribb, and Edmund Launert. *The Manual of Cultivated Orchid Species, Third Edition*. Cambridge, MA: The MIT Press, 1992.

Bell, C. Ritchie and Byron J. Taylor. *Florida Wild Flowers and Roadside Plants*. Chapel Hill, NC: Laurel Hill Press, 1982.

Berry, Fred and W. John Kress. *Heliconia, An Identification Guide*. Washington and London: Smithsonian Institution Press, 1991.

Black, Robert J. and Kathleen C. Ruppert. *Your Florida Landscape, A Complete Guide to Planting & Maintenance*. Gainesville, FL: Cooperative Extension Service, Institute of Food and Agricultural Sciences, University of Florida, 1995.

Blackmore, Stephen and Elizabeth Tootill, eds. *The Penguin Dictionary of Botany*. Middlesex, England: Penguin Books, Ltd., 1984.

Blombery, Alec and Tony Todd. *Palms*. London, Sydney, Melbourne: Angus & Robertson, 1982.

Bond, Rick and editorial staff of Ortho Books. *All About Growing Orchids*. San Ramon, CA: The Solaris Group, 1988.

Boning, Charles R. *Florida's Best Fruiting Plants*. Sarasota, FL: Pineapple Press, 2009.

Brookes, John. *The Book of Garden Design*. New York: Macmillan Publishing Co. and London: Dorling Kindersley Ltd., 1991.

Broschat, Timothy K. and Alan W. Meerow. *Betrock's Reference Guide to Florida Landscape Plants*. Cooper City, FL: Betrock Information Systems, Inc., 1991.

Brown, Deni. *Aroids, Plants of the Arum Family, Second edition*. Portland, OR: Timber Press, 2000.

Bush, Charles S. and Julia F. Morton. *Native Trees and Plants for Florida Landscaping*. Gainesville, FL: Florida Department of Agriculture and Consumer Services.

Calkins, Carroll C., ed. *Reader's Digest Illustrated Guide to Gardening*. Pleasantville, NY and Montreal: The Reader's Digest Association, Inc., 1978.

Campbell, Richard J., ed. *Mangos: A Guide to Mangos in Florida*. Miami: Fairchild Tropical Garden, 1992.

Courtright, Gordon. *Tropicals*. Portland, OR: Timber Press, 1988.

Dade County Department of Planning, Development and Regulation. *The Landscape Manual*. 1996.

Dunn, Teri and Walter Reeves. *Jackson & Perkins Selecting, Growing, and Combining Outstanding Perennials, Southern edition*. Nashville, TN: Cool Springs Press, 2003.

Editors of Sunset Books and Sunset Magazine. *Sunset National Garden Book.* Menlo Park, CA: Sunset Books, Inc., 1997.

Gerberg, Eugene J. and Ross H. Arnett, Jr. *Florida Butterflies.* Baltimore: Natural Science Publication, Inc., 1989.

Gilman, Edward F. *Betrock's Florida Plant Guide.* Hollywood, FL: Betrock Information Systems, 1996.

Graf, Alfred Byrd. *Tropica.* East Rutherford, NJ: Roehrs Co., 1978.

Hillier, Malcolm. *Malcolm Hillier's Color Garden.* London, New York, Stuttgart, Moscow: Dorling Kindersley, 1995.

Holttum, R.E. and Ivan Enock. *Gardening in the Tropics.* Singapore: Times Editions, 1991.

Hoshizaki, Barbara Joe. *Fern Growers Manual.* New York: Alfred A. Knopf, 1979.

Kilmer, Anne. *Gardening for Butterflies and Children in South Florida.* West Palm Beach: The Palm Beach Post, 1992.

Kramer, Jack. *300 Extraordinary Plants for Home and Garden.* New York, London, Paris: Abbeville Press, 1994.

Lamp'l, Joe. *The Green Gardener's Guide.* Franklin, TN: Cool Springs Press, 2007.

Lessard, W.O. *The Complete Book of Bananas.* Miami, 1992.

MacCubbin, Tom and Georgia Tasker. *Florida Gardener's Guide, Revised edition.* Franklin, TN: Cool Springs Press, 2002.

MacCubbin, Tom. *Florida Home Grown: Landscaping.* Sentinel Communications, Orlando, Florida, 1989.

MacCubbin, Tom. *Florida Lawn Guide.* Franklin, TN: Cool Springs Press, 2007.

MacCubbin, Tom. *Month-by-Month Gardening in Florida, Revised edition.* Franklin, TN: Cool Springs Press, 2005.

Mathias, Mildred E., ed. *Flowering Plants in the Landscape.* Berkeley, Los Angeles, London: University of California Press, 1982.

Meerow, Alan W. *Betrock's Guide to Landscape Palms.* Cooper City, FL: Betrock Information Systems, Inc., 1992.

Morton, Julia F. *500 Plants of South Florida.* Miami: E.A. Seemann Publishing, Inc., 1974.

Myers, Ronald L. and John J. Ewel, eds. *Ecosystems of Florida.* Orlando: University of Central Florida Press, 1991.

The National Gardening Association. *Dictionary of Horticulture.* New York: Penguin Books, 1994.

Neal, Marie. *In Gardens of Hawaii.* Honolulu: Bishop Museum Press, 1965.

Nelson, Gil. *Florida's Best Native Landscape Plants.* Gainesville, FL: University Press of Florida. 2003.

Nelson, Gil. *The Trees of Florida, A Reference and Field Guide.* Sarasota: Pineapple Press, Inc., 1994.

Perry, Frances. *Flowers of the World.* London, New York, Sydney, Toronto: The Hamlyn Publishing Group, Ltd., 1972.

Rawlings, Marjorie Kinnan. *Cross Creek.* St. Simons Island, GA: Mockingbird Books, 1942. Seventh Printing, 1983.

Reinikka, Merle A. *A History of the Orchid.* Portland, OR: Timber Press, 1995.

Rittershausen, Wilma and Gill and David Oakey. *Growing & Displaying Orchids, A Step-by-Step Guide.* New York: Smithmark Publishers, Inc., 1993.

Scurlock, J. Paul. *Native Trees and Shrubs of the Florida Keys.* Pittsburgh: Laurel Press, 1987.

Stearn, William T. *Stearn's Dictionary of Plant Names for Gardeners.* New York: Sterling Publishing Co., Inc. 1996.

Stevenson, George B. *Palms of South Florida.* Miami: Fairchild Tropical Garden, 1974.

Tasker, Georgia. *Enchanted Ground, Gardening With Nature in the Subtropics.* Kansas City: Andrews and McMeel, 1994.

Tasker, Georgia. *Wild Things, The Return of Native Plants.* Winter Park, FL: The Florida Native Plant Society, 1984.

Tomlinson, P.B. *The Biology of Trees Native to Tropical Florida.* Allston, MA: Harvard University, 1980.

Vanderplank, John. *Passion Flowers, Second Edition.* Cambridge, MA: The MIT Press, 1996.

Walker, Jacqueline. *The Subtropical Garden.* Portland, OR: Timber Press, 1992.

Warren, William. *The Tropical Garden.* London: Thames and Hudson, Ltd., 1991.

Watkins, John V. and Thomas J. Sheehan. *Florida Landscape Plants, Native and Exotic, Revised Edition.* Gainesville, FL: The University Presses of Florida, 1975.

Workman, Richard W. *Growing Native.* Sanibel, FL: The Sanibel-Captive Conservation Foundation, Inc., 1980.

INDEX OF COMMON NAMES

BOTANICAL INDEX

MEET THE AUTHORS

Tom MacCubbin is known to gardeners in Florida through his radio, television, and newspaper contributions. He retired from his position as an extension environmental horticulturist with the University of Florida in Orange County after 36 years and was promoted to the distinguished position of Extension Agent Emeritus with the University of Florida. Readers are familiar with Tom's question-and-answer gardening columns and feature articles for *The Orlando Sentinel*, while others may recognize him as a co-host of Orange County Gardening on cable television and weekly horticulture reports on Central Florida News 13. His radio program, *Better Lawns & Gardens*, is broadcast over twenty Florida stations.

The National Association of County Agriculture Agents has recognized his media contributions with numerous awards, including awards for the best state personal column, best news photo story, best news column, and best television program. Most recently, his *Better Lawns & Gardens* radio program was judged best in the nation for 1998 & 2000; in 1999, he was presented the AT&T Communications Award in the Best Videotape/Television category as a regional winner for his role as co-host of Orange County Gardening; in 2001 he received an Award of Excellence for work as a county horticulture agent and for effective involvement with media programming, from the National Council of State Garden Clubs, Inc. He has been honored with the Best Horticulture Writer Award by the Florida Nurseryman and Growers Association, and was granted the Garden Communicators Award by the American Nurseryman's Association. In June 2007 Tom was recognized nationally as the teacher-of-the-year by the American Horticultural Society. MacCubbin has authored more than eight gardening books for Florida including the *Florida Gardener's Guide*, *Month-by-Month™ Gardening in Florida*, *My Florida Garden: A Gardener's Journal*, and *The Florida Lawn Guide* with Cool Springs Press. Active in their community, MacCubbin and his wife, Joan, live near Apopka.

Georgia Tasker was the garden writer for the *Miami Herald* for more than thirty years. Recognized frequently for her outstanding work, Tasker was a Pulitzer Prize finalist for her writing on tropical deforestation and the Florida Nurserymen and Growers Association named her Outstanding Horticultural Writer. Following the destruction of Hurricane Andrew, Tasker was given the Media Award of Greatest Merit by the Florida Urban Forestry Council for her work to help save trees in areas devastated by the storm. She has also received Fairchild's highest honor, the Barbour Medal, and a lifetime achievement award from Tropical Audubon Society. Georgia currently writes and blogs for the Fairchild Tropical Botanic Garden, and is an avid photographer, gardener, and traveler. In addition to being co-author of the *Florida Gardener's Guide* with Tom MacCubbin, Tasker is the author of *Wild Things*, *The Return of Native Plants* and *Enchanted Ground: Gardening with Nature in the Subtropics*. Georgia lives in Coconut Grove.

Robert Bowden is currently the Executive Director of Leu Gardens in Orlando. He served in this capacity at Atlanta Botanical Gardens and as Director of Horticulture at the Missouri Botanical Garden. His photographs and fun-filled essays have appeared in such magazines as *Garden Design*, *Traditional Home*, *Southern Accents*, and *The New York Times*. He appears regularly on a variety of nationally syndicated television shows including, *Victory Garden* on PBS, Discovery Channel's *Home Matters*, HGTV's *Way To Grow!* and *Rebecca's Garden*. He travels extensively in the U.S. and Caribbean talking about growing vegetables, perennials, tropical and sub-tropical plants, and on flowering vines, trees, and shrubs.

Joe Lamp'l, aka joe gardener®, is the host of two national television shows: *GardenSMART* on PBS and DIY Network's *Fresh from the Garden*. His latest project includes producing and hosting a brand new series on PBS, *Growing a Greener World*. He's also a syndicated columnist and author, including his latest book, *The Green Gardener's Guide: Simple, Significant Actions to Protect & Preserve Our Planet*. Joe's passion and work related to gardening, sustainable living, and environmental stewardship through multiple media platforms has positioned him as one of the most recognized personalities in the "green" sector today. Find out more information about Joe and his work online at www.joegardener.com.